GOODRIDGE'S GUIDE TO FLEA MARKETS

Midwest Edition

Other regional editions of
Goodridge's Guide to Flea Markets

Northeast/Mid-Atlantic Edition
Southeast Edition
West/Southwest Edition

GOODRIDGE'S GUIDE TO FLEA MARKETS

Includes Swap Meets, Trade Days, Farmer's Markets, Auctions and Antique and Craft Malls

Midwest Edition

JIM GOODRIDGE

ADAMS PUBLISHING
Holbrook, Massachusetts

Copyright ©1995 by Jim Goodridge. All rights reserved.
No part of this work may be reproduced in any form, or by any means,
without the permission of the publisher. Exceptions are made for brief
excerpts to be used in published reviews.

Published by Adams Media Corporation
260 Center Street, Holbrook, MA 02343

ISBN: 1-55850-519-9

Printed in the United States of America

A   B   C   D   E   F   G   H   I   J

Library of Congress Cataloging-in-Publication Data
Goodridge, Jim.
    Goodridge's guide to flea markets. Midwest edition / Jim Goodridge.
       p.   cm.
    "Includes swap meets, trade days, farmer's markets, auctions, and
antique and craft malls."
    Includes bibliographical references and index.
    ISBN 1-55850-519-9
    1. Flea markets—Middle West—Directories. I. Title. II. Title: Flea
markets.
HF5482.G66   1995
381'.192'02577—dc20   94-46489
                                                                                      CIP

IMPORTANT NOTICE
Every effort has been made to ensure that the information contained in this
directory is accurate.
    However, due to the size and scope of the publication and the fluid
nature of the industry, market information is subject to change. Neither the
publisher nor the author assumes any responsibility for errors or omissions
in content or composition.
    Comments may be directed to the author c/o Adams Publishing, 260
Center Street, Holbrook, MA 02343.

*This book is available at quantity discounts for bulk purchases. For
information, call 1-800-872-5627.*

COVER DESIGN by Barry Littmann.

TABLE OF CONTENTS

Author's Notes 7
The Changing Face of America's Marketplace. 8
Flea Marketing—The Beat of a Different Drum. 9
Good Buys at the Flea Market 10
Flea Market Shoppers........................... 11
Flea Market Facts 12
The Evolution of Antique and Craft Malls. 13

FLEA MARKETS
(Includes Swap Meets, Trade Days,
and Farmer's Markets)

Illinois 17
Indiana 37
Iowa... 61
Kansas 65
Kentucky 71
Michigan 86
Minnesota 103
Missouri 109
Nebraska...................................... 129
North Dakota 133
Ohio 135
South Dakota 169
Wisconsin 172

ANTIQUE AND CRAFT MALLS

Illinois 185
Indiana....................................... 194
Iowa... 205
Kansas....................................... 207
Kentucky 214
Michigan..................................... 220
Minnesota 228
Missouri 230
Nebraska..................................... 245
North Dakota 247
Ohio 247

South Dakota 257
Wisconsin 257

AUCTIONS
Public Auctions. 263
Dealer Auctions 286

References. 289
Recommended Resources 298
Index. 301

Author's Notes

This manual was originally written for the professional vendor who travels the country setting up and selling at flea markets and various other events. The information contained in each market entry will also be useful to the concessionaire, who can refer to it for booking information. For example, a market's listing may indicate whether the market allows outside food vendors to sell on the premises.

All markets have some type of snack bar, with hamburgers, soda, etc. Many of the large markets have excellent restaurants run by professional food-service companies. Most have rest rooms, telephones, and basic services. Most markets do not have a campground. However, a lot of them allow traveling dealers to stay over on the premises. If you are vacationing, please call about local camping and lodging.

Outdoor markets operate seasonally, and all are affected by the weather. Many are closed during the winter, or have restricted hours. Call ahead to avoid disappointment. Markets that are held at locations such as fairgrounds and race tracks are subject to the availability of the facility. The market will not be operating during the fair's run or the racing season, for example. Always call ahead to verify information. I can't say it too often.

Almost all markets are open over three-day holiday weekends. (Either Monday or Friday is added to the market's schedule.) This includes, but is not restricted to, holidays like Memorial Day, Labor Day, etc. Also, many markets have special hours and days during the Christmas season.

Shopping or selling at flea markets is such a personal experience. If you're a shopper, one dealer can make your visit truly a pleasure, and the same is true if you're selling.

This is the reason we list all the markets we can locate. Some listings don't give much information; others give a lot. If the market has 1,000 dealers and none carries the cross-eyed widgets you collect, then it's not a good market. But, if it only has ten dealers and two of them have your widgets, then it's a great market.

Who's to judge what's a good market? Only you can decide what's interesting. So join me on the road to exploring *all* the markets. If you discover a great market, additional information, or would like to share your flea marketing experiences with me, please drop me a line.

Remember: whether you are buying or selling, markets are subject to all local ordinances, sales tax, licensing, etc. If you have any questions, ask the market operator.

THE CHANGING FACE OF AMERICA'S MARKETPLACE

I will never forget the first time I peddled at a flea market. It was at a place near my home in Oklahoma City, called Mary's Swap Meet. The spot was nothing more than a dusty, barren lot in the hot Oklahoma sun, on the corner of a busy intersection.

I had a load of pure junk in my old paint wagon: old pots and pans, dishes, appliances, books, records, and other assorted items, so worn they could just as well have been thrown away.

Thirty-four dollars was my take that day, and I'll never forget the feeling it gave me. Those were the days when $34 actually bought a respectable amount at the grocery store. "Wow," I thought. "More than a day's wages for getting rid of unwanted junk." The experience really set my fertile mind in gear. The idea of working on the weekend and having free time during the week to play was too much.

The whole concept of flea marketing was fascinating to me, and it was only a short while before I was in business for myself, full time, traveling the country, selling my wares here and there.

I can hardly believe the changes that have taken place in the flea market business over the years. First and foremost, flea markets have established themselves as a viable American industry.

In the bustling tourist mecca of Orlando, Florida, Flea World is second only to Disney World in number of visitors. Tour buses swamp the small Indiana community of Shipshewana every week, and in Canton, Texas, First Monday Trade Days are legendary. This market, like so many others with a long track record, is bursting at the seams with vendors, today numbering well over 4,000. The Rose Bowl Flea Market in Pasadena, California is a unique happening that has to be seen to be believed.

As for parties, Stewart Promotions's flea market at the fairgrounds in Louisville, Kentucky, over the New Year's holiday, is one of the country's best trade day celebrations.

The stereotypical image of flea market peddlers as part-time junkers, hobbyists, and amateur collectors is somewhat dated. Today, the industry is dominated by full-time commercial exhibitors.

Professionalism among the ranks has increased as dealers have realized and accepted their emerging role as knowledgeable businessmen and -women. As the face of America's marketplace continues to change, one thing is clear: both dealers and customers are more affluent and more sophisticated than ever before.

A few roadside markets still exist and are a nice stopover for a touch of local flavor and the possibility of finding a treasure among the bric-a-brac. But as we head into the next century, the gigantic commercial markets are going to continue to grow—and, in the wake of their success, more will spring up. These megamarkets are taking their rightful place today, alongside the large shopping malls, as a viable alternative for the American shopper.

From computers to crafts, produce to pearls, it's all at today's flea market. If you can pronounce it or describe it, a vendor somewhere has it for sale. Even the great name brands, Levi's, Calvin Klein, Dockers, Guess, Nike, etc., once the exclusive domain of the overpriced department stores, now line the flea market rows.

For everyone concerned, consumer or exhibitor, flea markets are good for America. Thousands of jobs are created, families fed, children educated, and consumers' needs met in a fair market system that is traditionally American.

Flea markets are big business. And even though they continue to change and affect this country's retail industry, some things will always be the same: flea markets are exciting.

FLEA MARKETING—THE BEAT OF A DIFFERENT DRUM

by Georgia Goodridge

Some of the most enjoyable times my family and I have had have been on the road in the summertime, traveling from one market to another. Our children have always traveled with us and have taken an active role in helping us sell. Their experiences have taught them lessons about life, business, and our country's free-enterprise system that no other form of schooling could have.

I am a strong believer in free enterprise. I believe in working for yourself, being responsible only to yourself, and making your own decisions about that which affects your life. As dealers, we travel to the beat of a different drum from most people today. The greater number of large companies and corporations has made it increasingly difficult for the independent businessman to make a go of it. I truly believe that the people who set up and sell at flea markets, fairs, festivals, and other shows are the real practitioners of free enterprise and the backbone of this nation.

The first principle you must accept when you decide to become a dealer—no matter what the product or service you offer—is that there are going to be risks. Working for yourself means that there are no guarantees.

If you have been selling for a while, you will know that what I am saying is true. If you work a nine-to-five job, you know that if you work x number of hours you will get x amount of money. If you set up at a flea market, a million and one variables are involved which will affect what you take home at the end of the day. You have no control over any of these—expenses, weather, number of people who are there, type of people who are there, time of the month; even the condition of the economy plays a part. Still, the potential for making big money is there, as with no other opportunity available to the average working man.

If you have the physical and inner strength it takes to be a dealer, to work twelve-to-fourteen hour days and eat a steady diet of concession food, if you can smile when your feet are so tired they are throbbing and be pleasant to belligerent customers though you would really like to tell them to take a flying leap, then you, like me, are hopelessly hooked on a way of life that is more rewarding than anything else I can imagine.

GOOD BUYS AT THE FLEA MARKET

by Georgia Goodridge

The most successful flea market shoppers are comparasion shoppers. Finding the good buys is a combination of luck at finding something you want and knowing whether it is priced above, at, or below local retail value.

The more you get out to stores, garage sales, flea markets, and auctions, the more knowledgeable you will be about current market values.

A great place to begin comparison shopping is the grocery store. Pick a few items you use all the time and compare prices between two or three stores. Make it a habit to comparison shop. You'll be glad you did when you transfer your skills to "swap shopping."

Some of the great buys I have found this year: a Mattel Fanner Fifty toy cap pistol. I paid $4 for the toy and sold it for $37. A Davy Crockett cookie jar, circa 1950. I paid $16 for it and sold it for $55. A set of silver-plated flatware (60 pieces), in the original wooden tray, for $3. I sold it for $72. A pair of ladies' high-button shoes, for fifty cents, which I sold for $22. An oak vanity, which I purchased for $20 and sold for $95. All it needed was furniture polish.

Great buys can still be made, and treasures can still be found, if you are persistent. It also doesn't hurt to shop early, as it is still true about the early bird getting the worm. Remember, even though you have a lot more competition when shopping now, not everyone collects or is looking for the same things as you. So don't give up. Persistence will bring rewards.

FLEA MARKET SHOPPERS

Take away the frills of heat in winter, air conditioning in summer, carpeting and wall coverings, and add plenty of fresh air and sunshine, a few tables, and loads of merchandise, and you have a flea market. The bargains are there, whether you are looking for something "cheap" or a value at a good price. You can find collectible items, antiques, someone's used clothing, outlet merchandise and just plain junk when you shop at a flea market.

For many people, shopping at a flea market is a way of life. Their income level prohibits shopping elsewhere. They don't carry credit cards, and generally credit cards are "out" at the markets, anyway. These shoppers have a fixed monthly income or overly stretched weekly paychecks. Some of them recognize a good value; others buy cheap Taiwan junk. All of them shop the no-frills flea markets for better prices than the more comfortable shopping malls can offer.

Other flea market shoppers are looking for something of value for very little money. These kinds of shoppers have specific items or types of items in mind. The low overhead of the flea market keeps prices down for the discriminating shopper.

Other shoppers are antiquers or collectors. They buy for resale or to furnish their homes. The resellers will talk you down on price when they already know they are buying at a steal. They take your "piece of junk" to their antique shop or mall space, jack up the price fifty times, and sell to antique collectors. The other antiquers or collectors are young middle-incomers furnishing their new homes. They've already been to the antique mall or shops and couldn't afford the prices. They spend weekend hours looking for a good antique bargain.

The last group of shoppers aren't shoppers at all. They are compulsive buyers. They walk around trying not to look at your merchandise, because they know if they stop to look, they'll buy something. You can recognize them because they walk around looking straight ahead or up in the air and never at your booth. These are the people you want to stop. Try getting them to stop and look, and you have a sure sell. Getting them to stop is the hard part.

Flea Market Facts

Did you ever wonder when or where the first flea market was held, or how flea markets actually got their name?

The story goes that the Marché des Puces (literally, market of fleas) in Paris was legalized in the 1890s for taxation purposes. It has been said that this is the largest flea market in the world.

Specializing in used items, flea markets date back as far as the middle ages, and are much the same today. However, more and more new, hot, popular merchandise has flooded the trade, giving the buyer an unending array of choices.

Our World War II soldiers, as well as travelers to European countries during that era, brought the name "flea market" back to the States.

Mythically speaking, the name "flea market" came about from thieves' practice of selling stolen wares in out-of-the-way places. When found, they would scatter like fleas to avoid the authorities.

Today, flea market vendors no longer gather in out-of-the-way locations or scatter when spotted. Quite the opposite is true. Flea marketing has turned into one of the most prosperous independent ventures of the times. As the old saying goes, one man's trash is indeed another man's treasure.

Traveling toward the West Coast, you will note that flea markets are called swap meets, and, in the South, trade days. Which is the correct name? This is a point I am sure each region would argue.

Flea markets are held at a wide variety of locations, ranging from drive-ins to fairgrounds to industry parking lots, with as great a variety of space as imaginable. Some charge admission; others do not. Some offer camping for their vendors, entertainment, and even restaurants.

Regardless of when, where, or how flea markets came to be, one thought remains: they will always be around. Where else can you sell or buy just about anything ever manufactured or created?

THE EVOLUTION OF ANTIQUE AND CRAFT MALLS

During the 1980s, antique and craft malls came into their own on a national basis as a legitimate arm of retailing. The nineties have seen an explosion in the mall concept of marketing fine antiques and collectibles, as well as handcrafted items.

The mall concept is a tremendous, yet very simple one. It combines the excitement and variety of an antique show or craft festival with the stability and convenience of a store.

Week after week, as dealers bring in new and different merchandise, one can find under one roof all the diverse and interesting items that were heretofore available only at shows. The pace of malls is rapid and exciting as new dealers move in, bringing with them new and different stock. Every trip to the mall is an adventure to see "what's here today".

By sheer numbers, the Midwest is the leader, with far more multidealer malls than the rest of the country. However, the

South and the West Coast are not far behind, as new malls are springing up daily. The East Coast—with the exception of Pennsylvania, which is mall heaven—is beginning to follow suit as the collectibles field booms and buyers hunger for these fabulous treasure centers.

At each mall, every member of your family or group will find something of interest.

One thing is certain: you will not find the same boring and uninteresting franchises and groups of young hooligans roaming the aisles that you now find in the large retail malls.

Happy flea marketing!

> In general...
>
> ✦ Admission and parking at flea markets are free unless otherwise noted.
>
> ✦ Figures for "average attendance" at flea markets are for the week. Figures for "average daily attendance" are for individual days.
>
> ✦ If a flea market is listed as meeting on the first weekend of the month, and the first day of the month is a Sunday, that is considered the first weekend, and the market is open that Saturday also.

FLEA MARKETS

(Includes Swap Meets, Trade Days, and Farmer's Markets)

ILLINOIS

Country charm and cosmopolitan chaos. Always a pleasure to travel through Illinois. Lovely country—the beautiful little towns, neat shops, great auctions, and some nifty flea markets, both large and small. I make it a point to stop at the small markets and out-of-the-way auctions—always a lot of interesting people at these places. Great buys and some real treasures can be found at these places. I, for one, no longer go into the city of Chicago. The north shore and O'Hare areas contain some really nice, safe shops and markets.

Best bets...

- **Belleville Flea Market, Belleville**
  St. Clair Fairgrounds. One of the country's better antique markets—an all-day stop you won't want to miss.

- **The Buyers Market, Chicago**
  One of the area's most popular markets, especially for hot, new, trendy items.

- **Kane County Flea Market, St. Charles**
  Great buys for antique dealers, serious collectors, investors, and decorators.

- **Sandwich Antiques Market, Sandwich**
  An excellent source market for the serious collector, shopkeeper, or decorator.

ALGONQUIN
Hello Open Air Flea Market and Farmers Market. Used merchandise, housewares, clothing, tools, electronics, toys, farm items, produce, new merchandise. Food available. *Saturdays and Sundays, 8:00 A.M. - dark.*

ALSIP
Tri-State Swap-O-Rama. 4350 W. 129th St. I-294 to Rt. 50. East 1 mile. Indoor/outdoor market. Lots of new merchandise: sportswear, sports-related merchandise. Collectibles, glassware, crafts, art, used merchandise. Average attendance 12,000. 700+

> ### Housewares vs. Household Goods
> In flea-market-speak, "housewares" usually refers to cookware, dishes, lamps, and other small items. "Household goods," on the other hand, is usually taken to mean furniture, appliances, and other large items for the home.

dealers. Snack bar, rest rooms, wheelchair accessible. Reservations required. Electricity available. No overnight camping. Contact: Jim Pierski, 4600 W. Lake St., Melrose Park, IL 60160. (708) 344-7300. *Wednesdays, Saturdays, and Sundays, 7:00 A.M. - 4:00 P.M.*

AMBOY
Antique Show and Flea Market. 4-H Fairgrounds. Rt. 30. Antiques, collectibles, primitives, jewelry, furniture and crafts, with some new merchandise. Excellent market. Approximately 80 dealers. Snack bar, rest rooms, wheelchair accessible. Ample parking. Admission charge. Space from $35. Camping available. Market conducts many special events. Contact: Bill Edwards, Box 99, Amboy, IL 61310. (815) 626-7601. *Third Sunday of each month, 8:00 A.M. - 4:00 P.M.*

AVON
Peddler's Days. New and used merchandise, crafts, produce, garage sale items. Snack bar. (309) 465-3855. *Saturdays and Sundays.*

BELLEVILLE
Belleville Flea Market. St. Clair Fairgrounds. Indoor/outdoor market. One of the country's better antique markets. For the collector or person interested in quality antiques, an all-day stop you won't want to miss. New merchandise: sportswear, electronics, and jewelry (fine, estate, and costume). Food available, rest rooms, wheelchair accessible. Ample parking. (618) 235-0666. *Third weekend of each month.*

BENSENVILLE
Swap-O-Rama. 1145 York Rd. New merchandise: sportswear, housewares, electronics. Used merchandise, crafts, collectibles, produce. Food available. (312) 774-3900. *Sundays.*

BISMARCK
Flea Market. Hwy. 1. Used merchandise, garage sale items, collectibles, farm items, produce, crafts, collectibles. Food available.

(217) 759-7102. *Saturdays and Sundays.*

CARBONDALE
Wildwood Flea Market. Giant City Rd. New and used merchandise, lots of flea market merchandise. Crafts, produce, collectibles. Food available. (618) 529-5878. *Saturdays and Sundays.*

CENTRALIA
Don's Flea Market. Junction of Rts. 161 and I-57. Indoor/outdoor market. Lots of secondhand and garage sale merchandise. Some new merchandise, crafts, and collectibles. Approximately 20 exhibitors. Space from $15. Contact: Don Mercer, 3846 State Rt. 161, Centralia, IL 62801. (618) 533-2949. *Fridays.*

CHAMPAIGN
"Giant Flea Market." Round Barn Banquet Centre. Springfield and Mattis Sts. Indoor market. New and used merchandise, small antiques and collectibles, crafts. Approximately 50 dealers. Food available, rest rooms, wheelchair accessible. Ample parking. Admission charge. Space from $12. Contact: John Crouch, Box 5058, Springfield, IL 62705. (217) 529-6939. *Last Sunday of each month.*

CHICAGO
Brighton Park Swap-O-Rama. 3429 W. 47th St. Near 47th and Archer. Indoor/outdoor market. Mountains of new merchandise: imports, gifts, decorator items, sportswear, electronics, sports merchandise. Used merchandise, collectibles. Average daily attendance 5,000. Approximately 300 dealers. Snack bars, rest rooms. Admission charge. Space from $14 to $18. Good market for commercial vendors. Reservations recommended. Electricity available. No overnight camping. Contact: Jim Pierski, 4600 W. Lake St., Melrose Park, IL 60160. (312) 344-7300. *Saturdays and Sundays.*

CHICAGO
The Buyers Market. 4545 W. Division St. Indoor market. Lots of new merchandise; some collectibles and used items. Great deals on new merchandise make this one of the area's most popular markets, especially for hot, new, trendy items. Average attendance 8000 - 10,000. Approximately 300 sellers. Snack bars, rest rooms, wheelchair accessible. Ample parking. Admission charge. Space from $12. Contact: Lenny Kraut, 4545 W. Divi-

sion St., Chicago, IL 60651. (312) 227-1889. *Saturdays and Sundays, 7:00 A.M. - 4:00 P.M.*

CHICAGO

Double Drive-In Flea Market. 2800 W. Columbus. Large commercial market with wide variety of new merchandise, some used merchandise, and lots of garage sale items. The market for the thrifty shopper—lots of great buys on new merchandise. Approximately 600 dealers. Snack bar, rest rooms. Ample parking and lots of walking. Contact: Ron Swislow, 2750 W. Columbus Ave., Chicago, IL (312) 925-9602. *Saturdays and Sundays, 6:00 A.M. - 5:00 P.M.*

CHICAGO

Great American Flea Market. 1400 S. Cicero. Large commercial market with great selection of new and used merchandise, crafts, collectibles. Average attendance 10,000. Approximately 250 dealers. Food available, rest rooms, wheelchair accessible. Space from $13. Contact: Don Horwitcz, 1400 S. Cicero, 60650. (312) 780-1600. *Saturdays and Sundays, 8:00 A.M. - 5:00 P.M.*

CHICAGO

International Amphitheater Swap-O-Rama. 4200 S. Halstead. New merchandise: upscale and trendy items, fine jewelry, sportswear, electronics, sports merchandise, collectibles. Snack bar, rest rooms. Parking available. Contact: Jim Pierski, (312) 344-7300. *Saturdays and Sundays.*

CHICAGO

Marketplace Flea Market. 101 S. Halstead St. New merchandise: sportswear, jewelry, housewares, outdoor items, sports merchandise. Used merchandise, garage sale items. Food available. (708) 756-1100. *Friday - Sunday.*

CHICAGO

Maxwell Street Flea Market. Junction of 14th Place, Halstead, and Roosevelt Rd. New and used merchandise, gifts, imports, lots of garage sale items, collectibles. Rest rooms, snack bar. Ample parking. *Daily.*

CHICAGO

Regency Flea Market. 4001 W. Grand Ave. New merchandise: sportswear, tools, electronics, jewelry, outdoor items, toys. Used merchandise, crafts, collectibles, produce. Average attendance 3,000. Approximately 125 sellers. Food available, rest rooms, wheelchair accessible. Contact: Andre, 4001 W. Grand Ave., Chicago, IL 60659. (312) 772-6685. *Saturdays and Sundays, 9:00 A.M. - 5:00 P.M.*

CHICAGO

Waukegan Drive-In Theater Flea Market. Rt. 41 and Washington. Antiques, collectibles, crafts, new and used merchandise, produce. Snack bar, rest rooms, wheelchair accessible. Ample parking. *Sundays.*

CICERO

Casa Blanca Flea Market. 3200 S. Cicero Ave. Indoor/outdoor market. Antiques, collectibles, new merchandise, musical instruments, used merchandise, housewares, electronics, crafts. Approximately 200 dealers. Snack bar, rest rooms, wheelchair accessible. Ample parking. Contact: Manager, 3200 S. Cicero Ave., Cicero, IL 60650. (312) 652-0867. *Daily, 8:00 A.M. - 5:00 P.M.*

CICERO

Cicero Swap-O-Rama. 1333 S. Cicero Ave. Lots of new merchandise: sports-related items, housewares, electronics. Used merchandise. Average attendance 3,000. Approximately 125 dealers. Snack bar. Ample parking. Indoor and outdoor space year round. Space from $15. Reservations recommended. Electricity available. No overnight camping. Contact: Jim Pierski, 4600 W. Lake St., Melrose Park, 60160. (708) 344-7300. *Saturdays and Sundays, 7:00 - 4:00 P.M.*

Shopping Tip #1

Bring cash or traveler's checks (cash preferred). Flea markets are a cash-and-carry business. Occasionally, vendors accept personal checks with identification, or credit cards, but you can't rely on that.

DANVILLE

North Vermillion Flea Market. 120 E. Wilson St., Danville, IL 61832. New merchandise: sportswear, tools, jewelry, housewares, toys, sports merchandise. Collectibles, crafts, glassware, produce. Food available, rest rooms, wheelchair accessible. Ample parking. Contact: Orville Johnson, (217) 431-4982. *Fridays, 4:00 P.M. - 9:00 P.M.; Saturdays and Sundays, 8:00 A.M. - 6:00 P.M.*

DANVILLE

Weekend Flea Market. Old Grant Schoolhouse. Antiques, collectibles, glassware, primitives, jewelry. New and used merchandise, crafts. Food available. (217) 446-5094. *Saturdays and Sundays.*

DECATUR

"Giant Flea Market." Civic Center. Indoor market. Antiques, crafts, collectibles, new and used merchandise. Approximately 75 dealers. Food available, rest rooms, wheelchair accessible. Admission charge. Space from $15 per table. Reservations required. Contact: John Crouch, Box 5058, Springfield, IL 62705. (217) 529-6939. *Second Sunday of each month, 8:30 A.M. - 4:30 P.M.*

DE KALB

Little Flower Flea Market. Antiques, collectibles, glassware, crafts. Food available, rest rooms. (815) 756-6620. *Second Sunday of each month.*

DES PLAINES

VFW Flea Market. 2067 Miner. Antiques, collectibles, crafts, quilts, new and used merchandise. Food available, rest rooms, wheelchair accessible. Ample parking. Contact: H. Dyeus, (312) 823-2511. *Third Sunday of each month.*

DIX

Dix Flea Market. Rt. 37. New indoor/outdoor market. Lots of antiques, collectibles, glassware, primitives, country items. Antique shop and auction company also located on the grounds. Food available. Space from $10 per day. (618) 266-7007. *Second weekend of each month.*

DOWNERS GROVE

Flea Market. 39th and Glendening Sts. New and used merchandise, gifts, imports, antiques, collectibles, crafts. Food available. (312) 969-6763. *First Sunday of each month.*

DUQUOIN

"Giant Flea Market." Fairgrounds. Antiques, collectibles, primitives, country, glassware, jewelry, silver. New and used merchandise, crafts. Approximately 100 dealers. Snack bar, wheelchair accessible. Ample parking. Admission charge. Space from $12 per table. Contact: John Crouch, Box 5058, Springfield, IL 62705. (217) 529-6939. *First Sunday of each month, 8:30 A.M. - 4:30 P.M.*

EAST DUNDEE

Dundee Drive-In Flea Market. Junction of Hwys. 72 and 25. Antiques, collect-

> ### *Pay Attention While Shopping*
> While shopping at flea markets, it is the responsibility of the buyer to "see" what he or she is buying. Many times we only assume that we have seen.
>
> Example: You see a serving tray with a nice brass handle facing you. You assume that it will have a second, equally nice handle on the opposite side. You look briefly, caught up in the color, style, and price being exactly what you are looking for. You buy it before someone else can snatch it up and only half look as the seller puts it in a bag for you.
>
> Later, at home, you remove your treasure and find that the handle that was away from you has been repaired with a large silver nut and washer. You're brokenhearted.
>
> Remember: it is no one else's responsibility to look after your wallet but you. So pay attention and take time to look items over well before purchasing them.

ibles, glassware, country, crafts, glassware, primitives. New and used merchandise. Food available, rest rooms. Ample parking. (312) 426-6736. *Sundays.*

ELMHURST

Flea Market. 310 W. Butterfield Rd., American Legion Hall. Market is primarily antiques and collectibles. Glassware, vintage clothing, coins, silver, jewelry, linens, advertising items, primitives. Some quality secondhand merchandise. Food available, rest rooms, wheelchair accessible. Ample parking. (312) 393-1795. *Second Sunday of each month.*

FAIRFIELD

Flea Market. Rt. 45, 3 miles south of Fairfield. New and used merchandise, garage sale items, bric-a-brac. Crafts, collectibles, produce. Food available, rest rooms. Ample parking. *First and third Mondays of each month.*

GENEVA

Kane County Antique Show and Flea Market. Fairgrounds. Rts. 64 and 30. Indoor/outdoor market. Quality antiques, collectibles, silver, coins, linens, vintage clothing, jewelry. Approximately 30 dealers. Food available, rest rooms, wheelchair accessible. Ample parking. Space from $15. Contact: Mrs. Robinson, 307 Sandholm, Geneva, IL 60134.

(312) 232-6264. *First Sunday of each month.*

GLENDALE
World Bazaar Giant Indoor/Outdoor Flea Market. 500 E. North Ave. One mile west of I-355. Lots of new merchandise, some used merchandise and collectibles. Great market for the thrifty shopper looking for new merchandise, both personal and household. Food available, rest rooms, wheelchair accessible. Ample parking. Admission charge. (708) 858-6410. *Saturdays and Sundays.*

GODFREY
Flea Market. Godfrey Community Center. Good flea market for the bargain hunter looking for new and nearly new finds, as well as for the collector looking for hidden treasure. (618) 466-2907. *First Sunday of each month.*

GOOD HOPE
Jerry's Variety Flea Market. Junction of Hwys. 9 and 67. Typical flea market fare, from jewelry trinkets to tools and everything in between. (309) 323-5777. *First weekend of each month.*

GRAFTON
Flea Market and Arts and Crafts Show. Reubel Hotel. Lots of secondhand bric-a-brac; good selection of crafts, as the name implies. (618) 254-9162. *Friday - Sunday.*

GRAYSLAKE
Flea Market. Lake County Fairgrounds. Lots of antiques and good-quality collectibles at this market. Primitives, advertising items, silver, fine and estate jewelry, coins, silver, linens, furniture. Approximately 75 dealers. Food available, rest rooms. Ample parking. Space from $12. (708) 223-1433. *Sundays.*

GRAYSLAKE
Grayslake Indoor Mart. Grayslake Auction Center. Rts. 120 and 83. Outdoor space. Contact: The Danners, (312) 223-9890 or 998-0428. *Saturdays and Sundays, 9:00 A.M. - 5:00 P.M.*

GRAYSLAKE
Grayslake Swap-O-Rama. Junction of Hwys. 120 and 83. New and used merchandise, garage sale items, crafts, collectibles, produce. Snack bar, rest rooms, wheelchair accessible. Ample parking. (414) 563-7398. *April - October; Sundays.*

GRIFFITH
Swap-O-Rama Flea Market. Ridge Road Drive-In. New and used merchandise. Flea

market fare, from bric-a-brac, crafts, and collectibles to produce. Food available, rest rooms, wheelchair accessible. Ample parking. (312) 774-3900. *Sundays.*

HARTFORD
Flea Market. Booths full of everything from the new and trendy to the nearly new and still desirable. (618) 254-2827. *Fourth Sunday of each month.*

HARVEY
Flea Market. 817 Chicago Ave. East. Contact: Joseph's Calumet College. Used merchandise, lots of garage sale vendors, and plenty of bric-a-brac. Food available, rest rooms, wheelchair accessible. Ample parking. *Thursdays.*

HAVANA
Flea Market. Rt. 97, South of town. Antiques, collectibles, new and used merchandise, crafts, produce. Food available, rest rooms, wheelchair accessible. Ample parking. (309) 543-4499. *First and third weekends of each month.*

HERRIN
Flea Market. (618) 942-7750. *April - November; Saturdays and Sundays.*

HIGHLAND
Highland Flea Market. Linden Dale Park. New and used merchandise, garage sale items, bric-a-brac, crafts, produce. Food available, rest rooms, wheelchair accessible. Ample parking. (618) 654-2581. *Second Sunday of each month.*

ITASCA
A and M Indoor Flea Market. A flea market with everything you expect to find, from pocket knives to birdhouses, T-shirts to baseball cards. (312) 529-1760. *Saturdays and Sundays.*

JOHNSTON CITY
Flea Market City. I-57, Exit 59. New and used merchandise, lots of garage sale and bric-a-brac items, country collectibles, produce, crafts. Food available. (618) 983-5548. *First weekend of each month.*

JOLIET
Derald's Indoor Flea Market. 219 Maple St. New merchandise: housewares, tools, sportswear, electronics, sports memorabilia. Used merchandise: jewelry, clothing, collectibles, crafts, and more. Food available, rest rooms. Ample parking. (815) 722-9232. *Saturdays and Sundays.*

KANKAKEE
Court Street Flea Market.

Shopping Essentials

Flea market shopping is a necessity for some, while for others it is a pastime or hobby. No matter what their motivation, all frequent buyers have one thing in common—they come prepared for anything. They have learned the hard way that you never know what you may find for sale at a flea market on a given day.

Seasoned shoppers often have a special jacket, tote bag, or backpack they keep packed with shopping essentials. A fishing vest makes a great piece of gear for a frequent shopper, because of all the small pockets.

Essentials include a tape measure, magnifying glass for inspecting small items, pocket poncho, rain bonnet or umbrella, notebook and pencil, pocket calculator, and a few sundries, such as aspirin, Band-Aids, suntan lotion, etc. Your own experience will add new things to this list. For instance, if you are a collector, you might carry a pocket price guide with you.

It is easy for the world of flea marketing to get into your blood, and your experiences will be even more fun and rewarding if you come prepared.

1933 E. Court St. I-57, Exit 312. Small indoor market. New and secondhand items, collectibles, crafts, gift and decorator items. Average daily attendance 200. Approximately 25 dealers. Snack bar, rest rooms. Ample parking. Admission charge. (708) 755-4931. *Saturdays and Sundays.*

KANKAKEE

Flea Market. Rt. 17. Clemens Auction Gallery. Antiques, collectibles, art, prints. Snack bar, rest rooms, wheelchair accessible. Ample parking. (815) 932-0565. *Second Sunday of each month.*

KANKAKEE

"Giant Flea Market." Fairgrounds. Indoor market. Antiques, collectibles, crafts, primitives, advertising items, paper goods, coins. Approximately 50 sellers. Snack bar, rest rooms, wheelchair accessible. Ample parking. Admission charge. Space from $12 per table. Contact: John Crouch, Box 5058. Springfield, IL 62705. (217) 529-6939. *Second Sunday of each month.*

Larkin
Big John's Flea Market. Rt. 6 East. Used merchandise, garage sale items, collectibles, gifts, imports. Rest rooms. Ample parking. 723-7472. *Daily.*

Le Grange
Antique Flea Market. 900 S. Le Grange Rd. American Legion Hall. Antiques (smalls), collectibles, primitives, glassware, silver, coins, linens, vintage clothing. Food available, rest rooms, wheelchair accessible. Ample parking. *Second Sunday of each month.*

Loves Park
The Peddlers Place Flea Market and Crafts Show. 6400 N. Second St. (Hwy. 251 South). Country crafts, collectibles, new and used merchandise. Snack bar, rest rooms. Ample parking. (815) 282-9739. *Saturdays and Sundays.*

Loves Park
Trash to Treasures Flea Market. Hwy. 251 North. Used merchandise, garage sale items, bric-a-brac, collectibles. Snack bar, rest rooms. Ample parking. (815) 397-6683. *Saturdays and Sundays.*

Marion
Flea Market. Fairgrounds. Lots of garage sale and used merchandise, new merchandise, collectibles, crafts, produce. Snack bar, rest rooms, wheelchair accessible. Ample parking. (618) 993-3764. *Saturdays.*

Melrose Park
A. M. Bargain Bazaar Flea Market. 1945 Cornell at North Ave. New and used merchandise, garage sale and bric-a-brac items, lots of good secondhand merchandise. Collectibles, gifts, decorator items. Snack bar, rest rooms, wheelchair accessible. Ample parking. Contact: Mary Gowenlock, 1945 Cornell, Melrose Park, IL 60160. (708) 450-0277. *Thursdays, Saturdays, and Sundays.*

Melrose Park
Ashland Avenue Swap-O-Rama. 4100 S. Ashland Ave. Indoor/outdoor market. Lots of sports merchandise and memorabilia, new merchandise, imports, collectibles, crafts, and used desirables. Approximately 450 dealers. Snack bar, rest rooms. Ample parking. Space from $17. (708) 344-7300. *Friday - Sunday, 7:00 A.M. - 4:00 P.M.*

Melrose Park
Flea Market. Shoppers will

find traditional flea market fare at this monthly venue. Sports memorabilia, jewelry, tools, household items, and more. (312) 366-5627. *Fourth Sunday of each month.*

MELROSE PARK

Melrose Park Swap-O-Rama. 4600 W. Lake St. Lake St. at Mannheim Rd. New merchandise: sports-related items, sportswear, new collectibles, electronics. Crafts, some used and garage sale merchandise. Good market for commercial vendors; excellent for bargain prices on new merchandise. Average attendance 6,000. Approximately 300 dealers. Snack bar, rest rooms, wheelchair accessible. Ample parking. Space from $15 to $18 inside, $8 outside. Reservations required. Electricity available. No overnight camping. Contact: Jim Pierski, 4600 W. Lake St., Melrose Park, IL 60160. (708) 344-7300. *Saturdays and Sundays, 7:00 A.M. - 4:00 P.M.*

MENDOTA

Fourth Sunday Flea Market. 810 Main St. Antiques, collectibles, primitives, country collectibles, farm items, new and used merchandise, crafts, produce. Snack bar, rest rooms, wheelchair accessible. Ample parking. (815) 539-7595. *May - September; fourth Sunday of each month.*

MONEE

County Line Swap-O-Rama. Rt. 50 to Cicero Ave. at Steger Rd. New merchandise: electronics, tools, housewares, sports items, outdoor wares, and sportswear. Also used merchandise, garage sale items, crafts, collectibles, and produce. Average daily attendance 2,500. Approximately 130 dealers. Food available, rest rooms, wheelchair accessible. Outside space only. Space from $5 to $8. Electricity available. No overnight camping. Contact: Jim Pierski, 4600 W. Lake St., Melrose Park, IL 60160. (708) 344-7300. *April - November; Sundays.*

MT. PROSPECT

Fourth Sunday Flea Market. Randhurst Shopping Center. Antiques, collectibles, new and used merchandise. Food available, rest rooms, wheelchair accessible. Ample parking. (312) 253-0117. *Fourth Sunday of each month.*

MURPHYSBORO

Southern Illinois TradeFair. Junction of Rts. 13 and 127 N. Indoor/outdoor flea market. New merchandise, imports, used merchandise, some collectibles, lots of secondhand merchandise. Fun market to poke around in. Good snack bar, rest rooms, wheelchair accessible. Ample parking. Space from $5 per day. (618) 684-3119 or 684-2849. *Fridays and Saturdays, 9:00 A.M. - 5:00 P.M.*

NAUVOO
Flea Market and Crafts Show. Indoor/outdoor market. Collectibles, farm items, religious items, used merchandise. Located in historic town with lots of interesting shops and sightseeing opportunities. Approximately 30 dealers. Snack bar. Space from $5. (319) 524-7611. *First Sunday of each month.*

NORMAL
"Giant Flea Market." Illinois State University Ballroom. Antiques, collectibles, primitives, coins, silver, new merchandise, gift items, decorator items, used merchandise, crafts. Approximately 50 dealers. Snack bar, rest rooms, wheelchair accessible. Ample parking. Admission charge. Space from $11 per table. Contact: John Crouch, Box 5058. Springfield, IL 62705. (217)

> ### Bargaining Savvy for the Beginner
> It is perfectly acceptable at a flea market to try to negotiate a lower price on an item. Most dealers expect you to, and have built bargaining room into their prices.

529-6939. *May - October; first Sunday of each month.*

NORTHBROOK
Flea Market. Sports Complex. Indoor Market. New and used merchandise, garage sale items, crafts, collectibles. Snack bar, rest rooms, wheelchair accessible. Ample parking. *Saturdays and Sundays.*

NORTHLAKE
Northlake Swap-O-Rama. 401 W. Lake St. Antiques, collectibles, new and used merchandise, crafts. Food available, rest rooms, wheelchair accessible. Ample parking. (312) 774-3900. *April - November; Sundays.*

OREGON
Trading Fair. Fairgrounds. Antiques, collectibles, primitives, country collectibles, housewares, linen, quilts, crafts. Food available, wheelchair accessible, rest rooms. Ample parking. Admission

> ## *Shopping for Your Pet*
> Shoppers can find almost anything they need for the family pet at a flea market. Aquariums, terrariums, dog houses, kitty cushions, even rhinestone-studded collars and leashes. You name it, and chances are, someone at a market is selling it. Pet supplies are a popular line among vendors, and you may be able to find shampoo, toys, flea collars, pet food of all brands and descriptions, and practically everything to keep your pet happy and healthy.
>
> We know of one market where a veterinarian holds periodic immunization clinics and does pet identification tattooing!
>
> At some markets, dealers sell personally engraved name tags for pets, "made to order" while you wait.
>
> Many great buys for your pet await you at the flea market, and for bargains and variety, this is the place to shop.

charge. (815) 239-1188. *Third Sunday of each month.*

OTTAWA
Flea Market and Bazaar. Rt. 1 West. Cooks Trailer Court. Used merchandise, garage sale items, bric-a-brac. Rest rooms. Ample parking. *Summer months only; Saturdays and Sundays.*

PANA
The Biggest Indoor Flea Market. Dutch Mill Building. East Rt. 16 and 51. Antiques, collectibles, memorabilia, advertising items, primitives, country, crafts, used merchandise, produce. Approximately 50 dealers inside and 25 outside. Snack bar, rest rooms, wheelchair accessible. Space from $10 daily or $25 for all 3 days. Tables and electricity available. Self-contained camping OK. Contact: Carl Spalding, Rt. 2, Box 268, Pana, IL 62557. (217) 562-4825. *Friday - Sunday, 9:00 a.m. - 4:30 p.m.*

PEORIA
"Giant Flea Market." Fairgrounds, Expo Gardens. Indoor market. New merchandise, tools, collectibles, used goods, crafts, art, and more. Approximately 100 sellers. Snack bar, rest rooms, wheelchair accessible. Ample parking. Admission charge. Space from $12 per table. Contact: John Crouch, Box 5058. Springfield, IL 62705. (217) 529-6939. *Fourth Sun-*

day of each month, 8:30 A.M. - 4:30 P.M.

PEOTONE
Antique Show and Flea Market. Will County Fairgrounds. 1 mile East of I-57. Space for 700 sellers. Wide variety of antiques and collectibles. Approximately 60 dealers. Admission charge $2. Space from $25. Contact: Robert Mitchell, Jr. 223 E. Main. Amboy, IL 61310. (815) 857-2253 or 857-3328. *Fourth Sunday of each month.*

PINCKNEYVILLE
Flea Market. Indoor/outdoor market. Contact: Shirley Woolsey, (618) 357-8110. *Fourth weekend of each month.*

PRAIRIE VIEW
Country Boy Flea Market. 193 Milwaukee Ave. New and used merchandise, lots of garage sale and bric-a-brac items. Crafts, collectibles, produce. Snack bar, rest rooms, wheelchair accessible. Ample parking. (312) 541-1952. *Wednesdays, Saturdays, and Sundays.*

PRINCETON
Second Sunday Flea Market. Fairgrounds. Antiques, collectibles, vintage clothing, silver, coins, linens, quilts. Food available, rest rooms, wheelchair accessible. Ample parking. (815) 643-2931. *Second Sunday of each month.*

QUINCY
Jack's Flea Market. 126 S. Fourth St. Used merchandise, garage sale items, gifts, imports, decorator items. Rest rooms. Ample parking. (317) 223-0695. *Saturdays and Sundays.*

ROCKFORD
Greater Rockford Indoor/Outdoor Antique and Flea Market. 3913 Sandy Hollow Rd. Rt. 20. Exit Alpine St. Approximately 200 outside spaces and 50 inside spaces. Good selection of collectibles, small antiques, primitives, country, advertising items, paper goods, coins, silver, glassware. New merchandise, crafts, and used merchandise. Snack bar, rest rooms, wheelchair accessible. Ample parking. Space from $20 for the weekend. Reservations required. Contact: Carol Shorkey, 6350 Canyon Wood Dr., Rockford, IL 61109. (815) 397-6683 or 874-3362. *Saturdays and Sundays, 9:00 A.M. - 4:00 P.M.*

ROCKFORD
Rockford Flea Market. Forest Hills Lodge. Rt. 173. New and used merchandise,

> ### *Junk vs. Junque*
> What is the difference between "junk" and "junque"?
>
> The word "junk" usually refers to castoff items which are no longer wanted or used and could be called secondhand at best.
>
> The word "junque" is a colloquialism that has come to mean high class, fancy, cute, better than average, junk.

garage sale items, crafts, collectibles, produce. Food available, rest rooms, wheelchair accessible. Ample parking. Admission charge. Contact: Paul Arduini, (815) 633-5328. *Saturdays and Sundays.*

ROYALTON
Flea Market. North Main St. Used merchandise, housewares, clothing, tools, bicycles, toys, some new merchandise. Rest rooms. Ample parking. (618) 984-1363. *Saturdays*

ST. CHARLES
Kane County Flea Market. Kane County Fairgrounds. Randall Rd. between Rts. 64 and 38. Indoor/outdoor market. Strong on quality antiques (both furniture and smalls). Great selection of collectibles; lots of fine jewelry and quality "junque." Some real quality dealers. Good market for antique dealers, serious collectors, investors, and decorators to make some great buys. Excellent attendance. Approximately 1000 dealers. Good home-cooked meals served, rest rooms, wheelchair accessible. Ample parking. Admission charge $4. Space from $110 indoors and $100 outdoors. Contact: Helen Robinson, Box 549, St. Charles, IL 60174. (708) 377-2252. *First weekend of each month. Saturdays, 1:00 - 5:00 P.M.; Sundays, 7:00 A.M. - 4:00 P.M.*

SANDWICH
Sandwich Antiques Market. Fairgrounds. State Rt. 34. Quality antique market; lots of furniture. Excellent for antique dealers and serious collectors. Great selection of collectibles, glassware, silver and fine jewelry. Great source market for the serious collector, shopkeeper or decorator. Approximately 500 exhibitors. Snack bar, rest rooms, wheelchair accessible. Ample parking. Admission charge $3. Contact: Robert Lawler, 1510 N. Hoyne. Chicago, IL 60622.

(312) 227-4464. *Monthly, 8:00 A.M. - 4:00 P.M.*

SAUGET
Archview Flea Market. Rt. 3. I-255, Exit 13 to Hwy. 157 to Rt. 3, north 3 miles. New indoor/outdoor market. New merchandise: furniture, sportswear, electronics. Used merchandise. Approximately 75 dealers. Snack bar, rest rooms, wheelchair accessible. Ample parking. Contact: Ron Newsome, 1401 Mississippi Ave., #5. Sauget, IL 62202. (618) 271-1021. *Saturdays and Sundays.*

SPARTA
The Olde Hotel Flea Market and Auction. A typical flea market in every sense. Even a bride-to-be could find what she needed at this market: something old, something new, something blue, and much more. Market also runs an auction service. (618) 295-2440. *Saturdays and Sundays.*

SPRINGFIELD
Flea Market. MacArthur at North Grand. New and used merchandise, garage sale bric-a-brac, crafts, produce, and more. Snack bar, rest rooms. (217) 523-6953. *Saturdays and Sundays.*

SPRINGFIELD
Flea Market. Springfield Drive-In. New merchandise: electronics, tools, housewares, toys, sportswear, sports merchandise. Used merchandise, garage sale items. Crafts, collectibles, produce. Snack bar, rest rooms, wheelchair accessible. Ample parking. (217) 496-2088. *April - November; Sundays.*

SPRINGFIELD
Flea Market. 2700 W. Lawrence. Soccer World. Ample parking. New merchandise: sportswear, housewares. Used merchandise, garage sale items. Snack bar, rest rooms. (217) 522-4105. *Saturdays.*

SPRINGFIELD
Frank's Gigantic Flea Market. Corner of Dirksen and Clearlake, at the entrance of the K-Mart Shopping Center. Clearlake exit from I-55, 1 mile. New and used merchandise; flea market finds, including crafts, collectibles and produce. Food available, rest rooms, wheelchair accessible. Ample parking. Outside space for 150 dealers from $1. Contact: Frank Reynolds, 3208 E. Clearlake, Springfield, IL 62703. (217)

544-3142. *Saturdays and Sundays, 6:00 A.M. - dark.*

SPRINGFIELD
"Giant Flea Market." Fairgrounds. Illinois Building. Indoor market. Heavy on antiques and collectibles. Some new and used merchandise. Approximately 100 exhibitors. Snack bar, rest rooms, wheelchair accessible. Ample parking. Admission charge. Contact: John Crouch, (217) 529-6939. *Call for schedule; 8:30 A.M. - 4:30 P.M.*

SPRINGFIELD
"Giant Flea Market." Holiday Inn East. Indoor market. Antiques, collectibles, silver, coins, linens, glassware, vintage clothing. Approximately 50 dealers. Ample parking. Admission charge. Food available, rest rooms, wheelchair accessible. Space from $12 per table. Contact: John Crouch, Box 5058, Springfield, IL 62705. (217) 529-6939. *Third Sunday of each month.*

SPRINGFIELD
Judy's Flea Market. Shaheens's Racetrack parking lot. New and used merchandise, lots of garage sale items, crafts, produce, collectibles. Snack bar, rest rooms, wheelchair accessible. Ample parking. (217) 528-3142. *Saturdays and Sundays.*

SPRINGFIELD
Ruby Sled Antique and Art Mart. 1142 S. Spring. Antiques, collectibles, primitives, glassware, silver, art, prints, crafts. Rest rooms, wheelchair accessible. Ample parking. (217) 523-3391. *Saturdays and Sundays.*

TINLEY PARK
I-80 Collectibles and Flea Market. I-80 and Oak Park Ave. Indoor/outdoor market. New and used merchandise, crafts, collectibles, antiques, produce. Food available, rest rooms, wheelchair accessible. Ample parking. Contact: Ralph Bruno, (708) 532-8238. *Saturdays and Sundays, 6:00 A.M. - dark.*

URBANA
Urbana Antiques and Flea Market. Fairgrounds. Indoor/outdoor market. Good selection of new and used merchandise here. Wide variety of collectibles, memorabilia, primitives, country, and advertising items. A good market for the collector, shopkeeper, or decorator. Approximately 150 exhibitors. Ample parking. Space from $20. Contact: Howard Goddard, 934 Amherst Dr., Urbana, IL 43078. (513) 653-

6013 or 653-6945. *First weekend of each month, 9:00 A.M. - 5:00 P.M.*

VERGENNES
Flea Market. Rts. 13 and 127. Antiques, collectibles, silver, glassware, farm items, crafts, produce, used merchandise. Food available, rest rooms, wheelchair accessible. (618) 684-6314. *Second weekend of each month.*

VOLVO
Volvo Sales Flea Market. Rt. 120, west of Rt. 12. New merchandise: closeouts, surplus, housewares, clothing. Used merchandise, garage sale items. Snack bar, rest rooms, wheelchair accessible. Ample parking. (815) 385-3896. *Saturdays and Sundays.*

WAPELLA
Flea Market. Wapella Auction House. New merchandise, surplus, closeouts, housewares, clothing, used merchandise, collectibles. Snack bar, rest rooms, wheelchair accessible. Ample parking. *Second Sunday of each month.*

WARREN
Flea Market, Antiques and Crafts. Fairgrounds. Antiques, collectibles, glassware, primitives, quilts, vintage clothing, jewelry, watches. Good selec-

---

Surplus vs. Overruns
In flea-market-speak, the word "surplus" refers to dated, leftover items, such as last year's model. "Overruns" refers to too many new, current items.

---

tion of locally made crafts. Food available, rest rooms, wheelchair accessible. Ample parking. (608) 759-3493. *Second Sunday of each month.*

WATERLOO
Flea Market. Knights of Columbus Hall. New market. New and nearly new goods, produce, and typical flea market finds. (618) 939-8105. *Second weekend of each month.*

WAUKEGAN
Waukegan Swap 'N Shop Flea Market. Belvedere Mall. Rt. 120 and Lewis Ave. Large indoor market. New and used merchandise, housewares, tools, sports items, sportswear, electronics, outdoor items, collectibles, jewelry. Snack bar, rest rooms, wheelchair accessible. Contact: Larry Lemer, (708) 263-0160. *Friday - Sunday, 9:00 A.M. - 6:00 P.M.*

WHEATON
Du Page Antique and Flea Market. Du Page County Fair-

grounds. Large indoor/outdoor antique and collectible market. Great selection of antiques, furniture, quality collector lines, silver, coins, glassware, farm items, advertising items, vintage clothing, jewelry. Food available, rest rooms, wheelchair accessible. Ample paved parking. Admission charge. Contact: Marilyn Sugarman, (708) 455-6090 or 668-6636. *Third Sunday of each month.*

WHEELING

Twin Flea Market. 1010 S. Milwaukee Ave. Large outdoor market with lots of new merchandise, hot new items for the fashion conscious, secondhand items, and some collectibles. Approximately 300 dealers. Snack bar, rest rooms, wheelchair accessible. Ample parking. Contact: Ron Swislow, (708) 537-8223. *Saturdays and Sundays, 6:00 A.M. - 9:00 P.M.*

YORKVILLE

Flea Market. Country Side Center. Rts. 34 and 47. Antiques, collectibles, new and used merchandise, crafts. Food available, rest rooms. Ample parking. (312) 553-0826. *Seasonal; third Sunday of each month.*

INDIANA

Hoosiers and covered bridges—quaint, charming, friendly and lovely. From urbane Indianapolis to the Amish of Shipshewana, megamarkets, picturesque country auctions, and some of the finest malls in the heartland are located here. Americana at its finest is displayed in the diversity of Indiana.

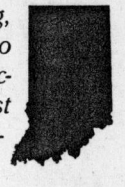

Every weekend seems to bring a quality event of some type at the Indiana State Fairgrounds, in Indianapolis—a really nice facility that has done an excellent job of booking interesting shows.

(Note: The State of Indiana and the City of Indianapolis both require a transient vendor's license. This requirement is actively enforced.)

Best bets...

✦ **White Farmers Market, Brookville**
  One of the most interesting tourist markets in the country. Livestock auction at 1:00 P.M. on Wednesdays.

✦ **Indiana Flea Market, Indianapolis**
  Collector's paradise; one of the better antique and collectible markets.

✦ **Shipshewana Auction and Flea Market, Shipshewana**
  If it's for sale, it's at this market. Over five auctions running simultaneously.

ALBANY
Albany Flea Market Mall. 324 W. State St. Indoor market. New and secondhand merchandise, collectibles, glassware, advertising items. Rest rooms, wheelchair accessible. Ample parking. Space from $15 per week. Contact: Jim Schultz, Box 112, Albany, IN 47320. (317) 789-8479. *Daily; closed Saturdays.*

ANDERSON
Olympia Expo Center Flea Market. 1312 W. 29th St. Indoor/outdoor market. New merchandise: housewares,

> ### *Dress for the Hunt!*
> ### *Tip #1*
> Dress in layers—weather is changeable and unpredictable, and you don't want to have to cut your trip short because you are too hot or too cold.

sportswear, electronics, sports merchandise, collectibles, glassware, primitives, country collectibles. Snack bar, rest rooms, wheelchair accessible. Ample parking. (317) 642-0550. *Saturdays and Sundays.*

ATTICA
Antiques and Collectibles Flea Market. National Guard Armory. Antiques, collectibles, glassware, coins, linens, primitives. Food available, rest rooms, wheelchair accessible. Ample parking. (317) 762-2727. *Second Sunday of each month.*

ATTICA
Flea Market. Rt. 28. Indian Lake Campgrounds. Secondhand merchandise, tools, clothing, garage sale items. Rest rooms, wheelchair accessible. Ample parking. (317) 362-2195. *Summer market; Saturdays and Sundays.*

AURORA
Aurora Flea Market. Rt. 50. New merchandise: electronics, tools, housewares, sportswear, toys. Used merchandise, garage sale items, crafts, collectibles, sportswear. Snack bar, rest rooms. Ample parking. (317) 423-3231. *Friday - Sunday.*

AUSTIN
Flea Market. South 4th St. Used merchandise, bric-a-brac, clothing, tools, toys. Rest rooms. Ample parking. (812) 794-3313. *Saturdays.*

AVON
Flea Market. Al Unser Industrial Park. New merchandise: sportswear, housewares, sports merchandise, electronics. Used merchandise. Snack bar, rest rooms, wheelchair accessible. Ample parking. (317) 272-0800. *Saturdays and Sundays.*

BARGERSVILLE
Bargersville Flea Market. Junction of Hwys. 135 and 144. Used merchandise, garage sale items, bric-a-brac, tools, toys, clothing. Rest rooms. Ample parking. (317) 535-4730. *Saturdays and Sundays.*

BIRDSEYE
Flea Market. Birdseye Auction Barn. New merchandise: sur-

plus, closeouts, clothing, housewares. Country collectibles. Used merchandise, garage sale items. Snack bar, rest rooms. Ample parking. *Second and fourth Sundays of each month.*

BLOOMINGTON

Bloomington Antique Show and Flea Market. Fairgrounds. Antiques, furniture, collectibles, glassware, advertising items, farm and ranch collectibles, coins, silver. Food available, rest rooms, wheelchair accessible. Ample parking. *Fourth weekend of each month.*

BLOOMINGTON

Starlite Drive-In Theater Flea Market. Old Hwy. 37 South. New merchandise: electronics, tools, sportswear, housewares, outdoor items, toys. Used merchandise, garage sale items. Crafts, collectibles, produce. Snack bar, rest rooms, wheelchair accessible. Ample parking. Contact: Carl Stewart, (812) 824-7911. *Saturdays and Sundays.*

BLOOMINGTON

Y and W Drive-In Theater Flea Market. Hwy. 37 North. New and used merchandise, collectibles, crafts, produce. Snack bar, rest rooms, wheelchair accessible. Ample parking. (812) 339-6319. *Sundays.*

BLUFFTON

Parlor City Flea Market. Hwy. 1, north of town. Used merchandise, garage sale items, bric-a-brac, crafts, produce. Approximately 25 dealers. Rest rooms. Ample parking. Space from $6. (219) 824-0528. *Saturdays and Sundays.*

BORDEN

Borden Flea Market. Hwy. 60, west of town. New and used merchandise, garage sale items, country collectibles, crafts, produce. Approximately 150 dealers. Rest rooms, snack bar. Ample parking. Space from $2. Camping available. Contact: Norma Wright, (812) 967-3033. *Seasonal market; Saturdays and Sundays.*

BROOKVILLE

White Farmers Market. 162nd St. at White Livestock Auction. Indoor/outdoor market, located on 160-acre farm in Amish country. New and used merchandise, collectibles, crafts, produce. One of the most interesting tourist markets in the country. Approximately 100 dealers. Livestock auction at 1:00 P.M. on Wednesdays; several special events held during the year. Snack bar, rest rooms, wheelchair accessible. Space from $8. Contact: Dane White, Box 53, Brookville, IN 47012. (317) 647-3574. *Wednesdays, daylight - early afternoon.*

BROWNSTOWN
Jackson County Flea Market. Fairgrounds. Antiques, collectibles, coins, silver, linen, glassware, primitives. Food available, rest rooms, wheelchair accessible. Ample parking. *Fourth weekend of each month.*

CARLISLE
Carlisle Flea Market. U.S. Hwy. 41. New and used merchandise, garage sale items, country collectibles, crafts, produce. Snack bar, rest rooms. Ample parking. (812) 839-4112. *Saturdays and Sundays.*

CARLISLE
Flea Market. Fairgrounds. Antiques, collectibles, glassware, primitives, jewelry, silver. Food available, rest rooms, wheelchair accessible. Ample parking. *Second and fourth weekends of each month.*

CEDAR LAKE
Barn and Field Flea Market. 151st and Parish Ave., 1 mile east of Rt. 41. Indoor/outdoor market. Heavy on fine antiques and quality collectibles, toys, dolls, jewelry, clothes, etc. Approximately 150 dealers. Has companion antique shops with many fine antiques and collectibles. Snack bar, rest rooms, wheelchair accessible. Space from $2 per day. Electricity available; camping onsite. Contact: D. Corey, Box 411, Cedar Lake, IN 46303. (219) 696-7368. *Saturdays and Sundays, 9:00 A.M. - 5:00 P.M.*

CEDAR LAKE
Uncle John's Flea Market. Rt. 41 south of U.S. 30. 15205 Wicker Ave. Indoor/outdoor market. Approximately 200 dealers. Space from $6. No overnight parking. Camping nearby. Contact: John Lail, 15205 Wicker Ave., Cedar Lake, IN 46303. (219) 696-7911. *Friday - Sunday, 8:00 A.M. - 5:00 P.M.*

CENTERVILLE
Beechwood Pavilion Flea Market. Hwy. 40 West. Indoor/outdoor market. New and used merchandise, garage sale items, collectibles, crafts, produce. Approximately 15 dealers. Snack bar, rest rooms. Ample parking. *Saturdays and Sundays.*

CENTERVILLE
Big Bear Flea Market. Centerville Rd. and I-70, Exit 145. Outdoor open-air and covered spaces. Antiques, collectibles, new and used merchandise, crafts. Approximately 100 dealers. Good food available. Campground with hookups. Contact: Ed Newman, (317) 855-3912. *Saturdays and Sundays, 7:00 A.M. - 5:00 P.M.*

CENTERVILLE
The Flea Marketeers. 103 W. Main St. Secondhand merchandise, garage sale items, gift items, imports, decorator items. Rest rooms. Ample parking. (317) 855-2231. *Monday - Saturday.*

CENTERVILLE
Webb's Antique Mall. 200 W. Union St. 2 miles south of I-70, Exit 145. 70,000 sq. ft. facility. Mall features high-quality dealers selling fine furniture, collectibles, glassware, and quality items of all descriptions. No junk. Over 400 booths. This market is one of my favorite stops. (317) 855-5542. Credit cards accepted. Nice restaurant in the mall. Clean restrooms, wheelchair accessible, lots of walking. Ample parking. *Daily, 9:00 A.M. - 6:00 P.M.*

CHARLESTOWN
Charlestown Flea Market. Hwy. 62, 1 mile east of town. New and used merchandise, garage sale merchandise, collectibles, produce, crafts. Snack bar, rest rooms, wheelchair accessible. Ample parking. Contact: Edward Davidson, (812) 256-3559. *Saturdays and Sundays.*

CLARKSVILLE
Trading Fair. 520 Marriott Dr. Indoor market. New merchandise: electronics, tools, housewares, sports merchandise, jewelry. Used merchandise: collectibles, glassware, advertising items. Snack bar, rest rooms, wheelchair accessible. Ample parking. (812) 288-0600. *Saturdays and Sundays.*

CLOVERDALE
Country Corner Flea Market. Hwy. 42 West. Indoor/outdoor market. New and used merchandise, collectibles, crafts, produce, bric-a-brac. Snack bar, rest rooms. Ample parking. Contact: Ted Howard, (317) 795-4501. *Friday - Sunday.*

COLUMBIA CITY
Flea Market. East on Rt. 30 at Auction Center. New merchandise: clothing, imports, housewares. Used merchan-

> **More Bargaining Savvy for the Beginner**
> Make sure your offer is reasonable. Don't expect a dealer to accept or be happy if you make a $2 offer on a $50 item.

dise and appliances. Rest rooms, wheelchair accessible. Ample parking. *Daily.*

CONNERSVILLE
Flea Market. 2207 Vermont. Secondhand merchandise, garage sale items, collectibles. Rest rooms. Ample parking. *Daily.*

DECATUR
Flea Market. Community Center. Indoor/outdoor market. Antiques, collectibles, glassware, silver, vintage clothing, new and used merchandise, crafts, produce. Food available, rest rooms, wheelchair accessible. Ample parking. Space from $5. (219) 724-3538. *First Sunday of each month.*

EATON
Indiana Avenue Flea Market. 107 W. Indiana Ave. New and used merchandise, garage sale items. Rest rooms. Ample parking. (317) 759-8932. *Saturdays and Sundays.*

EVANSVILLE
Diamond Flea Market. 1250 Diamond Ave. Collectibles, country, primitives, some antiques, new and used merchandise, crafts, produce. Average daily attendance 750. Approximately 75 dealers. Snack bar, clean rest rooms. Ample parking. Overnight camping nearby. Space from $20 for the weekend. Contact: Barbara Staub, 1250 E. Diamond Ave., Evansville, IN. (812) 464-2675. *Saturdays and Sundays 9:00 A.M. - 5:00 P.M.*

EVANSVILLE
Evansville Flea Market. 1800 Mesker Park Dr. New and used merchandise, garage sale items, collectibles, farm and ranch items, crafts, produce. Approximately 70 dealers. Snack bar, rest rooms. Ample parking. Space from $5. Market is located in an old amusement park. No alcohol, drug paraphernalia, or obscene items. (812) 422-2559 or 867-3425. *Saturdays and Sundays.*

EVANSVILLE
The Gallery Flea Market. 6724 Boonville Hwy. (812) 477-5988 or 479-6103. *Friday - Sunday, 9:00 A.M. - 6:00 P.M.*

FLORA
Flea Market. Moose Lodge. Collectibles, silver, new and

used merchandise. Food available, rest rooms, wheelchair accessible. Ample parking. (618) 622-2015 or 622-5385. *First Sunday of each month.*

FOUNTAINTOWN

Fountaintown Emporium. Old Green Field Rd. Located at old schoolhouse. Indoor/outdoor market. Antiques, collectibles, silver, glassware, primitives, advertising items, new and used merchandise. Food available, rest rooms, wheelchair accessible. Ample parking. Spaces from $5. Contact: Art Goodblood, (317) 861-7989 or 862-2187. *First Sunday of each month.*

FOUNTAINTOWN

Moonlite Flea Market and Crafts Show. Used and secondhand items, garage sale items, country collectibles, farm and ranch items, lots of locally made crafts, produce. Approximately 50 vendors. Food available, rest rooms. Ample parking. Space from $6 per day. Camping available. Contact: Donny Wyss, Box 104, Fountaintown, IN 46150. (317) 861-9775. *May - October; Saturdays and Sundays.*

FRANKLIN

Flea Market. Hwy. 31 North. New and used merchandise, garage sale items, collectibles, crafts, produce. Snack bar, rest rooms. Ample parking. *Saturdays and Sundays.*

FRANKLIN

Franklin Antique Show and Flea Market. Fairgrounds. Indoor market, excellent for antiques and quality collectibles. Some new merchandise. Approximately 50 dealers. Snack bar, rest rooms, wheelchair accessible. Space from $28 for the weekend. Contact: Elmer Judkings, 122 Woodland Dr., New Whiteland, IN 46184. (317) 535-5084. *Third Sunday of each month, 9:00 A.M. - 5:00 P.M.*

FRIENDSHIP

Friendship Flea Market. Hwy. 62, west of Dillsboro. One of the most fun markets to sell at or attend. Great place to see living American heritage in action. Strong attendance; usually over 100,000 for the spring show. Approximately 500 dealers. Space from $110 for entire show or $15 per day. Camping permitted at selling space. Contact: Tom Kerr, 654 Wayskin Dr., Covington, KY 41015. (606) 356-7114. *Held semiannually (spring and fall), in conjunction with the national black powder shoots.*

Ft. Wayne

Ft. Wayne Antique and Collectors Market. Memorial Coliseum. New market. Antiques, collectibles, crafts, and new merchandise. Special antique section. Admission charge $1. Snack bar, rest rooms, wheelchair accessible. Ample parking. Contact: Stewart Promotions, 2950 Breckenridge Lane, #4A. Louisville, KY 40220. (502) 456-2244. *Monthly. Usually last weekend of each month; call for dates. Fridays, 3:00 - 9:00 P.M.; Saturdays, 10:00 A.M. - 7:00 P.M.; Sundays, 11:00 A.M. - 5:00 P.M.*

Ft. Wayne

Ft. Wayne Flea Market. 6905 S. Hanna at U.S. Hwy. 27 South. Primarily indoor market; limited outdoor space. New merchandise: imports, gifts, sportswear, electronics. Approximately 100 dealers. Snack bar, rest rooms, wheelchair accessible. Contact: Dean Morris, (219) 447-0081. *Saturdays and Sundays.*

Ft. Wayne

International Park Consumer Center. 2701 S. Coliseum Blvd. Indoor/outdoor market. New merchandise: gifts, imports, surplus, closeouts, clothing, jewelry. Market has never caught on with the professional dealer. Snack bar, rest rooms, wheelchair accessible. Ample parking. Contact: International Park. 2710 S. Coliseum Blvd., Ft. Wayne, IN 46803. (219) 422-3737. *Friday - Sunday.*

Ft. Wayne

New Haven Flea Market. New Haven Drive-In Theater. New and used merchandise, large volume of garage sale items, collectibles, crafts, produce. Snack bar, rest rooms, wheelchair accessible. Ample parking. (219) 749-8314. *Sundays.*

Ft. Wayne

Speedway Mall Flea Market. 217 Marciel Dr., 2 blocks north of Glenbrook. Across from 84 Lumber. Flea market and farmers' market. Indoor/outdoor market. 150 spaces inside. New and used items, antiques, nostalgia, coins, stamps. Snack bar, rest rooms, wheelchair accessible. Inside and outside space from $5 per weekend. Contact: Mrs. Mills, (219) 484-1239. *Fridays, noon - 9:00 P.M.; Saturdays and Sundays, 10:00 A.M. - 5:00 P.M.*

Ft. Wayne

Shiloh Country Flea Market.

Indoor/outdoor market. New and used merchandise, antiques, collectibles, Lots of good farm items, crafts, produce, livestock. Food available, rest rooms, wheelchair accessible. Ample parking. (219) 637-3517. *Tuesdays and Wednesdays.*

GARY
Market City Flea Market. 4121 Cleveland St. Indoor/outdoor market. Crafts, art, memorabilia, decorator items. New merchandise, secondhand items, garage sale "junque." Some antiques and collectibles, but most of market is discounted new merchandise. 200+ dealers. Snack bar, rest rooms, wheelchair accessible. Ample parking. Space from $30. Contact: Manager, 4121 Cleveland, Gary, IN 46408. (219) 887-3522. *Saturdays and Sundays, 9:00 A.M. - 5:00 P.M.*

GARY
Village Flea Market. 1845 W. Ridge Rd. New and used merchandise, garage sale items, collectibles, crafts, produce. Snack bar, rest rooms. Ample parking. (219) 980-1111. *Friday - Sunday.*

GAS CITY
Country Village Flea Market and Craft Show. 241 E. Main St. Used merchandise,

---

> **Shopping Tip #2**
> Be ready to pounce on an item if you know it's exactly what you want. Chances are it won't be there for long, and it'll haunt you for the rest of your days if you don't snap it up.

---

garage sale items, gifts, imports, decorator items. Good selection of local craft items. Approximately 20 dealers. Rest rooms. Spaces $20 per week. Contact: Louie Alspach, (317) 674-3103. *Thursday - Sunday.*

GOSHEN
Peddlers Flea Market. 2626 Peddlers Village Rd. New merchandise: gifts, imports, sportswear. Used merchandise, garage sale items, collectibles. Snack bar, rest rooms. Ample parking. (219) 533-9723. *Tuesday - Saturday, 10:00 A.M. - 8:00 P.M.*

HAMMOND
41 Swap-O-Rama. 2500 Calumet. New and used merchandise, garage sale items, collectibles, produce, crafts. Snack bar, rest rooms. Ample parking. (312) 774-3900. *April - October; Sundays.*

HIGHLAND
Flea Market. Community

Expo Center. 8341 Indianapolis Blvd. Antiques, collectibles, crafts, new and used merchandise. Snack bar, rest rooms. Ample parking. (219) 838-3500. *Saturdays and Sundays.*

HOAGLAND

Monthly Flea Market. Hayloft. Antiques, collectibles, used merchandise, clothing, jewelry. Food available, rest rooms. Ample parking. Contact: Betty Stroebel, (219) 745-4060. *Fourth Sunday of each month.*

HOBART

Holiday's Barn Market. I-65 and Rt. 6. New and used merchandise, antiques, glassware, country collectibles, crafts. Approximately 100 dealers. Food available, rest rooms. Ample parking. Spaces $10. Contact: Robbie Robinson, 2785 Eleanor St., Portage, IN 46368. (219) 942-6682. *Saturdays and Sundays.*

INDIANAPOLIS

Antique Flea Market. 7159 E. 46th St. Antiques, collectibles, furniture, glassware, primitives, silver, linens, vintage clothing. Snack bar, rest rooms, wheelchair accessible. Ample parking. (317) 545-0339. *Saturdays and Sundays.*

INDIANAPOLIS

Big Red Flea Market. 11777 Lafayette Ave. Indoor/outdoor market. Antiques, collectibles, linens, quilts, glassware, primitives, advertising items, decorator items. An interesting market to poke around in. Auction held on Saturday nights. Snack bar, rest rooms, wheelchair accessible. Ample parking. Camping available. (317) 769-3266. *Friday - Sunday.*

INDIANAPOLIS

Big Top Flea Market. 1002 E. 52nd St. New merchandise: gifts, decorator items, imports. Used merchandise, garage sale items. Collectibles, crafts. Snack bar, rest rooms. Ample parking. (317) 283-7500. *Wednesday - Sunday.*

INDIANAPOLIS

Flea Market. 480 S. Tibb Ave. Tibb's Drive-In. New and used merchandise, antiques and collectibles, crafts, produce. Snack bar, rest rooms. Ample parking. (317) 243-6666. *Sundays.*

INDIANAPOLIS

Flea Market. 3302 E. 10th St. Used merchandise, garage sale items, bric-a-brac abounds. Crafts, collectibles, produce. Snack bar, rest rooms. Ample parking. (317)

637-5730. *Saturdays and Sundays.*

INDIANAPOLIS

Flea Market. 5101 W. Washington. Antiques, collectibles, primitives, advertising items, glassware. Used merchandise, crafts. Snack bar, rest rooms. Ample parking. (317) 266-0888 or 631-2972. *Sundays.*

INDIANAPOLIS

Flea Market. 2604 LaFayette Rd. New and used merchandise, collectibles, crafts, produce. Snack bar, rest rooms, wheelchair accessible. Ample parking. (317) 786-6672. *Saturdays and Sundays.*

INDIANAPOLIS

Indiana Flea Market. State Fairgrounds. Expo Hall. Indoor market. One of the better antique and collectible markets in the U.S. A collector's paradise. Some very high-quality dealers here, with great setups of high-grade merchandise. If you're looking for a great source market, this is it. This market will have you singing the old song "Back Home in Indiana." 500+ booths. Snack bar, rest rooms, wheelchair accessible, good security. Ample parking. Admission charge. Contact: Stewart Promotions, 2950 Breckenridge Lane, #4A, Louisville, KY 40220. (502) 456-2244. *Monthly. Usually held mid-month; call for dates. Fridays and Saturdays, 11:00 A.M. - 8:00 P.M.; Sundays, 11:00 A.M. - 5:00 P.M.*

INDIANAPOLIS

Lafayette Road Flea Market. 2366 Lafayette Rd. Indoor/outdoor market. New and used merchandise, garage sale items, crafts, collectibles, produce. Snack bar, rest rooms, wheelchair accessible. Ample parking. Space from $21. Contact: Jerry Williams, (317) 639-4292. *Friday - Sunday.*

INDIANAPOLIS

Liberty Bell Flea Market. 8949 E. Washington. Indoor/outdoor market. Antiques, collectibles, coins, paper, vintage clothing, country, primitives, advertising items. New and used merchandise, electronics, crafts. Wide range of merchandise. This market is a very worthwhile stop. Approximately 200 dealers. Snack bar, clean rest rooms, wheelchair accessible. Ample parking. Space from $45. Contact: Terry Rexrost, 8949 E. Washington St., Indianapolis, IN 46219. (317) 898-3180. *Fridays, noon - 8:00 P.M.; Saturdays, 10:00 A.M. - 7:00*

P.M.; *Sundays, 10:00 A.M. - 6:00 P.M.*

INDIANAPOLIS

Twin Drive-In Theater Flea Market. 3000 Southeastern Ave. Good commercial market, with lots of new merchandise: sportswear, electronics, jewelry, watches, housewares, sports merchandise. Used merchandise, garage sale items. Produce, crafts. This market is on my approved "good sales" market list. Approximately 200 dealers. Snack bar, rest rooms, wheelchair accessible, lots of walking. Ample parking. Space from $5. Contact: Don Ross, Twin Drive-In, 3000 Southeastern Ave., Indianapolis, IN 46201. (317) 631-8494. *Saturdays and Sundays, 9:00 A.M. - 5:00 P.M.*

INDIANAPOLIS

West Washington Flea Market. 6445 W. Washington St. New merchandise: sportswear, housewares, electronics, tools, sports merchandise, toys. Used merchandise, garage sale items. Crafts, farm collectibles, produce. Approximately 100 dealers. Snack bar, rest rooms, wheelchair accessible. Ample parking. Space from $20. Contact: Mr. Baig, (317) 244-0941. *Fridays, 1:00 - 9:00 P.M.; Saturdays, 11:00 A.M. - 7:00 P.M.; Sundays, 11:00 A.M. - 6:00 P.M.*

JACKSONBURG

Flea Market. Jacksonburg Rd. Used merchandise, garage sale items, crafts, collectibles, produce. Snack bar, rest rooms. Ample parking. (317) 489-4066. *Saturdays and Sundays.*

JEFFERSONVILLE

Antiques Center and Flea Market. A typical flea market, with some great antiques and nice collector items amidst the booths of new and nearly new "junque" of all descriptions. (812) 288-4251. *Saturdays and Sundays.*

KINGMAN

Festival Flea Market. Junction of Hwy. 41 and State Rd. 234. 300 spaces. Antiques, collectibles, glassware, linen, silver, primitives, country collectibles. Market has many special holiday promotions. Open for ten days straight during the Covered Bridge Festival, one of Indiana's better special events (second week in October). Snack bar. Ample parking. Overnight camping available. Contact: Festival Flea Market, Rt. 1, Box 21, Kingman, IN 47952. (317) 397-8352. *May -*

October; Friday - Sunday, 9:00 A.M. - 5:00 P.M.

KINGSLAND
Flea Market. State Rt. 1 and US Hwy. 224. Indoor/outdoor market. Antiques, collectibles, glassware, silver, vintage clothing, primitives, decorator items. Used merchandise, crafts, produce. Food available, rest rooms. Ample parking. (219) 597-7375. *Second Sunday of each month.*

KOKOMO
Flea Market. Kokomo Home Center. 1940 S. Elizabeth St. New merchandise: electronics, sportswear, tools, jewelry, sports merchandise, toys. Used merchandise and garage sale items. Approximately 75 dealers. Snack bar, rest rooms, wheelchair accessible. Ample parking. Space from $28 for the weekend. (317) 453-7000. *Friday - Sunday.*

KOKOMO
The Merchants Market. 211 E. Morgan. Farm Co-Op Building. Indoor/outdoor market. New merchandise: jewelry, gifts, imports. Used merchandise, garage sale items, collectibles. Snack bar, rest rooms, wheelchair accessible. Ample parking. Contact: Nan Statler, (314) 452-9800. *Saturdays and Sundays.*

> **More Bargaining Savvy for the Beginner**
> Resist the urge to knock an item's worthiness in order to make your offer stand. It is a bit insulting to a seller, and actually makes the buyer doing it look silly for wanting an item of such inferior character.

LAFAYETTE
East Drive-In Flea Market. 3500 State Rt. 26. Used merchandise, garage sale items, collectibles, farm items, crafts, produce. Average attendance 1000. Approximately 35 sellers. Snack bar, rest rooms. Ample parking. Space from $5. Contact: Glenda Hart, (317) 447-2771 or 463-3111. *Sundays, 8:00 A.M. - 4:00 P.M.*

LAFAYETTE
Flea Market. 20 Elston Rd. Used merchandise, garage sale items, imports, crafts, collectibles, produce. Rest rooms. Ample parking. (317) 474-6114. *Saturdays and Sundays.*

LAKE STATION
Central Avenue Flea Market. 2750 Central Ave. I-94 to Reapel St. Indoor/outdoor market. New and used merchandise, antiques,

collectibles, crafts, produce. Approximately 75 dealers. Snack bar, rest rooms. Overnight parking available. Contact: Delbert Miller, 2750 Central Ave., Lake Station, IN 46405. (219) 962-5524. *Saturdays and Sundays, 9:00 A.M. - 5:00 P.M.*

LAKE STATION

Dunes Swap-O-Rama. Dunes Drive-In Theater. 1227 Ripley St. New and used merchandise, antiques, collectibles, crafts, produce. Snack bar, rest rooms, wheelchair accessible. Ample parking. (312) 774-3900. *Sundays.*

LA PORTE

Wildwood Park Farm and Flea Market. 4938 W. Hwy. 20. Indoor/outdoor market. New and used merchandise, garage sale items, collectibles, primitives, jewelry, produce, crafts. Average weekend attendance 3,500. Approximately 100 dealers. Snack bar, rest rooms, wheelchair accessible. Ample parking. Space from $4. Camping available. (219) 879-5660. *Friday - Sunday.*

LAWRENCEBURG

Tri-State Antique Market. Rt. 50, off I-275 Exit 16. Indoor/outdoor market, strong on antique furniture and collectibles. No new merchandise or crafts. Approximately 175 dealers. Food available, rest rooms, wheelchair accessible. Admission charge. Space from $20. Contact: Bruce Metzger, Box 238, Miamitown, OH 45041. (513) 353-2688. *May - November; first Sunday of each month, 7:00 A.M. - 3:00 P.M.*

LEBANON

Old Canyon Works Flea Market. Bargain hunters will enjoy the array of diverse merchandise to poke through at this typical Indiana flea market. (317) 482-6180. *Saturdays and Sundays.*

LOGANSPORT

Peddlers Acre. RR No. 6. Four miles west of Logansport, on State Rd. 24. Used merchandise, garage sale items, clothing, collectibles, bric-a-brac. Approximately 15 dealers. Rest rooms, snack bar. Ample parking. Overnight parking. (219) 722-2031. *Friday - Sunday, noon - 7:00 P.M.*

LOWELL

Flea Market. 120 Washington St. Used merchandise, garage sale items, bric-a-brac. Rest rooms. Ample parking. *Saturdays and Sundays.*

LOWELL
Livery Stable Antique Mart. Rt. 45 East. Antiques, furniture, collectibles, glassware, primitives, advertising items, silver, coins, jewelry, watches. Food available, rest rooms. Ample parking. (219) 696-9395. *Saturdays and Sundays.*

LYNN
Parkers Flea Market. U.S. Hwy. 27 South. New merchandise: sportswear, tools, electronics, jewelry, watches, decorator items. Used merchandise, garage sale items, crafts, collectibles, produce. Approximately 100 dealers. Snack bar, rest rooms. Ample parking. Space from $2. Contact: Tom Ward, (317) 861-1015. *Saturdays and Sundays.*

MADISON
Rivertown Flea Market. 2670 Michigan Rd. Indoor market. New merchandise: sportswear, electronics, tools, jewelry, housewares, toys. Used merchandise, collectibles, gifts, decorator items. Snack bar, rest rooms, wheelchair accessible. Ample parking. (812) 276-1616. *Friday - Sunday.*

MARION
Marion Flea Market and Antiques. 26th St. and Bypass. Antiques, collectibles, new and used merchandise, gifts, crafts, glassware, coins, silver, jewelry, primitives. Snack bar, rest rooms, wheelchair accessible. Ample parking. (317) 674-2613 or 674-9258. *Friday - Sunday.*

MARION
Open Air Flea Market. On bypass between 30th and 31st Sts. State Rds. 9 and 15. Approximately 65 spaces. New and used merchandise, collectibles, crafts, produce. Snack bar, rest rooms. Ample parking. Space from $5. Free overnight camping. Contact: Fred Emmons, 3703 S. Western Ave., Marion, IN 46953. (317) 674-4408 or 674-2613. *Seasonal market; Friday - Sunday.*

MARTINSVILLE
The Collector's Fair. Hwys. 37 and 252. Indoor/outdoor market. Antiques, collectibles, glassware, jewelry, coins, silver, primitives, advertising items. Snack bar, rest rooms, wheelchair accessible. Ample parking. (317) 342-6833. *Saturdays and Sundays.*

MEMPHIS
Burtons Farmers and Collectors Flea Market. I-65 and Memphis Rd. Exit. Used merchandise, collectibles, farm ranch items, produce, livestock. Approximately 25 deal-

> **Shopping Tip #3**
> Carry a big tote bag—many vendors run out of purchase sacks. For big purchases, station wagons or vans are worth driving.

ers. Snack bar, rest rooms. Ample parking. (812) 294-4685. *Friday - Sunday.*

MERRILLVILLE
Hoosier Swap-O-Rama. 2821 E. Lincoln. (Hwy. 30). New and used merchandise, collectibles, glassware, decorator items, coins, jewelry, bric-a-brac. Snack bar, rest rooms, wheelchair accessible. Ample parking. (219) 774-3900. *Sundays.*

MERRILLVILLE
Y and W Drive-In Flea Market. 6600 Broadway. New and used merchandise, garage sale items, crafts, produce, collectibles. Snack bar, rest rooms, wheelchair accessible. Ample parking. (219) 769-2203. *Sundays.*

METAMORA
Cracker Ridge Flea Market. U.S. Hwy. 52. 4 miles west of Metamora. Used merchandise, collectibles, glassware, primitives, jewelry, crafts, produce. Snack bar, rest rooms. Ample parking. Contact: Larry Mannie, Box 76, Metamora, IN 47030. (317) 698-2311. *May - November; Saturdays and Sundays.*

MICHIGAN CITY
Lilac Park Country Fair Craft and Flea Market. 2612 W. 1000 N. Approximately 150 spaces. Lots of crafts, new and used merchandise, some collectibles, vintage clothing, and jewelry. Snack bar, rest rooms. Ample parking. Contact: Leona Turner, (219) 874-6048. *April - October; Saturdays and Sundays.*

MISHAWAKA
Kamms Island Antique and Flea Market. 100 Center St. Center Complex. Antiques, collectibles, glassware, jewelry, vintage clothing, silver. Food available, snack bar, rest rooms. (219) 256-6611. *Sundays.*

MITCHELL
Ed's Gift Shop and Flea Market. State Rt. 60 East. New merchandise, gifts, imports, decorator items, jewelry. Used merchandise, garage sale items. Rest rooms. Ample parking. (812) 849-4815. *Saturdays and Sundays.*

MODOC
Halfway Flea Market. State Rt. 36 and Carlos. New and used merchandise, advertis-

ing items, primitives, farm items. Crafts, sports memorabilia, and produce. Snack bar, rest rooms, wheelchair accessible. Ample parking. (317) 853-5029. *Sundays.*

MONTICELLO
Norway Flea Market. 309 W. Norway Rd. Used merchandise, garage sale items, collectibles, crafts. Approximately 25 dealers. Rest rooms. Ample parking. Contact: Guy Harrison, (219) 583-3058. *Saturdays and Sundays.*

MONTICELLO
Twin Lakes Flea Market. 1617 W. Shafer Dr. Indoor/outdoor market. Lots of memorabilia, collectibles, books, vintage clothing, used merchandise, some new merchandise. Approximately 25 dealers. Contact: Guy Harrison, 3016 W. Shafer Dr., Monticello, IN 47960. (219) 583-4145. *May - September; Daily, 9:00 A.M. - 5:00 P.M.*

MORGANTOWN
Flea Market. Cross St. Indoor market. Antiques, collectibles, secondhand items, miscellaneous. *Saturdays and Sundays.*

MUNCIE
Flea Market. 1928 E. Memorial Dr. New and used merchandise, antiques, collectibles, jewelry, glassware, sports merchandise. Food available, rest rooms, wheelchair accessible. Ample parking. (317) 288-1218. *Sundays.*

MUNCIE
Greenwalts Flea Market. Fairgrounds. I-69, Exit 332, 7 miles to Wheeling Ave., south to fairgrounds. Primarily antiques, collectibles, primitives, memorabilia, advertising items, and decorator items. Market has a wonderful traditional family atmosphere. Approximately 75 sellers. Snack bar, rest rooms, wheelchair accessible. Ample parking. Space from $35 for the weekend. Contact: Mary or Keith Greenwalt, Rt. 9, Box 34, Muncie, IN. (317) 289-0194. *Call for schedule; 9:00 A.M. - 5:00 P.M.*

MUNCIE
Kilgore Flea Market. 2004 Kilgore Ave. Indoor/outdoor market. New and used merchandise, collectibles, jewelry, glassware, housewares, gifts, crafts. Snack bar, rest rooms, wheelchair accessible. Ample parking. Contact: Charles Terry, (317) 747-6069. *Saturdays and Sundays.*

MUNCIE
Main St. Flea Market. 1710 E. Main St. Indoor/outdoor mar-

ket. New and used merchandise, secondhand items. Gifts, imports, decorator items. Crafts, produce. Snack bar, rest rooms, wheelchair accessible. Ample parking. Contact: Leonard Lewis, (317) 289-5394. *Saturdays and Sundays, 9:00 A.M. - 5:00 P.M.*

MUNCIE

Sky-Hi Flea Market. Ski-Hi Drive-In Theater. Hwys. 3 and 28. New merchandise: electronics, jewelry, tools, sportswear, housewares, toys. Used merchandise, lots of wonderful junk. Crafts, collectibles and produce. Snack bar, rest rooms, wheelchair accessible. Ample parking. (317) 284-6411. *Sundays.*

MUNCIE

White River Flea Market. 2150 White River Rd. New and used merchandise, country collectibles, primitives, crafts, produce. Snack bar, rest rooms, wheelchair accessible. Ample parking. (317) 474-0253. *Saturdays and Sundays.*

NAPOLEON

Ye Olde Central House Flea Market. Main St. Used merchandise, garage sale items, collectibles. Approximately 25 dealers. Rest rooms. Ample parking. Space $3 per day. Contact: Richard Ramey, Rt. 2, Box 379, Osywood, IN 47037. (812) 689-4373. *First Sunday of each month.*

NAPPANEE

Borkholder Dutch Village Market. Restricted to antiques and collectibles. Great selection of smalls and quality and hard-to-find collector items. Auction on Tuesday evenings. Snack bar, rest rooms, wheelchair accessible. Ample parking. (219) 773-2828. *Tuesdays, Fridays, and Saturdays, 7:00 A.M. - 6:00 P.M.*

NASHVILLE

Old Time Flea Market. State Rt. 46. New and used merchandise, garage sale items, farm and ranch items, collectibles, glassware. Approximately 50 dealers. Snack bar, rest rooms, wheelchair accessible. Ample parking. Outside and covered space available. Space from $5. Overnight parking available. Contact: Bill and Helen Martin. Rt. 2, Box 242, Nashville, IN 47448. (812) 988-2346. *April - November; Saturdays and Sundays.*

NEW ALBANY

Flea Market. 3020 Grantline Rd. New and used merchandise, garage sale items, crafts, produce, collectibles.

Snack bar, rest rooms, wheelchair accessible. Ample parking. Contact: Norman Myers, (812) 948-8390 or 944-6401. *Saturdays and Sundays.*

NEW ALBANY
Pine Ridge Flea Market. 3328 Corydon Pike. 4 miles west of downtown. Indoor/outdoor market. Antiques, collectibles, farm items, primitives, used merchandise. Snack bar, rest rooms. Ample parking. Space from $10. Contact: David Upchurch, 3714 Klerner Lane, New Albany, IN 47150. (812) 941-1111. *Fridays, Saturdays, and Sundays.*

NEW ALBANY
Spring Street Flea Market. 1403 E. Spring St. Used merchandise, garage sale items, gift items, jewelry, clothing, housewares. Rest rooms. Ample parking. Contact: Roger Campbell, (812) 944-5577. *Daily.*

NEW CASTLE
Flea Market. 1331 Brood St. New and used merchandise, garage sale items, crafts, collectibles, advertising items. Snack bar, rest rooms, wheelchair accessible. Ample parking. Contact: Carol Cassidy, (317) 529-6077. *Fridays and Saturdays*

NEW HAVEN
Indoor Flea Market. 3003 Ryan Rd. Jewelry, sportswear, imports, tools, collectibles, sports memorabilia. Snack bar, rest rooms. Ample parking. Space from $5. (219) 482-4529. *Saturdays and Sundays.*

NEW WHITELAND
New Whiteland Flea Market. U.S. Hwy. 31 and Tracy Rd. New and used merchandise, garage sale items, crafts, collectibles, produce. Snack bar, rest rooms, wheelchair accessible. Ample parking. (317) 535-5900. *Saturdays and Sundays.*

NORTH LINTON
Flea Market. Everything from the necessary to the frivolous. Lots and lots of this-n-that. (812) 847-2870. *Saturdays and Sundays.*

NORTH VERNON
Green Meadows Flea Market. Hwy. 7 N. Indoor/outdoor market. New and used merchandise, decorator items, gifts, imports, clothing, tools, kitchenware. Snack bar, rest rooms, wheelchair accessible. Ample parking. Camping available. Contact: Charles Conehan, (812) 346-1990. *Friday - Sunday.*

NORTH WEBSTER
Flea Market. Land O'Lakes Barn. Antiques, collectibles, jewelry, vintage clothing, farm and ranch items, used merchandise. Snack bar, rest rooms. Ample parking. (219) 834-7014. *Saturdays and Sundays.*

OSCEOLA
Highway 20 Flea Market. 10156 McKinley. New and used merchandise, garage sale items, bric-a-brac. Snack bar, rest rooms, wheelchair accessible. Ample parking. (219) 674-8334. *Friday - Sunday.*

PERU
Reservation Campground Flea Market. 3 miles east of town, on Hwy. 24. Used merchandise, garage sale items, bric-a-brac, mostly local sellers. Rest rooms. Ample parking. (317) 473-4647. *Sundays.*

PETERSBURG
Antiques and Collectibles Flea Market. Hwy. 57 South. Antiques, collectibles, furniture, jewelry, glassware, silver, coins, primitives, advertising items, decorator items. Food available, rest rooms, wheelchair accessible. Ample parking. *Second and fourth weekends of each month.*

PORTLAND
Antique Show and Flea Market. Fairgrounds. U.S. Hwy. 27. Antiques, collectibles, furniture, glassware, knives, jewelry, watches, vintage clothing, advertising items, primitives. Lots of bargain prices on nice items at this market. A good buyers' market. Food available, rest rooms, wheelchair accessible. Ample parking. (219) 726-4150. *Saturdays and Sundays.*

RENSSELAER
Rensselaer Antique and Flea Market. McKinley and Merrioll Sts. Indoor/outdoor market. Antiques, collectibles, furniture, jewelry, sports cards, watches, vintage clothing, reproductions, gifts, used merchandise and decorator items. Popular local market. Snack bar, rest rooms, wheelchair accessible. Ample parking. (219) 866-7493. *Sundays.*

RICHMOND
Eastern Indiana Flea Market. Fairgrounds. Primarily antiques and collectibles. Contact: John Ford, Box 68, Springport, IN 47386. (317) 755-3565. *Monthly.*

RICHMOND
Wayne County Flea Market. 4-H Fairgrounds, Kuhlman

> ## *How Many Flea Markets Are There in the U.S.?*
> According to our research, there are 3,582 flea markets in the United States, although be well advised that keeping up with flea markets is sort of like keeping up with rabbits. They come and they go. Always call ahead to verify that the market is still in business.
>
> On more than one occasion, I have gone to a market, only to find that the market is no longer open. It happens to all of us, so call first.

Center. Salisbury Rd. Indoor/outdoor market. Wide variety of new and used merchandise. Antiques, collectibles, jewelry, housewares, electronics, glassware. Snack bar, rest rooms, wheelchair accessible. Ample parking. (317) 966-9074. *Usually first or second weekend of each month; call for dates. 9:00 A.M. - 5:00 P.M.*

RICHMOND

Yesteryears Antique and Collectible Mall and Flea Market. Old Melody Skating Rink. 1505 S. 9th St. Antiques, furniture, collectibles, decorator items, linen, jewelry, coins, silver, primitives, advertising items. Approximately 75 dealers. Snack bar, rest rooms, wheelchair accessible. Ample parking. Contact: Lysle Sheeley, 1505 S. 9th St., Richmond, IN 47374. (317) 966-0594 or 935-9865. *Thursday - Sunday*.

ROANOKE

Flea Market. Thunderbird Lodge. A little of this and a little of that, from used desirables to the new and trendy. *Third Sunday of each month.*

ROCHESTER

Flea Market. 20309 E. Edison St. New and used merchandise, garage sale items, collectibles, crafts, produce. Snack bar, rest rooms, wheelchair accessible. Ample parking. *Saturdays and Sundays.*

RUSHVILLE

Inside Flea Market. State Rd. 3 South. Behind Lloyd's Motors. Strong on antiques and collectibles. A good buyers' market; quality items at very desirable prices. Food available, rest rooms, wheelchair accessible. Ample parking. *Saturdays and Sundays, 8:00 A.M. - 5:00 P.M.*

SALEM

Farmers Flea Market. 209 W. Market St. Indoor/outdoor market. Used merchandise, garage sale items, bric-a-brac, produce, livestock, crafts, collectibles. Approximately 30 dealers. Food available, rest rooms, wheelchair accessible. Ample parking. Space from $3. Contact: Johnnie Saylor, (812) 883-6824. *Daily.*

SCOTTSBURG

Moonglo Treasure Chest Flea Market. U.S. Hwy. 31 South. (Old drive-in theater.) New merchandise: electronics, tools, housewares, sports merchandise, toys, sportswear, jewelry. Used merchandise, lots of garage sale items. Average attendance 2000. Approximately 100 vendors. Snack bar, rest rooms, wheelchair accessible. Ample parking. Space $4 to $7. Contact: Carl Spellman, Box 183, Scottsburg, IN 47170. (812) 752-6805. *Saturdays and Sundays.*

SEYMOUR

Crossroads Antique Mall. 311 Holiday Square, behind the Holiday Inn. Indoor antique mall with outdoor flea market. Antiques, collectibles, and country accessories. Approximately 150 dealers. Rest rooms, snack bar, wheelchair accessible. Ample parking. (812) 522-5675. *Saturdays.*

SHIPSHEWANA

Pumpkin Vine Junction. Collectibles, crafts, gifts, decorator items, lots of Amish items and food. Rest rooms. Ample parking. (219) 768-4011. *May - November; Tuesdays and Wednesdays.*

SHIPSHEWANA

Shipshewana Auction and Flea Market. Rt. 5, south of town. Excellent antique and wholesale market. Not just a flea market, but one of the outstanding events in America. If it's for sale, it's at this market. Over five auctions running simultaneously, including a livestock auction. Allow plenty of time for this market and the quaint Amish village it's located in. This market is so popular, it has a special large parking lot just for tour buses. Have motel reservations before going; area is a complete sellout when market is operating. A couple of very charming bed-and-breakfasts here—one has to reserve rooms months ahead, but it's worth it. Approximately 800 dealers. Great food, rest rooms, wheelchair accessible. Ample parking, but lots of walking. Space is at a premium here; make reservations early. Space from $25. Contact: Shipshewana Auction, Box 185, Shipshewana, IN 46565. (219) 768-4129. *Tuesdays and Wednesdays, 7:00 A.M. - dark.*

SOUTH BEND

Thieves Market. 2309 E. Edison, at Ironwood St. Permanent shops; outside flea market on weekends. Nice selection of collectibles, memorabilia, primitives, and lots of vintage jewelry and older fine jewelry, along with several specialty shops. Approximately 25 dealers. Space $5 per day. Contact: David Ciesiolka, Box 6114, South Bend, IN 46615. (219) 233-9820. *Saturdays and Sundays, 10:00 A.M. - 6:00 P.M.*

TERRE HAUTE

Terre Haute Flea Market. Virgo County Fairgrounds. Indoor/outdoor market. Antiques, collectibles, crafts, new merchandise, limited used items. Approximately 200 dealers. Food available, rest rooms, wheelchair accessible. Ample parking. Space from $15 per day outside. Contact: Stewart Promotions, 2950 Breckinridge Lane, #4A, Louisville, KY 40220. 9502) 456-2244. *Call for schedule; usually the first weekend of each month.*

TRAFALGAR

Trafalgar Antique Market. Hwys. 135 and 252. Quality-oriented indoor market. Antiques, good selection of furniture, collectibles, primitives, fine and estate jewelry, watches, coins, silver, linens, vintage clothing. Snack bar, rest rooms, wheelchair accessible. Ample parking. (317) 933-3402. *Saturdays and Sundays.*

WALDRON

Wilson Corners Flea Market. Rt. 1. 6 miles south. Used merchandise, garage sale items, country collectibles, crafts, produce. Rest rooms. Ample parking. *Saturdays and Sundays.*

WORTHINGTON

Green County Hill Flea Market. 4 miles north of Worthington, on Rt. 57. Antiques, collectibles, primitives, coins, glassware, new and used merchandise, crafts, produce. Food available, rest rooms, wheelchair accessible. Ample parking. Spaces from $25 for the weekend. Contact: Lynn McGarnsney, Rt. 4, Box 150, Franklin, IN 46131. (317) 736-4564. *Fridays and Saturdays,*

> ### *The World's First Flea Market*
> Did you ever wonder when or where the first flea market was held, or how flea markets actually got their name?
>
> The story goes that the Marché des Puces (literally, market of fleas) in Paris was legalized in the 1890s for taxation purposes. It has been said that this is the largest flea market in the world.
>
> Mythically speaking, the name "flea market" came about from the practice of thieves selling stolen wares in out-of-the-way places. When found, they would scatter like fleas to avoid the authorities.

first and third weekends of each month.

ZANESVILLE

Flea Market. 17727 Indianapolis Rd. Antiques, collectibles, primitives, glassware, new and used merchandise, garage sale items, crafts and produce. Snack bar, rest rooms, wheelchair accessible. Ample parking. (219) 638-4767. *Second and fourth weekends of each month.*

IOWA

Into the heartland of America—the great expanses of farms teeming with crops to feed the world. The heartbeat of America can be found in hard-working Iowa.

This is a tremendous area to find great antiques and collectibles at some very attractive prices. If you are in Iowa during the summer months, be sure to check out some of the many fine outdoor festivals held throughout the state.

Best bets...

✤ **Flea Market, Des Moines**
  Located on the State Fairgrounds, this is the area's leading market.

✤ **Bryants Flea Market, Keokuk**
  A good source market for the shopkeeper, dealer, serious collector or decorator.

✤ **Collectors Paradise Flea Market, What Cheer**
  Antiques and collectibles market with quality items, fine jewelry, toys, coins, primitives, and furniture.

BOONE
Ledges Road Flea Market. Hwy. 30. New and used merchandise, garage sale items, crafts, collectibles, produce. Snack bar, rest rooms. Ample parking. *Saturdays and Sundays.*

BOONE
Original Hillbilly Flea Market and Auction. 6 miles from town. Lots of used merchandise, farm collectibles, glassware, vintage clothing, primitives. Snack bar, rest rooms. Ample parking. *May - October, Saturdays and Sundays.*

COUNCIL BLUFFS
"Giant Flea Market." Antique Junction Mall. 14 miles south on I-29, at Glenwood, Exit 35. This market has it all, from tools to toys, household wares to decorator items. (712) 622-3532. *Held periodically; call for dates.*

COUNCIL BLUFFS
Tomes Flea Market. New and used merchandise, bric-a-

brac, garage sale items, farm and ranch collectibles. Average daily attendance 400 - 500. Approximately 25 vendors. Snack bar, rest rooms. Ample parking. Space from $10. Contact: Bud Tomes, (912) 366-0363. *Saturdays and Sundays.*

CRYSTAL LAKE

Crystal Lake Flea Market. A bargain hunter's treasure trove, with lots of nearly new and forget-me-not desirables of every description. (515) 565-3565. *Saturdays and Sundays.*

DAVENPORT

"Giant Flea Market." Holiday Inn, 5202 N. Brady St. Indoor market. Antiques, collectibles, crafts, new merchandise. Approximately 50 dealers. Food available, rest rooms, wheelchair accessible. Ample parking. Admission charge. Space from $12 per table. Contact: John Crouch, Box 5058, Springfield, IL 62705. (217) 529-6939. *Third Sunday of each month.*

DES MOINES

Flea Market. 806 S.E. 30th St. Used merchandise, garage sale items, decorator items, gifts, jewelry. Rest rooms. Ample parking. (514) 262-7322. *Tuesday - Sunday.*

DES MOINES

Flea Market. State Fairgrounds. East 30th St. and University Ave. Indoor market. Antiques, collectibles, glassware, vintage clothing, jewelry, coins, silver, sports memorabilia, advertising items. The area's leading market. Food available, rest rooms, wheelchair accessible. Ample parking. Space from $16. Reservations recommended. Contact: Evelyn Jennings, 1601 Capitol Ave., Des Moines, IA 50317. (515) 262-4282. *Monthly.*

DUBUQUE

Flea Market. Fairgrounds. 5 miles west of town on Hwy. 20. Indoor/outdoor market. Wide range of goods; lots of good-quality antiques and collectibles at very attractive prices. Good market for both the serious shopper and casual browser. Approximately 100 dealers. Admission charge. Space from $6. Contact: Norma Koppen, 1887 Carter Rd., Dubuque, IA 52001. (319) 583-7940. *Sundays.*

KEOKUK

Bryants Flea Market. River Rd. 6 miles north of city. Antiques, collectibles, primitives, furniture, jewelry, coins, silver, primitives, advertising items. Good source market for the shopkeeper, dealer, serious collector, or decorator. Approximately 200 dealers. Food available, snack bar, rest rooms, wheelchair accessible. Space from $6. (319) 463-7727. *Third Sunday of each month.*

LA PORTE CITY
Flea Market. Pat's Country Barn. 109 W. Main St. Used merchandise, garage sale items, country collectibles, crafts. Rest rooms. Ample parking. *Saturdays and Sundays.*

MANLEY
Flea Market. Typical this-n-that flea market. Contact: Manley Chamber of Commerce. *Saturdays and Sundays.*

MARSHALLTOWN
Central Iowa Flea Market. Fairgrounds. Indoor/outdoor market. Lots of different items, including pets, birds, chickens, and other live animals. Approximately 50 dealers. Space from $5. Contact: Arnold Klaas, (515) 483-2781, or Central Iowa Fair, (515) 753-3671. *Monthly.*

MASON CITY
Olde Central Antique Mall. 317 S. Delaware St., across from Southbridge Mall. 2 levels, 8,000 sq. ft., 40 dealers.

> "The great thing about flea markets is that they have absolutely no effect on anything."
> —Jim Goodridge

Antiques, collectibles, gift and decorator items, jewelry, glassware, linens. Snack bar, rest rooms, wheelchair accessible. Ample parking. Dealers welcome. (515) 423-7315. *Monday - Saturday, 10:00 A.M. - 5:00 P.M; Sundays, 11:00 A.M. - 4:00 P.M.*

MUSCATINE
King's Flea Market. 1700 Grandview. Held in an old lumber yard, under cover. Used merchandise, collectibles, antiques, furniture, glassware, clothing, jewelry, housewares. Approximately 100 dealers. Space from $20. Snack bar, clean rest rooms. Admission charge. Overnight camping available. (319) 264-8190. *April - October. Usually the third weekend of each month, but schedule varies; call for information.*

OTTUMWA
Collectors Fair. Coliseum Basement. Hwys. 34 and 63. Indoor market. Collectibles, used merchandise, tools, toys, lots of secondhand items. Approximately 40 dealers.

Snack bar, rest rooms. Ample parking. Admission charge $.50. Space from $12.50. Contact: Dwight Jones, (515) 684-6719. *Saturdays and Sundays, 9:00 A.M. - 4:00 P.M.*

PACIFIC JUNCTION

Antique Junction Mall. 14 miles south of Council Bluffs on I-29, at Glenwood, Exit 35. 24,000 sq. ft. One of the midwest's newest and finest malls, worth visiting. 138 booths, 80+ dealers. Tearoom. Air-conditioned. Market also conducts two large flea markets, spring and fall; call for dates. (712) 622-3532. *Monday - Saturday, 10:00 A.M. - 5:00 P.M.; Sundays, noon - 5:00 P.M.*

SIOUX CITY

Flea Market. City Auditorium. Antiques, collectibles, jewelry, sports cards, coins, silver, linens, primitives, advertising items. New and used merchandise. Approximately 200 dealers. Food available, rest rooms, wheelchair accessible. Ample parking. Space from $13. Contact: Ed Benson, Box 286, Sioux City, IA 57101. (605) 332-4554. *First weekend of each month.*

VINCENT

Vincent Antique Galleries. Northeast of Ft. Dodge. Antiques, collectibles, lots of estate items. Approximately 100 exhibitors. Dealers welcome. (515) 356-4000. *Wednesday - Sunday.*

WASHINGTON

Midway Shop and Swap. Used merchandise, bric-a-brac, collectibles. Rest rooms. Ample parking. (206) 878-1802. *Saturdays and Sundays.*

WATERLOO

Kozy Corner Flea Market. 7023 Osage Rd. Used merchandise, bric-a-brac, imports, gifts, collectibles, crafts. Rest rooms. Ample parking. *Saturdays and Sundays.*

WHAT CHEER

Collectors Paradise Flea Market. Keokuk County Fairgrounds. I-80, Exit 201 south, 20 miles. Indoor/outdoor market. Antiques and collectibles market with quality items, fine jewelry, toys, coins, primitives, furniture. Excellent source market for dealers. Approximately 400 dealers. Food available, rest rooms, wheelchair accessible. Ample parking. Admission charge $1. Contact: Larry Nicholson, Box 413, What Cheer, IA 50268. (515) 634-2109. *Usually the first weekend of each month; call for schedule. 7:00 A.M. - 5:00 P.M.*

KANSAS

Ah, sweet land of Oz. Some of America's prettiest and friendliest small towns are located here. Just a block from the superhighway lies the churning, powerful heart of the American people. Stop off at a few of these towns, and be sure to eat at the local "City Cafe." You'll wonder why anyone would ever live in a big city.

Best bets...

✦ **Hutchinson Flea Market, Hutchinson**
Antiques and collectibles, good selection of memorabilia, primitives, and advertising items.

✦ **Flea Market, Topeka**
The usual flea market items, as well as quilts, primitives, and farm collectibles.

✦ **Wichita Flea Market, Wichita**
Wide range of merchandise; lots of good-quality small antiques, collectibles, memorabilia, antique toys, advertising items.

ARKANSAS CITY
Arkansas City Flea Market. 712 W. Washington St. 7 blocks west on Washington, off Hwy. 77. Indoor market. New merchandise: electronics, housewares, tools, jewelry, toys, sportswear. Used merchandise: antiques, collectibles, glassware, primitives, farm and ranch collectibles. Approximately 80 dealers. Snack bar, rest rooms, wheelchair accessible. Ample parking. Space $10. Reservations recommended. Camping available. Contact: Don Jackson, Box 290, Arkansas City, KS 67005. (316) 442-0848 or 442-9566. *Seasonal market; first Sunday of each month.*

CHAUTOUQUA
Chautouqua Flea Market. City Park. Used merchandise, garage sale items, crafts, produce, some collectibles. Primarily local exhibitors. Snack bar, rest rooms. Ample parking. *Seasonal market; Saturdays and Sundays.*

CHETOPA
Country Cupboard Antiques Flea Market. Downtown. Corner of GH and Maple Sts. Collectibles, garage sale items, crafts, produce, lots of used merchandise and farm items. Food available, rest rooms. Ample parking. (316) 236-7045. *Fourth Saturday of each month.*

CHETOPA
Peters Flea Market. 4th and Delaware Sts. New and used merchandise, garage sale items, bric-a-brac. Rest rooms. Ample parking. (316) 236-7815. *Saturdays and Sundays.*

COLUMBUS
Helen's Market. 805 E. Sycamore St. Indoor market. Used merchandise, garage sale items, gifts, decorator items, collectibles. Rest rooms. Ample parking. (316) 429-3300. *Daily.*

CONCORDIA
Concordia Flea Market. 1 mile north of town. New and used merchandise, collectibles, decorator items, farm items. Market does special promotions and has a great selection of locally made crafts. Contact: Charles Chartier, Box 98, Clyde, KS 66938. (913) 446-3411. *Saturdays and Sundays.*

EUREKA
Country Flea Market and Antique Mall. 6 miles east of town, on Hwy. 54. Old Tonovay School building; 7,000 sq. ft. facility. Furniture, jewelry, cookie jars. Approximately 200 dealers. Rest rooms. Ample parking. Dealers welcome. (316) 583-5245. *Daily.*

GARNETT
Garnett Flea Market. Hwy. 59 North. Above Bouman's Carpet and Furniture store. Lots of glassware, good collectibles, and clocks. Approximately 15 dealers. Rest rooms. Ample parking. (913) 448-3216. *Daily.*

HUTCHINSON
Hutchinson Flea Market. Kansas State Fairgrounds. 20th and Main Sts. Indoor market. Antiques and collectibles, good selection of memorabilia, primitives, advertising items. Approximately 200 dealers. Snack bar, rest rooms, wheelchair accessible. Ample parking. Admission charge $.50. Space from $15. Contact: Schartz Enterprises, Box 1585, Hutchinson, KS 67504. (316) 663-5626. *First Sunday of each month, 9:00 A.M. - 4:00 P.M.*

Junction City
Flea Market. Municipal Auditorium. Antiques, collectibles, new and used merchandise, crafts, silver, sports memorabilia, coins, country items. Food available, rest rooms, wheelchair accessible. Ample parking. (913) 238-5296. *First Saturday of each month.*

Kansas City
Armourdale Collectibles and Flea Market. 823 Osage St. Antiques, collectibles, glassware, pottery, crafts, books, trains and accessories. Rest rooms, wheelchair accessible. Ample parking. (913) 342-3654. *Monday - Saturday, 10:00 A.M. - 5:00 P.M.; Sunday, noon - 5:00 P.M.*

Kansas City
Boulevard Drive-In Swap Shop. 1051 Merriam Ln. New merchandise: electronics, tools, housewares, sports merchandise, toys, sportswear. Also used flea market finds, garage-sale-type items, crafts, collectibles, produce. Average daily attendance 1200. Approximately 150 dealers. Snack bar, rest rooms. Ample parking. Admission charge. Space from $3. Contact: Wes Neal, (913) 262-2414. *Saturdays and Sundays, 7:00 A.M. - dark.*

Kansas City
Flea Market. 63rd St. Drive-In Theater. Traditional flea market wares, from baseballs to bracelets, flower bulbs to cowboy boots. (816) 353-1628. *Saturdays and Sundays.*

Kansas City
Flea Market. 817 Westport Rd. New and used merchandise, garage sale items, bric-a-brac, lots of "junque." Rest rooms. Ample parking. *Saturdays and Sundays.*

Lawrence
Quantrill's Antique Mall and Flea Market. 811 New Hampshire St. Downtown. 10,000 sq. ft., 3 rooms, 45 booths. New and used merchandise, collectibles, primitives, glassware, crafts. Company also operates an antique mall on the premises, with a good selection of antiques and collectibles. Snack bar, rest rooms, wheelchair accessible. Ample parking. (913) 842-6616. *Friday - Sunday, 10:00 A.M. - 5:00 P.M. Antique mall is open daily, 10:00 A.M. - 5:00 P.M.*

Manhattan
Airport Flea Market. Near Manhattan Airport. Indoor/outdoor market. New and used merchandise, crafts, collectibles, produce. Snack

bar, rest rooms, wheelchair accessible. Ample parking. Space from $8 daily outdoors and $10 daily indoors. Contact: Market Manager, 723 Moro St., Manhattan, KS 66502. (913) 776-6906. *Saturdays and Sundays.*

OPOLIS

Opolis Flea Market. Hwys. 171 and 57. Indoor/outdoor market. At the Missouri state line. Market is heavy on antiques, collectibles, and antique auto parts. Auto enthusiasts will find some really nice and very unusual antique auto items and accessories at this market. Lots of old Volkswagen stuff. Approximately 15 dealers. Snack bar, rest rooms. Ample parking. Space from $8. Contact: Norma Kukovich, Box 42, Opolis, KS 66760. (316) 231-2543. *Saturdays and Sundays, 9:00 A.M. - 5:00 P.M.*

OSWEGO

Circle C Trading Post. 518 Commercial St. Antiques, collectibles, crafts, leaded glass, gifts. Furniture, both new and used; lots of nice reproduction oak furniture. Snack bar, rest rooms. Ample parking. (316) 795-3081. *Tuesday - Saturday, 11:00 A.M. - 5:00 P.M.*

OSWEGO

Oswego Flea Market. Junction of Hwys. 59 and 96. Country market, with used merchandise, bric-a-brac, housewares, clothing, crafts, collectibles, produce. Food available, rest rooms. Ample parking. (316) 795-4415. *Saturdays.*

OTTAWA

Ottawa Flea Market. 110 W. First St. New and used merchandise, collectibles, crafts. Rest rooms. Ample parking. (913) 242-4095. *Saturdays and Sundays.*

PARSONS

Old Glory Flea Market, Antiques and Craft Mall. 5021 W. Main St. Hwy. 160 West. Antiques, crafts, glassware, collectibles, primitives, decorator items, silver, linens, quilts. Longaberger basket consultant on premises. 75+ dealers. (316) 421-6326. *Monday - Saturday, 9:00 A.M. - 6:00 P.M.; Sunday, 1:00 - 6:00 P.M.*

PITTSBURG

Jayhawk Antique/Craft Mall and Flea Market. 4030 N. Hwy. 69. General line of antiques and collectibles. Large selection of locally made crafts and decorator items. 175+ dealers. Snack bar, rest rooms, wheelchair accessible. Ample parking. *Daily, 10:00 A.M. - 6:00 P.M.*

PITTSBURG
Needful Things Flea Market. 113 W. 5th St. Antiques, dishes, dolls, books, quilts. Good selection of Tiara dinnerware, both new and used. Rest rooms. Ample parking. *Daily, 11:00 A.M. - 5:00 P.M.*

PITTSBURG
The Warehouse. 612 S. Broadway. Indoor market. Antiques, collectibles, primitives, advertising items, farm items, toys, some new merchandise and secondhand items. Approximately 50 dealers. Rest rooms. Ample parking. Contact: Jody Monsour, 612 S. Broadway, Pittsburg, KS 66762. (316) 231-6429. *Monday - Saturday, 9:00 A.M. - 6:00 P.M.; Sunday, 1:00 P.M. - 6 P.M.*

TOPEKA
Flea Market. Fairgrounds. Antiques, collectibles, coins, linens, silver, quilts, primitives, advertising items, knives, farm collectibles. One of the better markets in the area. Food available, rest rooms, wheelchair accessible. Ample parking. (913) 233-4444. *Third Sunday of each month.*

Shopping Tip #4
Go for the best price. No one is offended if you ask, "Is that firm?" (But don't haggle too long if the vendor is selling firearms.) It's OK to make the vendor an offer.

TOPEKA
Highland Crest Flea Market. 3000 S.E. Fremont. New and used merchandise, garage sale items, bric-a-brac. Rest rooms. Ample parking. (913) 266-5966. *Saturdays and Sundays.*

TOPEKA
Topeka Antique Mall and Flea Market. 5247 S.W. 28th Court. Indoor market. New merchandise, gifts, decorator items, sportswear, tools, housewares, electronics, toys. Used desirables, collectibles, crafts. Furniture, stoneware, quilts, jewelry, Flow Blue, Oriental, primitives, pottery. 50 booths in the antique mall. Space from $11 per day. Snack bar, rest rooms, wheelchair accessible. Food vendors allowed. (913) 273-2969. Mall is open *Tuesday - Sunday, 9:00 A.M. - 5:00 P.M.; flea market on weekends.*

Wichita

The Market. Wichita Greyhound Park. New market. New merchandise: electronics, housewares, tools, sportswear, coins, sports items. Used merchandise, flea market merchandise. Rest rooms, snack bar, wheelchair accessible. Ample parking. Admission charge. Space from $10. Contact: The Market, P.O. Box 277, Valley Center, KS 67147. (316) 755-2440. *Saturdays and Sundays.*

Wichita

New Ponderosa Flea Market. 2427 W. Pawnee St. Indoor/outdoor market. New merchandise: gifts, imports. Used desirables, collectibles. Snack bar, rest rooms, wheelchair accessible. Ample parking. Contact: Carroll Ghan, (316) 941-9953. *Friday - Sunday.*

Wichita

Treasure Plaza Flea Market. 4201 S. Seneca. Indoor market. New merchandise, antiques, collectibles, giftware, crafts. Market has retail consignment auction on Sundays. Snack bar, rest rooms, wheelchair accessible. Ample parking. Space $44 weekly or $125 monthly. Mainly permanent spaces. Contact: James Smith, (316) 522-9480. *Daily.*

Wichita

Village Flea Market. 2301 S. Meridian. Indoor/outdoor market. Antiques, collectibles, primitives, crafts, produce, lots of secondhand and garage sale merchandise. Approximately 100 dealers. Snack bar, rest rooms, wheelchair accessible. Ample parking. Space from $27 per weekend. Contact: Dale Cooper, 2302 S. Meridian, Wichita, KS 67213. (316) 942-8263 or 942-8264. *Fridays, Saturdays, and Sundays, 9:00 A.M. - 6:00 P.M.*

Wichita

Wichita Flea Market. Kansas Coliseum. North 85th St. and I-135. Large indoor market with a wide range of merchandise. Lots of good-quality small antiques, collectibles, memorabilia, antique toys, advertising items. Average attendance 5,000. Approximately 700 dealers. Snack bars, clean rest rooms, wheelchair accessible. Ample parking. Admission charge $.50. Space from $15. Reservations required. Contact: Schartz Enterprises, Box 1585, Hutchinson, KS 67504. (316) 663-5626. *Fourth Sunday of each month, 9:00 A.M. - 4:00 P.M.; call to confirm dates.*

KENTUCKY

What a beautiful state—the gently rolling countryside, the horse farms, the fields. How nice some of the towns are. "My Old Kentucky Home." I could sure sing that song if I were ever to be fortunate enough to live in one of those beautiful little Kentucky towns.

Some great markets here—flea markets, malls, and auctions. From the tremendous markets of Louisville to the small-town malls, great buys and great shopping.

Best bets...

- **Burlington Antique Flea Market, Burlington**
  A collector's paradise; wide range of quality collectibles and small antiques.

- **Country World Flea Market, Georgetown**
  A fun, country-style market. Pleasant, friendly people, from sellers to management.

- **Kentucky Flea Market, Louisville**
  One of America's greatest markets. This market has it all.

- **Richwood Flea Market, Richwood**
  Market is heavy on new merchandise: sportswear, electronics, housewares, and collectibles.

ASHLAND

A B and D Flea Market. 635 Winchester Ave. Indoor/outdoor market. Lots of goodies at this market. New and used merchandise, great selection of decorator items and bric-a-brac, country and farm collectibles. Jewelry, coins, sportswear, crafts. Approximately 200 dealers. Snack bar, rest rooms, wheelchair accessible. (606) 324-2429. *Thursdays and Fridays.*

ASHLAND

Hillbilly Flea Market. U.S. Hwy. 23 North. Indoor/outdoor market. Good mix of merchandise. New and used merchandise, imports, souvenirs. Some antiques, collectibles, primitives, memorabilia, books, jewelry, coins, advertising items. Aver-

dance 5000. Approximately 150 dealers. Restaurant, clean rest rooms, wheelchair accessible. Air-conditioned and heated. Camping available. Contact: Bonnie Taylor, 4547 N. Dixie, Elizabethtown, KY 42701. (606) 329-9824 or 329-1058. *Friday - Sunday, 7:00 A.M. - 5:00 P.M.*

AURORA

Hillbilly Peddlers Flea Market. Junction of Rts. 68 and 80, Kentucky Lake. Used merchandise, garage sale items, crafts, produce. Snack bar, rest rooms. Ample parking. Space from $5. Contact: Bobby Morris, Box 5, Benton, KY 42025. (502) 527-0836. *Summer market; Saturdays and Sundays. Market open on holidays.*

BARDSTOWN

White's Flea Market. Hwy. 62. Used merchandise, garage sale items, bric-a-brac, collectibles, crafts, produce. Rest rooms. Ample parking. (502) 346-4677. *Saturdays and Sundays.*

BEAVER DAM

Flea Market. Silvers Restaurant parking lot. New and used merchandise, crafts, collectibles, produce. Food available, rest rooms. Ample parking. *Mondays.*

BEAVER DAM

Kay's Flea Market. Hwy. 231 South. Country and farm collectibles, used merchandise, crafts, produce. Clean rest rooms. Ample parking. Camping available. Electricity. No drugs, alcohol, or pornographic items. Contact: Kay's, Rt. 4, #256, Beaver Dam, KY 42320. *Thursdays.*

BEREA

Robbie's Antique and Flea Market. Hwy. 25 South. Antiques, collectibles, furniture, silver, glassware, lots of country collectibles. Food available, rest rooms. Ample parking. *Saturdays and Sundays.*

BEREA

Robby's Flea Market. 3 miles south of town on Route 3. Used merchandise, garage sale items, clothing, jewelry, tools. Rest rooms. Ample parking. Contact: Dale Robinson, Rt. 3, Box 456, Berea, KY 40403. *Daily; closed Wednesdays.*

BEREA

Todd's Antique Mall and Flea Market. Hwy. 21 West. Mainly permanent booths with antiques and collectibles. Great selection of merchandise, from Flow Blue to Griswold skillets. Rest rooms, wheelchair accessible. Ample parking. (606) 986-9961. *Daily.*

BOONEVILLE
Boonville Flea Market. Rt. 3. Used merchandise, flea market merchandise, farm collectibles, crafts, produce. Food available, rest rooms. Ample parking. *Wednesdays.*

BURLINGTON
Burlington Antique Flea Market. Fairgrounds. A collector's paradise. Wide range of quality collectibles and small antiques. Approximately 50 dealers. Food available, rest rooms, wheelchair accessible. Ample parking. (606) 341-7394 or 341-1400. *Monthly; call to confirm dates.*

CAMP NELSON
Camp Nelson Flea Market. Old U.S. Hwy. 27. Secondhand and flea market merchandise, some new items, collectibles, crafts, produce. Snack bar, rest rooms. Ample parking. (606) 885-9304. *Saturdays and Sundays.*

CARROLLTON
Carroll County Flea Market. Hwy. 42. Used merchandise, garage sale items, country collectibles, crafts. Snack bar, rest rooms. Ample parking. (502) 732-5851. *Saturdays and Sundays.*

CENTRAL CITY
Flea Market. Hwy. 70. Farm items, used merchandise, country collectibles, crafts, produce, livestock. Food available, rest rooms. Ample parking. *Wednesdays.*

CLARKSVILLE
Clarksville Flea Market. Downtown. Used merchandise, lots of great collectibles, crafts, imports. Rest rooms. Ample parking. *Friday - Sunday.*

CORBIN
Lily Trading Post and Flea Market. Hwy. 25. London Corbin Rd. Indoor/outdoor market. Used merchandise, farm and country collectibles, glassware, primitives. Average daily attendance 300. Approximately 25 dealers. Snack bar, rest rooms, wheelchair accessible. Ample parking. Space from $2. Camping available. (606) 528-9298. *Daily.*

CORBIN
Ridners Flea Market. U.S. Hwy. 25. West at Ridners Motel. Used merchandise, farm and country collectibles, crafts, produce. Approximately 40 dealers. Snack bar, rest rooms. Ample parking. Space from $2. *Daily.*

CORBIN

Sammy's Flea Market and Auction. 25 "C" St. Indoor/outdoor market. New merchandise: surplus, closeouts, housewares, sports merchandise, sportswear. Used merchandise, collectibles, crafts. Approximately 75 dealers. Snack bar, rest rooms. Ample parking. Contact: Sammy Issao, 704 Vine St., Corbin, KY 40701. (606) 528-5260. *Saturdays and Sundays.*

COVINGTON

American Legion Flea Market. 203 Daytonia St. New and used merchandise, garage-sale-type items, crafts, collectibles, produce. Snack bar, rest rooms, wheelchair accessible. Ample parking. (605) 291-8834. *Saturdays.*

COVINGTON

By Buy Enterprise Flea Market. 728 Madison Ave. Flea market merchandise, garage sale items, country collectibles, advertising items, primitives. Rest rooms. Ample parking. Contact: Glen Brewer, Box 41012-2038, Covington, KY. (606) 292-8929. *Daily.*

CRESTWOOD

Flea Market. 6346 W. Hwy. 146. Used merchandise, garage sale items, gifts, imports, collectibles, crafts. Ample parking. Snack bar, rest rooms. (502) 222-0229. *Monday - Thursday.*

DAYSVILLE

Old Southern Flea Market. Hwy. 68-80, 5 miles east of Elkton, 10 miles west of Russelville. Indoor/outdoor market. New and used merchandise, great selection of country and farm collectibles, advertising items, primitives, glassware, crafts, produce. Live entertainment. Food available, rest rooms, wheelchair accessible. Overnight parking onsite. Contact: Kathy Walker, (502) 265-2630 weekends or 265-2338 weekdays and nights. *Saturdays, 9:00 A.M. - 9:00 P.M.; Sundays, 9:00 A.M. - 6:00 P.M.*

ELIZABETHTOWN

Bowling Lanes Flea Market. 4547 N. Dixie. Indoor/outdoor market. New merchandise: electronics, housewares, sportswear. Used merchandise, collectibles, crafts, produce. Food available, rest rooms, wheelchair accessible. Ample parking. Electricity and showers available. Contact: Bonnie Taylor, (502) 737-5755. *Saturdays and Sundays, 8:00 A.M. - 6:00 P.M.*

ELIZABETHTOWN
Flea Market Mall. Hwy. 31 West. New and used merchandise, antiques, collectibles, furniture, vintage clothing, silver, linens, glassware. Snack bar, rest rooms, wheelchair accessible. Ample parking. (502) 769-5374. *Friday - Sunday.*

ELIZABETHTOWN
Starlite Drive-In Theater Flea Market. Hwy. 31 West. Large commercial market, with wide variety of new merchandise, used desirables, antiques, collectibles, glassware, primitives, advertising items, lots of farm and ranch collectibles, crafts, produce. A good market to poke around in for treasures or bargains. Approximately 250 dealers. Snack bar, rest rooms, wheelchair accessible. Ample parking. Space from $3. Contact: Don Ford, Lake Shore Dr., Hardinsburg, KY 40143. (502) 769-3937. *Sundays.*

FLORENCE
Flea Market. Boone/Kenton Warehouse, 8471 Hwy. 42. New and used merchandise, garage sale items, antiques, collectibles, glassware, primitives, silver, linens, advertising items, good selection of tobacco collectibles. Interesting market, with a wide variety of "things." Approximately 250 dealers. Snack bar, rest rooms, wheelchair accessible. Ample parking. Contact: Shirlie Elliott, Box 834, Florence, KY 41042. (606) 525-7066. *Saturdays and Sundays.*

FRANKFORT
Flea for All Flea Market. Hwy. 60. Used merchandise, garage sale items, bric-a-brac. New merchandise: gifts, imports, collectibles, country crafts, produce. Snack bar, rest rooms, wheelchair accessible. Ample parking. (804) 340-7579. *Friday - Sunday.*

FRANKLIN
South Central Kentucky Flea Market. 210 Cherry St. New and used merchandise, garage sale items, crafts, produce. Snack bar, rest rooms. Ample parking. (502) 586-9058. *Saturdays and Sundays.*

> ***Dress for the Hunt!***
> ***Tip #2***
> Wear comfortable shoes —a must, due to the amount of walking it usually takes to cover a flea market. Also, a lot of the terrain at markets is unpaved, with gravel or soil to walk on.

> ### Sort of Like Baseball...
> The word seasonal refers to those markets that operate during seasons of the year in which suitable weather permits, i.e., in the northeast during the winter it is too frigid, and in the southwest during the summer it is too hot. Sort of like baseball. Always remember that bad weather, snow, rain, etc., cancels outdoor markets.

GEORGETOWN
Country World Flea Market. U.S. Hwy. 460 East. Lots of antiques, collectibles, primitives, country, crafts, and farm items, along with new merchandise and secondhand items. This is a very fun, country-style market. Pleasant, friendly people, from sellers to management. Approximately 300 vendors. Food available, rest rooms, wheelchair accessible. Camping available. Space from $8. Contact: Glen Juett, 111 Montgomery Ave., Georgetown, KY 40324. (502) 863-0474 or 863-0289. *April - November; Open continuously from 7:00 A.M. Friday - Sunday evening.*

GEORGETOWN
Horse Park Flea Market. Connector Rd. I-75, Exit 125. Strong commercial market, with lots of new and good used merchandise. Crafts, country collectibles, produce. Approximately 100 dealers. Snack bars, rest rooms, wheelchair accessible. Ample parking. Contact: Tanis Pickard, (606) 293-2268 or 863-5151. *Saturdays and Sundays.*

GILBERTSVILLE
Welk's Flea Market. Hwy. 641. New and used merchandise, garage sale items, bric-a-brac, crafts, collectibles, produce. Snack bar, rest rooms. Ample parking. (502) 362-8514. *Friday - Sunday.*

GLASGOW
Antique Flea Market. 31 E. South St. Antiques, collectibles, furniture, silver, glassware, advertising items, tobacco items, country and farm collectibles, toys, primitives. Snack bar, rest rooms. Ample parking. (502) 678-4620. *Saturdays and Sundays.*

GREENVILLE
Town and Country Flea Market. Hwy. 62, Rt. 1. Antiques, collectibles, livestock, poultry, crafts, produce, and new merchandise. Furniture, both

new and used. Very nice market to attend as a buyer or a seller. Scenic area with lakes and motels; neighboring antique and specialty shops. This market provides a great backdrop for a most enjoyable early-week adventure. Approximately 250 sellers. Snack bar, rest rooms, Ample parking. Space from $3. Camping available. No alcohol, drugs, or pornographic items allowed. Contact: Luke Robinson, Hwy. 62 W., Greenville, KY 42345. (502) 338-4920. *Mondays and Tuesdays, 8:00 A.M. - dark.*

GUTHRIE

Southern Kentucky Flea Market. U.S. Hwy. 41, between Tiny Town and Guthrie. Indoor/outdoor market. New and used merchandise, lots of country collectibles, toys, advertising and tobacco items. Locally made crafts, gifts, imports. Approximately 125 dealers. Snack bar, rest rooms. Ample parking. Contact: James Covington, Box 566, Guthrie, KY 42234. (502) 483-2166. *Daily.*

HENDERSON

Ellis Park Flea Market. Ellis Park Race Track. Indoor/outdoor market. Good market for new merchandise and antiques. Good selection of quality collectibles, primitives, and advertising items. Approximately 300 dealers. Contact: Stewart Promotions, 2950 Breckinridge Ln., #4A, Louisville, KY 40220. (502) 456-2244. *Monthly; call to confirm dates.*

HENDERSON

Flea Market. 3199 Hwy. 41 North. New and used merchandise, farm and sport collectibles, crafts, produce. Snack bar, rest rooms. Ample parking. *Sundays.*

HENDERSON

Flea Market. 2100 S. Green St. Indoor/outdoor market. New and used merchandise, lots of used housewares, tools, clothing, outdoor items. Crafts, collectibles, produce. Auctions on Friday evenings. Snack bar, rest rooms, wheelchair accessible. Ample parking. (502) 826-6263. *Thursday - Saturday.*

HOPKINSVILLE

Twin Street Flea Market. Main and Virginia Sts. Used merchandise, collectibles, gifts, advertising items, primitives. Rest rooms. Ample parking. Contact: Everett Brawner, (502) 886-3447. *Daily.*

INDEPENDENCE
North Kentucky Flea Market. 5209 Madison Pike. New and used merchandise, garage-sale-type items, crafts, collectibles, produce. Snack bar, rest rooms. Ample parking. Contact: Dick Young, 1602 Crossridge Ln, Louisville, KY 40222. (606) 356-9602. *Friday - Sunday.*

IRVINGTON
Drive-In Theater Flea Market. U.S. Hwy. 60. New merchandise: electronics, tools, sportswear, jewelry, housewares. Used merchandise, garage sale fare, crafts, produce, collectibles. Snack bar, rest rooms, wheelchair accessible. Ample parking. (502) 769-3937. *Saturdays and Sundays.*

KUTTAWA
Antique Flea Market. U.S. Hwy. 62. Antiques, furniture, glassware, silver, linens, advertising items, primitives, jewelry, decorator items. Rest rooms. Ample parking. Contact: Randy Jeffress, (502) 388-2175. *Daily.*

LEITCHFIELD
Bratcher's Flea Market. Hwy. 62 East. 1 mile east of town. Antiques, collectibles, crafts, new merchandise, produce, and used items. Approximately 100 dealers. Ample parking. Space from $6. Contact: Gladys Bratcher, Hwy. 62, Leitchfield, KY 42754. (502) 259-3571. *Wednesdays and Saturdays; opens at sunup.*

LEXINGTON
Lexington Antique and Flea Market. Lexington Civic Center. Lots of high-quality antiques and collectibles, along with some new merchandise. Snack bar, rest rooms, wheelchair accessible. Downtown location; parking is difficult. Ample paid parking. Contact: Stewart Promotions, 2950 Breckenridge Ln., #4A, Louisville, KY 40220. (502) 456-2244. *Usually held mid-month; call for dates. Fridays and Saturdays, 11:00 A.M. - 8:00 P.M.; Sundays, 11:00 A.M. - 5:00 P.M.*

LEXINGTON
Mid-State Flea Market. 753 Newtown Rd. New and used merchandise, farm and sports collectibles, crafts, produce. Snack bar, rest rooms. Ample parking. (502) 255-7419. *Friday - Sunday.*

LEXINGTON
Show and Sell Flea Market. 2592 Palumbo Dr. Indoor market. New merchandise: housewares, outdoor items, sportswear, novelties, jewelry.

Used merchandise, collectibles, crafts, sports merchandise. Average daily attendance 4,000. Snack bar, rest rooms, wheelchair accessible. Ample parking. (800) 442-1324 or (606) 269-8141. *Friday - Sunday.*

LONDON
Dean Tobacco Warehouse Flea Market. I-75 and Exit 41. Dean Tobacco Warehouse. New and used merchandise, farm and ranch collectibles, tobacco collectibles. Approximately 50 dealers. Snack bar, rest rooms, wheelchair accessible. Ample parking. Contact: Carl Tuttle, Rt. 2, Box 333, London, KY 40741. (606) 864-2185. *Friday - Sunday.*

LONDON
Flea World Flea Market. 192 Bypass and Hwy. 229. 2 miles east of I-75, Exit 38. Approximately 100 spaces outside and 250 spaces inside. Large commercial market with lots of new merchandise, general flea market merchandise, country collectibles, advertising items, primitives, glassware, silver, coins, sports merchandise, crafts, produce. Snack bar, rest rooms, wheelchair accessible. Ample parking. Contact: Brenda Hait, (606) 864-3532. *Saturdays and Sundays, 9:00 A.M. - 5:00 P.M.*

LOUISVILLE
Bargain Bazaar. 9070 Dixie Hwy. Pleasure Ridge Park. Indoor market. New and used merchandise, housewares, clothing, electronics, glassware, jewelry, sports cards, crafts, collectibles, decorator items. Approximately 50 dealers. Rest rooms. Ample parking. Contact: John Young, 9070 Dixie Hwy., Louisville, KY 40258. *Daily.*

LOUISVILLE
Clay Street Flea Market. 120 N. Clay St. Indoor market. New and used merchandise, collectibles, silver, advertising items, primitives. Rest rooms. (502) 584-9942. *Daily.*

LOUISVILLE
Country Fair and Flea Market. 3502 7th St. New and used merchandise, garage-sale-type items, produce. Good market. Excellent selection of crafts. Snack bar, rest rooms, wheelchair accessible. Ample parking. (502) 368-6186. *Saturdays and Sundays.*

LOUISVILLE
Derby Park Traders Circle Flea Market. 2900 S. 7th St. Rd. ½ mile from Churchill

> ### More Bargaining Savvy for the Beginner
> If you have never tried haggling over a price before, now's your chance. The first thing you might do is walk around at your local market, window shop a bit, and try to eavesdrop on others who are bargaining. Pay particular attention to what they say, how the dealer reacts, etc. When you are ready try it yourself—remember the adage "Nothing ventured, nothing gained." That certainly pertains to the world of flea market bargaining.

Downs. Look for the huge green-and-white billboards. Indoor/outdoor market. Antiques, collectibles, primitives, memorabilia, country, antique toys, new and used merchandise, crafts, art. 50 - 60 dealers. Snack bar, rest rooms, wheelchair accessible. Ample parking. Space from $21 for the weekend. RV parking, electrical hookups, showers. Contact: Radeana Parker, 2900 Seventh St., Louisville, KY 40216. (502) 636-3532 or 636-5817. *Fridays, Saturdays, and Sundays, 8:00 A.M. - 6:00 P.M.*

LOUISVILLE
Flea Market. National Turnpike and Outer Loop. New and used merchandise, lots of farm and ranch items, collectibles, crafts, produce. Approximately 50 dealers. Snack bar, rest rooms, wheelchair accessible. Ample parking. Space from $3 a day. Contact: Maxine Moran, 4021 Crittenden Dr., Louisville, KY 40209. (502) 367-1397. *Saturdays and Sundays.*

LOUISVILLE
High Grove Antiques and Flea Market. Junction of Hwys. 31E and 48. 22 miles south of town. Antiques, collectibles, farm and ranch items, tobacco items, new and used merchandise, country crafts, produce. Country store next door. Food available, rest rooms. Ample parking. (502) 895-7585. *Tuesday - Sunday, 10:00 A.M. - 5:00 P.M.*

LOUISVILLE
Kentucky Flea Market. Fairgrounds. Indoor market. One of America's greatest markets; this market has it all. Excellent for the wholesale buyer as well as the retail shopper and decorator. Large section devoted solely to quality antique dealers. Attendance at the monthly market

is 30,000 - 50,000. Market also hosts a special event over the New Year holiday. This is one of the most popular events in America. The holiday market has from 1,000 - 2,000 dealers. Over 100,000 shoppers attend the special promotions and holidays. Admission charge. Space from $60. Reserve space early. Contact: Stewart Promotions, 2950 Breckinridge Ln., #4-A, Louisville, KY 40220. (502) 456-2244. *Monthly. Usually held early in the month; call for dates. Fridays, noon - 8:00 P.M.; Saturdays 10:00 A.M. - 8:00 P.M.; Sundays, 11:00 A.M. - 6:00 P.M.; Mondays, 10:00 A.M. - 5:00 P.M.*

MAYFIELD
Mayfield-Graves County Park Flea Market. Fairgrounds. Antiques, furniture, collectibles, farm and ranch items, glassware, silver, jewelry, tobacco collectibles, primitives, knives, books, art. Approximately 150 dealers. Food available, rest rooms, wheelchair accessible. Ample parking. (502) 247-0049. *Second and third Mondays of each month.*

MONTICELLO
Kay's Fleaground. Kelley Lane Rd. New and used merchandise, garage sale items, bric-a-brac, crafts, produce, collectibles. Snack bar, rest rooms, wheelchair accessible. Ample parking. *Friday - Sunday.*

MT. STERLING
Mt. Sterling Flea Market. 120 S. Queen St. Used merchandise, collectibles, glassware, jewelry. Rest rooms. Ample parking. *Daily.*

MURRAY
Murray Drive-In Theater Flea Market. South 4th St. New and used merchandise. Typical flea market treasures: antiques, collectibles, glassware, silver, farm and ranch items, crafts, produce. Average daily attendance 2,000. Approximately 100 dealers. Snack bar, rest rooms, wheelchair accessible. Ample parking. Space from $2. Contact: Tommy Brown, Box 229, 42071, Murray, KY (502) 753-8084. *First and fourth Mondays of each month.*

NEW LONDON
New London Flea Market. Tobacco Rd. Tobacco Warehouse #4. Indoor market. New and used merchandise, garage sale items, souvenirs, novelties, sportswear, country collectibles, glassware, jewelry, tobacco collectibles. Food available, rest rooms,

wheelchair accessible. Ample parking. Contact: Graham Cole, (606) 878-9000. *Friday - Sunday, 7:00 A.M. - dark,*

NICHOLSVILLE

Windmill Flea Market. Hwy. 27 South. Windmill Restaurant parking lot. New and used merchandise, garage sale items, collectibles, crafts, produce. Food available, rest rooms, wheelchair accessible. Ample parking. Contact: Charles Curtis, (606) 498-4722. *Saturdays and Sundays.*

OWENSBORO

Flea Market. Consumers Mall. 2930 E. 4th St. New merchandise: electronics, sportswear, housewares, sports memorabilia, tools. Used merchandise, garage-sale-type treasures. Also crafts, collectibles, produce. Snack bar, rest rooms, wheelchair accessible. Ample parking. (502) 685-3592. *Saturdays and Sundays.*

OWENSBORO

Hog Heaven Flea Market. 8424 Hwy. 60 East. 7 miles from Owensboro. Approximately 200 spaces. New indoor/outdoor market. New merchandise, used merchandise, lots of farm and country collectibles, advertising items, glassware, primitives. Country crafts, produce, livestock. Food available, rest rooms, wheelchair accessible. Ample parking. (502) 246-4420. *Saturdays and Sundays.*

PAINTSVILLE

Flea Market. Hwy. 172. New and used merchandise, garage sale items, collectibles, crafts, produce. Snack bar, rest rooms. Ample parking. (606) 297-3991. *Friday - Sunday.*

RADCLIFF

Hardin County Flea Market. Knox Blvd. and Wilson Rd., at Redmar Plaza. Indoor market. Located next to Fort Knox. Nice market, with wide range of merchandise. Snack bar, rest rooms. Ample parking. Air-conditioned and heated. Contact: B. J. Dozier, 1487 W. Elm Rd., Radcliff, KY 60160. (502) 351-0200 or 351-1118. *Fridays, Saturdays, and Sundays.*

RICHWOOD

Richwood Flea Market. 10915 Dixie Hwy. U.S. Hwy. 25, Exit 175 on I-175. 4 miles south of Florence, 13 miles south of Cincinnati, OH. Indoor/outdoor market. Market is heavy on new merchandise: sportswear, electronics, housewares, and collectibles. Good market for commercial vendors. Average attendance 6,000 per weekend. Approximately 320 dealers. Good snack bar/cafe, rest rooms, wheelchair accessible. Ample parking. Camping available. Space from $60 per weekend. Contact: Terri White, 10915 Dixie Hwy., Florence, KY 41042. (606) 371-5800. *Tuesdays, daylight - dark; Saturdays, and Sundays, 9:00 A.M. - 5:00 P.M.*

RICHMOND

Risk Flea Market. Rt. 8. Old Irvine Rd. Indoor/outdoor market. Used merchandise, garage sale type items. Everything from trash and treasures to produce, crafts, and collectibles. Food available, rest rooms. Ample parking. *Saturdays and Sundays.*

ROCHESTER

Rochester Flea Market. Rochester Ball Park. Used merchandise, garage sale items, bric-a-brac, crafts, produce. Approximately 25 dealers. Snack bar, rest rooms. Ample parking. Contact: Steve Rubuno, (502) 934-4024. *Fridays.*

RUSSELL

Hillbilly Flea Market. Rt. 23 North. Used merchandise, garage sale items, country and advertising collectibles, primitives, crafts, produce. Rest rooms. (606) 329-9821. *Saturdays and Sundays.*

RUSSELL SPRINGS

Russell Springs Flea Market. Hwy. 80. New and used merchandise, bric-a-brac, collectibles, crafts, produce. Snack bar, rest rooms. Ample parking. *February - November; Friday - Sunday.*

SHELBYVILLE

Shelbyville Flea Market. Hwy. 60 East at the Big Top Warehouse. Antiques, glassware, primitives, advertising and tobacco items, silver, knives, jewelry. Lots of used merchandise, garage-sale-type items, crafts. Approximately 50 dealers. Food available, rest rooms, wheelchair accessible. Ample parking. Space $15 per weekend. (502) 633-1244. *March - October; first weekend of each month.*

SHEPHARDSVILLE

Bullett County Flea Market. I-65 and Hwy. 24 South, at the Fairgrounds. Antiques, glassware, linens, silver, jewelry, watches, knives, farm and country collectibles. Lots of interesting collector lines here. New and used merchandise, crafts. Approximately 100 dealers. Food available, rest rooms, wheelchair accessible. Ample parking. Contact: Claude Lundy, Box 915, Knob Creek Rd., Brooks, KY 40109. (502) 955-8967. *Second weekend of each month.*

SIMPSONVILLE
Shelby County Flea Market. I-64, Exit 28. Indoor/outdoor market. New and used merchandise, flea market merchandise, collectibles, decorator items, giftware, crafts, produce. Snack bar, rest rooms, wheelchair accessible. Ample parking. (502) 722-8883. *Saturdays and Sundays, 9:00 A.M. - 5:00 P.M.*

SOUTHGATE
Beverly Flea Market. 601 Alexandria Pike. New and used merchandise, garage sale items, bric-a-brac, crafts, collectibles, produce. Snack bar, rest rooms, wheelchair accessible. Ample parking. (502) 356-5622. *Saturdays and Sundays.*

UNION CITY
Union City Flea Market. Fairgrounds. Antiques, collectibles, jewelry, silver, glassware, advertising items, primitives, farm and country items. New and used merchandise, crafts. Food available, rest rooms, wheelchair accessible. Ample parking. (502) 469-5663. *Second weekend of each month.*

WALTON
Lakewide Flea Market. Hwy. 25. Large selection of new and used merchandise, good secondhand items, farm and ranch items, country collectibles, glassware, jewelry, silver, primitives, crafts, produce, livestock. Approximately 100 dealers. Food available, rest rooms, wheelchair accessible. Ample parking. Space from $4. (606) 356-9473. *Tuesdays.*

WAYNE
Flea Market. 3420 Sullivan Dr. Used merchandise, garage sale items, collectibles, crafts, produce. Snack bar, rest rooms, wheelchair accessible. Ample parking. (502) 443-8706. *Friday - Sunday.*

WILLIAMSBURG
Helping Hand Flea Market. Old Hwy. 25 West. 9 miles south of town. Used merchandise, lots of junk, some good collectibles, glassware, primitives. Approximately 10 dealers. Rest rooms. Ample parking. (606) 549-2337. *Daily.*

WINCHESTER
Winchester Flea Market. 4400

> ### *Trading with Traders*
>
> Wheeling and dealing. Old-fashioned "horse trading." It can be fun and profitable. If you have something you'd like to trade—a nice pocketknife, for instance—and a dealer has something you're interested in, ask if he'll swap. The value of the two items will need to be comparable.
>
> If the dealer thinks he can make money with your pocketknife, if it will enhance his knife inventory in some way, he may just trade with you.
>
> Remember, you'll never know until you ask. Swapping, after all, is the very essence of the open-air marketplace. It's how it all began. A lot of bartering is still going on today. Like anything else, there is a certain skill to it that comes with practice and experience.
>
> A shrewd trader can come out making a good profit from his dealings. That is the challenge and fun of learning this art.

Oliver Rd. Exit 94 off I-64. New and used merchandise, collectibles, glassware, silver, jewelry and antiques. Average daily attendance 1,000. Approximately 60 dealers. Snack bar, rest rooms, wheelchair accessible. Ample parking. Inside space from $10 daily; outside space from $5 daily. Tables furnished. Camping and electricity available. Contact: Raymond Huls, 202 Boone, Winchester, KY 40391. (606) 744-1179 or 745-4332. *Saturdays and Sundays, 8:00 A.M. - 5:00 P.M.*

WINCHESTER

Winchester Flea Market. 1465 W. Lexington Ave. Indoor market. New and used merchandise, collectibles, jewelry, crafts, decorator items, advertising items. Approximately 75 dealers. Rest rooms. Ample parking. (606) 744-4510. *Seasonal market; Saturdays and Sundays.*

WINCHESTER

Winchester Flea Market. 5000 W. Lexington Ave. New and used merchandise, garage sale treasures, bric-a-brac, crafts, country and new collectibles, produce. Snack bar, rest rooms, wheelchair accessible. Ample parking. (606) 745-4332. *Friday - Sunday.*

MICHIGAN

The sheer physical beauty of Michigan is overwhelming. The Upper Peninsula is one of God's finer creations. The same is true of the pretty little coastal cities, such as Benton Harbor—one of my favorite stops—however, I do find it prudent to avoid Detroit.

Great markets in Michigan, and someday maybe great football. Some of the finest antique markets in the country are located here—some great malls, also. This entire state is a happy hunting ground for collectors.

Best bets...

- **Ann Arbor Antiques Market, Ann Arbor**
  One of the finest antiques markets in the entire country; many, many fine investment-quality pieces here.

- **Caravan Antiques Market, Centerville**
  Held periodically, this quality-oriented market is limited to antiques, fine art, and high-caliber collectibles.

- **Giant Trade Center Flea Market, Flint**
  Large selection of new merchandise at severely discounted prices; great bargains on personal, household, and recreational items.

- **Ionia Antique and Collectibles Market, Ionia**
  Great antique and collectible market, with excellent selection and wide range of booths.

- **Reits Flea Market, Paw Paw**
  Good market for commercial vendors; clean, friendly, and well-managed.

ANN ARBOR

Ann Arbor Antiques Market. 5055 Saline Rd. Strong on memorabilia and collectibles, with lots of fine antiques. A very quality-oriented market. This is one of the finest antiques markets in the entire country. Many, many fine investment quality pieces here—a collector's paradise. Fun, friendly, well managed.

Great attendance. Approximately 350 dealers. Food available, rest rooms, wheelchair accessible, and lots of walking. Ample parking. Contact: Margaret Brusher, P.O. Box 1512, Ann Arbor, MI 48106. (313) 429-9838. *April - November; third Sunday of each month.*

ANN ARBOR
Flea Market. 410 N. 4th Ave. Shoppers will find a broad array of new and used merchandise, collectibles, bric-a-brac, etc. *Saturdays and Sundays.*

ARMADA
Armada Outdoor Flea Market. 25381 Ridge Rd. Antiques, collectibles, country and farm collectibles, glassware, silver, vintage clothing. Shoppers will find a good selection and wide range of merchandise. Farmers' market also. Average daily attendance 1,000+. Approximately 250 dealers. Good food available on premises. Ample parking. Space from $10. (313) 784-9194. *May to October; Tuesdays and Sundays, 6:00 A.M. - 3:00 P.M.*

BIRCH RUN
Flea Market. Pine Ridge Park. Rows of great flea market finds, including new and used merchandise, garage sale bric-a-brac, handicrafts, collectibles, produce. Food available. (517) 624-9729. *May - September; Saturdays and Sundays.*

BRIGHTON
Sports Flea Market. 6080 Grand River. New and used merchandise, garage sale items, crafts, collectibles, produce. Snack bar. (517) 546-8270. *Saturdays and Sundays.*

BURTON
"Giant Flea Market." 4204 Davison St. Used desirables, lots of garage sale bric-a-brac, some new merchandise, crafts, collectibles, produce. Food available. (313) 742-5371. *Saturdays and Sundays.*

CEDAR SPRINGS
Northern Exchange Flea Market. 12595 Northland Dr. New and used merchandise, antiques, collectibles, crafts, produce. Snack bar. (616) 696-0125. *Tuesdays, Fridays, and Saturdays.*

CENTERVILLE
Caravan Antiques Market. Fairgrounds. Hwy. M-86. Large indoor/outdoor antique market. Real quality-oriented market, limited to antiques, fine art, and high-caliber

collectibles. Approximately 600 dealers. Food available. Admission charge. Space from $50. Contact: Jordon Humberstone. 1510 N. Hoyne St. Chicago, IL 60622. (313) 571-0452. *Usually held five times per year, mostly in the spring and summer. Call for schedule.*

CHARLOTTE

Jackie's I-69 Super Flea Market. 2525 Lansing Rd. New merchandise: gifts, souvenirs, imports. Used merchandise, collectibles, silver, glassware, linens. Approximately 25 dealers. Snack bar, rest rooms, wheelchair accessible. Space from $4. Overnight parking. Contact: Jackie Holmes, 2527 Lansing Rd., Charlotte, MI 48813. (517) 543-5315 or 663-5300. *Daily, 10:00 A.M. - 5:00 P.M.*

CHARLOTTE

1761 Flea Market. 1761 Lansing Rd. (Hwy. 69). New indoor/outdoor market. New merchandise: sportswear, tools, electronics, housewares, sports merchandise, toys, jewelry, lots of new collectibles. Also used merchandise, glassware, china, decorator items. Snack bar, rest rooms, wheelchair accessible. Ample parking. (517) 543-0707. *Thursday - Monday.*

CHARLOTTE

Weekend Flea Market. 202 Pearl St. The bargain-conscious shopper will enjoy this typical market, with lots of new and used merchandise, crafts, collectibles, produce, and more. Food available. *Friday - Sunday.*

COLOMA

Farmers Market. 6671 Red Arrow Hwy. New and used merchandise, garage sale this-n-that, handcrafted treasures, collector items, farm and country desirables, produce, livestock. Food available, rest rooms, wheelchair accessible. Ample parking. (616) 468-5200. *Saturdays and Sundays.*

COPEMISH

Copemish Flea Market. Rt. 115. New merchandise, lots of flea market items, crafts, collectibles, glassware, silver, primitives, farm and ranch collectibles, produce. Approximately 100 dealers. Snack bar, rest rooms. Ample parking. Space from $4.50. Contact: Marguerite Weaver, Box 116, Copemish, MI 49625. (616) 378-2430. *May - October; Saturdays and Sundays, 8:00 A.M. - 6:00 P.M.*

DAVISON
Midway Flea Market. 205 Davison Rd. Indoor/outdoor market. New and used merchandise, jewelry, clothing, housewares, sports merchandise. Also handmade gifts, collectibles, produce. Snack bar. Space from $18 for both days. Contact: Ken Lamson, 504 N. Dayton, Davison, MI 48423. (313) 653-8766. *Saturdays and Sundays.*

DAVISON
Richfield Center Flea Market. 6006 N. State. Rt. 15. New and used merchandise, garage sale items, crafts, collectibles, produce. Food available. Contact: S. Miner, Box 81, Pottler Lake, Davison, MI 48464. (313) 653-5893 or 793-2773. *Saturdays and Sundays, 10:00 A.M. - 6:00 P.M.*

DETROIT
B and B Flea Market. 17507 Van Dyke St. New merchandise: electronics, jewelry, housewares, sportswear. Used merchandise, garage sale items, crafts, collectibles, produce. Food available. (313) 365-4071. *Friday - Sunday.*

DETROIT
Big D Flea Market. 2311 E. Vernon Hwy. New merchandise, used merchandise, general flea market goods. Some collectibles, handcrafts, produce. Snack bar, rest rooms. Ample parking. *Saturdays and Sundays.*

DETROIT
Close Out - Blow Out Flea Market. 3700 Central. Indoor/outdoor market. Wide variety of new and used merchandise. Approximately 40 dealers. Restaurant. (313) 841-2100. *Thursday - Sunday.*

DETROIT
8 Mile Trade Center. 6400 E. 8 Mile Rd. New and used merchandise, garage sale bric-a-brac, crafts, collectibles, produce. Snack bar. (313) 893-5879. *Friday - Sunday.*

DETROIT
Northland Flea Market. 14615 West 8 Mile Rd. Used merchandise, garage sale items, collectibles, decorator items. Approximately 15 dealers. Space $50 weekly. Contact: Albert Vertison, (313) 862-5451. *Daily 9:00 A.M. - 7:00 P.M.*

DETROIT
Penn-Huron Flea Market. 17076 Huron Dr. Indoor/outdoor market. Wide range of merchandise; especially heavy on new merchandise. Much like shopping at a severely discounted department store. Approximately 150 dealers.

> **Flea Market**
> "Market where one can purchase fleas."
> — J. Davis, age 6

Snack bar, rest rooms, wheelchair accessible. Ample parking. Space from $7. Contact: Richard Slater, 8100 Longworth, Detroit, MI 48209. (313) 841-2196 or 753-4133. *Saturdays and Sundays.*

DOWAGIAC

Dowagiac Flea Market. M-51 South at Peavine. Indoor/outdoor market. New and used merchandise, lots of garage sale items and bric-a-brac. Also crafts, jewelry, collectibles, produce. Approximately 50 dealers. Food available. Rest rooms, wheelchair accessible. Space from $3. Contact: Robert Gant, Sr., M-51 South, Dowagiac, MI 49047. (616) 782-3668. *Friday - Sunday.*

ELBA

Elba Flea Market. State Rt. M-21. Used merchandise, garage sale items, collectibles, jewelry, housewares, clothing, new merchandise, crafts, household wares, produce. Food available. (517) 843-6104. *Saturdays and Sundays.*

FLINT

Giant Trade Center Flea Market. 4204 Davison Rd. Large selection of new merchandise at severely discounted prices. Great market for bargains on personal, household, and recreational items. Better prices than any discount store on many things. Average attendance 5000 - 6,000. Approximately 80 dealers. Ample parking. Space from $45 for 3 days. Contact: Jerry Keeley, 4204 Davison Rd., Flint, MI 48509. (313) 742-5371. *Friday - Sunday, 10:00 A.M. - 7:00 P.M.*

GAYLORD

The Purple Flea. McVannell Rd. and M-32. New and used merchandise, lots of garage sale items, collectibles, crafts, produce. Food available. (517) 732-5335. *Saturdays and Sundays.*

GRAND RAPIDS

Beltline Drive-In Flea Market, Beltline Drive-In Theatre. 1400 W. 28th St., S.W. Large commercial market, with great selection of new merchandise. Lots of good secondhand items and garage sale merchandise. Also some antiques, collectibles, glassware, silver, coins, primitives, farm and ranch collectibles, produce. Come dressed for a great deal of walking. Average attendance of 5,000 for the weekend. Approximately 350 dealers. Snack bar, rest rooms, wheelchair accessible. Ample parking. Admission charge. Space from $8. Contact: Don Moinet, 1400 W. 28th St., S.W. 49509. (616) 532-6302. *Seasonal market open May - October; flea market held on Saturdays and Sundays.*

GRASS LAKE

Grasslake Mini-Mall Flea Market. Burtch Rd. New merchandise, used desirables, country collectibles, gifts, imports, crafts, produce. Average attendance 200. Approximately 40 dealers. Food available. Space from $2.50. Overnight parking. Contact: E.C. Caler, 242 Burtch Rd., Grass Lake, MI 49240. (517) 522-8810. *Saturdays and Sundays, 10:00 A.M. - 6:00 P.M.*

HILLSDALE

Andy Adams Sale Barn Flea and Farmers Market. Fairgrounds. Indoor/outdoor market. New and used merchandise, antiques, collectibles, produce, livestock. Market has been at the same location for over 80 years. Livestock and consignment auction on Saturday mornings. Average daily attendance 2,000. Approximately 25 dealers. Food available. Space from $10. Camping and electricity available. (517) 437-7230. *Saturdays.*

HILLSDALE

Flea Market. 3390 Beck Rd. Indoor/outdoor market. This is a new market, with antiques, collectibles, and a lot of secondhand items. Good family-style restaurant next door. (517) 437-0012 or 439-1815. *Wednesdays and Thursdays.*

HOLLY

Flea Market. 3005 Grange Hall Rd. Used merchandise, garage sale items, crafts, collectibles, decorator items, produce. Food available. (313) 634-2828. *Saturdays and Sundays.*

HOLTON

C.V. Auction and Flea Market. Rt. 120. Sarr Track Arena. Antiques, collectibles, used merchandise, glassware, housewares, clothing, outdoor and farm items. Snack bar, rest rooms. Ample parking. (616) 828-4146. *Sundays, 6:00 A.M. - 2:30 P.M.*

HOMER

Thurstons Flea Market. M-60, 5 miles east of I-69. Antiques, collectibles, jewelry, coins, linens, vintage clothing, primitives, advertising items. Also plenty of used merchandise, crafts, decorator items, produce. Average attendance 1,000. Approximately 30 dealers. Food available. Space from $5. Camping available. (517) 568-3851. *Sundays.*

HOUGHTON LAKE
Flea Market. 2451 W. Houghton Lake Dr. New and used merchandise, garage sale items, crafts, collectibles, produce. Snack bar. (517) 366-8531. *June - November; Thursday - Monday.*

HOWARD CITY HEIGHTS
Burley Park Swap Meet. Hwy. 131 North, Exit 120. Primarily antiques and collectibles. Great selection of offerings for collectors of just about everything. Lots of quality items, including furniture. Popular market. Clean, friendly, and well managed. Approximately 600 dealers. Space from $10. Camping available. Contact: Judy Rogers, 4540 Bailey Rd., Coral, MI 49322. (616) 354-6354. *Seasonal market. Opens Memorial Day; Saturdays and Sundays.*

HOWELL
Howell Flea and Farmers Market. 2300 E. Grand River. Auction Barn. New and used merchandise, housewares, jewelry, collectibles, clothing, kitchen items, lots of farm items. Also large farmers' market. Approximately 40 dealers. Snack bar, rest rooms, wheelchair accessible. Ample parking. Space from $6. Contact: David Anderson, 2205 Oak Grove Rd., Howell, MI 48843. (517) 546-0136 or 548-3300. *Wednesdays, 8:00 A.M. - 5:00 P.M.*

IONIA
Country Store Antique Flea Market. Rt. M-66. Antiques, collectibles, glassware, silver, coins, jewelry, watches, farm and ranch collectibles. Food available, rest rooms. Ample parking. *Wednesday - Sunday.*

IONIA
Ionia Antique and Collectibles Market. Fairgrounds. Indoor/outdoor market. Great antique and collectible market, with excellent selection and wide range of booths. Excellent market for quality items. Food available, rest rooms, wheelchair accessible, lots of walking. Ample parking. Space from $30. Tables available. Reservations recommended. Overnight camping on your rented space outside. $5 electricity charge. Contact: Judith

Kramer, 496 S. State St., P.O. Box 3, Pewamo, MI 48873. (517) 593-3316. *Sundays.*

JACKSON

Spikes Flea Market. 2190 Brooklyn Rd. New and used merchandise, garage sale items, crafts, produce, collectibles. Company also conducts weekly public auction from its premises. Snack bar, rest rooms. Ample parking. (517) 423-6312. *Saturdays and Sundays.*

KALAMAZOO

Eastland Outdoor Market. Sprinkle and Mille Rd. New merchandise, general flea market lines, crafts, collectibles, produce. Snack bar, rest rooms. Ample parking. (616) 381-7084. *Thursday - Sunday.*

LAKE CITY

Lake City Flea Market. 518 Union St. Indoor/outdoor market. Secondhand merchandise, collectibles, memorabilia, primitives, bric-a-brac, housewares. Average attendance 1,000. Approximately 30 dealers. No food available. Space from $4. Camping nearby. (616) 839-3206. *May - November; daily, 9:00 A.M. - 5:00 P.M.*

LAMBERTVILLE

Jo's Ceramic Art and Flea Market. 8177 Sector Rd. 3 miles north of Toledo, OH. Used merchandise, collectibles, decorator items, gifts, imports, crafts, produce. Approximately 20 dealers. Snack bar. Space from $25 for the weekend. Contact: Jo Peart, Box 387, Lambertville, MI 48144. (313) 856-8000. *Friday - Sunday.*

LAMBERTVILLE

Lambertville Antique Market. Rt. 29. (River Rd.) Market features a bit of Americana, from the offbeat to the highly collectible. For the serious collector, shopkeeper, dealer, or decorator, this market is a most interesting stop. Food available, snack bar, rest rooms. (609) 397-0456. *Saturdays and Sundays.*

LANSING

Flea Market. 2016 E. Michigan. Collectibles, glassware, jewelry, used merchandise, gifts, imports, souvenirs, decorator items. Reservations needed. (517) 372-5356. *Daily.*

LANSING

Lansing Classic Flea Market. 7275 E. 189th St. New and used merchandise, garage sale items, crafts, collectibles, produce. Snack bar, rest rooms. *Friday - Sunday.*

LANSING
Lansing Flea Market. 3215 S. Pennsylvania Ave. General flea market lines, new and used merchandise, collectibles, crafts, produce. Approximately 35 dealers. Snack bar, rest rooms, wheelchair accessible. Ample parking. Contact: Joe Scrattan, 4240 Love Joy Rd., Perry, MI 48872. (517) 394-7047 or 625-7262. *Friday - Sunday, 9:00 A.M. - 6:00 P.M.*

LAPEER
Lions Club Flea Market. County Center building. Antiques, collectibles, fine jewelry, vintage clothing, glassware, country collectibles, kitchen collectibles, silver, knives, toys. Snack bar, rest rooms, wheelchair accessible. Ample parking. *May - September; Sundays.*

LEXINGTON
Lexington Harbor Bazaar. 5590 Main St. New merchandise: gifts, jewelry, souvenirs, novelties, sportswear, clothing; lots of trendy new items in the boutique section. Used merchandise: garage sale items, collectibles, glassware, antiques, silver, vintage clothing. Approximately 200 dealers. Food available, rest rooms, wheelchair accessible. Ample parking. Space from $25 for weekend or $40 per week. Reservations required. Contact: E.R. Kingley, 5590 Main St., Lexington, MI 48450. (313) 359-5333. *Boutiques open daily; central market open Saturdays and Sundays; 10:00 A.M. - 5:00 P.M.*

MASON
Antique Flea Market. Mason St. Lots of quality antiques, furniture, collectibles, fine jewelry, vintage clothing, art, prints, books, military items, memorabilia, quality decorator pieces. Approximately 60 dealers. Food available, rest rooms. Space from $8. Contact: David Fincock, (517) 676-9753. *Wednesdays, Saturdays, and Sundays; 10:00 A.M. - 6:00 P.M.*

MERRILL
Tillies Treasures Flea Market. Hwy. M-46. Indoor market. New and used merchandise, sportswear, decorator items, souvenirs, collectibles, gifts, imports. Snack bar, rest rooms, wheelchair accessible. Ample parking. (517) 643-7516. *Saturdays and Sundays, 10:00 A.M. - 5:00 P.M.*

MONROE
Dallas Corner Flea Market. 15300 S. Dixie Hwy. New and used merchandise, lots of garage sale items. Collectibles, imports, crafts,

produce. Snack bar. Contact: Norman Sayer, (313) 242-6284. *Friday - Sunday.*

MT. CLEMENS
Gibraltar Trade Center. I-94 and N. River Rd. (Exit 237). Large indoor market with mostly permanent booths. Limited outdoor space available. Gibraltar is known mainly for its massive array of new merchandise: discount-house type, sweats, cookware, etc. Some collectibles. Market also conducts many special events. Snack bars, rest rooms, wheelchair accessible. Ample paved parking. Admission charge. Market management not very friendly to traveling commercial dealers. Contact: Jan Sullivan, (313) 465-6440 or 287-2000. *Fridays, noon - 9 P.M.; Saturdays, 9:00 A.M. - 9:00 P.M.; Sundays, 9:00 A.M. - 6:00 P.M.*

MT. CLEMENS
Old Timers Flea Market. 36000 Grosbeck Rd. Antiques, collectibles, silver, jewelry, vintage clothing, primitives, advertising items, memorabilia. Also plenty of new and used merchandise, garage sale items, crafts, gifts, imports, decorator items and produce. Average daily attendance 2,000 - 4,000. Approximately 100 dealers. Food available, rest rooms, wheelchair accessible. Space from $30. Contact: Dora Pet, 36000 Grosbeck Rd., Mt. Clemens, MI 48043. (313) 792-1612. *Friday - Sunday, 10:00 A.M. - 6:00 P.M.*

MT. MORRIS
Mt. Morris Mini Market. 11718 Saginaw. Used merchandise, collectibles, gifts, imports. Approximately 15 dealers. Space from $35 for 2 days. Contact: Ester Johnson, (313) 687-1560. *Friday - Sunday.*

MUSKEGON
Gold Token Flea Market. 1300 E. Laketon Ave. Indoor/outdoor market. Lots of secondhand and garage sale merchandise and new imports. Some antiques and collectibles. Approximately 75 dealers. Snack bar, rest rooms. Ample parking. (616)

Shopping Tip #5
Take a chance. Even if a high price is declared to be firm, be patient and return near closing time. A vendor may opt for a lower profit margin instead of packing the piece back home until the next week.

773-1137. *Saturdays, 6:00 A.M. - 2:00 P.M.*

MUSKEGON

The Great American Market Place. 1940 Henry St. Indoor market. New and used merchandise, gifts, decorator items, imports, souvenirs. Contact: Frank Rubin, (616) 755-4604. *Daily; closed Tuesdays.*

MUSKEGON

Select Auditorium Flea Market. 1445 Laketon Ave. U.S. Hwy. 31 and Laketon Ave. New and used merchandise, collectibles, art, crafts, gifts, decorator items, produce. Contact: Bud Kelly, 1445 E. Laketon Ave., Muskegon, MI 49442. (616) 726-5707. *Daily, 6:00 A.M. - 6:00 P.M.*

MUSKEGON HEIGHTS

Farmers Market Flea Market. 700 Yuba St. Large, wide-open market, with lots of new and used merchandise, antiques, collectibles, housewares, farm items, clothing, produce, livestock, crafts. Average attendance 3,000. Approximately 250 dealers. Food available, snack bar, rest rooms, wheelchair accessible. Lots of walking. Ample parking. Space from $5. Contact: John Albertie, (616) 722-3251 or 728-6433. *May - October; Wednesdays, 6:00 A.M. - 6:00 P.M.*

NEW BALTIMORE

Penn-Huron Flea Market. 17076 Huron Dr. Indoor/outdoor market. Wide range of merchandise; especially heavy on new merchandise. Much like shopping at a severely discounted department store. Approximately 150 dealers. Snack bar, rest rooms, wheelchair accessible. Ample parking. Space from $7. Contact: Richard Slater, 8100 Longworth, Detroit, MI 48209. (313) 841-2196 or 753-4133. *Saturdays and Sundays.*

NILES

Four Flats Flea Market. 2424 U.S. Hwy. 31. Antiques to "junque." Treasures are here if you have the patience to sort through it all. (616) 684-5051. *Saturdays and Sundays, 8:00 A.M. - 4:00 P.M.*

NORTHVILLE

Northville Flea Market. 301 S. Center, Northville Downs Race Track. Antiques, collectibles, silver, linens, coins, memorabilia, toys, vintage clothing, country collectibles. Approximately 40 dealers. Food available, rest rooms, wheelchair accessible. Ample parking. Space from $5. Contact: Chamber of Commerce,

(313) 349-7640. *Second Saturday of each month.*

Paw Paw

La Rue's Flea Market. 37908 Red Arrow Hwy. 1 mile west of Paw Paw, via I-94. Indoor/outdoor market. Wide selection of new and used merchandise, antiques, collectibles, jewelry, gifts, decorator items, crafts. Market conducts retail consignment auction on Sundays. Average daily attendance 1,000. Approximately 75 dealers outdoors and 100 indoors. Ample parking. Space from $3. Camping available. Contact: Donald LaRue, Jr., (616) 657-3533. *Saturdays and Sundays 9:00 A.M. - 6:00 P.M.*

Paw Paw

Reits Flea Market. 1/2 mile north on I-94. Exit 56. Lots of new merchandise. Also collectibles, antiques, glassware, used merchandise, crafts, art, and more. This is a good market for commercial vendors. Clean, friendly, and well-managed. It is always a pleasure to sell at or shop here. Average attendance 10,000. Approximately 450 dealers. Plenty of good food. Good restaurant. Rest rooms, wheelchair accessible. Ample parking. Space from $8 daily. Camping from $3. Electricity available. $1 space charge without Michigan sales tax license. Fireworks, martial arts, pornography, and alcohol prohibited. Contact: Bill Reits, 45293 Red Arrow Hwy. Paw Paw, MI 49079. (616) 657-3428 or (219) 259-8292. *May - October; Saturdays and Sundays, 8:00 A.M. - 4:00 P.M. Also open on holidays.*

Pontiac

Dixieland Flea Market. 2045 Dixie Hwy. End of Telegraph Rd. Indoor/outdoor market. Large, classic commercial market, with wide range of new merchandise, from hot new trendy to necessaries. Used merchandise, lots of antiques, collectibles, silver, coins, glassware, primitives. Crafts, produce, decorator items. Average daily attendance 8,000. Approximately 400 dealers. Food available, rest rooms, acres of walking. Ample parking. Good security. Overnight parking available. Reservations recommended. Space from $8 per day. Contact: Charles Sorkins, (313) 338-3220. *Fridays and Saturdays, 4:00 A.M. to 9:00 P.M.; Sundays 10:00 A.M. to 6:00 P.M.*

> ### *Where Was the First American Flea Market?*
> The consensus among most historians, although admittedly there are very few historians of flea markets in this country, seems to be that the fabulous First Monday Trade Days in Canton, Texas, a small city eighty miles southeast of Dallas, was the first American flea market to open and to remain open on a regular basis.
>
> Still thriving today, First Monday Trade Days are held on the weekend preceding the first Monday of each month. The Saturday and Sunday are always hopping, with Sunday being the biggest day of this event. Monday can be counted on to provide shoppers with lots of activity, but is generally the slowest day of the event.

PORT HURON
Farmers and Flea Market. 2424 10th Ave. Large selection of used merchandise, garage sale items, crafts, collectibles, glassware, produce, etc. Food available. *Thursdays.*

PORT HURON
Wurzel Flea Market, Inc. Rt. 136, north of Port Huron. New and used merchandise. General flea market lines of all types, including crafts, collectibles, and produce. Average attendance 2,500. Approximately 90 dealers. Space from $7 outside and $12 inside. Electricity available. Contact: Anna Weeks, 6575 Fredmoore Hwy., St. Clair, MI 48079. (810) 358-4283. *Saturdays and Sundays.*

PORTLAND
Portland Flea Market. 143 Kent St. Used merchandise: collectibles, gifts, imports, decorator items, country collectibles, vintage clothing, jewelry. Approximately 25 dealers. Contact: Richard Parkhouse, 143 Kent St., Portland, MI 48875. (517) 647-4484 or 647-7337. *Wednesdays, Saturdays, and Sundays.*

RAVENNA
Ravenna Flea Market. Folcum Rd. 2 miles north of the Ravenna Livestock Sales Grounds. I-96, Coopersville exit, north 13 miles. Lots of country stuff and country collectibles here. Primitives and advertising items abound. This is a market for the collector or decorator. Average attendance 4,000. Approximately 200 dealers. Company also conducts large

public auctions on Mondays. Space from $5. Contact: Jim Lund, 1685 19-Mile Rd., Cedar Springs, MI 49319. (616) 696-1247 or 853-2952. *Mondays, 7:00 A.M. - dark.*

ROMULUS

Green Line Road Flea Market. 16447 Middlebelt Rd. Primarily new and used merchandise, some crafts, limited antiques and collectibles. Snack bar, rest rooms, wheelchair accessible. Approximately 250 exhibitors. Ample parking. Space from $12. Contact: William Pai, (313) 941-6930. *Saturdays and Sundays, 7:00 A.M. - 4:00 P.M.*

ROYAL OAK

Flea and Farmers Market. 316 East Eleven Mile Rd. Indoor/outdoor market. Antiques, collectibles, decorator items, country treasures. New and used merchandise: jewelry, sportswear, housewares. Crafts, produce, livestock. Approximately 120 dealers. Food available. Space from $12. Contact: Steve Sendek, 316 E. Eleven Mile Rd., Royal Oak, MI 48067. (313) 548-8822. *Sundays.*

SAGINAW

Giant Public Market. 3435 Sheridain. Corner of Sheridain and Williamson. Clean, well-managed market in a modern building. New merchandise: imports, sportswear, gifts. Collectibles, decorator items, crafts, art, coins, jewelry, glassware. Average attendance 5,000. Approximately 100 dealers. Snack bar, rest rooms, wheelchair accessible. Space from $15. Contact: Bob Reiss, (517) 754-9090. *Fridays and Saturdays, 10:00 A.M. - 7:00 P.M.; Sunday, 10:00 A.M. - 6:00 P.M.*

SAGINAW

Saginaw Flea Market. Fairgrounds. Antiques, collectibles, silver, jewelry, new and used merchandise, crafts, produce. Average attendance 4,000. Approximately 100 dealers. Food available, rest rooms, wheelchair accessible. Ample parking. Contact: Deloris Holtrop, 420 Fisher, Saginaw, MI 48604. (517) 754-6004. or 753-4408. *Thursdays.*

SAGINAW

Tri-City Trade Center. 3860 Dixie Hwy. New and used merchandise, garage sale items, crafts, collectibles, produce. Food available. *Saturdays and Sundays.*

SAUGATUCK

Saugatuck Flea Market. 3604 64th St. Used merchandise, collectibles, gifts, imports. Approximately 20 dealers.

Space from $5. Contact: Everett Slendz, 3604 64th St., Saugatuck, MI 49419. (616) 857-2726. *Saturdays and Sundays, 8:00 A.M. - 5:00 P.M.*

SEARS
U.S. 10 and M-66 Flea Market. 6964 M-66. New and used merchandise, collectibles, crafts, produce. Cafe, rest rooms, camping. (616) 734-9112. *Friday - Sunday; April - October.*

SHELBY
Shelby Pavilion Flea Market. 508 N. State St. Used merchandise, lots of garage sale booths, crafts, produce. Approximately 25 dealers. Food available. Space from $3. Contact: Nick Elliott, 508 N. State St., Shelby, MI 49455. (616) 861-2200. *April - October; Tuesdays and Fridays.*

SIX LAKES
Flea Market. 303 N. Railroad St. Junction of Rts. M-46 and M-66. New and used merchandise, garage sale items, gifts, imports, decorator pieces, country collectibles, outdoor items, produce. Average daily attendance 300. Approximately 50 dealers. Food, rest rooms. Space from $5. Camping available. (517) 365-9057. *April - October; Saturdays and Sundays.*

SOUTH HAVEN
North Star Flea Market. Blue Star Hwy. and North Shore Dr. New and used merchandise, crafts, collectibles. Snack bar. (616) 637-3680. *Saturdays and Sundays.*

STANDISH
J and V Flea Market. 5108 S. Huron. Mile 13. Used merchandise, garage sale items, crafts, produce, collectibles. Approximately 25 dealers. Space from $5. Contact: Jim Wells, 5108 S. Huron Rd., Standish, MI 48658. (517) 846-4437. *Saturdays and Sundays.*

STERLING HEIGHTS
Flea Market. Utica Amusement Park. Van Dyke Rd. New and used merchandise, souvenirs, clothing, crafts, and a variety of flea market lines. Food available. (313) 268-0746. *Wednesdays.*

ST. JOHNS
Becks Farm Market. 7522 Hwy. 27, 6 miles north of town. Collectibles, farm items, used merchandise, housewares, clothing, produce. Food available. (517) 224-2351. *May - September; Saturdays and Sundays.*

TAYLOR
Gibraltar Trade Center. See listing for Mt. Clemens. *Friday - Sunday.*

THREE OAKS

Featherbone Flea Market. 11 N. Elm St. Indoor market. Antiques, collectibles, silver, coins, fine and estate jewelry, vintage clothing, art, prints, books, toys, primitives, advertising items. Approximately 40 dealers. Space rented by the month only. Contact: Jim Wisner, Box 393, Three Oaks, MI 49128. (616) 756-7320 or 426-3015. *Daily.*

TRUFANT

Trufant Auction and Flea Market. 303 North St. Large, wide-open market. Antiques to imports, used merchandise to fine jewelry. This is an excellent one-day market, with a wide variety of booths. Approximately 250 dealers. Company also conducts weekly public auctions. Snack bar, rest rooms, wheelchair accessible, lots of walking. Ample parking. Space from $5. Contact: Maurice Peterson, Rt. 1, Box 201, Trufant, MI 49347. (616) 984-2168. *April - September; Thursdays.*

UTICA

Country Fair Flea Market. 45300 Mound Rd. At Rt. M-59. Indoor market. Good mixture of merchandise, with lots of antiques and collectibles. Approximately 150 dealers. Snack bar, rest rooms, Ample parking. Space from $30. Contact: Country Fair, 45300 Mound Rd., Utica, MI 48087. (313) 254-7110. *Friday - Sunday.*

WARREN

Country Fair Antique Flea Market. 20900 De Quindre. 1 block north of 8-Mile Rd. Indoor market. Market has well-publicized area known as "Famous Antique Village." Also new and used merchandise. Approximately 350 dealers. Space from $40. Overnight parking available. Good security. Contact: Country Fair, 20900 Dequindre Blvd., Warren, MI 48034. (313) 757-3740 or 757-3741. *Fridays, 4:00 A.M. - 9:00 P.M.; Saturdays and Sundays, 10:00 A.M. - 6:00 P.M.*

WAYNE

Merri Trail Market. 35240 Michigan Ave. New and used merchandise, collectibles, crafts, produce. Approximately 50 dealers. Snack bar. Space from $35. (313) 729-3030. *Fridays and Saturdays.*

WAYNE

Wayne Farmers and Flea Market. 38000 Michigan Ave. New and used merchandise, antiques, collectibles, crafts, produce, livestock. Food available. (313) 422-0694. *Saturdays and Sundays*.

WESTLAND

Merri-Trail Flea Market. 82444 Merriman Rd. Used merchandise, garage sale items, new merchandise, collectibles, crafts, produce. Snack bar. *Saturdays and Sundays*.

WYOMING

Beltline Drive-In Flea Market, Beltline Drive-In Theatre. 1400 W. 28th St., S.W. Large commercial market, with great selection of new merchandise. Lots of good secondhand items and garage sale merchandise. Also some antiques, collectibles, glassware, silver, coins, primitives, farm and ranch collectibles, produce. Come dressed for a great deal of walking. Average attendance of 5,000 for the weekend. Approximately 350 dealers. Snack bar, rest rooms, wheelchair accessible. Ample parking. Admission charge. Space from $8. Contact: Don Moinet, 1400 W. 28th St., S.W. 49509. (616) 532-6302. *Seasonal market open May - October; flea market held on Saturdays and Sundays*.

YPSILANTI

Bunky's Flea Market. 822 Michigan Ave. Used and garage sale merchandise, crafts, collectibles, produce, new merchandise, and much more to attract collectors and bargain-conscious shoppers. Snack bar, rest rooms, wheelchair accessible. (313) 483-8336. *Friday - Sunday*.

YPSILANTI

Giant Flea Market. 214 E. Michigan, at Park. Indoor/outdoor market. Mainly antiques, collectibles, jewelry, and lots of classic flea market items. Great market for pleasurable shopping. Interesting booths and friendly people. Average attendance 3,000 - 5,000. 150 - 200 dealers. Space from $24 per weekend. Camping nearby. Contact: C. Hanna, 214 E. Michigan, Ypsilanti, MI 48197. (313) 971-7676 or 480-1539. *Friday - Sunday*.

Minnesota

One of America's real treasures—a beautiful state, with some of the cutest small towns one will ever see. Great shops, restaurants—a day of endless sunshine strolling around in some of these towns.

Tremendous auctions here, with great volumes of quality items at some of the sales. Sunup to dark, sometimes two and three rings going at one time. Need some mighty deep pockets to snatch up all the treasures.

Best bets...

✦ **Smitty's Flea Market, Mankato**
Outdoor market with approximately 100 dealers.

✦ **Orchard Fun Market, Monticello**
Between two and five hundred dealers, depending on the season. Entertainment and kids' rides.

✦ **Traders Market, New Market**
One of the area's better antiques and collectibles markets, with many special events.

✦ **Olmstead County Gold Rush Antique Show and Flea Market, Rochester**
A don't-miss event if you are looking for quality antiques.

ANNANDALE
Wright County Swap Meet. Rt. 3. 2 miles west of city. Collectibles, used merchandise, country treasures, handcrafts, produce. Snack bar. (612) 274-9005. *April - October; Saturdays and Sundays.*

BATTLE CREEK
Rainbow Bait Flea Market. Hwy. 78. Used merchandise, gifts, all sorts of classic flea market bric-a-brac, souvenirs, collectibles. (218) 864-5569. *Saturdays and Sundays.*

BLAINE
Blaine Flea Market. 10980 Central Avenue N.E. Hwy. 65, downtown. Large indoor flea market. New and used merchandise, furniture, lots of secondhand and garage sale items, plenty of bric-a-brac and gift items. Snack bar,

rest rooms, wheelchair accessible. Ample parking. Rent is by the month only. (612) 757-9906. *Saturdays and Sundays, 10:00 A.M. - 8:00 P.M.*

BLOOMINGTON

Mann-France Drive-In Theater Flea Market. France Ave. and Hwy. 494. Antiques, collectibles, decorator finds, jewelry, coins, sports cards, new merchandise, used merchandise, crafts, produce. Snack bar. *Sundays.*

BRAINERD

Searcy Flea Market. Hwy. 210. 6 miles west of city. Used merchandise, country and farm collectibles. Crafts, produce. Pleasant country market. Food available. *Friday - Sunday.*

BRECKENRIDGE

Auctions Unlimited Flea Market. Antiques, collector items, housewares, clothing, secondhand desirables, farm collectibles, jewelry. Snack bar, rest rooms, wheelchair accessible. Ample parking. *Third weekend of each month.*

DETROIT LAKES

Shady Hollow Flea Market. Hwy. 59, 5 miles south of town. Antiques, collectibles, silver, glassware, toys, new and used merchandise, crafts. Food available. Contact: Ardis Hanson, (218) 847-9488. *Sundays.*

FAIRBAULT

Flea Market. A typical weekend market, with a little of everything, from baseballs to clocks, electronics to T-shirts. (507) 334-5159. *Saturdays and Sundays.*

HACKENSACK

Flea Market. Catholic Church on Hwy. 371. New and used merchandise, antiques, collectibles, jewelry, crafts. Approximately 50 dealers. Food available. Contact: Chamber of Commerce, (218) 675-6135. *Monthly.*

HINCKLEY

Hinckley Flea Market. Hwy. 48. I-35, Exit 183. Indoor/outdoor market, some covered spaces. New merchandise: sportswear, imports, handmade crafts, art, collectibles, antiques, advertising items, imports, antique toys, and more. Average daily attendance 500+. Approximately 125 dealers. Snack bar, rest rooms, wheelchair accessible. Ample parking. Space from $7. Camping available. Contact: Walter Nilsen, 2413 Hughitt Ave., Superior, WI 54880. (612) 384-9911 or 394-3526. *April - October; Thurs-*

> ### *Tenets of Shopper Courtesy*
>
> Everyone appreciates a courteous shopper, and this is especially true at flea markets. Because of the freewheeling spirit at markets, buyers often forget that dealers selling their wares are not there for enjoyment, but are in their place of business, trying to make a living.
>
> Sellers and shoppers alike can get the most from the flea market experience if everyone will follow these tenets of shopping courtesy:
> 1. If you break something, offer and plan to pay for it.
> 2. Never walk into blocked-off areas of a booth.
> 3. Don't make rude comments about a person's booth or insult his merchandise.
> 4. Bargaining is a part of the flea market scene, but be reasonable and courteous when making an offer.

day - Sunday, 9:00 A.M. - 6:00 P.M.

HOPKINS
Main Street Antique Mall. 901 Main St. 20 minutes west of Minneapolis. General line of antiques and collectibles, art, prints, books. Approximately 65 dealers. (612) 931-9748. *Daily; closed holidays.*

JENKINS
Flea Market. Hwy. 371. Used merchandise, garage sale items, crafts, farmers' market. Food available. Contact: Tillman Rude, (218) 947-3313. *Seasonal market. Thursdays and Sundays during warm-weather months.*

LITCHFIELD
Meeker County Swap Area. New and used merchandise, crafts, collectibles, produce. Snack bar. Contact: Jerry Krambler, 501 Pleasant Ave., Litchfield, MN 55355. (612) 693-7698. *Saturdays and Sundays.*

MANKATO
Smitty's Flea Market. Hwy. 371. 1½ miles south of Nisswa. Antiques, collectibles, books, vintage clothing, advertising items, farm items, antique toys, primitives, lots of fishing collectibles. Approximately 100 dealers. Snack bar, rest rooms, wheelchair accessible. Ample parking. Space from $15 per day. Contact: Jim Schmidt, P.O. Box 585, Mankato, MN 56002. (507) 931-2449. *May -*

September; Saturdays, dawn - dark.

MINNEAPOLIS
Flea Market. Lyndale and Glenwood Sts. New and used merchandise, tools, garage sale items, crafts, housewares, produce. Food available. *Saturdays.*

MINNEAPOLIS
Flea Market. Midway Shopping Center. Snelling and Hwy. 36. Used merchandise, garage sale items, crafts, collectibles, produce. Food available. *Saturdays.*

MONTICELLO
Orchard Fun Market. Orchard Rd. 3 miles west of stoplight in Monticello. Indoor/outdoor market. Antiques, collectibles, crafts, used merchandise, and some new merchandise. Entertainment and kids' rides. 200 - 500 dealers, depending on season. Good food available onsite, rest rooms, wheelchair accessible. Ample parking. Space from $10. Contact: Orchard Fun Market, Rt. 1, Box 373, Monticello, MN 55362. (612) 295-2121. *Saturdays and Sundays.*

MOORHEAD
Buds Flea Market. Hwys. 10 and 75. Indoor market. New and used merchandise: jewelry, housewares, clothing, sports items, gifts, decorator items. Approximately 50 dealers. Snack bar, rest rooms, wheelchair accessible. Space from $23 for the weekend. Contact: Bud Granfor, Perley, MN 56574. (218) 861-6635. *Saturdays and Sundays.*

NEW MARKET
Traders Market. I-35 South. County Rd. 2. Elko/New Market Exit. One of the area's better antiques and collectibles markets. Crafts, produce, used merchandise. Snack bar, rest rooms, wheelchair accessible. Ample parking. Market hosts many special events; call for schedule. (612) 461-2400 or 435-7327. *Saturdays and Sundays.*

NISSWA
Flea Market. Hwy. 371 North. Used merchandise, garage sale items, crafts, collectibles, produce. Snack bar. (218) 963-2844. *Fridays and Saturdays.*

OMEGA
Wild Cat Swap Meet. New merchandise: tools, electronics, sportswear, toys, housewares, sports merchandise. Also used merchandise, garage sale items, crafts, produce, collectibles, and sometimes antiques. Approximately 100 dealers. Snack bar, rest rooms. Ample parking. Con-

tact: Dave Mertens, Box 94, Omega, MN (218) 983-3325. *Saturdays and Sundays.*

OTTERTAIL
Carol's Flea Market. Hwy. 78. Indoor market. New merchandise: jewelry, sportswear, electronics, housewares. Used merchandise: collectibles, glassware, silver, vintage clothing, art, books. Snack bar, rest rooms, wheelchair accessible. Ample parking. (218) 367-2742. *Saturdays and Sundays.*

PINE CITY
Flea Market. Downtown. Used merchandise, mostly garage sale items, crafts, some collectibles, produce. Food, rest rooms in the area. *Wednesdays.*

REDWING
Flea Market. Gibson's Parking Lot. Antiques, collectibles, country and farm items, new and used merchandise, crafts, produce. Food available. *Sundays.*

ROCHESTER
Olmstead County Gold Rush Antique Show and Flea Market. Fairgrounds. 50-acre facility, with 12 - 14 buildings in use for this combination show and market. Indoor/outdoor antiques only. This is a don't-miss event if you are looking for quality items. Strong attendance. Over 1,000 vendors selling high-quality antiques. Plenty of good food. Ample parking and miles of walking. Ample rest rooms. Admission charge. Space from $40 indoors and $30 outdoors. Reservations necessary. Contact: Joyce Fuchs, Rt. 2, Box 2X, Pine Island, MN 55963. (507) 356-4461. *Second weekend of May and third weekend of August.*

ST. CLOUD
Flea Market. Armory. 8th St. (612) 251-9189. *Usually held one weekend per month.*

ST. PAUL
Flea Market. Armory. 1530 E. Maryland. Antiques, collectibles, jewelry, silver, linens, new and used merchandise. Food available, rest rooms, wheelchair accessible. Ample parking. (612) 457-4999. *Three weekends per month, Saturdays and Sundays.*

TWIN CITIES
Flea Market. Washington County Fairgrounds. Indoor/outdoor market. Antiques, collectibles, jewelry, silver, vintage clothing, art, farm items, glassware. Food available, rest rooms, wheelchair accessible. Ample parking. Contact: Ron Johnstone,

> ### *Barter*
>
> Almost every flea market dealer likes to trade—especially if he can trade stock for stock. The first rule of thumb that I use in a trade is that both of us have to be using the same "dollar"—such as my wholesale price, your wholesale price, or retail to retail. I will not trade if we are using different dollars or if you want cash back as part of the deal.
>
> For no particular reason, I will not add anything "to boot" in a trade. I will take cash as part of the trade. Some of the things I like to trade for: fine jewelry, coins, quality small antiques. It goes without saying that if I can trade for any household or personal necessities, things I would have to pay cash for, then I am definitely interested.
>
> Over the years, I have traded for real estate, dental work, gold, silver, coins, fine jewelry, lodging, food, restaurant credit, and different kinds of merchandise that I can resell. The opportunity for trades are always present at a market.
>
> I always put up two signs: 1. Buy, Sell, Trade. Wholesale-Retail. 2. All sales final.

(612) 439-3183. *Seasonal market; fourth weekend of each month.*

WABASHA

Wabasha Indoor/Outdoor Flea Market. Hwy. 61 and Industrial Ct. New and used merchandise, furniture, lots of garage sale items and small newer collectibles. Food available. Contact: Don Carlson, (612) 565-4767. *Saturdays and Sundays, 9:00 A.M. - 5:00 P.M.*

WINONA

Flea Market. Levee Plaza Mall. Used merchandise, lots of garage sale items, bric-a-brac, crafts, produce. Food, rest rooms, wheelchair accessible. Ample parking. *Saturdays.*

MISSOURI

The Missouri Ozarks—the crown jewel in the beauty of America. Biscuits and gravy in the morning and hee-haw at night in the capital of the Ozarks, Branson. Many a time I have spent the entire day—and a long day, at that—making the short trip from Rogers, Arkansas, to Branson, Missouri. Just too many wonderful shops.

Great flea markets abound across the state. Missouri seems to have an unusually large number of flea markets—small, medium, and large. There is no shortage of flea markets. There is an equally large number of malls, a lot of them stocked with a tremendous selection of goods. Great country auctions wherever you are. With all the fun places to visit in Missouri, it's a shame that football is not played in the state.

Best bets...

* **Jeff Williams Original Kansas City Flea Market, Kansas City**
  Market is wide open for all types of items, from antiques to electronics.

* **Parkland Pavilion Antiques and Auction Gallery, Leadington**
  One of my favorite malls to shop—some real treasures here, at very good prices. Very pleasant, helpful people operate this mall.

* **Nana's Antique Mall, Mt. Vernon**
  Well-stocked mall operated in the true Ozark manner; a very enjoyable place to stop and shop.

* **Pevely Flea Market, St. Louis**
  Excellent market year-round for all types of merchandise.

ASBURY

Stateline Trade Center and Flea Market. Hwy. 171, 10 miles southeast of Pittsburg, KS. Used merchandise, country and farm collectibles, decorator items, advertising items, primitives. *Fridays and*

> **Dress for the Hunt!**
> **Tip #3**
> Take some sort of tote bag for carrying your purchases—even if you don't plan on buying anything.

Saturdays, 10:00 A.M. - 8:00 P.M.; Sundays, 1:00 - 6:00 P.M.; Mondays, 10:00 A.M. - 6:00 P.M.

AURORA
Highway 39 Merchants Flea Market. 4½ miles south of Walmart Store. Used merchandise, garage sale items, country collectibles, crafts, produce. Food available, rest rooms. (417) 678-6314. *Tuesday - Sunday, 9:00 A.M. - 6:00 P.M.*

AURORA
Houn Dawg Flea Market. Hwy. 39. 16 W. Olive St. Downtown. Indoor market. Lots of dolls, including some good collector dolls. Christmas decorations, Precious Moments, comics, crafts, quilts, glassware, pottery, furniture. *Daily.*

AVA
Granny's Attic Flea Market. 412 NW 12th Ave. 1 block north of town square. Business Rt. 5 and Hwy. 14. Antiques, collectibles, memorabilia, nice reproduction furniture, souvenirs, glassware, gifts. Also new merchandise: imports, sportswear. Close to Branson. Approximately 150 indoor booths, with 100 outdoor exhibitors on weekends. Snack bar. Ample parking. Space from $4 outdoors. Contact: Ronald Hammer, (417) 683-5776 or 683-3395. *Monday - Thursday, 9:00 A.M. - 5:00 P.M.; Fridays and Saturdays, 9:00 A.M. - 7:00 P.M.; Sundays, 10:00 A.M. - 5:00 P.M.*

AVA
Hammers Junktique Flea Market and Swap Meet. Hwy. 5. Used merchandise, country collectibles, primitives, glassware. Space from $5. Camping available. (417) 683-5776 or 683-3385. *Friday - Sunday.*

BARNHART
Barnhart Flea Market. 6850 Hwy. 61-67. Approximately 250 indoor spaces and 300 outdoor spaces. Mostly new merchandise and a lot of great "junque." A local market, not recommended for the traveling commercial vendor. 7 acres of parking. Space from $12 daily. Dealer setup Thursdays and Fridays, 8:00 A.M. - 8:00 P.M. Quantity

rates available. Food concessions by prior approval only. No firearms or alcohol sales permitted. Contact: Ed Samnee or Joyce Suermann, 6850 Hwy. 61-67, Imperial, MO 63052. (314) 464-5503. *Saturdays and Sundays.*

BELTON

Belton Antique Mall and Flea Market. 1016 N. Scott St. New market. Antiques, furniture, collectibles, jewelry, glassware. (816) 322-5688. *Monday - Saturday, 10:00 A.M. - 5:00 P.M.; Sundays, noon - 5:00 P.M.*

BILLINGS

Holstein Antiques and Flea Market. Hwy. 60. Antiques, collectibles, glassware, primitives, memorabilia, lots of Holstein cow stuff. 45 dealers. (417) 744-4193. *Monday - Saturday, 10:00 A.M. - 5:00 P.M.; Sunday, 1:00 - 5:00 P.M. Closed Tuesdays.*

BOLIVAR

Hidden Treasures Flea Market. Old Morrisville Rd. and Hwy. 13. (417) 326-4499. Antiques, primitives, collectibles, books, furniture, glass pottery. 75 dealers. *Daily.*

BONNE TERRE

Indoor Flea Market. Main St. downtown. Collectibles, crafts, decorator items, used merchandise, garage sale items. Approximately 15 dealers. *Wednesday - Sunday.*

BRANSON

Caldwells Flea Market. 114 Main St. Indoor market. Collectibles, country crafts, used merchandise, bric-a-brac, mountains of pure junk, souvenirs. (417) 334-5051. *Daily.*

BRANSON

Coffelt Country Crossroads. State Hwy. 165. $1/4$ mile south of Hwy. 76. Very interesting and enjoyable country market. All types of merchandise. Market is located in the heart of country music's new "Nashville." 13 permanent shops—ice cream shop, candle shop, quilts, wood signs, etc. Branson is packed with tourists during the summer months. Average daily attendance 300. 20-100 dealers. Snack bar, rest rooms, wheelchair accessible. Space from $5 daily. Tables and electricity available. Contact: Sandra Smith, HCR 5, Box 1829, Branson, MO. (417) 334-7611 or 335-4185. *Friday - Sunday.*

BRANSON

Flea Bag Market. 120 N. Sycamore. Used merchandise, bric-a-brac, collectibles, glassware, jewelry. (417) 334-5242. *Daily.*

Branson
Stacey Flea Market. Hwy. 76 West. Country collectibles, gifts, souvenirs, decorator items, imports, Snack bar, rest rooms. Ample parking. (417) 335-4305. *Daily.*

Butler
III Mile Junction Flea market. Used merchandise, collectibles, crafts, produce. Snack bar. (816) 679-6016. *Saturdays and Sundays.*

Cabool
Lloyds Flea Market. Hwy. 63. Country and farm collectibles, glassware, clothing, jewelry, used merchandise, garage sale items. Average attendance 1,000. Approximately 30 dealers. Snack bar, rest rooms. Space from $3. Contact: Lloyd Ayers, Sr., Rt. 1, Box 211, Houston, MO 65483. (417) 967-4473. *Saturdays and Sundays.*

Cape Girardeau
Antique Flea Market. Fairgrounds. Nice country market, with crafts, collectibles, antiques, food, and some new items. (314) 334-2451. *Monthly.*

Carthage
Carthage Route 66 Antique Mall and Flea Market. 1221 Oak St. New and used items, air-conditioned, lots of good Rt. 66 collectibles. 100+ dealers. (417) 359-7240. *Daily.*

Carthage
Deants Antique Mall and Flea Market. 1200 Oak St. Indoor market. Lots of good collectibles and secondhand merchandise. Over 100 booths. (417) 358-6104. *Daily.*

Carthage
Flea Market. Old Furniture Building. Collectibles, furniture, glassware, silver, jewelry, lots of secondhand merchandise, trash, and treasures. (417) 358-1901. *Daily, 10:00 A.M. - 5:00 P.M.*

Carthage
71 Flea Market. Hwy. 71. Used merchandise, garage sale items, crafts, sports memorabilia, new merchandise, souvenirs, produce. Snack bar. (417) 358-1988 or 358-FLEA. *Friday - Sunday.*

Cassville
De Ole Garage Antique Mall and Flea market. Hwy. 112 South. New market. Antiques, collectibles, primitives, glassware, jewelry, tools, linens. Lots of secondhand merchandise. (417) 847-5919. *Monday - Saturday, 10:00 A.M. - 5:00 P.M.; Sundays, 12:30 - 5:00 P.M.*

Cassville
E and E Flea Market. 5

miles north of town, on Hwy. 37. Used merchandise, garage sale items, collectibles, decorator items. Contact: Elizabeth Schaar, Rt. 1, Box 1567, Cassville, MO 65625. (417) 847-3888. *Daily, 9:00 A.M. - 5:00 P.M.*

CHILLICOTHE
North 65 Swap and Show. Rt. 5 North. New and used merchandise, collectibles, crafts, produce. Food available. Space from $2.50 per day. Camping available. (816) 646-9704. *April - October; Saturdays and Sundays.*

COLE CAMP
Flea Market. Hwy. 65. Used merchandise, garage sale items, bric-a-brac, crafts, produce, country collectibles. Food available, rest rooms. Ample parking. *May - November; Saturdays and Sundays.*

COLUMBIA
Midway Antique Center and Flea Market. Exit 121, I-70 and Hwy. 40. 3 miles west of Columbia. Used merchandise, collectibles, garage sale items, crafts. Food available, rest rooms, wheelchair accessible. Ample parking. 45 dealers. (314) 445-6717. *Daily 10:00 A.M. - 5:00 P.M.*

> **Shopping Tip #6**
> Be practical. Even though that velvet Elvis print might look darn handsome at the flea market and the vendor is giving a good spiel about its collector value, think long and hard about how it will look in your house.

COLUMBIA
Morton's Flea Market. Hwy. 63 South. Indoor market. New and used merchandise, souvenirs, collectibles. Approximately 25 dealers. (314) 449-6306. *Saturdays and Sundays.*

COLUMBIA
Stop N Scratch Flea Market and Antiques. 1907 N. Providence Plaza Antiques, sports memorabilia, glassware, primitives, advertising items, toys, linens, collectibles. (314) 443-8275. *Monday - Friday, 9:00 A.M. - 7:00 P.M.; Saturdays, 9:00 A.M. - 6:00 P.M.; Sundays, 11:00 A.M. - 6:00 P.M.*

CROCKER
Bear Ridge Antique and Collectible Flea Market. Hwy. 17, 7 miles north of Waynesville. Glass, jewelry, crafts, paper items, Americana, dolls. (417) 736-5858. *Monday - Satur-*

day, 9:00 A.M. - 5:00 P.M.; Sundays, 1:00 - 4:00 P.M.

DEXTER
Old Timers Flea Market. Hwy. 60 West. Collectibles, farm and ranch items, used merchandise, garage sale items, bric-a-brac. (314) 624-8288. *Daily.*

DOOLITTLE
Indoor Flea Market. I-44 Frontage Rd. and MM 179. New and used merchandise, gifts, souvenirs, jewelry, glassware, silver, crafts. Snack bar. Contact: Alice Jones, (314) 762-2065. *Saturdays and Sundays.*

EAGLE ROCK
Antiques and Uniques Flea Market. Hwy. 86. Building covers 2 floors. Lots of secondhand merchandise and some good "junque"; treasures are here—somewhere. (314) 271-4509. *Daily.*

ELDON
Eldon Flea Market. Hwy. 54. New market. Used merchandise, garage sale items, bric-a-brac, crafts, produce. Food available. Space from $3 per day. Camping available. (314) 365-2534. *April - October; Saturdays and Sundays.*

FAIR GROVE
Old Mill Flea Market. Main St. Market covers 6,000 sq. ft. Kitchenware, antiques, collectibles, glass, furniture, quilts, toys. (417) 759-2040. *Monday - Saturday, 10:00 A.M. - 5:00 P.M.; Sundays, noon - 5:00 P.M.*

FARMINGTON
Fairgrounds Flea Market. Fairgrounds. Hwy. 67 North. Antiques, collectibles, memorabilia, primitives, country, sports items, brewery items, crafts, art, etc. Also new and used merchandise. Average attendance 3,000. 60 - 80 vendors. Snack bar, rest rooms, wheelchair accessible. Space from $3. Contact: Dave Tripp, Rt. 1, Box 233, Farmington, MO 63640. (314) 756-1691. *Saturdays and Sundays, 9:00 A.M. - 4:00 P.M.*

GOODMAN
Kelly Springs Antique Mall and Flea Market. Hwy. 71, south of town. Collectibles, Coca-Cola memorabilia, cast iron items, quilts, dolls, glassware. Rest rooms. Ample parking. (417) 364-8508. *Thursday - Sunday, 10:00 A.M. - 5:00 P.M.*

GRANBY
Granby Flea Market. 4 miles east of Alternate Hwy. 71 on Hwy. 60. Collectibles, flea market items, antiques. 40 inside dealers. Outdoor setups available on

weekends, weather permitting. Camping with electricity available. (417) 472-3532. *Daily, 9:00 A.M. - 5:00 P.M.*

GREENVILLE
Hillbilly Park Flea Market. Hwy. 67, 8 miles south of Greenville. New market. New merchandise, used merchandise, crafts, collectibles, furniture, produce. Food available. Space from $8. (314) 297-3522. *Fridays, Saturdays, and Sundays.*

HANNIBAL
Bonanza Flea Market. 110 Church St. Indoor/outdoor market. Used desirables, new merchandise, collectibles, crafts, produce. Snack bar. (314) 248-1505. *Saturdays and Sundays.*

HOLDEN
Iron Kettle Antiques and Flea Market. South of Hwy. 50 on Hwy. 131. 9 miles from Holden; east on Hwy. 58, 3 miles. Glassware, furniture, collectibles, baseball cards, jewelry. (816) 732-4031. *Saturdays, 1:00 - 5:00 P.M.; Sundays, 1:00 - 6:00 P.M.*

HOUSTON
Lloyd's Flea Market. Hwy. 17, east of town. New and used merchandise, some small antiques, good selection of collectibles and memorabilia. Approximately 50 dealers. Snack bar, rest rooms, wheelchair accessible. Space from $3. Contact: Lloyd Ayers, Sr., Rt. 1, Box 211, Houston, MO 65483. (417) 932-6656. *Friday - Sunday.*

JOPLIN
Joplin Flea Market. 1200 Virginia Ave. Indoor/outdoor market. 40,000 sq. ft. of exhibit space. Heavy on used and flea market items, some antiques and collectibles. Approximately 150 dealers. Space from $5. Contact: LaVerne Miller, 2572 Markwardt Ave., Joplin, MO 64801. (417) 623-6328 or 623-3743. *Saturdays and Sundays.*

JOPLIN
North Main Street Antique/Craft Mall and Flea Market. 5 miles north of I-44 on Hwy. 43, (Main St.), behind Lumberjack Carpet. New market. 100+ booths inside with general line of antiques and collectibles. Air conditioned. Outside space available on weekends, weather permitting. Rest rooms, wheelchair accessible. Ample parking. (417) 781-9700. *Monday - Saturday, 9:00 A.M. - 5:00 P.M.; Sundays, noon - 5:00 P.M.*

JOPLIN
Rusty Nail Flea Market. 3004

Buying Toys at a Flea Market
Safety Check Tip #1

There are always a lot of toys to be found when shopping the markets. If you have little ones, especially if they are with you, it is hard to resist the temptation to buy them something they spy—most of us can't do it. A consumer safety tip, however: the same precautions should be taken with used toys that are taken when buying new ones at the store. Be sure to buy a toy that is age-appropriate for the child—no loose pieces or tiny wheels to pull off, for instance, that a baby or toddler might put in its mouth and perhaps choke on.

Here's a good idea: Take the empty cardboard tube from a roll of toilet tissue along with you on your shopping trip. Before you buy a toy for a young child, make sure that none of the pieces can fall through the tube. The tube is approximately the size of a child's airway. For your child's safety, if the toy or any piece of it falls through the tube, don't buy it.

Also, many of the new toys found at the markets are imports. Remember that many of these do not have to meet the same safety standards as the ones at a toy store.

Silver Creek Dr. 2 blocks south of I-44 on Hwy. 71. Exit 8A. Antiques, collectibles, dolls, furniture, crafts, jewelry, primitives. (417) 624-7157. *Thursday - Monday, 9:00 A.M. - 5:00 P.M.*

KAHOKA

Hickory Hills Flea Market. Hwy. 136, between Kahoka and Wayland. 15 miles east of Keokuk, IA. Antiques, collectibles, used merchandise. Food available. Space from $4 daily. Camping available. Contact: Gloria Johnsierken, Rt. 3, Box 65, Kahoka, MO. (816) 727-3769. *Monthly.*

KANSAS CITY

Heart Swap Meet. 6403 E. Hwy. 40. New merchandise: electronics, jewelry, sportswear, tools, housewares, sports merchandise, toys, decorator items, gifts. Used merchandise, lots of garage sale items. Also crafts, produce, collectibles. Average daily attendance 4,000. Approximately 500 dealers. Snack bars, rest rooms, wheelchair accessible. Ample parking. Admission charge. Space from $3 to $25. Camping available. (816) 923-3366. *Saturdays and Sundays.*

Kansas City
Jeff Williams Original Kansas City Flea Market. Governor's Building at the American Royal Center. Market is wide open for all types of items: antiques, collectibles, coins, jewelry, silver, glassware. New merchandise: sportswear, imports, electronics. Used merchandise. Average daily attendance 4,000. Approximately 500 dealers. Snack bar, rest rooms, wheelchair accessible. Ample parking. Space from $30. Contact: Jeff Williams, Box 543, Blue Springs, MO 64013. (816) 228-5811. *Monthly; 8:00 A.M. - 4:00 P.M.*

Kansas City
The Kansas City Flea Market. Governor's Building, next to Kemper Arena. I-435 and Front St. Large indoor one-day show, with lots of new merchandise. Snack bar, rest rooms, wheelchair accessible. Ample parking. Admission charge $1. Contact: Peak Shows, 1153 Evergreen Parkway, #M-250, Evergreen, CO 80439. (800) 333-FLEA or (303) 526-5494. *Monthly.*

Kansas City
Nate's 63rd Street Swap Meet. Drive-In Theater. Hwy. 50 East and I-435. New and used merchandise, crafts, collectibles, produce. Snack bar. *Saturdays and Sundays.*

Kansas City
Things Unlimited. 817 Westport Rd. Indoor market. New merchandise: sportswear, tools, jewelry, watches, sports merchandise, housewares, electronics. Used merchandise, glassware, primitives, kitchen collectibles, crafts. Approximately 75 dealers. Snack bar, rest rooms, wheelchair accessible. (816) 931-1986. *Saturdays and Sundays.*

Kansas City
Waldo's Antiques and Flea Market. 226 W. 75th St. 25 individual antique shops offering a general line of antiques and collectibles. There is an outdoor flea market on weekends with used merchandise, garage sale items, and some new merchandise. Snack bar, rest rooms, wheelchair accessible. Ample parking. *Open daily; flea market held on Saturdays and Sundays.*

Kansas City
Westport Flea Market. 817 Westport Rd. (816) 931-1986. Oldest indoor market in the area. Lots of collector plates, baseball cards, primitives, postcards, knives, new merchandise, and secondhand

merchandise. Excellent restaurant next door. 30+ dealers. *Daily.*

KENNET
Kennet Flea Market. Indoor/outdoor market. Used merchandise, farm and ranch collectibles, toys, glassware, crafts, produce. Approximately 60 vendors. Snack bar, rest rooms. *Saturdays and Sundays.*

KNOB NOSTER
Flea Market. North Vaughn St. Used merchandise, collectibles, primitives, silver, glassware, and a little bit of everything you might expect to find at a flea market. (816) 563-9766. *Saturdays and Sundays.*

KNOB NOSTER
Knob Noster Flea Market. 585 N. Jefferson. Souvenirs, gifts, jewelry, used merchandise, collectibles. (417) 588-7430. *Saturdays and Sundays.*

LAMAR
Treasure Seekers Antique Mall and Flea Market. West side of town square. New market. Antiques, collectibles, furniture, jewelry, silver, coins, glassware, primitives, advertising items, art, prints, books. (417) 682-2900. *Monday - Saturday, 9:00 A.M. - 5:00 P.M.; Sundays, 1:00 - 5:00 P.M.*

LEBANON
The Country Corner Flea Market and Antiques. 585 N. Jefferson, Just off I-44. Indoor market. 7,500 sq. ft. facility. Mostly permanent booths, with lots of flea market goods and tourist items. Approximately 40 dealers. Space from $5. Contact: Marilyn Allen, 585 Jefferson St., Lebanon, MO 65536. (417) 588-1430. *Monday - Saturday, 9:00 A.M. - 6:00 P.M.; Sundays, noon - 6:00 P.M.*

LEBANON
Remember When Flea Market. 577 N. Jefferson. Antiques, collectibles, furniture, used merchandise, primitives. Dealers welcome. (417) 588-1029. *Daily.*

LINN CREEK
Hillbilly Al's Flea Market. Junction of Hwy. 54 and A-road. New and used merchandise, crafts, collectibles, produce. Snack bar. (314) 346-5890. *Saturdays and Sundays.*

LOWRY CITY
J and L Flea Market. Hwy. 13 South. Antiques, collectibles, used merchandise. (417) 644-2929. *Monday - Saturday,*

> **More Tenets of Shopper Courtesy**
> 1. When shopping with children, keep them under control. Do not let them handle or grab merchandise. Be prepared to help them yourself.
> 2. Never allow horseplay in and around booths. Be prepared to pay for anything your children might damage.
> 3. The flea market can be a great learning place for children. It's up to parents (and grandparents) to make those lessons good ones.

9:00 A.M. - 6:00 P.M.; Sundays, 1:00 - 6:00 P.M.

MACON
Flea Market. Hwy. 63 South. Used merchandise, garage sale items, bric-a-brac, crafts, produce, and plenty of hidden flea market treasures. Snack bar. *Saturdays and Sundays.*

MARIONVILLE
Kountry Korner Flea Market. Junction of Hwys. 60 and 265. Railroad items, antiques, primitives, furniture, glass, Indian artifacts, western items, books. Picture gallery collection. Rest rooms, wheelchair accessible. Ample RV and bus parking. Contact: Don and Ruth Rickman, (417) 463-2923. *Monday - Saturday, 10:00 A.M. - 5:00 P.M.; Sundays, 1:00 - 5:00 P.M.*

MARSHFIELD
Bobbie's Wishing Well. 222 S. Crittenden. Exit 100 off I-44. Antiques, "junque," collectibles. Lots of interesting shops in Marshfield make this a great stop. 20 dealers. Contact: Bobbie Reed, (417) 468-6380. *Monday - Saturday, 9:30 A.M. - 5:00 P.M.; Sundays, 12:30 - 5:00 P.M.*

MARSHFIELD
Hidden Treasures Antiques and Flea Market. 301 S. Clay. Exit 100 off I-44. Antiques, furniture, glass, advertising items, crocks, collectibles, toys, tools, clocks, baskets, teddy bears, primitives, books. Contact: Donna Arehart, (417) 468-6088 or 468-4165. *Monday - Saturday, 9:00 A.M. - 5:00 P.M.; Sundays, 10:00 A.M. - 4:00 P.M.*

MOUNTAIN VIEW
Weavers Auction and Flea Market. 9 miles west of Mountain View. Flea market, animal swap meet, auction on Saturday nights. Camping available. RV hookups from

> ### *Green Cash*
> In the world of flea market selling, a cash sale is one that is paid in U.S. currency—what I like to call "Yankee greenbacks." Checks and credit cards are not "cash."
>
> When I am negotiating with a customer, I always ask, "What kind of funds are you going to pay with?" Credit cards cost the dealer money to process, and if he is selling on the road, both credit cards and checks have to be sent home to be processed, delaying him in obtaining the funds.

$7.50 nightly. Contact: Wayne Weaver, Rt. 3, Box 102, Mountain View, MO 65546. (417) 934-2160 or 469-3351. *Daily.*

MT. VERNON
Mt. Vernon Flea Market. Rt. 1. Indoor/outdoor market. Used merchandise, new merchandise, gifts, souvenirs, collectibles. (417) 466-2422. *Daily, closed Wednesdays.*

NEOSHO
Chea's Place. 523 N. College St. Antiques and collectibles. (417) 451-2511. *Tuesday - Saturday, 10:00 A.M. - 5:00 P.M.; Sundays and Mondays, 1:00 - 5:00 P.M.*

NEOSHO
Neosho Gallery and Flea Market. 900 N. College St. Business Rt. 60. Antiques, furniture, collectibles, glassware, and toys. 100+ booths. Rest rooms, wheelchair accessible. Ample parking. (417) 451-4675. *Tuesday - Sunday. 9:00 A.M. - 5:00 P.M.*

NEOSHO
71 Craft and Flea. Rt. 8, 1.5 miles north of town on Hwy. 71. Furniture, primitives, ceramics, collectibles, wood crafts, gifts, books, antiques and secondhand items. Air-conditioned. (417) 451-9575. *Tuesday - Saturday, 9:00 A.M. - 5:00 P.M.; Sundays, 11:00 A.M. - 5:00 P.M.; closed Mondays.*

NEOSHO
Verns Flea Market. 1 mile south of junction of 60 and 71A. Collectibles, new and used merchandise, dinnerware, glassware, depression glass, guns, antiques, tools, jewelry. Outdoor setups available on weekends, weather permitting. *Monday - Friday, 9:00 A.M. - 6:00 P.M.; Saturdays and Sundays, 6:00 A.M. - 6:00 P.M.*

Nixa
Camel Back Antiques and Flea Market. Junction of Hwy. 160 and Northview Rd. Antiques, primitives, collectibles and glassware. (417) 725-5125. *Monday - Saturday, 10:00 A.M. - 5:00 P.M.; Sundays, 11:00 - 5:00 P.M.*

Nixa
Red Barn Flea Market and Antiques. 1 mile west of Hwy. 160/14. This market has a little bit of everything, from antiques, dishes, and collectibles to furniture, memorabilia, and concrete yard ornaments. (417) 725-3338. *Thursday - Monday.*

Oak Grove
Inge's Oak Grove Flea Market. 1120 Broadway. Antiques, collectibles, furniture, tools. Credit cards accepted. (816) 625-8885. *Monday - Saturday, 10:00 A.M. - 6:00 P.M.; Sundays, 1:00 - 6:00 P.M.*

Old Mines
Starlite Flea Market. 5 miles north of Potosi on Hwy. 21. Used merchandise, garage sale items, bric-a-brac, and junk. Average weekly attendance 2,500. Snack bar. Space from $4. Camping available, with electricity. Contact: Terry Mercille, Rt. 2, Box 123, Cadet, MO 63630. (314) 438-4974. *Friday - Monday.*

Osceola
Trade Fair Market. Trade Fair Mall. Hwy. 13. New merchandise, used merchandise, crafts, produce. Snack bar. (417) 647-8085. *Wednesday - Monday.*

Osceola
Wisner's Flea Market and Antiques. Hwy. 13. Collectibles, jewelry, glassware, primitives, memorabilia, souvenirs, used merchandise. (417) 646-8555. *Daily.*

Ozark
Country Junction Flea Market and Baird's Antiques. Junction of Hwys. 14 and 65 South. Large selection antique furniture, glass, jewelry, linens, housewares. (417) 485-8116. *Monday - Saturday, 9:30 A.M. - 5:00 P.M.; Sundays, 1:30 - 5:00 P.M.*

Ozark
Ozark Flea Market. 519 S. Town Center. (East Hwy. 14). Antiques, furniture, Coke items, quilts, toys, tools, primitives, advertising signs. (417) 485-8544. *Daily.*

Park Hills
Jose's Flea Market. 233 W. Main St. New merchandise and new and secondhand furniture, bric-a-brac, garage

sale items. *Monday - Saturday, 9:30 A.M. - 5:30 P.M.*

PARK HILLS
The Little Red School House Flea Market. Vo-Tech Rd, south of Bonne Terre. Antiques, collectibles, secondhand items, tools, bric-a-brac, new merchandise. (314) 358-0570. *Thursday - Sunday, 10:00 A.M. - 6:00 P.M.*

PEVELY
Pevely Flea Market. Hwy. 61 South Drive-In Theater. Indoor, outdoor, and covered spaces. Excellent market year-round for all types of merchandise. Good market for the traveling dealer. Strong attendance. Approximately 500 dealers. Arrive early for space. Contact: Ken Smith, 211 Broadway, Pevely, MO 63070. (314) 479-5400. *Saturdays and Sundays.*

POPLAR BLUFF
Flea Market. Next to livestock market. Used merchandise, garage sale items, farm and ranch items, housewares, clothing, produce. Food available, rest rooms. Ample parking. *Thursdays and Fridays.*

POTOSI
Mainstreet Market. 207 E. High St. Antiques, glassware, collectibles, period furniture, toys, books, quilts, Indian articles, western memorabilia, coins. (314) 438-7731. *Daily.*

REPUBLIC
West County Flea Market. 336 N. Hwy. 60. Antiques, collector items, dolls, Precious Moments collectibles. (417) 732- 8415. *Monday - Saturday, 10:00 A.M. - 5:00 P.M.; Sundays, 1:00 - 5:00 P.M.*

RUTLEDGE
Dog, Gun, Hillbilly Consignment Auction and Flea Market. Contact: Irvin Johnson, (816) 883-5816 or 883-5322. *Monthly.*

SEDALIA
Sedalia Flea Market. Hwy. 65 South. Souvenirs, used merchandise, garage sale items, glassware, dolls, toys, jewelry. (816) 827-5860. *Daily.*

SELIGMAN
Highway 37 Flea Market. 9 miles from Roaring River State Park. Indoor/outdoor market. Used merchandise, country and farm collectibles, souvenirs, novelties, handcrafts, giftware. Great trout fishing in the area. Camping available. Market open to food vendors. (417) 662-3890. *Daily.*

SEYMOUR
The Living Rock Sell R' Swap. 226 Clinton Ave. Old

Hwy. 60. Antiques, collectibles, crafts and lots and lots of secondhand "junque." Contact: David Winter (417) 935-2743. *Monday - Saturday, 10:00 A.M. - 6:00 P.M.*

SIKESTON

Sikeston Trade Fair. Blodgett Rd. New and used merchandise, garage sale items, crafts, produce. Snack bar, rest rooms. (314) 472-2683. *Friday - Sunday.*

SIKESTON

Tradewinds Flea Market. 875 Malone Ave. Indoor market. Wide-open market; lots of new merchandise: sports-related merchandise, sportswear. Some good collectible booths, glassware, silver. Also crafts, art, decorator items. Good market for wintertime selling. Average daily attendance 3,500. Approximately 200 dealers. Snack bar, rest rooms, wheelchair accessible. Ample parking. Space from $5. Contact: Tradewinds Flea Market, 165 Lee St., Sikeston, MO 63801. (314) 471-3965. *Thursday - Sunday, dawn - dusk.*

SPRINGFIELD

Cherry Tree Flea Market. 1459 E. Cherry. Used furniture, collectibles, comics, clothing, jewelry, new and

> ## *Springfield Attractions*
> Springfield is the gateway to the Ozarks vacationland and springboard to Branson, home of today's country music. Many fine shops and attractions are located in Springfield, and many excellent restaurants. Plan to spend a few days exploring.

used electronics. (417) 831-7230. *Monday - Saturday, 10:00 A.M. - 6:00 P.M.; Sundays, noon - 5:00 P.M.*

SPRINGFIELD

Country Corner Flea Market. 351 Booneville. Antiques, collectibles, records, books, tapes, toys, jeans, furniture. (417) 862-1597. *Monday - Saturday, 10:00 A.M. - 5:00 P.M.; Sundays, noon - 5:00 P.M.*

SPRINGFIELD

Flea Market and Swap Meet. University Plaza Trade Center. Approximately 200 dealers. RV hookup available. Space from $20. Contact: Floyd Cillabough, 809 E. Hill, Springfield, MO 65803. (417) 833-1380. *Monthly; opens at 7:30 A.M.*

SPRINGFIELD

G and W Antiques and Collectible Flea Market. 400 W. Commercial. Glass, furniture,

> ### *Sure-Fire, Don't-Miss Markets for the Midwest!*
>
> | | |
> |---|---|
> | Belleville Flea Market | Belleville, Illinois |
> | Kane County Flea Market | St. Charles, Illinois |
> | Indiana Flea Market | Indianapolis, Indiana |
> | Kentucky Flea Market | Louisville, Kentucky |
> | Burley Park Swap Meet | Howard City Heights, Michigan |
> | Ionia Antique and Collectibles Market | Ionia, Michigan |
> | Gibraltar Trade Center | Mt. Clemens, Michigan |
> | Country Fair Antique Flea Market | Warren, Michigan |
> | Olmstead County Gold Rush Antique Show and Flea Market | Rochester, Minnesota |
> | Caesar Creek Flea Market | Caesar Creek, Ohio |
> | Springfield Antique Show and Flea Market | Springfield, Ohio |
> | Washington Court House Flea Market | Washington, Ohio |

jewelry, railroad items, quilts, linens, primitives, toys. Credit cards accepted. (417) 869-0061. *Monday - Saturday, 10:00 A.M. - 6:00 P.M.*

SPRINGFIELD
Great Discoveries Flea Market and Antique Furniture. 416 W. Commercial. Collectibles, glass, linens, jewelry, primitives, books. Credit cards accepted. (417) 869-9101. *Monday - Saturday.*

SPRINGFIELD
I-44 Swap Meet. 1724 W. Kearney. I-44 and Neergard, fronts onto I-44. Lots of new merchandise: sportswear, electronics, imports, gifts, sports-related merchandise. Farm items. secondhand and garage sale merchandise. 200+ dealers. Snack bar, rest rooms. Ample parking. Space from $5 per day. (417) 864-4340 or 864-6508. *March - December; Saturdays and Sundays, dawn - dusk.*

SPRINGFIELD
Kountry Korner Flea Market. 1917 W. Atlantic. Collectibles, crafts, new merchandise, glass, jewelry, used furniture, tools, lots of secondhand

merchandise. (417) 865-9510. *Monday - Saturday, 9:00 A.M. - 5:00 P.M.; summer hours, 9:00 A.M. - 6:00 P.M.*

SPRINGFIELD
Northtown Flea Mart. 3310 N. Glenstone. Indoor market. Some antiques and collectibles, mostly used and flea market merchandise, lots of bric-a-brac. Approximately 20 permanent dealers. Monthly rentals only. Contact: Peggy Humbird, 3310 N. Glenstone Ave., Springfield, MO 65801. (417) 833-3533. *Daily; closed Wednesdays.*

SPRINGFIELD
Olde Towne Flea Market. 600 Booneville Ave. Antiques, collectibles, furniture. Approximately 100 dealers. Monthly rentals only, from $125. Contact: Olde Towne Flea Market. 600 Booneville Ave., Springfield, MO 65801. (417) 831-6665. *Monday - Saturday, 9:30 A.M. - 5:00 P.M.; Sundays, 1:00 - 5:00 P.M.; closed Tuesdays.*

SPRINGFIELD
Park Central Flea Market. 429 Booneville. 2 floors. Antiques, primitives, glass, linens, toys, collectibles, china, furniture, sports cards. (417) 831-7516. *Monday - Saturday, 10:00 A.M. - 5:00 P.M.; Sundays, noon - 5:00 P.M.*

SPRINGFIELD
South Peer Antique Mall and Flea Market. 317 South Ave. South of town square. Furniture, glass, china, linens, jewelry, primitives, toys, books. 60 dealers. (417) 831-6558. *Daily. 9:30 A.M. - 5:00 P.M.*

SPRINGFIELD
Sac River Trade and Antique Mall. Hwy. 13. Antiques, furniture, collectibles, silver, coins, linens, quilts, glassware, kitchen collectibles, books, art, prints. Snack bar, rest rooms, wheelchair accessible. Ample parking. (417) 756-2201.

SPRINGFIELD
Southtown Flea Market. 2139 S. Campbell. 2 blocks south of Bass Pro. 5,000 sq. ft. facility. Antique furniture, advertising items, glassware, lots of miscellaneous items. Free coffee. 35+ dealers. (417) 882-1707. *Monday - Saturday, 9:30 A.M. - 5:00 P.M.; Sundays, noon - 5:00 P.M.*

SPRINGFIELD
Springfield Flea Market. Fairgrounds. New indoor/outdoor market. Strong on antiques, collectibles, and new merchandise. (417) 833-5119. *Second weekend of each month.*

Springfield

S.T.D. East Flea Market (formerly known as The Variety Shop). 1820 E. Trafficway. Glassware, baseball cards, toys, crafts, books, furniture, collectibles, antiques. (417) 831-6367. *Daily, 10:00 A.M. - 6:00 P.M.*

Springfield

S.T.D. West Flea Market (formerly known as The Variety Shop). 651 S. Kansas. Glassware, antiques, collectibles, furniture, books, crafts, toys, baseball cards. (417) 831-6331. *Daily, 10:00 A.M. - 6:00 P.M.; Fridays until 9:00 P.M.*

Springfield

Treasure Finders Antiques and Flea Market. 1722 S. Seiger, behind Andy's. Antique furniture, tools, baseball cards, glass, toys, dolls, general secondhand merchandise. (417) 883-3373. *Monday - Saturday, 9:00 A.M. - 6:00 P.M.; Sundays, noon - 5:00 P.M.*

Springfield

Viking Flea Market. 626 W. Chase. Indoor market. Approximately 30 permanent dealers. Contact: Viking Flea Market. 626 W. Chase, Springfield, MO 65803. (417) 869-4237. *Daily, closed Wednesdays.*

St. Genevieve

Antique Mart. 305 N. Main St. Indoor market. Primarily antiques and collectibles, with lots of primitives, kitchenware, and advertising items. (314) 883-7333. *Daily.*

St. Louis

Flea Market. VFW Hall. 7208 W. Florissant St. Contact: Billie Dickemper, (314) 383-1919. *Seasonal market. Usually first weekend of each month; call for dates.*

St. Louis

Flea Market and Antique Show. Page and Hwy. 270. Approximately 40 dealers. $20 per table. Contact: Betty Roberts, (314) 521-5544. *Fourth Sunday of each month.*

St. Louis

Frisom Flea Market. 7025 St. Charles Rock Rd. Approximately 300 spaces. New merchandise: sportswear, imports, gifts, lots of new decorator and collectible items. Lots of used and secondhand merchandise. Average attendance 1,200. Snack bar, rest rooms, wheelchair accessible. Ample parking. Space from $10 daily. Electricity available. Contact: Jack Frisom, 7025 St. Charles Rock Rd., St. Louis, MO 63133.

> ### *Try It Before You Buy It!*
> Most dealers will tell you that the electric appliance they are selling works "all the way." Reputable ones will advise you of any defects or quirks they know of. However, a rule of thumb is to ask to try it before you buy it.
>
> Ninety-five percent of all flea markets will have an electrical outlet somewhere designated for this purpose. If a dealer refuses to allow you to test an item, pass on it—no matter how great the bargain or how good it looks on the outside. That defective microwave you fail to check out first could become an awfully large bookend in your kitchen, and a hard reminder.

(314) 727-0460. *Friday - Sunday, 8:00 A.M. - 5:00 P.M.*

ST. LOUIS
Pevely Flea Market. Hwy. 61 South Drive-In Theater (Pevely). Indoor, outdoor, and covered spaces. Excellent market year-round for all types of merchandise. Good market for the travelling dealer. Strong attendance. Approximately 500 dealers. Arrive early for space. Contact: Ken Smith, 211 Broadway, Pevely, MO 63070. (314) 479-5400. *Saturdays and Sundays.*

ST. ROBERT
Freddy Bees Flea Market. I-44 and 160 mile marker. New and used merchandise, garage sale items, bric-a-brac, crafts, produce. Snack bar. Camping available. (314) 336-4750. *Thursday - Sunday.*

UNION
Mason-Dixon Line Flea Market. I-44 and Hwy. 50. Primarily new merchandise and secondhand "junque." Snack bar, rest rooms, wheelchair accessible. Ample parking. *Saturdays and Sundays.*

WARRENSBURG
B and B Swap and Shop, Flea Market and Large Variety Mall. Hwy. 50 and Southside Rd. 1/2 mile east of Knob Noster. Antiques, collectibles, crafts, glassware, primitives, canopies, sports cards, furniture, and new merchandise. *Tuesday - Sunday, 9:30 A.M. - 5:30 P.M.*

WARSAW
AJ's Trade Fair. Hwy. 7 and Truman Dam. Indoor/outdoor market, with some covered spaces. New and used merchandise, some collect-

ibles and primitives. Restaurant and bakery. Market is located in center of resort area and often has live entertainment. Approximately 75 dealers. Ample parking. Camping and electricity available. Space from $43 per day. (816) 438-5707. *Daily, 9:00 A.M. - 7:00 P.M.*

WASHINGTON
Washington Flea Market. 217 Elm St. Collectibles, glassware, primitives, farm items, new merchandise, crafts, produce. Snack bar. (314) 239-5386. *Wednesday - Sunday.*

WENTZVILLE
Wentzville Flea Market. Main St. Indoor/outdoor market. New and used merchandise, garage sale items, crafts. Snack bar. (314) 327-6358. *Sundays.*

WEST PLAINS
Monthly Flea Market. Fairgrounds. Antiques, collectibles, new and used merchandise, crafts. Food available, rest rooms, wheelchair accessible. (417) 256-2198. *Monthly.*

> **Dress for the Hunt!**
> **Tip #4**
> Keep a blanket, empty cardboard box, and a few newspapers in the trunk of your car in case you need to pad something you buy, or to protect small items. Nylon cord or a piece of clothesline can also come in handy.

Indoor market. Mostly collectibles, advertising items, primitives, country, collectible glassware and silver. New and used merchandise. Approximately 50 dealers. Ample parking. Rental by month only. Contact: Andrea Lee, 3235 S. Locust Ave., Grand Island, NE 68801. (308) 381-4075. *Monday - Saturday, 10:00 A.M. - 5:00 P.M.; Sundays, noon - 5:00 P.M.; closed holidays.*

HENDERSON

County Collectibles Market. I-80 at Henderson. New and used merchandise, farm items, lots of western collectibles, gifts, jewelry, housewares, crafts, produce. Food available, rest rooms, wheelchair accessible. Ample parking. (402) 423-4770. *Mondays and Saturdays.*

INVALE

Invale Flea Market. 6 miles west of Red Cloud. Used merchandise, farm and houseware items, western and Indian collectibles, lots of garage sale finds. Crafts, produce. Food available. *Saturdays and Sundays.*

LINCOLN

The Antique Market. 48th St. and Old Cheney Rd. General line of antiques and collectibles with some nice furniture. 55 dealers. Snack bar, rest rooms, wheelchair accessible. Ample parking. (402) 423-4805. *Daily.*

LINCOLN

Foxy Grandma's Flea Market. 3880 N. 66th Ave. New and used merchandise, jewelry, collectibles, vintage clothing, decorator items. (402) 466-3870. *Saturdays and Sundays.*

LINCOLN

Indoor Flea Market. Pershing Auditorium. 226 Centennial Mall South. Good selection of antiques, antique furniture, collector items, farm-related fare, handcrafted treasures, new and used merchandise. Snack bar, rest rooms, wheelchair accessible. Admission charge. Space from $40. Contact: Derek Anderson, Box 81126, Lincoln, NE 68501. (402) 471-7500. *Usually held*

NEBRASKA

Land of endless plains and no football. If you are fortunate enough to be in Nebraska during harvest, not only is it tremendously hot, but watching the giant harvest tractors harvesting what seem to be endless fields of corn, wheat, etc., is a never-ending fascination. As a young laddiebuck, I had the unfortunate pleasure of working on the hay harvest. Now I just watch.

Best bets...

* **Indoor Flea Market, Lincoln**
  One can usually find a good selection of antiques, antique furniture, and hand-crafted treasures at this market. Quality items are very reasonably priced in the Lincoln area.

* **Sunrise Sunset Flea Market, Lincoln**
  This large, commercial market offers a little bit of everything including antiques, collectibles, farm and ranch items, western and Indian jewelry, and decorator items. The Nebraska State Fairgrounds hosts many fine events, so be sure to call for a schedule when you are in the area.

* **Flea Market, South Sioux City**
  Located at the Sioux Land Convention Center, this market offers quality antiques, collectibles, primitives, farm items, farm toys, jewelry and more. Always some fine bargains on quality items. A must-see for shopkeepers, dealers, and collectors!

COLUMBUS
Columbus Flea Market. Platte Ct. New and used merchandise, lots of bric-a-brac, country memorabilia items, collectibles, crafts, produce. Food available, wheelchair accessible, rest rooms. Ample parking. (605) 361-1717. *May - October; weekends.*

GRAND ISLAND
Great Exchange Indoor Flea Market. 3235 S. Locust Hwy. Junction of Hwy. 34. I-80, Exit 312, north 5 miles.

in the middle of the month; 10:00 A.M. - 5:00 P.M.

LINCOLN

Sunrise Sunset Flea Market. State Fairgrounds. Approximately 600 spaces. Large midwestern commercial market with a wide range of goods. A bit of everything, including new merchandise, used desirables, garage sale items, antiques, collectibles, farm and ranch items, western and Indian jewelry, art, decorator items, and collectibles. Food available, rest rooms, wheelchair accessible. Ample paved parking. Space from $10 daily for 22 x 18. Contact: Box 4212, Lincoln, NE 68504. (402) 467-4836 or 466-0334. *Saturdays and Sundays.*

NORTH PLATTE

The Antique Place. 418 E. 4th St. (Co-op). General line of furniture, glass, primitives, toys. (308) 534-4344. *Daily.*

OMAHA

CLBC Flea Market. 11000 N. 72nd St. Indoor/outdoor market. New and used merchandise, housewares, jewelry, sportswear, garage sale items, western wear and collectibles, T-shirts, and plenty of this-n-that. Approximately 40 dealers. Food available. Space from $6. Contact: Richard Bechtloff, 12434 Westwood Ln., Omaha, NE 68144. (402) 572-9568 or 333-4507. *Saturdays and Sundays.*

OMAHA

Flea Market. Mueller Recreation Hall. 36th & 'W' Sts. Antiques, collectibles, western and Indian jewelry, art and collectibles, kitchen collectibles, toys, farm and ranch collectibles, glassware, primitives, coins, silver, vintage clothing. Average attendance 1,000. Approximately 100 dealers. Ample parking. Space from $8.50. Contact: Ronald Beranek, 16606 Iske Dr., Omaha, NE 68123. (402) 291-6280. *Second Sunday of each month.*

OMAHA

Maurices Flea Market. 13th and Martha. Soko Hall. New and used merchandise, collectibles, antiques, silver, glassware, tools, toys, coins, sports cards, jewelry. Approximately 100 dealers. Food available, rest rooms, wheelchair accessible. Ample parking. Admission charge. Space from $12.50. (402) 493-0133. *Last Sunday of each month.*

OMAHA

New City Flea Market. I-80 and 84th Sts. New merchan-

> **Shopping Tip #7**
> Always call before traveling long distances!

dise, used and garage sale items, crafts, collectibles, produce. Snack bar. (402) 339-0800. *Saturdays and Sundays.*

OMAHA
Swap and Flea Market. 5610 Redick. New and used merchandise, flea market merchandise, collectibles, western items, crafts, produce. Food available, rest rooms, wheelchair accessible. Ample parking. (402) 571-5712. *Saturdays and Sundays.*

SOUTH SIOUX CITY
Flea Market. Sioux Land Convention Center. Corner 5th St. and "C" Ave. Good antiques, collectibles, primitives, farm items and farm toys, glassware, silver, furniture, jewelry. This market is always worth attending—always some fine bargains on quality items. Approximately 250 dealers. Snack bar, rest rooms, wheelchair accessible. Ample street parking. Admission charge. Space from $16 per day. Contact: Ed Benson, Box 236, South Sioux City, NE 57101. (605) 361-1717. *Second weekend of each month; Saturdays, 9:00 A.M. - 5:00 P.M.; Sundays, 11:00 A.M. - 4:00 P.M.*

SOUTH SIOUX CITY
Siouxland Flea Market. 2009 Dakota Ave. Indoor market. Antiques, collectibles, ceramics, art, memorabilia, advertising items, collectible glassware and silver. New and used merchandise, housewares. Approximately 100 dealers. Snack bar. Monthly rentals only. Contact: Roberta Gallup, 2009 Dakota Ave., South Sioux City, NE 68776. (402) 494-3221. *Monday - Saturday, 9:00 A.M. - 6:00 P.M.*

VALENTINE
Flea Market. Sandhills Drive-In Theater. Hwy. 20 West. New merchandise, used merchandise, lots of bric-a-brac, farm and ranch items, crafts, coins, collectibles, produce. Approximately 50 dealers. Snack bar, rest rooms, wheelchair accessible. Ample parking. Space from $4. (402) 376-3711. *Second Sunday of each month.*

NORTH DAKOTA

Welcome to the high plains—land of endless skies and no people. Be patient; you will come to a town. Wonderful towns and wonderful people here—real cowboys. The flea markets and auctions are brimfull of fine-quality antiques, especially primitives and furniture.

Best bets...

- ✈ **Dakota Midwest Flea Market and Antique Show, Bismarck**
  This new market offers antiques, collectibles, furniture, dolls, toys, vintage clothing, jewelry, and books, country primitives, and Victorian-era items. With friendly people, interesting farm and ranch stores, and saddle shops, Bismarck is a great city that takes one back to an earlier time.

- ✈ **Magic City Flea Market, Minot**
  Good selection of quality farm and ranch collectibles and a great variety of western and Indian items. This is the area's leading flea market.

BISMARCK

Dakota Midwest Flea Market and Antique Show. Mandan Community Center. New market. Antiques, collectibles, glassware, furniture, dolls, toys, vintage clothing and jewelry, books, country primitives and Victorian-era items, new and used merchandise of the general garage sale variety. Food available, rest rooms. Contact: Leo Mattern, 2738 Gateway Dr., #8, Bismarck, ND 58501. (701) 258-5623. *Monthly.*

FARGO

Farmers and Flea Market. River Mall. New and used merchandise: farm and ranch items, housewares, home furnishings, clothing, children's goods, tools, fashion accessories, sundries, CDs, videotapes, tools, western collectibles, Indian items. Crafts, produce. Food available, rest rooms. *Saturdays and Sundays.*

GRAND FORKS

Flea Market and Craft Show.

> **Shopping Tip #8**
> Information is subject to change—always call first!

South Forks Plaza Pavilion. South Fork Plaza. 1700 S. Washington. New indoor market. 150 spaces. New and used merchandise, collectibles, crafts, gifts, imports, decorator items, jewelry. Average attendance 1,500. Snack bar, rest rooms. Electricity available. Contact: Leo Saucedo, (701) 772-8121. *Fridays and Saturdays.*

GRAND FORKS

Greater Grand Forks Area Flea Market. Antiques, collector items, country primitives and Victorian-era items, glassware, heirloom offerings of all kinds. Also plenty of garage-sale-type bric-a-brac and new necessities, like household goods and home furnishings, clothing, etc. *Fourth Saturday of each month.*

MANDAN

Midwest Flea Market and Antique Show. Mandan Community Center. 901 Division St. I-94, Exit 152. Indoor market. Antiques, collectibles, art, crafts, new and some used merchandise. Approximately 75 dealers. Snack bar, rest rooms, wheelchair accessible. Ample parking. Space from $10 per day. Contact: Leo Nattern, 2738 Gateway Dr., Bismarck, ND 58501. (701) 258-5623. *First weekend of each month.*

MINOT

Magic City Flea Market. State Fairgrounds. Highway 2. Indoor market, with some outdoor spaces during the summer. Antiques, collectibles, and crafts, as well as new and used merchandise of all kinds. This is the area's leading flea market. Average attendance 3,000. Approximately 125 dealers. Snack bar, rest rooms, wheelchair accessible. Ample parking. Space from $10. Contact: Richard Timboe, Box 1672, Minot, ND 58702. (701) 852-1289 or 838-1150. *Second weekend of each month, 9:00 A.M. - 4:00 P.M.*

OHIO

The Buckeye State. Miles of endless beauty. Some of the most interesting small towns in America. Great people. This is a great state for flea marketing. Lots of flea markets, large, well-stocked malls, and auctions everywhere.

At the Ohio State Fairgrounds in Columbus, almost every weekend brings a great event—various antique and collectible shows, some of them as good as can be found. If in the area, always check with the fairgrounds office as to what shows are going on.

Best bets...

- **Pymatuning Lake Drive-In Flea Market, Andover**
  Large, classic midwestern flea market, with great selection.

- **Aurora Farms Flea Market, Aurora**
  Clean, friendly, well managed market—a real pleasant, upbeat country atmosphere here.

- **Hartville Flea Market, Hartville**
  A wide-open marketplace, with lots of new merchandise and a good selection of small antiques, collectibles, sports items, and memorabilia.

- **Springfield Antique Show and Flea Market, Springfield**
  Emphasis on quality antiques; an excellent market for the advanced collector, dealer, or shopkeeper.

- **Washington Court House Flea Market, Washington Court House**
  This market runs the gamut of goods; one could take the entire weekend to see it all.

AKRON

Gala Flea Market. 2215 E. Waterloo. Gala Drive-In Theater. New and used merchandise, lots of garage sale items. Collectibles, crafts, produce. Snack bar, rest rooms, wheelchair accessible. Ample parking. (216) 733-2354. *Saturdays and Sundays.*

> ### *What State Has the Most Flea Markets in the U.S.?*
> According to my research, Florida has 296 flea markets, followed by California with 275, and Texas with 250 markets. This dispels a couple of long-held popular beliefs: In some things Texas is third, not first, and California is not first in everything.

AKRON
Lisa Maries Flea Market and Antique Mall. 4100 State Rd. (Rt. 8) Antiques, collectibles, furniture, jewelry, vintage clothing. (216) 920-9050. *Saturdays and Sundays.*

AKRON
Montrose Drive-In Flea Market. West Market St. New merchandise: electronics, children's items, sportswear, housewares, tools, modern collectibles, crafts. Secondhand merchandise, produce. Snack bar, rest rooms, wheelchair accessible. Ample parking. (216) 666-3000. *Saturdays and Sundays.*

ALLIANCE
Alliance Flea Market. 1500 S. Mahoning Ave. New and used merchandise, mountains of bric-a-brac, collectibles, crafts, produce. Contact: Gary Johnson, (216) 823-2342 or 823-2303. *Saturdays and Sundays.*

ALLIANCE
Farmers Auction and Flea Market. Rt. 62. 18 miles northeast of Canton. New merchandise, antiques, collectibles, crafts, large selection of new furniture. This is a real pleasant country market; mark your map so you don't miss this one. Approximately 50 dealers. Average attendance 500 - 1000. Snack bar, rest rooms, wheelchair accessible. Ample parking. Space from $20. Overnight parking. Contact: George Pilla, 1500 S. Mahoning Ave., Alliance, OH 44601. (216) 823-2302 or 823-8242. *Saturdays and Sundays, 9:00 A.M. - 5:00 P.M.*

AMENDE
Flea Market. Hwy. 159. Used merchandise, garage sale items, farm items, housewares, home furnishings and decorations, country collectibles and crafts. Food available. *Saturdays and Sundays.*

AMHERST
Jamies Flea Market. Rt. 113.

See South Amherst listing. Contact: Manager, P.O. Box 69, Amherst, OH 44001. (216) 986-4402. *Wednesdays and Saturdays, 8:00 A.M. - 5:00 P.M.*

ANDOVER

Pymatuning Lake Drive-In Flea Market. South of town. Large, classic midwestern flea market, with great selection of collector lines, small antiques, primitives; sometimes loads of antique furniture here. Wide range of new and used merchandise. Approximately 400 dealers. Food available, rest rooms, wheelchair accessible, lots of walking. Ample parking. Admission charge. Space from $2.75. (216) 293-7757. *Sundays.*

ASHTABULA

Indoor Flea Market. Lake Ave. Plaza. Modern collectibles, collector items, new and used merchandise, decorator items and crafts, home furnishings, jewelry, clothing, electronics. Snack bar, rest rooms, wheelchair accessible. Ample parking. (216) 993-3962. *Saturdays and Sundays.*

ASHTABULA

Tannery Hill Farmers Flea Market. Main Ave. Extension. Used merchandise, collector items, jewelry, housewares, clothing. Average weekend attendance 15,000. Approximately 200 dealers. Space from $5. Contact: Arthur Eronson, Box 592, Ashtabula, OH 44004. (216) 997-1440. *Friday - Sunday.*

AURORA

Aurora Farms Flea Market. 549 S. Chillicothe Rd. 1 mile south of Rt. 82. (Rt. 43) Indoor/outdoor market. Antiques, collectibles, crafts. This is a clean, friendly, well-managed market. Real pleasant, upbeat country atmosphere here. Market also conducts retail consignment auctions. Space from $7. Average attendance 8,000 - 10,000. Approximately 400 - 600 dealers. Contact: Tom Nero, 549 S. Chillicothe, Aurora, OH 44202. (216) 562-2000. *Wednesdays, Saturdays, and Sundays, 8:00 A.M. - 4:00 P.M.*

AVON

French Creek Flea Market. 37340 French Creek Rd. New and used merchandise, housewares, sportswear, fashion accessories, children's goods, tools, electronics, decorator items, collectibles. Call for dates: (216) 934-9232. *Weekends.*

BEACH CITY

Shady Rest Flea Market. Hwys. 250 and 93. New merchandise, lots of used garage sale items and bric-a-brac. Approximately 100 dealers. Snack bar, rest rooms, wheelchair accessible. Ample parking. Space from $6 per day. Contact: Nildred Miller, 1762 Johnstown Rd., N.E., Dover, OH 44622. (216) 343-9508. *April - October; Sundays, daylight - dark.*

BELLEFONTAINE

Bellefontaine Flea Market. Fairgrounds. Lake Ave. Antiques, collector lines, silver, jewelry, vintage clothing, new and used merchandise. Approximately 75 dealers. Snack bar, rest rooms, wheelchair accessible. Ample parking. Space from $16. Contact: W. S. Meyer, 616 Hilltop Dr., Bellefontaine, OH 43311. (513) 599-4300. *June - September; Saturdays and Sundays.*

BETHEL

Bethel Flea Market. 1095 Union St. Used merchandise, garage sale items, farm items, collectibles. Approximately 30 dealers. Space from $12 for the weekend. Contact: Robert White, 512 High St., Milford, OH 45150. (513) 248-0621 or 734-6928. *Friday - Sunday.*

BLOOMFIELD

Bloomfield Auction and Flea Market. Rt. 87. 1/2 mile west of town. Indoor/outdoor market. Crafts, antiques, collectibles, new and used merchandise, produce. Approximately 150 dealers. Snack bar, rest rooms, wheelchair accessible. Ample parking. Space from $6. Contact: Charles Roscoe, 8183 Rt. 193, Farmdale, OH 44417. (216) 876-4993 or 983-5084. *Thursdays, 6:00 A.M. - 4:00 P.M.*

BOWLING GREEN

Bowling Green Flea Market. Rt. 64 and Poe Rd. Indoor/outdoor market at Junior Fair Building. Antiques, collectibles, furniture, jewelry, vintage clothing, kitchen collectibles, advertising items. New and used merchandise. Food available, rest rooms. Ample parking. Camping available. *Saturdays and Sundays.*

BOWLING GREEN

Wood County Indoor and Outdoor Antiques and Flea Market. Antiques, collectibles, country primitives and Victorian-era items, dolls, toys, glassware, advertising items, furniture, used desirables of

138 FLEA MARKETS

> ### *Have You Made Your Nut Yet?*
> If you have ever heard one dealer saying to another dealer "Have you made your nut yet?," you are hearing them speak of an old, time-honored tradition of flea marketing.
>
> In the nineteenth century, dealers would arrive at the trade grounds in their wagons—usually with a lot of items, produce, or animals to sell or trade and no money to pay the operator of the trade grounds his rent.
>
> The market proprietor would remove the king nut from the wagon, effectively disabling it. When the dealer received enough money to pay his privilege (rent) to the market owner, he would receive his king nut back.
>
> Dealers still use this expression when speaking to other dealers about having done enough business to earn back the cost of their space.

all descriptions, handcrafted treasures, some reproductions. *Third weekend of each month.*

BROOKLYN
Flea Market. 10643 Memphis Ave. New and used merchandise, garage sale items, farm items, housewares, home furnishings, crafts, collectibles, produce. (216) 941-2892. *Saturdays and Sundays.*

BROOKVILLE
Brookville Flea Market. U.S. Hwy. 52. Collector lines, antiques, furniture, farm and country items, household goods, home furnishings, fashion accessories, clothing, jewelry, crafts, produce. Food available, rest rooms, Ample parking. *Wednesdays.*

BRUNSWICK
Highway 42 Drive-In Theater Flea Market. Hwy. 42. Antiques, furniture, collectibles, new and used merchandise, novelties, country collectibles, home furnishings, decorator items, sportswear, jewelry, crafts, produce. Food available, rest rooms, wheelchair accessible. Ample parking. (216) 225-3200. *Sundays.*

BRYAN
Flea Market. Holiday Inn. Rt. 15. New merchandise, collector lines, silver, coins, sports cards, vintage clothing, imports, giftware. Food avail-

> ### *More Tenets of Shopper Courtesy*
> 1. When shopping with children, keep them under control. Do not let them handle or grab merchandise. Be prepared to help them yourself.
> 2. Never allow horseplay in and around booths. Be prepared to pay for anything your children might damage.
> 3. The flea market can be a great learning place for children. It's up to parents (and grandparents) to make those lessons good ones.

able, rest rooms. Ample parking. (517) 764-1247. *Sundays.*

BRYAN
Flea Market. Hwy. 6 and Rt. 10. Antiques, collectibles, farm items, country collectibles. Lots of new and used merchandise for home, work, and play. Crafts, produce. Food available. *Third Sunday of each month.*

BUCKEYE LAKE
Gardners Warehouse Flea Market. Rt 79. 30 miles east of Columbus. Indoor/outdoor market. New merchandise, with lots of closeouts and surplus. Modern collectibles, used merchandise, clothing, housewares. Approximately 50 dealers. Space from $10 per weekend. Camping nearby. Contact: Janie Poarch, Lakeside Rd., Millersport, OH 43046. (614) 928-6746. *Friday - Sunday.*

CAESAR CREEK
Caesar Creek Flea Market. Junction of I-71 and SR #73, near Wilmington. Antiques, crafts, lots of new and used merchandise. One of the area's better markets—real clean and friendly, with a great variety of booths. Average daily attendance 5,000. Approximately 350 dealers. Snack bar, rest rooms, wheelchair accessible. Ample parking. Admission charge. Camping available. Market open to food vendors. Contact: Allen Levin, 7763 Rt. 73. Wilmington, OH 45171. (513) 382-1669 or 223-0222. *Saturdays and Sundays.*

CAMBRIDGE
Flea Market. Junction I-77 and Hwy. 22. Used merchandise, garage sale items, farm collectibles. Crafts, home furnishings, household goods, decorator items, produce. Food available. (614) 439-4241. *Saturdays and Sundays.*

CANTON
Canton Flea Market. Meyers Lake Plaza Shopping Center. Whipple Rd. New and used merchandise, housewares, home furnishings and decorator items, clothing, fashion accessories, children's goods, tools, electronics, garage sale items. (216) 477-3259. *Saturdays.*

CANTON
Flea Market. Flea market fare includes new merchandise and imports, housewares, clothing, used secondhand merchandise, electronics. (216) 364-6089. *Saturdays and Sundays.*

CANTON
Flea Market and Antique Show. Stark County Fairgrounds. 305 Wertz. Indoor/outdoor market. Antiques, good variety of collector lines—military, RR, dolls, coins, toys. Also furniture, silver, sports cards, country, and Victorian-era items. New and used merchandise, crafts. Food available, rest rooms, wheelchair accessible. Ample paved parking. (216) 478-1602. *Monthly.*

CHILLICOTHE
Ross County Flea Market. 344 Fairgrounds Rd. Fairgrounds. Indoor/outdoor market. Antiques, furniture, collector lines, silver, coins, sports cards, vintage clothing, jewelry, primitives, advertising items. Approximately 50 dealers. Food available, rest rooms, wheelchair accessible. Ample parking. Space from $3. Camping available on premises. Contact: Bob Whitten, 144 Andersonville Rd., Chillicothe, OH 45601. (614) 775-0012. *Sundays, 8:00 A.M. - 5:00 P.M.; no market in August.*

CINCINNATI
Finneytown Flea Market. 1047 W. Northbend Rd. Indoor market. New merchandise: electronics, housewares, decorator items and home furnishings, jewelry, sports merchandise, children's items. Used merchandise, garage sale items, collector items. Snack bar, rest rooms, wheelchair accessible. Ample parking. (513) 681-7250. *Friday - Sunday.*

CINCINNATI
Groesbeck Flea Market. 9058 Colevain Ave. Used merchandise, garage sale items. Housewares, electronics, fashion accessories, clothing, gifts, lots of bric-a-brac. (513) 385-3356. *Thursday - Tuesday.*

CINCINNATI
Kellogg Flea Market. 3742 E. Hwy. 52. Used merchandise, garage sale items, new merchandise, decorator items and home furnishings, collectibles, crafts, produce. Snack bar, rest rooms. Ample parking. *Friday - Sunday.*

CINCINNATI
London Village Flea Market. 4781 Hamilton and Ash Tree. New and not-so-new merchandise. Housewares, clothing, decorator items, trendy imports, crafts. *Saturdays and Sundays.*

CINCINNATI
Midtown Flea Market. 3421 Montgomery Rd. New and used merchandise, collectibles, imports, giftware, clothing, artwork, tools, electronics. (513) 791-1021. *Saturdays and Sundays.*

CINCINNATI
Paris Flea Market. Ferguson Hills Drive-In Theater. 2310 Ferguson Rd. Lots of new merchandise: imports, gifts, housewares, electronics, sportswear. Some antiques and collectibles, crafts, produce. One of the area's better flea markets. Always a great opportunity to find some real treasures or super buys at this market. Average attendance 9,000. Approximately 250 dealers. Snack bar, wheelchair accessible. Ample parking. Space from $4.50. Contact: Ferguson Hills Drive-In, 2310 Ferguson Rd., Cincinnati, OH 45238. (513) 223-0222 or 451-1271. *Saturdays and Sundays, 7:00 A.M. - 4:00 P.M.*

CINCINNATI
Peddlers Flea Market. 4344 Kellogg Ave. East of downtown, on Ohio River. Indoor/outdoor market. Large commercial market, with lots of new merchandise, used merchandise, farm collectibles, wide variety of collector lines. Crafts, produce. Average attendance 5,000. Approximately 400 dealers. Snack bars, rest rooms, wheelchair accessible, lots of walking here. Ample parking. Space from $22. Contact: Manager, 4343 Kellogg Ave., Cincinnati, OH. *Saturdays and Sundays.*

CINCINNATI
Rinks Flea Market. 7900 Beechmont Ave. New and garage-sale-type finds. Housewares, home furnishings and decorator items, collectibles, electronics, tools, toys, sports memorabilia, handcrafted items. (513) 791-1021. *Saturdays and Sundays.*

All Sales Final

For the most part, what I have for sale I want you to look at. Examine it, handle it, smell it, taste it, and then make a decision. If you want it, pay the price and take it home with you.

I only wish to deal with responsible adults. If you make up your mind to buy something and it is as represented and does not have hidden factory damages, keep it. What you buy is yours—to keep.

If you like to buy items that have guarantees, then you should shop at Sears or WalMart. Generally, items sold at flea markets are sold the same as at auctions: "Where is, as is."

If you are buying electric items, most markets have an outlet where you can plug the item in and test it. It is your responsibility to check out the item.

Most dealers will exchange new items, especially items that are factory-sealed in boxes if there is hidden damage. However, if the item is damaged by misuse, you are out of luck. The rules are not the same as at the discount house.

CINCINNATI

Stickers Grove Flea Market. Rt 128. 1 mile south of Ross. Antiques, furniture, collector lines, new and used merchandise. Approximately 100 dealers. Food available, rest rooms, wheelchair accessible. Ample parking. Contact: Ohio Valley Promotions, 9468 Reading Rd., Cincinnati, OH 45215. (513) 733-5885. *June - September; Thursdays, 9:00 A.M. - 5:00 P.M.*

CINCINNATI

Traders World. 601 Union Rd. Off I-75, exit 29. 500 indoor spaces and 200 covered outdoor spaces. One of the area's better markets with acres of booths. Primarily new merchandise and crafts. Large selection of discounted, surplus, and closeouts on new, personal, and household merchandise. Special promotions and live entertainment. Average daily attendance 8,000. Food available, rest rooms, wheelchair accessible, and miles of walking. Ample parking. Admission charge. Space from $18 per day outside. (513) 424-5708. *Saturdays and Sundays.*

CINCINNATI

Turtle Creek Flea Market. I-75 and SR 63. New market. Inside, covered, and outside spaces. New merchandise, souvenirs, sportswear, housewares, sports cards, jewelry, secondhand merchandise, some collectibles. A smaller, local market. Not recommended for commercial vendors. *Saturdays and Sundays.*

CINCINNATI

Village Flea Market. 2100 Losantville Ave. New and used merchandise, collectibles, crafts, produce, household goods, home furnishings, clothing, imports and gift items. Snack bar. *Saturdays and Sundays.*

CIRCLEVILLE

Pickaway County Flea Market. U.S. Rt. 22 East. Antiques; always a great selection of collector lines and country and farm collectibles. Country primitives. New and used merchandise, garage sale items. Approximately 90 - 100 dealers. Food available, rest rooms, wheelchair accessible. Ample parking. Space from $10. Camping with showers available. Electricity available. Reservations recommended for inside space. No drug paraphernalia sales allowed. Contact: John or Melissa Rodgers, Box 93, Williamsport, OH 43164. 986-8274. *Monthly.*

CLEVELAND

The Bazaar. 4979 W. 130th St. Corner of Brook Park Rd. and W. 130th St. Lots of collectibles and secondhand items. Primarily permanent dealers on a monthly basis. Contact: John Grace, (216) 362-0022. *Friday - Sunday, 10:00 A.M. - 6:00 P.M.*

CLEVELAND

Broadway Flea Market. 6116 Broadway St. New and used merchandise, lots of garage sale and secondhand items. Household, imports, crafts. *Saturdays and Sundays.*

CLEVELAND

Clark Avenue Flea Market. 5109 Clark Ave. Indoor/outdoor market. Antiques, collectibles, jewelry, glassware. Indoors is mostly permanent shops, with some nice-quality items. Clean, friendly market. Approximately 60 dealers. Excellent restaurant, clean rest rooms, wheelchair accessible. Ample parking. Outside space from $4. Contact: Fred Scafe, (215) 398-5283. *Thursday - Sunday, 11:00 A.M. - 6:00 P.M.*

CLEVELAND

Cloverland Drive-In Theater Flea Market. Rts. 22 and 17. New and used merchandise. Collector lines. Snack bar, rest rooms. wheelchair accessible. Ample parking. (216) 524-2929. *Saturdays and Sundays.*

CLEVELAND
East Lake Drive-In Theater Flea Market. 34280 Vine St. New merchandise, wide variety. Used merchandise, lots of garage sale booths here. Snack bar, rest rooms, wheelchair accessible. Ample parking. (216) 942-2663. *Saturdays and Sundays.*

CLEVELAND
Lee Road International Market. 4115 Lee Rd. Indoor market. New merchandise, closeouts, surplus, decorator items, gift items. Good shoppers' market. (216) 491-9058. *Saturdays and Sundays.*

CLEVELAND
Memphis Drive-In Theater Flea Market. 10543 Memphis Ave. New merchandise: housewares, electronics, jewelry, clothing, children's items, sportswear, sports merchandise. Used merchandise, garage sale items. Snack bar, rest rooms, wheelchair accessible. Ample parking. (216) 941-2892. *Saturdays.*

COLUMBIANA
Theron's Country Flea Market. 1641 Rt. 164. Indoor/outdoor market. Primarily

---

> ***Dress for the Hunt! Tip #5***
> If you wear glasses—don't forget to bring them for inspecting prospective purchases.

---

antiques and collectibles market. Good selection of smalls. Market conducts general household auctions on Saturday nights. Approximately 50 dealers. Country restaurant, rest rooms, wheelchair accessible. Ample parking. Contact: Jack Brown, Rt. 164, Lisbon Rd., Columbiana, OH 44408. (216) 482-4327. *Wednesdays and Sundays, 9:00 A.M. - 5:00 P.M.*

COLUMBUS
Antiques and Collectibles Show. Ohio State Fairgrounds. I-71, Exit 17th Ave. W. Indoor/outdoor market. Large, quality market, antiques and collectibles only. One of the better-quality antique events in the country. For those in the trade, this is a great source market. 1,000+ dealers. Food available, rest rooms, wheelchair accessible. Ample paved parking; $3 parking charge. Inside space from $75, outside from $54. Contact: Don Scott, Box 60, Bre-

men, OH 43107. (614) 569-4112. Fax (614) 569-7595. *Usually held the third weekend of each month.*

COLUMBUS
Columbus Flea Market. 1857 S. Parsons. Used merchandise, garage sale items, junk. The kind of place a diligent shopper might find a real bargain or treasure. Contact: Harold Wilson, (614) 444-0122. *Daily.*

COLUMBUS
Livingston Court Indoor Flea Market. 3575 E. Livingston Ave. Large outdoor market. New and used merchandise, lots of bric-a-brac, some antiques, collectibles, and crafts. Approximately 350 dealers. Snack bars, rest rooms, wheelchair accessible. Ample parking. Space from $10 per day. Contact: Doug Hott, 856 King Ave., Columbus, OH 43212. (614) 275-4444 or (614) 231-7726. *Friday - Sunday, 10:00 A.M. - 7:00 P.M.*

COLUMBUS
Rainbow's Giant Amos Indoor Flea Market. 3454 Cleveland Ave. Large indoor market, with primarily new merchandise: electronics, sportswear, housewares, tools, jewelry, clothing, new collectibles. Approximately 225 dealers. Snack bar, rest rooms, wheelchair accessible. Ample parking. Space from $13 per day. Contact: Doug Hott, 865 King Ave., Columbus, OH 43212. (614) 291-3133 or 275-4444. *Friday - Sunday, 10:00 A.M. - 7:00 P.M.*

COLUMBUS
The Red Barn Flea Market. I-70 and State Hwy. 310 East. Indoor/outdoor market. New and used merchandise, decorator items, country and farm collectibles, primitives, kitchen collectibles, jewelry, clothing, housewares. Snack bar, rest rooms, wheelchair accessible. Ample parking. Space from $4. (614) 927-1234. *Saturdays and Sundays.*

COLUMBUS
The South Drive-In Theater Flea Market. Rt. 40. 1 mile east of Reynoldsburg. Large outdoor market, with mostly new merchandise and used and garage sale dealers. Approximately 400 dealers. Space $4 on Saturday/Sunday and $.50 on Wednesday. Contact: Doug Hott, 865 King Ave., Columbus, OH 43212. (614) 275-4444 or 291-3133. *Wednesdays, Saturdays, and Sundays.*

COLUMBUS
Swap Shop and Flea Market. CCC Twin Drive-In Theater. 1375 Harrisburg Pike. New

and used merchandise, garage sale items, home furnishings, household goods, clothing, collectibles, crafts, produce. Snack bar, rest rooms, wheelchair accessible. Ample parking. (614) 275-4444. *Saturdays and Sundays.*

COLUMBUS

Trader Ned's Flea Market. Fairgrounds. Indoor/outdoor market. Antiques, collector lines, furniture, silver, coins, sports cards, jewelry, vintage clothing, kitchen collectibles. Food available, rest rooms, wheelchair accessible. Ample parking. Space from $20 per day. Camping available. Reservations recommended. Contact: B.S. Enterprises, Box 21347, Columbus, OH 43221. *Third weekend of each month.*

COLUMBUS

Westland Indoor Flea Market. 4170 W. Broad St. New market. Large indoor market, with primarily new merchandise: electronics, sportswear, sports items, housewares, tools, some collectibles and used merchandise. Snack bar, rest rooms, wheelchair accessible. Ample parking. Space from $17 per day. Contact: Doug Hott, 865 King Ave., Columbus, OH 43212.

(614) 275-4444 or 272-5678. *Friday - Sunday.*

CONNEAUT

Swap and Shop Flea Market. Rt. 2. Antiques, collectibles, used merchandise, jewelry, clothing, housewares. Food available. (216) 593-2042. *Sundays.*

CUYAHOGA FALLS

Oakwood Antiques and Collectibles Market. 3265 Oakwood Dr. Indoor/outdoor market. Small market, with mostly secondhand and garage sale items, some collectibles and decorator items. Approximately 10 dealers. Snack bar, rest rooms. Ample parking. Space from $10 per day. Contact: Bill Kern, (673-4762. *Friday - Sunday.*

DAYTON

Dayton Traffic Circle Flea Market. 3700 Keats. Indoor/outdoor market. New merchandise: housewares, sportswear, electronics, jewelry, children's items, tools, sports merchandise, decorator items, gift items. Average attendance 4,000. Approximately 400 dealers. Snack bar, rest rooms, wheelchair accessible. Ample parking. Contact: Jerry Richie, 3700 Keats, Dayton, OH 45414. (513) 275-4759. *Friday - Sunday 10:00 A.M. - 5:00 P.M.*

> **Shopping Tip #9**
> Information is subject to change—always call ahead to avoid disappointment!

DAYTON
Dixie Stop Flea Market. 4170 N. Dixie Dr. New and used merchandise, garage sale items. Crafts, collectibles, produce. Food available, rest rooms, wheelchair accessible. Ample parking. (513) 890-2184. *Friday - Sunday.*

DAYTON
Flea Market. 3998 Salem Ave. New and used merchandise, garage sale items, household goods, tools, clothing, jewelry, decorator items, crafts, children's merchandise. (513) 277-0133. *Saturdays and Sundays.*

DAYTON
London Flea Market. Forest Park Plaza. New merchandise, used merchandise, garage sale items, modern collector lines, clothing, jewelry, housewares. Food available, rest rooms, wheelchair accessible. Ample parking. (513) 277-5208. *Friday - Sunday.*

DAYTON
London Flea Market. 4400 N. Main St. Used merchandise, garage sale items, collectibles. Approximately 40 dealers. Ample parking. Space from $25. Contact: Ahmen Harchaovi, (513) 277-5208. *Thursday - Sunday.*

DAYTON
Paris Flea Market. 6201 N. Dixie Dr. Dixie Drive-In Theater. Good selection of antiques and collectibles, crafts, new and used merchandise. Average daily attendance 1,500. Approximately 50 dealers. Snack bars, rest rooms, wheelchair accessible. Admission charge. Ample parking. Space from $10. Contact: Gary Castle, (513) 890-5513. *Saturdays and Sundays, 7:00 A.M. - 4:00 P.M.*

DEFIANCE
Wheel and Deal Indoor Flea Market. New merchandise, surplus, closeouts, housewares, jewelry, clothing, children's lines. Snack bar, rest rooms. Ample parking. *Saturdays and Sundays.*

DELAWARE
Country Bazaar. Hwy. 23. I-480 and I-71. Indoor/outdoor market. Antiques, collector lines, furniture, silver, coins, sports cards, fine and costume jewelry, vintage clothing, lots of country collectibles, decorator items.

This is one of the area's better all-around markets. Approximately 150 vendors. Food available, rest rooms, wheelchair accessible. Space from $6 per day. Most inside spaces rented to sellers on a monthly basis. Contact: Doug Hott, (614) 275-4444 or 291-3133. *Sundays, 10:00 A.M. - 6:00 P.M.*

DELAWARE

Kingman Drive-In Theater Flea Market. Rt. 23 North. Approximately 8 miles north of I-270. New merchandise, crafts, produce, some antiques, good selection of collectibles. Approximately 200 dealers. Snack bar, rest rooms, wheelchair accessible. Ample parking. Admission charge. Space from $5. Contact: Dale Zinn, (614) 548-4227 or 275-4444. *March - October; Saturdays and Sundays, 7:00 A.M. - 3:00 P.M.*

DOVER

Dover Flea Market. 120 N. Tuscarawas Ave. Indoor/outdoor market. New merchandise: sportswear, housewares, jewelry, sports merchandise, clothing, children's items. Used merchandise, decorator wares, collectibles, primitives. Snack bar, rest rooms, wheelchair accessible. Ample parking. Contact: H. Ricer, (216) 364-3959. *Saturdays and Sundays.*

DOVER

Sunny Acres Flea Market. Sugarcreek and Cover Rds. New and used merchandise, garage sale items, farm items, crafts, collectibles, produce. Snack bar, rest rooms, wheelchair accessible. Ample parking. (216) 364-6807. *Fridays and Saturdays.*

EATON

Flea Market. Frederick Community Building. Antiques, collectibles, new and used merchandise, crafts, decorator items. Food available, rest rooms, wheelchair accessible. Ample parking. *Fourth weekend of each month.*

EATON

Preble County Flea Market. Rt. 122 South. Fairgrounds. Indoor/outdoor market. Antiques, collectibles, farm and country collectibles. Silver, coins, jewelry, vintage clothing. Approximately 75 dealers. Food available, rest rooms, wheelchair accessible. Ample parking. Eaton is also the home of the Preble County Pork Festival, one of Ohio's better special events. The festival is held in early September. Contact: Myron Peer, (513) 456-4709. *First weekend of each month.*

ELYRIA

Halls Flea Market. 41957 N. Ridge Rd. (Rt. 254). Indoor/outdoor market. Good selection of new merchandise, lots of used items, many collector booths, crafts, produce, country and farm collectibles. Average daily attendance 500 - 1,000. Approximately 150 dealers. Food available, rest rooms, wheelchair accessible. Space from $5. Overnight parking and camping nearby. Contact: Connie Hall, 41957 N. Ridge Rd., Elyria, OH 44035. (216) 324-4166 or 233-8613. *Friday - Sunday, 10:00 A.M. - 6:00 P.M.*

ETNA

Etna Flea Mart. 3360 Pike St. Indoor/outdoor market. Used merchandise, garage sale items, crafts, decorator items. Approximately 25 dealers. Space from $6 daily. Contact: Louise Courts, Box 110, Pataskala, OH 43062. (614) 928-1544 or 471-1222. *Friday - Sunday.*

ETNA

Park 'N Swap Flea Market. Lions Park. Antiques, collectibles, new and used merchandise, crafts. Food available, rest rooms, wheelchair accessible. Ample parking. Contact: Ernest Bowers, (614) 927-5763. *Monthly.*

FAIRBORN

Fairborn Flea Market. 136 N. 1st St. New and used merchandise, imports, home furnishings, housewares, gifts, clothing, tools, electronics, collectibles. (513) 878-0606. *Saturdays and Sundays.*

FERNALD

Web Flea Market. 7500 New Haven Rd. Indoor/outdoor market. Large, classic midwestern market, with a great selection of new and used merchandise. Many booths of collector lines, silver, glassware, primitives, advertising items. Also housewares, clothing and fashion accessories, giftware. Approximately 300 dealers. Food available, clean rest rooms, wheelchair accessible, lots of walking. Ample paved parking. Contact: Marge Weber, 3411 Spring Grove Ave., Cincinnati, OH 45225. (513) 738-2678. *Saturdays and Sundays.*

FINDLEY

Findley Flea Market and Antique Show. 1017 E. Sandusky St. One of the area's leading antique and collector markets, with many booths of quality items. Food available, rest rooms, wheelchair accessible. Ample parking. (419) 423-2415. *Second weekend of each month.*

FRANKLIN
Schome Flea Market. 8862 Dayton Oxford Rd. New merchandise, used merchandise, garage sale items, farm items, clothing, housewares. Average daily attendance 1,500. Approximately 125 dealers. Snack bar, rest rooms, wheelchair accessible. Ample parking. Admission charge. Space from $5. Contact: Frank Sublett, (513) 746-0389. *Saturdays and Sundays.*

FREMONT
Fremont Flea Market. Fairgrounds. 4 miles south of Turnpike, Exit 6. Indoor/outdoor market. Primarily used merchandise, lots of bric-a-brac, some collectibles and new merchandise. Average daily attendance 1,500. Approximately 90 dealers. Snack bar, rest rooms, wheelchair accessible. Ample parking. This market conducts several nice special events during the year. Space $10 daily, tables $2. Reservations recommended. Camping available onsite. Contact: Gary Kern, 821 Rawson Ave., Fremont, OH 43420. (419) 332-1200 or 332-6937. *Second Saturday and Sunday of each month; 10:00 A.M. - 5:00 P.M.*

GALLIPOLIS
French 500 Flea Market. Fairgrounds. Hwy. 35 and 60. Antiques, collectibles, silver, jewelry, sports cards, vintage clothing. Used merchandise. Food available, rest rooms, wheelchair accessible. Ample parking. *Second weekend of each month.*

GALLIPOLIS
Gallipolis Flea Market. Rt. 35. New and used merchandise, garage sale items, crafts, collectibles, produce. Snack bar. (614) 446-7037. *Saturdays and Sundays.*

GERMANTOWN
Flea Market. Lindy's Auction Barn. Rt. 725. New and used merchandise, housewares, clothing, jewelry. Antiques, collectibles, farm items. Food available, rest rooms, wheelchair accessible. Ample parking. *Second Sunday of each month.*

GRAND RAPIDS
Flea Market. Hwy. 24. Antiques, collectibles, new and used merchandise, crafts, farm and country items, produce. Food available, rest rooms, wheelchair accessible. Ample parking.

(419) 832-7054. *First weekend of each month.*

GREENVILLE

Company B NCO Club Flea Market. 1434 Celina Rd. New merchandise, used merchandise, lots of garage sale booths, crafts. Average attendance 1,000. Approximately 50 dealers. Food available, rest rooms. Space from $10. Contact: Roscoe Hikle, (513) 647-6308. *First weekend of each month.*

HARRISON

Harrison Flea Market. 1110 Harrison Ave. Indoor/outdoor market. New and used merchandise, collectibles, decorator items, modern collector items. Snack bar, rest rooms. Ample parking. Contact: Henry Ferguson, (513) 367-9162. *Friday - Sunday.*

HARTVILLE

Buyers Flea Market. 900 Edison St., N.W. Indoor/outdoor market, strong on antiques, crafts, and collectibles. Good selection of quality items. Admission charge. (216) 877-6433. *Mondays and Thursdays.*

HARTVILLE

Hartville Flea Market. 788 Edison St. Rt. 619 East from I-77 north of Canton. Indoor/outdoor market. A wide-open marketplace, with lots of new merchandise and a good selection of small antiques, collectibles, sports items, and memorabilia. Average attendance 10,000. Approximately 800 - 1,000 vendors. Snack bar, rest rooms, wheelchair accessible. Ample parking. Space from $6 on Monday; this is the big day at this market. Contact: Marian Cobleata, 788 Edison St., Hartville, OH 44632. (216) 877-9860. *Mondays and Thursdays, 7:00 A.M. - 6:00 P.M.*

HUBBARD

Hubbard Liberty Flea Market. Rt. 304. New merchandise: clothing, housewares, children's items, jewelry, sports merchandise, collector lines, crafts, gifts. Used merchandise. Approximately 100 dealers. Snack bar, rest rooms, wheelchair accessible. Ample parking. Contact: Mel Revelis, (216) 534-9855. *Wednesdays, Saturdays, and Sundays.*

HUBER HEIGHTS

Brandt Pike Flea Market, Huber Heights. 6123 Brandt Pike. Marion Meadows Shopping Center. New and used merchandise, lots of garage sale booths, collectibles, crafts. Market is in an interesting city of all-brick homes.

> ### *Where Is the Largest Flea Market in the United States?*
>
> Everybody claims to be the biggest and best in every endeavor, and it is no different with flea markets. Numerous markets lay claim to being the largest market in America.
>
> The San Jose, California market advertises itself as the "World's Largest Flea Market." Many think the Rose Bowl Flea Market in Pasadena, California is the biggest, while others vote for Flea World or the Wagon Wheel Flea Market, both in Florida. Champions proclaim "It's First Monday in Canton, Texas; that's the world's largest," and still others will say it's the Tennessee Flea Market at Nashville.
>
> Me, I have personally been to each of these markets, and my guess—and it truly is a guess—is that it is a market located in a tiny flyspeck of a town in the middle of Amish country in Indiana: Shipshewana, Indiana. That is my unofficial guess for the largest flea market in America. What is not a guess is that it is one of the most interesting markets and places in all of this country. Visitors can be assured of one thing: A trip to any of these megamarkets is an experience they will not soon forget.

Contact: Ron Kronenberger, (513) 236-5003. *Friday - Sunday, 9:00 A.M. - 5:00 P.M.*

KETTERING

Hills and Dales Flea Market. 1448 W. Dorothy Ln. New and used merchandise, crafts, decorator items, collectibles. Snack bar, rest rooms, wheelchair accessible. Ample parking. Contact: Everett Cost, 294-0876. *Thursday - Sunday.*

LAFAYETTE

Anderson Flea Market. 20 Elisdorf St. New and used merchandise, surplus, closeouts, clothing, housewares, jewelry. Collectibles, antiques, silver. Market also conducts retail auctions on first and third Saturdays of each month at this location. Food available, rest rooms, wheelchair accessible. Ample parking. (317) 474-6114. *Fourth weekend of each month.*

LAFAYETTE

Fort Firelands Flea Market. 5850 E. Harbor Rd. (Rt. 163). New and used merchandise, housewares, home furnishings, clothing, country and farm items, garage sale

> **Shopping Tip #10**
> Days, dates, and markets are subject to change!

items. Food available. (419) 734-1237. *May - September; Friday - Sunday.*

LANCASTER
Dumontville Flea Market. 1 mile north of Coonpath Rd., on Rt. 158. Sports cards, glassware, collectibles, miniatures, secondhand merchandise, housewares. (614) 756-4457. *Thursdays, 1:00 - 6:00 P.M.; Friday - Sunday, 10:00 A.M. - 6:00 P.M.*

LIMA
Grand Oaks Flea Market. 1007 Grand Ave. Indoor/outdoor market. New and used merchandise, garage sale items. Housewares, imports, electronics, clothing. Food available. Space from $5. Contact: William West, (419) 643-4402. *Friday - Sunday.*

LIMA
Lima Antique Show and Flea Market. Fairgrounds. Indoor market. Antiques, collectibles, silver, jewelry, sports cards, vintage clothing, primitives, advertising items. Approximately 50 dealers. Food available, rest rooms, wheelchair accessible. Ample parking. Admission charge. Contact: Aubrey Martin, 716 S. Main St., Lima, OH 45804. (419) 228-1050. *May - September; Saturdays and Sundays.*

LIMA
Lima Antique Show and Flea Market. Fairgrounds. 2750 Hardin Hwy. I-75, Exit Hwy. 309-E. Indoor market. Antiques, collectibles, memorabilia, primitives, advertising items, sports items. This is a good market for those looking for quality collector items at great prices. Snack bar, rest rooms, wheelchair accessible. Ample parking. Contact: Aubrey Martin, 716 S. Main St., Lima, OH 45804. (419) 228-1050. *First weekend of each month, 9:00 A.M. - 5:00 P.M.*

LIMA
Northland Plaza Shopping Center Flea Market. New and used merchandise. Large number of garage sale booths here. Imports, name-brand fashions and accessories, decorator items, crafts, collectibles. Food available. (419) 227-8239. *Saturdays and Sundays.*

LOVELAND
Loveland Flea Market. Maderia Rd. New and used merchandise, garage sale items,

country collectibles, collector items. Also home furnishings, brand-name household goods and fashion clothing, imports, gift items, crafts. Food available. *Friday - Sunday.*

MALVERN

Flea Market. New merchandise, housewares, imports, gifts, decorator items, clothing, used goods, garage-sale-type bric-a-brac. (216) 862-1659. *Saturdays and Sundays.*

MANSFIELD

C and G Flea Market. Rt. 39. New and used merchandise, garage sale items, collectibles, glassware, jewelry. Contact: Gary Grogg, 1147 Lucas Rd., Mansfield, OH 44905. 589-9440 or 524-7405. *Fridays, Saturdays, and Sundays.*

MANSFIELD

Mansfield Flea Market. County Fairgrounds. Indoor market. Primarily antiques and collectibles. This is always a buyer's market, with lots of quality items at great discount prices. Approximately 300 dealers. Snack bar, rest rooms, wheelchair accessible. Ample parking. Admission charge. Space from $30 for the weekend. Contact: J. Stark, 784 Vernon Rd., Columbus, OH 43209. (614) 237-3689. *Usually held the last weekend of each month.*

MARENGO

Straw Factory Flea Market. 637 Rt. 61. I-40 and I-71. Indoor/outdoor market. New merchandise: surplus, closeouts, clothing, housewares, jewelry. Used merchandise. Collectibles, good selection of various collector lines, decorator items, advertising items. Market is adding new exhibit building. Average daily attendance 2,000. 50-60 dealers. Food available, rest rooms, wheelchair accessible. Ample parking. Space from $6 per day. (419) 258-FLEA. *Saturdays and Sundays.*

MARIETTA

Flea Market. Hilltop Speedway. Rt. 7. Antiques, collectibles, new and used merchandise, farm and country collectibles, clothing, jewelry, home furnishings and decorator items. Food available, rest rooms, wheelchair accessible. Ample parking. *Sundays.*

MARION

Antique Show and Flea Market. Fairgrounds. Antiques, collector lines including country and Victorian-era items, RR, clocks and watches, advertising, china,

OHIO **155**

vintage jewelry. Furniture, decorator items. Contact: Ronald Hilbert, Box 67, Unionville Center, OH 43077. (614) 873-4552. *Held periodically; call for schedule.*

MEDINA

Antique and Collectible Market. Fairgrounds. 735 Lafayette Rd. U.S. Hwy. 42. This is a great midwestern antique market with a wide range of collector booths. Many quality items here. Approximately 150 dealers. Food available, rest rooms, wheelchair accessible, and lots of walking. Ample parking. Admission charge. Space from $16. Overnight parking. Contact: Ron Denbow, Rt. 3, W. Salem, OH 44287. (419) 945-2296 or 289-6027. *Sundays.*

MIDDLEFIELD

Middlefield Farmers and Flea Market. Rt. 608 and Nauvoo Rd. New and used merchandise, farm items, produce, crafts, collectibles. Food available, rest rooms, wheelchair accessible. Ample parking. (216) 632-1001. *Saturdays and Sundays.*

MIDDLETOWN

Dixie Flea Market. 3009 S. Main St. Indoor/outdoor market. New merchandise: clothing, electronics, children's lines, housewares, outdoor items, collector lines, crafts, produce. Snack bar, rest rooms, wheelchair accessible. Ample parking. (513) 423-2431. *Friday - Sunday.*

MILAN

Firelands Flea Market. Ohio Turnpike, Exit 7. Antiques, collectibles, new and used merchandise, home furnishings, electronics, imports, giftware, crafts. Food available. (419) 499-4254. *Sundays.*

MONROE

Congress Inn Antiques and Flea Market. Rts. 63 and I-75. Antiques, collector lines, silver, vintage clothing, fine jewelry. Food available, rest rooms, wheelchair accessible. Ample parking. *Third weekend of each month.*

MONROE

Traders World. 601 Union Rd. Off I-75, exit 29. 500 indoor spaces and 200 covered outdoor spaces. One of the area's better markets with acres of booths. Primarily new merchandise and crafts. Large selection of discounted, surplus, and closeouts on new, personal, and household merchandise. Special promotions and live entertainment. Average daily attendance

8,000. Food available, rest rooms, wheelchair accessible, and miles of walking. Ample parking. Admission charge. Space from $18 per day outside. (513) 424-5708. *Saturdays and Sundays.*

MONTPELIER

Fairgrounds Flea Market. 619 Main St. (S.R. 107). New and used merchandise, antiques, collectibles, crafts, produce. Approximately 50 dealers. Food available, rest rooms, wheelchair accessible. Ample parking. Contact: Sam Kunsman. 316 N. Emmet St, Bryan, OH 43506. (419) 636-1635 or (419) 485-9963. *Thursdays.*

MONTPELIER

Flea Market and Auction. 619 S. Main St. (S.R. 107). New and used merchandise, closeouts, surplus, housewares, children's lines, home furnishings, clothing, jewelry, collectibles. Lots of garage sale items. Approximately 50 dealers. Food available, rest rooms, wheelchair accessible. Ample parking. Contact: Sam Kunsman, 316 N. Emmet St, Bryan, OH 43506. (419) 636-1635 or (419) 485-9963. *First Saturday of each month.*

NAVARRE

Indoor Flea Market. Rt. 21. New and used merchandise, garage sale items, Household goods, home furnishings, fashions and fashion accessories, imports, crafts, collectibles. Snack bar, rest rooms. Ample parking. *Saturdays and Sundays.*

NEW WATERFORD

Rogers Community Auction and Open Air Market. 4640 Raley Rd. Rt. 154 West. Indoor/outdoor market. Excellent all-around market with great variety of items and a fun, upbeat atmosphere. This is a great market for the dealer, shopkeeper, or decorator—an excellent source market. General retail consignment auction on Fridays at 6:00 P.M. Average summer attendance of 20,000. Approximately 900 dealers. Good food, rest rooms, wheelchair accessible, and lots of walking. Space from $10. Contact: Rogers Open Air Market, 5640 Raleyroad, New Waterford, OH 44445. (216) 227-3233. *Fridays.*

NEWARK

Newark Flea Market. 161 Union St. New and used merchandise, garage sale items, crafts, produce, collectibles. Food available. (614) 349-8337. *Friday - Sunday.*

> **More Bargaining Savvy for the Beginner**
> If a seller goes to the trouble to haggle over price with you, show him the courtesy of buying the item right then. Do not ask him to hold it until later unless money changes hands. It is unfair to expect him to pass up other sales opportunities, only to have you change your mind after leaving his stand and not return. If you are sure you want the item, be prepared to do business then and there.

NEWCOMERSTOWN

Country Lane Flea Market. U.S. Rt. 36. Used merchandise, garage sale items, farm collectibles, crafts, produce. Food available, rest rooms, wheelchair accessible. Ample parking. (614) 454-0405. *Saturdays and Sundays.*

NILES

Howland Drive-In Flea Market. 5772 Youngstown Warren Rd. (Rt. 422). Used merchandise, glassware, collectibles, jewelry, used merchandise, garage sale items. Approximately 20 dealers. Space from $3. Contact: Ivan Cooson, 5772 Youngstown Warren Rd., Niles, OH 44446. (216) 652-4454. *Sundays, 9:00 A.M. - 5:00 P.M.*

NORTH BLOOMFIELD

North Bloomfield Auction and Flea Market. Approximately 1 mile west of Bloom Center on Hwy. 87. Indoor/outdoor market. New and used merchandise, clothing, collectibles, housewares, garage sale items. Average daily attendance 1,000. Approximately 200 dealers. Company also conducts monthly public auctions from its premises. Food available, rest rooms, wheelchair accessible. Ample parking. Space from $6. Contact: Charles Roscoe, 8183 Rt. 193, Farmdale, OH 44417. (216) 876-4993. *Thursdays, 9:00 A.M. - 4:00 P.M.*

NORTHFIELD

Northfield Flea Market. Northfield Star Drive-In Theater. Northfield Rd. (Rt. 9). New and used merchandise, collectibles, crafts, produce, garage sale items. Food available. *Sundays.*

NORWALK

Fireland Public Market. Rt. 20 East. Indoor/outdoor market. New and used merchandise, lots of garage sale booths, collectibles, decorator items, crafts, produce.

Average attendance 1,000. Approximately 30 dealers. Food available, rest rooms, wheelchair accessible. Ample parking. Space from $5. Contact: Victor Mooney, Rt. 20 Laylin Rd., Norwalk, OH 44857. (419) 499-2086. *Mondays, 8:00 A.M. - 5:00 P.M.*

NORWICH

Stagecoach Antique Mall Market. I-70 and Exit 164. General line of antiques, furniture, collectibles and decorator items. Food available, rest rooms, wheelchair accessible. Ample parking. (614) 872-3720. *Second weekend of each month.*

NORWOOD

Lens Odds and Ends. 3846 Montgomery. Used merchandise, garage sale items. Housewares, bric-a-brac. Contact: Len Frye, (513) 531-4465. *Friday - Sunday.*

OBERLIN

East Oberlin Flea Market. 43433 Rt. 20 East. (US Hwy. 20). Located 2 miles east of Oberlin. Indoor market. New merchandise, lots of surplus and closeouts. Clothing, children's lines, sports merchandise, housewares, jewelry, gift items. Market has a department-store atmosphere. Approximately 100 dealers. Food available, rest rooms, wheelchair accessible. Space from $5. Camping nearby. Contact: Dewey Served, 43433 US Rt. 20, East Oberlin, OH 44074. (216) 774-4312 or 775-1395. *Friday - Sunday.*

ORRVILLE

Route 30 Flea Market. Rt. 30 East. Used merchandise, garage sale items, country collectibles. Food available.(216) 682-9976. *Wednesdays.*

PAINESVILLE

Fairgrounds Flea Market. 1301 Mentor Ave. On Rt. 20. Antiques, collectibles, jewelry, silver, coins, farm and country collectibles, crafts, produce. Average daily attendance 2,000. Approximately 80 exhibitors. Food available, rest rooms, wheelchair accessible. Space from $8. Contact: Jim or Dick, (216) 943-2730 or 943-5452. *Saturdays and Sundays.*

PATASKALA

Red Barn Flea Market. 10501 Columbus Expressway Pk. Hwy. I-70. Indoor/outdoor market. Excellent market, with a good mix of vendors. This is a very interesting market to poke around in. I have found some real treasures here at terrific prices. Snack bar, rest rooms, wheelchair accessible. Ample parking. Space from $5. Contact: Dave Smith, (614) 927-1234. *Friday - Sunday, 10:00 A.M. - 6:00 P.M.*

PERRYSBURG

Antique and Flea Market. Indoor/outdoor market. General line of antiques and collectibles. Food available. Space from $25. Contact: Lynn Savial, 23260 Dunbridge Rd., Perrysburg, OH 43551. *May - October; second Sunday of each month.*

PERRYSBURG

Lakeview Hall Flea Market. 26879 Lakeview Dr. Perrysburg Freeman Exit. Used merchandise, garage sale items, sometimes new merchandise, collectibles. Average attendance 100. Approximately 20 dealers. Space from $16. Overnight parking. Contact: Carol Hauder, 203 Edgewood Dr, Perrysburg, OH 43551. (419) 874-5013. *Sundays, 7:00 A.M. - 4:00 P.M.*

PIKESTON

Pikeston Flea Market. U.S. Hwy. 23 South. New and used merchandise, clothing, children's items, housewares, jewelry, collectibles, crafts, produce. Food available, rest rooms, wheelchair accessible. Ample parking. (614) 289-2593. *April - October; Fridays and Saturdays, 6:00 A.M. - 5:00 P.M.*

PIQUA

Antique and Collectible Flea Market. National Guard Armory. 623 E. Ash St., Exit 82. Antiques, collectibles, jewelry, coins, silver, glassware, sports cards, fine jewelry. Approximately 30 dealers. Food available, rest rooms, wheelchair accessible. Ample parking. Space from $40. Contact: Richard Coble, 1215 Forest Ave, Piqua, OH 45356. (513) 773-3780. *Monthly.*

PIQUA

Rich Mart Flea Mart. 9071 State Rt. 66. New and used merchandise, garage sale items. Housewares, home furnishings, clothing, imports, Crafts, collectibles, produce. Snack bar. Contact: Martha Wolfe, (513) 295-3108. *Friday - Sunday.*

PISGAH

Pisgah Flea Market. 8460 Columbus/Cincinnati Rd. Rt. 42. Indoor/outdoor market. New and used merchandise, farm and country items, clothing, jewelry, housewares. Food available, rest rooms, wheelchair accessible. Ample parking. Contact: Virginia Kerr, (513) 777-9866. *Saturdays and Sundays.*

POLAND
Poland Flea Market. State Rd. 224. Antiques, collectibles, used merchandise, jewelry, clothing and fashion accessories, imports, art, crafts. Food available. (216) 536-6702. *Sundays.*

PORTAGE
Portage Flea Market. Rt. 25. Antiques, collectibles, jewelry, silver, sports cards, used merchandise. Food available. (419) 352-1861. *First and third Sundays of each month.*

PROCTORVILLE
Proctorville Flea Market. Rt. 7, Indoor and limited outdoor market. Antiques, collectibles, crafts, coins, new merchandise, housewares, sportswear, tapes, lots of used garage sale merchandise. Approximately 200 dealers. Snack bar, rest rooms, wheelchair accessible. Ample parking. Space from $20 per day inside and $3 outside. Contact: Todd Riley, (614) 886-8207. *Friday - Sunday, 8:00 A.M. - 5:00 P.M.*

RAVENNA
Flea Market and Swap Shop. 2735 Hwy. 59. Used merchandise, household goods, home furnishings and decorator items, imports, bric-a-brac, collectibles. (216) 296-9829. *Saturdays and Sundays.*

RAVENNA
Ravenna Flea Market. 5555 Newton Falls. New and used merchandise, collectibles, crafts. Food available. (216) 678-4000. *Fridays.*

REYNOLDSBURG
40 East Drive-In Theater Flea Market. Rt. 40. 1 mile east of town. New merchandise: electronics, sportswear, housewares, jewelry, sports merchandise, children's lines. Used merchandise, crafts, collectibles, produce. Approximately 100 dealers. Snack bar, rest rooms, wheelchair accessible. Ample parking. Admission charge. Space from $3. Contact: Rainbow Theaters, 865 King Ave., Columbus, OH 43212. (614) 291-3133. *Sundays.*

RICELAND
Wooster Bargain Barn. Rt. 30 east. 7 miles east of Wooster. Indoor/outdoor market. New merchandise: surplus, closeouts, clothing, children's items, housewares, collectibles. Snack bar, rest rooms, wheelchair accessible. Ample parking. Space from $4 per day. Contact: Luther Hothem, 531 N. Market, Riceland, OH 44691.

(216) 682-9058 or 264-3854. *Wednesdays and Sundays.*

ROSS
Strickers Grove Flea Market. Rt. 128. 1 mile south of town. Indoor/outdoor market. Good selection of small antiques, collectibles, crafts. Lots of primitives, advertising items, and used merchandise. 50+ dealers. Space from $10 per day. Contact: Gladys Jordan, (513) 733-5885. *Thursdays, 8:00 A.M. - 1:00 P.M.*

SABINA
Sabina Antique Village and Flea Market. Rt. 22. General line of antiques, collectibles, furniture, jewelry and used merchandise. Food available, rest rooms, wheelchair accessible. Ample parking. (513) 584-2531. *Saturdays and Sundays.*

SANDUSKY
Nikana Flea Market. 1914 Cleveland Rd. Indoor/outdoor market. New and used merchandise, crafts, collectibles, produce. Snack bar, rest rooms, wheelchair accessible. Space from $6. Contact: Nicholas Meyerden, Box 1473, Sandusky, OH 44870. (419) 625-8586. *Tuesdays and Thursdays.*

SOUTH AMHERST
Jamie's Flea Market. Rt. 113. Approximately 1 mile west of Rt. 58. Indoor/outdoor market. Market has wide range of goods and is one of the area's oldest markets. Good selection of antiques and collectibles. Lots of crafts. Average daily attendance 5,000. Approximately 150 dealers. Snack bar, rest rooms, wheelchair accessible, and lots of walking. Space from $5 per day. Contact: Ralph Mock, 198 S. Leavitt Rd., Amherst, OH 44001. (216) 986-5681 or 986-4402. *Wednesdays and Saturdays, 8:00 A.M. - 5:00 P.M.*

SPRINGFIELD
Springfield Antique Show and Flea Market. Exit 59 on I-70. Clark County Fairgrounds. Indoor/outdoor market. Emphasis on quality antiques. This is an excellent market for the advanced collector, dealer, or shopkeeper. 600 - 800 dealers. Snack bar, rest rooms, wheelchair accessible. Ample parking. Admission charge. Contact: Bruce Knight, P.O. Box 2429, Springfield, OH 45501. (513) 325-0053 or 568-4266. *Usually third weekend of each month; call for dates.*

> ### *"Top 10" All-American Marketplace Award Winners!*
>
> The following list was compiled from letters we received praising and condemning markets, ballots sent in voting for the "Top 10" flea markets, and from our own personal travels around the country visiting different markets. They are listed alphabetically by state and then by city. Each of these markets is super in itself and is a pleasure to visit. If you feel that we left out a good market or your favorite market, please let us know.
>
> | | |
> |---|---|
> | Apache Park-N-Swap | Apache Junction, Arizona |
> | Rose Bowl Flea Market | Pasadena, California |
> | The Flea Market | San Jose, California |
> | Thunderbird Swap-Meet | Fort Lauderdale, Florida |
> | Flea World | Orlando, Florida |
> | Shipshewana Auction and Flea Market | Shipshewana, Indiana |
> | The Flea Market, Tennessee State Fairgrounds | Nashville, Tennessee |
> | First Monday Trade Days | Canton, Texas |
> | Trader's Village Flea Market | Grand Prairie, Texas |
> | Rummage-O-Rama | Milwaukee, Wisconsin |

ST. CLAIRSVILLE

Flea Market. Alderson Airport. Antiques, collectibles, used merchandise, crafts. Food available, rest rooms, wheelchair accessible. Ample paved parking. *Sundays.*

ST. MARYS

The Flea Mart. 1108 E. Spring St. New and used merchandise, garage sale items, collectibles, glassware, jewelry, primitives. Snack bar, rest rooms. Space from $25. Contact: Ronald Selby, Box 525, St. Marys, OH 45885. *Friday - Sunday.*

STRAUSBERG

Garver Flea Market. 134 N. Wooster Ave. U.S. Hwy. 21. Antiques, collector lines, silver, coins, sports cards, jewelry, new and used merchandise. Average attendance 2,000. Approximately 100 dealers. Food available, rest rooms, wheelchair accessible. Ample parking. Space from $8. Overnight parking. Contact: Vic Gessner, 134 N. Wooster, Straus-

> ### *Flea Market Return Policy*
> When making a purchase at a flea market, be aware that most dealers do not accept returns. Before buying, look around the booth to see if the dealer has posted his policy on a sign. If you don't see one, don't be afraid to ask. Many dealers will accept exchanges on items, but there is only one hard and fast rule at a flea market: buyer beware.

berg, OH 44680. (216) 878-5664. *Sundays, 8:00 A.M. - 5:00 P.M.*

TIFFIN
Tiffin Flea Market. Seneca County Fairgrounds. Southwest side of Tiffin, off State Rt. 53, 224, or 18. Indoor/outdoor market. Antiques, collectibles, new and used merchandise. Average weekend attendance 5,000 - 10,000. Approximately 100 dealers. Good food, wheelchair accessible. Ample parking. Admission charge. Space from $8 per day. Tables $4 per weekend. Reservations recommended. Overnight camping available. Contact: Mr. and Mrs. Don Ziegler, 6627 S. SR 173, Bloomville, OH 44818. (419) 983-5084. *April - October; Saturdays and Sundays.*

TIFFIN
Tiffin Mall Flea Market. 870 W. Market St. Rt. 18. New and used merchandise, decorator items, art, prints, jewelry, collectibles. Snack bar, rest rooms, wheelchair accessible. Ample parking. (419) 447-1866. *Saturdays and Sundays.*

TOLEDO
Bassett Flea Market. 600 Bassett St. Wide variety of new merchandise, used merchandise, farm items. Crafts, collectibles, produce. Approximately 150 dealers. Snack bar. Camping available. Contact: Al Cartier, (419) 729-0601. *Saturdays and Sundays.*

TOLEDO
Big B's Flea Market. 7200 Airport Hwy. Used merchandise, garage sale items, new merchandise, surplus, imports, crafts, collectibles, produce. Approximately 50 dealers. Food available. Space from $10 per day. Contact: Marge Buckley, (919) 865-6669. *Friday - Sunday.*

TOLEDO
Farmers and Flea Market.

1500 Navarre Ave. Used merchandise, garage sale items, housewares, home furnishings, clothing, children's items, farm items, collectibles. Food available. *Saturdays.*

TOLEDO
Flea Market. Langolis Auction House. 640 N. Lallendorf Rd. New and used merchandise, closeouts, surplus, electronics, housewares, clothing, used furniture, jewelry. Food available, rest rooms, wheelchair accessible. Ample parking. (419) 698-3412. *Saturdays and Sundays.*

TOLEDO
"Giant" Outdoor Flea Market. Westgate Shopping Center. Secor Rd. New and used merchandise, garage sale items, tools, electronics, imports, crafts, collectibles, produce. Food available. *Wednesdays, Saturdays, and Sundays.*

TOLEDO
Outdoor Flea Market. 5260 Telegraph Rd. Used merchandise, garage sale items. Plenty of bric-a-brac, housewares, home furnishings, imports, novelties. *Saturdays and Sundays.*

TOLEDO
Toledo Trade Market. 1258 W. Alexis Rd. Indoor market. New merchandise, lots of hot new trendy items. Collectibles, silver, decorator items, glassware. Snack bar, rest rooms, wheelchair accessible. Ample parking. Contact: Mike Tatro, (419) 478-1001. *Friday - Sunday.*

TORONTO
Tri-State Jockey Lot Flea Market. Indoor/outdoor market. Large commercial market, with lots of new merchandise, used merchandise, mountains of garage sale junk. Collectibles, housewares, children's items, jewelry, crafts, produce. Average daily attendance 4,000 - 5,000. Approximately 150 dealers. Food available, rest rooms, wheelchair accessible. Ample parking. Space from $10 per day. Contact: Dan Calabreese, Box 120, Toronto, OH 43964. (614) 537-9241. *Friday - Sunday.*

TROY
Flea Market. 1375 Union St. Used and new merchandise, housewares, home furnishings, imports, surplus goods, crafts, collectibles. Snack bar, rest rooms, wheelchair accessible. Ample parking. (513) 339-9387. *Saturdays and Sundays, 9:00 A.M. - 5:00 P.M.*

> ### *Would You Take?*
>
> All dealers, with few exceptions, have a little bit of flexibility in their pricing structure. One of the real fun things about flea markets is that you can negotiate with the dealer.
>
> A lot of factors are involved in just what a dealer will take for an item. He may need travel money, he may need money to pay the phone bill, he may have just had the item too long and doesn't want to pack it up one more time.
>
> The first rule is, don't insult the dealer. Don't tell him what a piece of junk the item is while you are trying to buy it. Courtesy and a pleasant personality will get you a lot further than tacky and abrasive comments.
>
> The best method is to ask the dealer, "Would you take... ?" and then name a number. The dealer will then tell you yes or will make you a counteroffer. He may say, "I can't take $10, but I can sell it for $8." Then it's up to you. It's always okay to say, "I'll pass."

URBANA

Antique Show and Flea Market. Fairgrounds. Indoor/outdoor market. Market features quality antiques and collectibles and is an excellent all-around event. Approximately 150 dealers inside; approximately 150 dealers outside during the summer. Contact: Howard Goddard, 934 Amherst Dr., Urbana, OH 43078. (513) 653-6013 or 788-2058. *Usually held the first weekend of each month; call for dates.*

URBANA

South Point Flea Market. Junction of Rts. 35 and 68. Antiques, collectibles, crafts, ball cards, toys, pictures, old tools, and lots of miscellaneous items. (513) 652-4691. *Friday - Sunday.*

VALLEY VIEW

Flea Market Bazaar. 5300 W. Canal Rd. Used merchandise, housewares, clothing, children's items, garage sale items. Snack bar, rest rooms, wheelchair accessible. Ample parking. (216) 524-9260. *Saturdays and Sundays.*

WALDO

Flea Market. Jessie's Auction House. New and used merchandise, closeouts, surplus, clothing, jewelry, housewares, children's items, lots of bric-a-brac. Snack bar, rest rooms, wheelchair accessible. Ample parking. *Second Sunday of each month.*

WARREN
Skyway Drive-In Flea Market. Levit Rd. Used merchandise, garage sale items, new merchandise, home furnishings, decorator items, collectibles, crafts, produce. Snack bar, rest rooms, wheelchair accessible. Ample parking. *Sundays.*

WARREN
Warren Flea Market. 428 S. Main St. Indoor/outdoor market. New and used merchandise, collectibles, decorator items, bric-a-brac. Snack bar. Contact: Alfred Raghanti, (216) 399-8298. *Tuesday - Saturday, 8:00 A.M. - 5:00 P.M.*

WASHINGTON COURT HOUSE
Washington Court House Flea Market. Fairgrounds. Rts. 3 and 22. A lot of everything here. This market runs the gamut of goods; one could take the entire weekend to see it all. Large truckloads of new surplus merchandise. Quality antiques and collectibles. Approximately 1,000 dealers. Good food, rest rooms, wheelchair accessible, and lots of walking. Ample parking, but due to huge crowds it can be difficult. Admission charge. Space from $6. Contact: Coy and Stookey, 134 E. Ohio, Washington Court House, OH 43160. (614) 278-2721. Washington hosts an annual city-wide festival and flea market. This popular event is known as "Ohio's Favorite Flea Market." *Monthly.*

WESTCHESTER
Flea Market. Queen City Speedway. Antiques, collectibles, new and used merchandise. Household goods, fashions and fashion accessories, imports. Snack bar, rest rooms, wheelchair accessible. Ample parking. *Sundays.*

WOODSFIELD
Lil Rebel Flea Market. Radson Shopping Center. New and used merchandise, garage sale items, bric-a-brac, crafts, produce. Food available. *First and third Saturdays of each month.*

WOODSFIELD
Radsons Flea Market. Rt. 78, Lewisville Rd. New and used merchandise, garage-sale-type bric-a-brac, home furnishings, children's goods, tools, electronics. Contact: Boyd Vananess, (614) 458-1740. *Semi-monthly.*

YOUNGSTOWN

Austintown Flea Market. 5370 Clarkins Drive. (I-80 and Rt. 46) Used merchandise, garage sale items, collector lines, glassware, jewelry. Food available. Contact: Sally Shipley, (216) 799-1325. *Saturdays and Sundays, 9:00 A.M. - 5:00 P.M.*

YOUNGSTOWN

Four Seasons Flea and Farmers Market. Rt. 422 and McCartney Rd. New and used merchandise, clothing, housewares, children's items, jewelry, farm items, produce, collectibles. Food available, rest rooms, wheelchair accessible. Ample parking. (216) 744-5050. *Wednesdays and Sundays.*

ZIONSVILLE

Big Red's Flea Market. U.S. Hwy. 52. 11777 Lafayette Rd. Used merchandise, garage sale items, collectibles, glassware, primitives, jewelry, decorator items. Contact: Mason Promotions, (317) 769-3260. *Daily.*

SOUTH DAKOTA

The high plains, endless miles, few people, and skies with no boundaries. Just keep faith—there really are towns in South Dakota. Granted, not many, and the ones there sure are small—but so frontier-like lovely. Here live people who embody everything great about the American character.

Best bets...

✦ Blackhills Flea Market, Rapid City
This is an all-day market with many friendly dealers, quality items, and lovely grounds. The perfect spot to wander around and enjoy the sheer beauty of life!

✦ Rapid City Flea Market, Rapid City
This market always has a lot to offer, including a great selection of country crafts and authentic Indian jewelry and art. Rapid City is a delightful vacation spot, especially in the summer when some great festivals and events are held.

✦ Flea Market, Sioux Falls
Located in the Expo Building, this is a good source market for dealers, shopkeepers, decorators, and collectors. Great buys on quality antiques and small, desirable collectibles. Prices here are far below those in the East.

RAPID CITY
Blackhills Flea Market. 5500 Mt. Rushmore Rd. U.S. Highway 16. Indoor/outdoor market. Wide variety of collectibles, antiques, advertising items, farm items. Good selection of locally made crafts. New merchandise. Very scenic market. Approximately 125 dealers. Lots of good food. Ample parking. Space from $8. Camping nearby. Contact: Paul Ashland, 909 St. Francis, Rapid City, SD 57701. (605) 343-6477 or 348-1981. *May - September; Saturdays and Sundays, 7:00 A.M. - dark.*

RAPID CITY
Rapid City Flea Market. Civic Center. 444 Mt. Rushmore Rd. Indoor market. Antiques,

> **Shopping Tip #11**
> Always call ahead to verify dates and information!

collectibles, sports items, new merchandise. Lots of secondhand items and country crafts. Market always has a great selection of authentic Indian jewelry and art. 50 - 75 dealers. Snack bar, rest rooms, wheelchair accessible. Ample parking. Space from $25. Contact: Robert Orlup, HC 1741, Deadwood, SD 57732. (605) 342-2524. *Usually held the first and third weekends of each month; call for dates. 9:00 A.M. - 5:00 P.M.*

SIOUX FALLS

Antiques and Flea Market. 1103 N. Main St. Antiques, furniture, collector lines, crafts, western and Indian jewelry and art. Snack bar, rest rooms, wheelchair accessible. Ample parking. (605) 338-0297. *Saturdays and Sundays.*

SIOUX FALLS

Flea Market. Expo Building, 12th St. and Fairgrounds. 5th and Main Sts. Indoor market. Nice overall market, with a good selection of collectibles, new merchandise, used merchandise, and crafts. Approximately 250 dealers. Snack bars, clean rest rooms, wheelchair accessible. Ample parking on adjacent streets. Space from $19. Contact: Ed Benson, Box 236, Sioux Falls, SD 57102. (605) 361-1717. *First weekend of each month, 9:00 A.M. - 5:00 P.M.*

SIOUX FALLS

Flea Market. 3515 N. Cliff Ave. New and used merchandise, garage sale items, lots of bric-a-brac, imports, clothing, farm items, collectibles. (605) 338-8975. *Tuesday - Thursday.*

YANKTON

Flea Market. City Auditorium. Antiques, collectibles, Indian jewelry and art. Western collectibles. (605) 361-1717. *Monthly.*

YANKTON

Lewis and Clark Traders. Hwy. 52, 1 mile west or 1 mile east of Gavins Point Dam. 75 spaces. New and used merchandise, farm and ranch items, Home furnishings, housewares, collectibles, Western and Indian art and artifacts, crafts, produce. Snack bar, rest rooms, wheelchair accessible. Ample parking. Space $5. Camping and electricity available. Contact: D. Larson,

800 East 4th, Yankton, SD 57078. (605) 665-2231. *Friday - Sunday.*

YANKTON

Yankton Flea Market. 601 Burleigh St. Used merchandise, garage sale items, bric-a-brac, collectibles. An occasional treasure can be unearthed here, amid the great amounts of pure flea market "junque." (606) 665-8130. *Daily.*

WISCONSIN

Wisconsin is such an aesthetically beautiful state. Lovely cities and towns. Beautiful countryside. Farms, dairy herds, all the folks busy feeding the world. When in Wisconsin, I always stock up on the locally produced foods—cheese, sausage, brats, etc. No one makes this type of food the way they do in Wisconsin.

Great markets in Wisconsin, some really great local festivals. Check these out.

Best bets...

✤ 7 Mile Fair, Caledonia
Large commercial market, with worlds of new and trendy merchandise, imports, and new collectibles.

✤ Northeastern Wisconsin's Biggest Craft Sale and Flea Market, Green Bay
This is probably my favorite Wisconsin market. I'm always able to find good wholesale buys here for resale.

✤ Rummage-O-Rama, Milwaukee
Always several demonstrators/pitchmen here, selling the latest in kitchenware and trendy gadgets. Lots of new items, collectibles, and more.

✤ Shawano Flea Market, Shawano
Large, popular market; clean, friendly, well-managed.

ABBOTSFORD
Flea Market. Hwy. 13 North. Used merchandise, home furnishings, decorator items, tools, new merchandise, imports, clothing, gifts, farm items, collectibles. *Saturdays and Sundays.*

ADAMS
Adams Flea Market. 556 S. Main St. Hwy. 13 South. Indoor/outdoor market. Antiques, collectibles, coins, vintage clothing, jewelry. Approximately 50 dealers. Camping available. Contact: Irene Steffen, (608) 339-3192.

Saturdays and Sundays, 6:00 A.M. - dark.

ADAMS

Adams Flea Market. Indoor/outdoor market. New and used merchandise, bric-a-brac, imports, prints, tools, collectibles, crafts. Snack bar, rest rooms. (608) 339-3606. *Saturdays and Sundays.*

BELOIT

White Horse Flea Market. 136 W. Grand Ave. New and used merchandise, garage sale items, decorator items, crafts, collectibles. Snack bar, rest rooms. (608) 362-8220. *Saturdays and Sundays.*

CALEDONIA

7 Mile Fair. 2720 W. 7 Mile Rd. I-94 and 7 Mile Rd. Exit 15 miles south of Milwaukee. Indoor/outdoor market. Large commercial market, with worlds of new and trendy merchandise, imports, and new collectibles. Management does not wish this flea market referred to as a flea market, so when you're at their market ... call it a fair. But by its nature it really is a flea market, and an exceptionally fine one at that. Approximately 750 dealers. Indoor space from $15; outdoor space available. Plenty of food, rest rooms. Ample parking. No outside food or beverage concessions allowed, as the market has the exclusive. Produce OK. Contact: Scott Niles, 2720 W. 7 Mile Rd., Caledonia, WI 53108. (414) 835-2177. *Saturdays and Sundays, 6:00 A.M. - 5:00 P.M.*

COLUMBUS

Sunday Flea Market. Antiques, lots of collector booths, crafts, used merchandise. Home furnishings, housewares, apparel, fashion accessories, crafts, Food available, rest rooms. Contact: Chamber of Commerce, (414) 623-3699. *June - September; Sundays.*

EAU CLAIRE

The Golden Indoor/Outdoor Flea Market. Melby Rd., off Rt. 53. Antiques, furniture (used and antique), many collector booths, jewelry, coins, sports cards, clothing, housewares, bric-a-brac, fishing collectibles, used merchandise. Snack bar, rest rooms, wheelchair accessible. Ample parking. (715) 832-8605. *Friday - Sunday, 9:00 A.M. - 6:00 P.M.*

EDGERTON

Wisconsin Flea Market. Hwys. 90 and 59. New and used merchandise, garage sale and farm items. Lots of bric-a-brac, crafts, collectibles, produce. Food available, rest rooms. (608) 884-3994. *Saturdays and Sundays.*

ELKHORN

Antique and Flea Market. Fairgrounds. Indoor/outdoor market. Good market for antiques, primitives, and collectibles. A tremendous source market, with literally hundreds of booths crammed full of desirable collector items. 500+ dealers. Food, rest rooms, wheelchair accessible, lots of walking. Admission charge $1. Contact: PROmotions, Box 544, Elkhorn, WI 53121. (414) 723-5651. *Monthly.*

FOND DU LAC

Flea Market. Fairgrounds. Antiques, collectibles, furniture, new and used merchandise. Lots of bric-a-brac, clothing, imports, gifts, tools, home furnishings. Food available, rest rooms, wheelchair accessible. Ample parking. (414) 583-3358. *Monthly.*

FOND DU LAC

Flea Market. Wescott Plaza Mall. New and used merchandise, gifts, souvenirs, jewelry, sportswear. (414) 923-5190. *Daily.*

FRANKLIN

St. Martin Flea Market. Antiques, collectibles, farm and country items, fishing tackle, sports merchandise, clothing, jewelry, housewares, lots of garage sale items, crafts. Food available, rest rooms. Contact: City Hall, (414) 425-7500. *First Monday of each month.*

GILLETT

Flea Market and Sidewalk Sale. Main St. New and used merchandise, collectibles, clothing, imports, lots of crafts, produce. Food available, rest rooms. (414) 855-6166. *Saturdays.*

GREEN BAY

Northeastern Wisconsin's Biggest Craft Sale and Flea Market. Brown County Arena. 1901 S. Oneida. Next to Lambeau Field. Great selection of antiques, collectibles, fine jewelry, collectible glassware and silver. Lots of crafts. Some new and used merchandise. This is probably my favorite Wisconsin market. I'm always able to find good wholesale buys here for resale. Average daily attendance 3,000. Approximately 300 dealers. Snack bars, rest rooms. Ample parking. Admission charge. Space from $14. Reservations required. Camping available. No outside food concessions allowed. Contact: J.H. Van

> ### *More Bargaining Savvy for the Beginner*
> If you come across a dealer who acts insulted when you try to dicker over price, move on to another booth. Chances are this dealer is new and doesn't understand that bargaining is part of traditional flea market etiquette. It might also be that he has not bought wisely for resale and can't bargain without taking a loss. In either case, he has a lot to learn about flea marketing. You needn't waste your time in this booth—there are plenty of other dealers who will wheel and deal. By moving on, you have just taught this dealer a valuable lesson. If he is smart, he will take a hard look at his operation and make adjustments.

Stechhelman, Box 10566, Green Bay, WI 54307. (414) 494-9507 or 494-3401. *Monthly, 8:30 A.M. - 3:30 P.M.*

HAUGEN
Barn Flea Market. Hwy. 53. Used merchandise, lots of used farm and country items, collectibles, crafts, produce. Food available, rest rooms. (715) 234-2615. *Thursday - Sunday.*

HAYWARD
Hayward Flea Market. Hwy. 27 and County Rd. "B." Indoor/outdoor market. Good selection of collectibles, lots of used merchandise, and some new goods. Approximately 75 dealers. Contact: Jan Thiry, (715) 634-4794. *Tuesdays and Wednesdays, dawn - dark.*

HAYWARD
St. Joseph's Flea Market. St. Joseph's Catholic Church. New and used merchandise, lots of garage sale booths, clothing, housewares, bric-a-brac. Lots of locally made crafts, produce. Food available, rest rooms. (715) 634-4061. *June - August; Mondays.*

JAMESVILLE
Jamesville Flea Market. Corner of Avalon and Prairie Rd. New and used merchandise, garage sale items, clothing, housewares, auto and fishing items, collectibles, crafts, produce. Food available, rest rooms. (608) 755-9830 or 752-7264. *Saturdays and Sundays.*

JEFFERSON
Jefferson Bargain Fair. Jefferson Speedway grounds. Hwy. 18. Antiques, collector booths, mountains of used

merchandise, clothing, furniture, farm items, fishing and marine items, auto items, great selection of crafts and decorator items. Food available, rest rooms. Ample parking. (414) 835-1168. *Seasonal market. Summer months; Sundays.*

KENOSHA
Bargain Showcase Indoor/Outdoor Market. 8501 75th St. New and used merchandise. Lots of new fashion and decorator items, newer collector lines. Snack bar, rest rooms, wheelchair accessible. Ample parking. Contact: Bill Utaski, (414) 697-9770. *Friday - Sunday, 9:00 A.M. - 5:00 P.M.*

KENOSHA
Kenosha Flea Market. 5535 22nd Ave. New and used merchandise, collector booths, good selection of fishing collectibles, art, prints, jewelry, clothing, housewares. Snack bar, rest rooms, wheelchair accessible. Ample parking. Contact: Beth Goll, (414) 658-3532. *Friday - Sunday.*

KENOSHA
Mid-City Outdoor Theater Flea Market. Hwy. 32. Antiques, collector booths, furniture, new and used merchandise, clothing, housewares, sports and fishing items, farm items, crafts, produce. Snack bar, rest rooms, wheelchair accessible. Ample parking. *Sundays.*

LADYSMITH
Van Wey's Community Auction and Flea Market. Rt. 2. 4 miles west of town on Hwy. 8. This is a classic country market that will take you back to an earlier time. Antiques, collectibles, primitives, farm items, new and used merchandise, crafts. Market has been in existence since 1926. Average attendance 3,500. Approximately 200 dealers. Cafe, rest rooms, wheelchair accessible. Ample parking. Space from $7. Camping nearby. Contact: Cecil Van Way, (715) 532-6044 or 532-3661. *April - October; 5th and 20th of each month.*

MADISON
The Forum Flea Market and Collectors Show. Dane County Expo Center. Indoor market. One of the area's most popular markets. Primarily antiques and collectibles, with wide range of booths of quality items. This is a very clean, well-managed market that is always a pleasure to shop. Approximately 100 dealers. Snack

bars, rest rooms, wheelchair accessible. Ample parking. Admission charge. Space from $25. Contact: Ed Haferman, Box 1361, Madison, WI 53701. (608) 837-5666. *Monthly, 9:00 A.M. - 4:00 P.M.*

MAUSTON

Mauston Antique Mall and Flea Market. 101 N. Union St. General line of antiques, collectibles, furniture. Used and new merchandise, home furnishings, decorator items. (608) 847-7559. *Daily.*

MENOMENEE FALLS

Starlite Swap-O-Rama. North Fond Du Lac Ave. Hwys. 145 and 41. Antiques, collector booths, furniture, new merchandise, lots of used merchandise, bric-a-brac, farm items, clothing, housewares. Approximately 75 dealers. Food available, rest rooms, wheelchair accessible. Ample parking. (312) 774-3900. *May - November; Sundays.*

MERRILL

Bargain Bin Flea Market. Hwy. K South. Used merchandise, garage sale and farm items, collectibles, clothing, housewares, crafts. Snack bar, rest rooms. *Saturdays and Sundays.*

MILWAUKEE

Flea Market. 4845 N. Tautonia. Used merchandise, garage sale items, home furnishings, clothing, crafts, collectibles. (715) 445-2082. *Tuesday - Thursday.*

MILWAUKEE

Mega Market. 7793 W. Appleton Ave. New merchandise: tools, fishing tackle, electronics, housewares, sportswear, toys, jewelry, sports merchandise, lots of new collector lines, decorator items. Snack bar, rest rooms, wheelchair accessible. Ample parking. Admission charge. (414) 464-8277. *Saturdays and Sundays.*

MILWAUKEE

Rummage-O-Rama. State Fair Park. All types of merchandise can be found here. Many one-of-a-kind treasures and plenty of traditional flea market bric-a-brac. Always several demonstrators/pitchmen, selling the latest in kitchenware and trendy gadgets. Lots of new items, collectibles, and more. This is a strong market with exceptional attendance. 500+ dealers. Food, rest rooms, wheelchair accessible. Ample parking. Admission charge. Space from $63. Camping available. Contact: J. Rasner, Box 51619, New Berlin, WI 53151. (414) 521-2111. *Usually*

> **Dress for the Hunt! Tip #6**
> Whatever you wear, make sure to dress for comfort. Casual is the name of the game when shopping at flea markets.

held once a month, occasionally twice a month; 10:00 A.M. - 5:30 P.M.

MINOCQUA
Maze Flea Market. 7576 Hwy. 51 South. Used merchandise, garage sale items, collectibles, crafts. Snack bar, rest rooms. (715) 356-7238 or 356-1440. *Saturdays and Sundays.*

MINOCQUA
Minocqua Flea Market. Hwy. 51 South. New and used merchandise, antiques, collectibles, crafts. Snack bar, rest rooms. (715) 356-5149. *Saturdays and Sundays.*

MONTELLO
Candy's Flea Market. 6 miles south of Montello on Hwy. 22. Indoor/outdoor market. New and used merchandise, lots of bric-a-brac. Antiques, collector booths, crafts. Average attendance 200. Approximately 25 dealers. Snack bar, rest rooms, wheelchair accessible. Space from $5 per day. Contact: Candy Howell, Rt. 1, Box 175A, Montello, WI 53949. (608) 297-2489. *May - October; Saturdays and Sundays.*

MONTELLO
Granite City Antique Mall and Flea Market. 145 Clay St. Indoor/outdoor market. The flea market features new and used merchandise, antiques, collectibles, and crafts. Average daily attendance 300 - 500. Approximately 50 dealers. Snack bars, rest rooms, wheelchair accessible. Outdoor space from $12. Camping available. (608) 297-7925. *Saturdays and Sundays.*

NEENAH
G and L Auction Company Flea Market. Neenah Labor Temple. New and used merchandise, surplus, closeouts, clothing, housewares, collectibles, crafts. Food available, rest rooms, wheelchair accessible. Ample parking. (715) 886-4031. *First Sunday of each month.*

NEW LONDON
Pin River Amusement Park Flea Market. Pin River Amusement Park. New merchandise, souvenirs, novelties, used merchandise, crafts. Food available, rest rooms. (414) 726-4302. *Sum-*

mer months only; Saturdays and Sundays.

OXFORD

Oxford Flea Market. Downtown. New merchandise, used merchandise, lots of garage sale booths, collectibles, crafts. Food available, rest rooms. Contact: Chamber of Commerce. *Second and fourth Saturdays of each month.*

PRINCETON

Princeton Flea Market. City Park. New merchandise, trendy fashion items, used merchandise, lots of garage sale booths, collectibles, crafts. Food available, rest rooms. Contact: Chamber of Commerce, (414) 295-3877. *May - October; Saturdays and Sundays.*

RHINELANDER

North Town Trade Center. 3846 Shawnee Ln. North on Hwy. 17 to Chippewa Dr. Turn right, then 1 block. Indoor market. New merchandise: gifts, electronics, fishing tackle, auto items, tools, sportswear, housewares, sports merchandise, jewelry, toys. Used merchandise, garage sale items. Antiques, collector booths, crafts. 150 - 200 dealers. Snack bar, rest rooms, wheelchair accessible. Space from $7.50 per day or $14 for the weekend. Camping available on premises. Prior approval for any food or beverage sales. Contact: Ernest or Michael Feight, (715) 369-3068. *Saturdays and Sundays.*

SHAWANO

Shawano Flea Market. Fairgrounds. Hwy. 29. Large market, clean, friendly, well-managed. Food, special events, antiques, collectibles, new merchandise, crafts, and produce are just some of the variety that this popular market has to offer. Approximately 200 dealers. Ample parking. Admission charge $1. Delightful tourist area, with many interesting shops and attractions. Contact: Bob Zurko, 211 W. Green Bay St., Shawano, WI 54166. (715) 526-9769. *April - mid-November; Sundays, daylight - 5:00 P.M.*

SPOONER

Millard's Flea Market. Hwys. 53 and 63. Used merchandise, garage sale items, home furnishings, housewares, imports, tools, farm items, crafts, produce. (715) 635-3801. *Fridays.*

ST. CROIX FALLS

Pea Picking Flea Market. Hwys. 8 and 35. 5 miles

> ### *Buying Toys at a Flea Market*
> ### *Safety Check Tip #2*
>
> Many new toys are to be found at flea markets, and you may want to take advantage of the great buys.
>
> For your children's safety, however, you should know that many of these toys are imports and do not meet American standards for child protection. Boxes are not always marked with the age of the child the toy is intended for. Also, foreign manufacturers often use materials for their toys that are safety hazards for children—hard plastics, for example, in such things as projectiles, or warrior battle gear that encourages fighting and could actually cause injury if a child is hit with it.
>
> As a parent, use your best judgment when buying toys at flea markets. Inspect the item thoroughly. Consider the child who will be using the toy and how he or she will be using it. Take the child's age, physical development, and maturity into consideration. If it meets your tough safety standards—buy it!

east of town. Indoor/outdoor market. Collectibles, country and farm items, crafts, used furniture. Lots of local food items, cheese, etc. Approximately 75 dealers. Space from $7 daily. Contact: Leonard Sommers, (715) 483-9460. *Saturdays and Sundays, 6:00 A.M. - 5:00 P.M.*

ST. GERMAINE

Flea Market. Village Park. Used merchandise, lots of garage sale booths, crafts, produce. Food available, rest rooms. *Mondays, 6:00 A.M. - 4:00 P.M.*

WAUSAU

Marathon Park Indoor Flea Market. 1810 Stewart Cir. Lots of new merchandise, used merchandise, furniture, garage sale items, collector booths, crafts, gifts. Snack bar, rest rooms, wheelchair accessible. Ample parking. (715) 359-9500. *April - October; Saturdays and Sundays.*

WAUTOMA

Wautoma Flea market. Junction of Rts. 73 and 21. Collectibles, crafts, furniture, used and garage sale items. 20 - 25 dealers. Space from $8. Contact: Milton Sommer, (414) 787-2300. *Mid-April - November; Saturdays and Sundays, 7:00 A.M. - dark.*

WESTFIELD

Westfield Flea Market.
Antiques, furniture, many collector booths, used merchandise, crafts. Food available. Contact: Chamber of Commerce, (608) 296-2462. *Seasonal market. Summer months; Sundays.*

WESTOVER

Westover Drive-In Theater Flea Market. New and used merchandise, garage sale items, antiques, collector booths, crafts, produce. Snack bar, rest rooms, wheelchair accessible. Ample parking. *Sundays.*

WOODSTOCK

Woodstock Antique and Flea Market. Fairgrounds. Antiques, furniture, many fine quality collector booths, used merchandise, farm items, auto items, fishing and marine items, some new merchandise. Crafts, local food items, produce. Food available, rest rooms, wheelchair accessible. Ample parking. (715) 526-9769. *Monthly.*

ANTIQUE AND CRAFT MALLS

Antique and Craft Malls

Antique malls, multi-dealer markets that are booming in popularity, have revolutionized the way antiques are bought and sold. In fact, they are considered to be the fastest-growing segment in the retailing field today. In this book we have listed only multi-dealer marketplaces (no individual shops). If you have information about a mall that we missed, please let us know about it.

ILLINOIS

Albany
Albany Antique Mart. Great River Rd. Hwy. 84. I-80, Exit 1, then 18 miles north. Antiques, collectibles, furniture, glassware, china, primitives, postcards, and a nice selection of vintage Christmas collectibles. (309) 887-4850. *Monday - Saturday, 10:00 A.M. - 5:00 P.M.; Sundays, noon - 5:00 P.M.*

Arcola
Emporium Antiques. 201 E. Main St. Antiques, collectibles. Glassware, china, silver, pottery, paper and advertising items. (217) 268-4523. *Monday - Saturday, 9:00 A.M. - 5:00 P.M.; Sundays, noon - 5:00 P.M.*

Atlanta
Route 66 Antique Mall. I-55, Exit 140, west 4 blocks. Quality antiques and collectibles in all categories, from furniture to small desirables. (217) 648-2321. *Monday - Saturday, 10:00 A.M. - 5:00 P.M.; Sundays, noon - 5:00 P.M.*

Avon
Avon Antique Mall. Main St. Glassware, china, linens, quilts, dolls, toys. Good selection of antiques and collectibles in all categories. (309) 465-7387. *Open daily.*

Beardstown
Beardstown Antique Mall. Rt. 125 East. 7,000 sq. ft. Antiques, collectibles, quilts, glassware, furniture. (217) 323-4569. *Monday - Saturday, 10:00 A.M. - 5:00 P.M.; Sundays, noon - 5:00 P.M.*

Belleville
Antique Gallery Mall. 201 W. Main St. Vintage clothing and

jewelry, china, silver, glassware, lamps, kitchen collectibles. (618) 233-0700. *Daily, 10:00 A.M. - 5:00 P.M.*

BLOOMFIELD

Memory Lane Antique Mall. 208 E. Franklin St. Antiques and collectibles. 60 dealers. (515) 664-1714. *Monday - Saturday, 8:00 A.M. - 5:00 P.M.; Sundays, 1:00 - 5:00 P.M.*

BLOOMINGTON

Antique Mall. 102 N. Center St. Front and Center Building. Quilts, country primitives, Victorian items, glassware, pottery, advertising items. 40+ dealers. (309) 828-1211. *Mondays, 10:00 A.M. - 7:00 P.M.; Tuesday - Saturday, 10:00 A.M. - 5:00 P.M.*

BOURBONNAIS

Indian Oaks Antique Mall. North Hwy. 50 and Larry Power Rd. Antiques, collectibles, gift items and crafts. 150+ dealers. Credit cards accepted. *Saturday - Wednesday, 10:00 A.M. - 5:30 P.M.; Thursdays and Fridays, 10:00 A.M. - 8:00 P.M.*

BROOKFIELD

Antique World Annex. 3100 Grand Blvd. Antiques and collectibles in all categories, from furniture to small desirables. (708) 387-2040. *Monday - Wednesday, 11:00 A.M. - 6:00 P.M.; Thursdays, 11:00 A.M. - 5:00 P.M.; Fridays and Saturdays, 11:00 A.M. - 6:00 P.M.; Sundays, 11:00 A.M. - 5:00 P.M.*

CHAMPAIGN

Vintage Antiques. 117 N. Walnut. Downtown. 2 floors. Nice selection of antiques and collectibles. Glassware, china, primitives, Victorian and Art Deco items. 10 dealers. (217) 359-8747. *Monday - Saturday, 10:00 A.M. - 5:00 P.M.*

CHENOA

The Antique Mall. I-55, Chenoa exit. 9,000 sq. ft. mall. Great selection of quality glassware, advertising items, toys, kitchenware, quilts, children's china and dolls. 32 dealers. Credit cards accepted. Several additional interesting shops are located in the vicinity, making this a terrific stop. Nancy Callis, (815) 945-7594. *Monday - Saturday, 10:00 A.M. - 6:00 P.M.; Sundays, 1:00 - 5:00 P.M.*

CHICAGO

Armitage Antique Gallery. 1529 W. Armitage. Lots of fine-quality antiques and collectibles. Glassware, china, pottery, country primitives, kitchenware, dolls, toys, banks. 40 dealers. (312) 227-

7727. *Daily, 11:00 A.M. - 6:00 P.M.*

CHICAGO
Wrigleyville Antique Mall. 3336 N. Clark St. Good variety of antiques and collectibles in all categories. 25 dealers. (312) 868-0285. *Monday - Saturday, 11:00 A.M. - 6:30 P.M.; Sundays, noon - 6:00 P.M.*

CLINTON
Clinton Antique Mall. Junction of Hwys. 51 and 54. General line of antiques and collectibles. 70+ dealers. (217) 935-8846. *Monday - Saturday, 10:00 A.M. - 5:00 P.M.; Sundays, noon - 5:00 P.M.*

DIVERNON
Lisa's Antique Mall. I-55, Exit 82, Hwy. 104. 12 miles south of Springfield. 2 large buildings, 40,000 sq. ft. Glassware, quilts, linens, lamps, paper and advertising items. 150 dealers. Credit cards accepted. (217) 628-1111 or 628-3333. *Daily, 10:00 A.M. - 6:00 P.M.*

DIXON
Brinton Avenue Antique Mall. 725 N. Brinton Avenue. Antiques, collectibles, art glass, lamps, toys, furniture, antique dolls, pottery. (815) 284-4643. *Daily, 10:00 A.M. - 5:00 P.M.*

EAST MOLINE
Antique and Treasure Trove. 611 15th Avenue. New mall, 2,400 sq. ft. Antiques, collectibles, gifts. Credit cards accepted. (309) 755-2525. *Monday - Friday, 10:00 A.M. - 5:00 P.M.; Saturdays, 10 - 3:00 P.M.*

EAST PEORIA
Pleasant Hill Antique Mall and Tea Room. 315 S. Pleasant Hill Rd. 30,000 sq. ft. Large, well-stocked mall, with a full line of antiques and collectibles. Tearoom and full family restaurant. (309) 694-4040. *Mondays and Tuesdays, 7:00 A.M. - 7:00 P.M.; Wednesday - Saturday, 7:00 A.M. - 10:00 P.M.; Sundays, 7:00 A.M. - 5:00 P.M.*

ELK GROVE VILLAGE
Antiques Mart. 1170 W. Devon Ave. Booths full of antiques and collectibles of every description. Glassware, china, silver, coins, advertising items, country and Victorian pieces, vintage jewelry. Approximately 125 dealers. (708) 894-8900. *Monday - Friday, 11:00 A.M. - 7:00 P.M.; Saturdays and Sundays, 10:00 A.M. - 5:00 P.M.*

ELK GROVE VILLAGE
Landmark Antiques. 1110 Nerge Rd. Quality antiques. Quilts, furniture, dolls, glass-

ware, toys, lamps, art glass, pottery. 35 dealers. (708) 924-5220. *Monday - Friday, 11:00 A.M. - 7:00 P.M.; Saturdays and Sundays, 10:00 A.M.- 5:00 P.M.*

FINDLAY

The Arches Antique Marketplace. 200 Main St. Quality antiques and collectibles of all descriptions. Books, glassware, decorator items, and plenty of small desirable collector finds. 20+ dealers. (217) 756-8243. *Sunday - Thursday, 11:00 A.M. - 5:00 P.M.; Fridays and Saturdays, 11:00 A.M. - 9:00 P.M.*

FOX LAKE

Antique Alley Mall. 415 S. Washington St. 3,000 sq. ft. mall, located in a former bowling alley. Antiques and collectibles. Collector finds, including depression and pattern glass, pottery, lamps, vintage clothing and lamps, trunks, kitchenware, Victorian-era items. (708) 587-0091. *Monday - Friday, 11:00 A.M. - 5:00 P.M.; Saturdays and Sundays, 11:00 A.M.- 4:00 P.M.*

GENESEO

Geneseo Antique Mall. 117 E. Exchange Avenue. I-80, Exit 19 downtown. Good selection of antiques and collectibles for every taste and budget. Credit cards accepted. (309) 944-3777. *Monday - Saturday, 9:00 A.M. - 5:00 P.M.*

GENESEO

Heartland Antique Mall. 4169 S. Oakwood Ave. A bit of everything at this mall. Antique furniture, lots of small desirables. Pam Ropp, (309) 944-3373. *Daily, 9:00 A.M. - 5:00 P.M.*

GENEVA

Geneva Antiques Market. 227 S. Third St. Antiques, collectibles. (708) 208-1150. *Monday - Saturday, 10:00 A.M. - 5:00 P.M.; Sundays, 11:00 A.M. - 4:00 P.M.*

GRAYSLAKE

Antique Warehouse. 2 S. Lake St. Lots of quality antiques and collectibles. No reproductions. 65 dealers. (708) 223-9554. *Monday - Saturday, 10:00 A.M. - 5:00 P.M.; Sundays, noon - 4:00 P.M.*

HAMILTON

Antique Mini Mall and Flea Market. Rt. 136. Collectibles of every description, and great antique finds for every taste and budget.

HENNEPIN

J and S Antiques Mall. Junction of State Hwy. 88 and I-80. Exit 45. 8,000 sq. ft. Loaded with quality antiques and collectibles. Jim and

Sandy Boender, (815) 454-2066. *Monday - Saturday, 9:00 A.M. - 5:00 P.M.; Sundays, noon - 4:00 P.M.*

JACKSONVILLE
Jacksonville Antique Mall. Corner of Lafayette and Pine Sts. Glassware, china, quilts, linens, antique furniture. 25 dealers. (217) 243-3219. *Monday - Saturday, 10:00 A.M. - 5:00 P.M.; Sundays, noon - 5:00 P.M.*

JACKSONVILLE
South Jacksonville Antique Mall. 1852 S. Main St. Good selection of antiques and collectibles. Nice decorator items. *Daily, 10:00 A.M. - 5:00 P.M.*

KANKAKEE
Bull Dog Antiques. 440 N. 5th Avenue. Antiques and collectibles. 12 dealers. (815) 936-1701. *Monday - Saturday, 10:00 A.M. - 5:00 P.M.; Sundays, noon - 4:00 P.M.*

KANKAKEE
Kankakee Antique Mall. 145 S. Schuyler. Downtown. I-57, Exit 312, West 1½ miles to Schuyler Ave. 65,000 sq. ft. Well-stocked mall, with a virtually unlimited range of items for the antiquer or collector. 225 individual dealer booths. (815) 937-4957. *Daily, 10:00 A.M. - 5:00 P.M.*

KANKAKEE
River Valley Antique Mall. Rt. 45/52, I-57, Exit 308, south 4 miles. A nice variety of good antiques and plenty of collector items in all categories. (815) 697-3040. *Daily, 10:00 A.M. - 5:00 P.M.*

KEITHSBURG
Commercial House Antiques. 413 Main St. Antiques, furniture, decorator items, lots of fine jewelry, sheet music, primitives. 10 dealers. Gail and Rupert Wenzel, (309) 374-2330. *Monday - Saturday, 10:00 A.M. - 5:00 P.M.; Sundays, noon - 4:00 P.M.; closed Tuesdays.*

LA GRANGE
Antique World. 1005 E. 31st St. 1½ miles west of Brookfield Zoo. *Monday - Wednesday, 11:00 A.M. - 6:00 P.M.; Thursdays, 11:00 A.M. - 8:00 P.M.; Saturdays, 11:00 A.M. - 6:00 P.M.; Sundays, 11:00 A.M. - 5:00 P.M.*

LEROY
On the Park Antiques. 104 E. Center St. Antiques, collectibles, primitives, glassware. 20 dealers. (309) 962-2618. *Monday - Saturday, 10:00 A.M. - 5:00 P.M.; Sundays, noon - 5:00 P.M.*

LINCOLN
Route 66 Antique Mall. 1409

Short 11th St. I-55 Exit 126. Use fairgrounds frontage road. Antiques, collectibles, books, small antiquarian items of all kinds. (217) 732-RT66. *Monday - Saturday, 10:00 A.M. - 5:00 P.M.; Sundays, noon - 5:00 P.M.*

LOMBARD
Village Green Antique and Gift Mall. 404 E. North Ave. Nice line of antiques, collectibles, gift items. Repair service. 60+ dealers. (708) 268-0086. *Open daily.*

MAHOMET
Second Story Antique Mall. 408 E. Main St. Upstairs location, 5,000 sq. ft. Country, oak, and walnut furniture, china, collectibles and books. 20 individual shops. Many fine shops located adjacent. (217) 586-5902. *Open daily.*

MARYVILLE
Maryville Antique Mall. Hwy. 159. 1 mile north of I-55/70. Good selection of quality antiques and collectibles, glassware, toys. 35 dealers. (618) 345-5533. *Monday - Saturday, 10:00 A.M. - 6:00 P.M.; Sundays, noon - 5:00 P.M.*

MATTOON
Mattoon Antique Mart. 908 Charleston Ave. Hwy. 16. Glassware, books, vintage jewelry, china. 20 dealers. (217) 234-9707. *Monday - Saturday, 10:00 A.M. - 5:00 P.M.; Sundays, 1:00 - 5:00 P.M.*

MCLEANSBORO
Southfork Antique Mall. 105 E. Broadway. 12,000 sq. ft. Antiques, collectibles. (618) 643-4458. *Monday - Saturday, 10:00 A.M. - 5:00 P.M.; Sundays, 1:00 - 5:00 P.M.*

METROPOLIS
Ferry Street Mall. 212 Ferry St. Antiques, collectibles, crafts. This town is the home of Superman, of comic-book fame. They host an annual Superman Festival here that is a don't-miss event. 60+ dealers. (618) 524-4805. *Daily, 10:00 A.M. - 5:00 P.M.*

MOMENCE
Cal-Jean Shops. 127 E. Washington St. Antiques and collectibles. (815) 472-2667. *Monday - Saturday, 9:00 A.M. - 5:00 P.M.; Sundays, noon - 5:00 P.M.*

NEWTON
Country Seed House Antique Mall. 604 E. Jourdan St. Antiques, collectibles, primitives, Victorian. No crafts. (800) 642-0390. *Wednesday - Saturday, 10:00 A.M. - 5:00 P.M.; Sundays, noon - 5:00 P.M.*

OREGON
Silo Antiques. Hwy. 2 North. 5,000 sq. ft. Good selection of furniture: walnut, cherry, pine, and oak. Also glassware and smalls of every description. (815) 732-4042. *Daily, 10:00 A.M. - 5:00 P.M.*

OSWEGO
Oswego Antique Shops. Rt. 34 and Main St. Glassware, toys, dolls, kitchen collectibles, decorator items. 7 shops, 50+ dealers. (708) 554-3131. *Open daily.*

PEORIA
Illinois Antique Center. 100 Walnut St. 35,000 sq. ft, 2 stories. Over 170 booths, with more than 100 showcases displaying quality antiques and collectibles. Good selection of architectural items. No crafts or reproductions. Very nice sandwich shop. (309) 673-3354. *Monday - Saturday, 9:00 A.M. - 5:00 P.M.; Sundays, noon - 5:00 P.M.*

PETERSBURG
Petersburg Peddlers. Town square, west side. 2-story building. Antiques, collectibles, country, primitives, furniture, quilts. Mall has an excellent tearoom. (217) 632-2628. *Tuesday - Sunday, 10:00 A.M. - 5:00 P.M.*

PLAINFIELD
Plainfield Antique Mart. 502 W. Lockport St. Downtown. Good selection of antiques and collectibles in all categories. (815) 436-1342. *Monday - Saturday, 10:00 A.M. - 6:00 P.M.; Sundays, 11:00 A.M. - 5:00 P.M.*

POCAHONTAS
TG's Antique Mall. I-70, Exit 36. Antiques, collectibles. From glassware to books, perfumes to banks. 45 dealers. (618) 669-2969. *Daily, 10:00 A.M. - 5:00 P.M.*

PRINCETON
Sherwood Antique Mall. 1661 N. Main St. I-80, Exit Rt. 26. New mall, 40,000 sq. ft facility. Furniture, glassware, small desirables in all categories. (815) 872-2580. *Daily, 10:00 A.M. - 9:00 P.M.*

QUINCY
Broadway Antique Mall. 1857 Broadway. Primitives, collectibles and antiques. (217) 222-8617. *Monday - Saturday, 9:30 A.M. - 5:30 P.M.; Sundays, noon - 5:00 P.M.*

QUINCY
Yesteryear Antique Mall. 615 Maine St. Antiques and collectibles. 100 booths. (217) 224-1871. *Monday - Saturday, 10:00 A.M. - 6:00 P.M.; Sundays, noon - 5:00 P.M.*

RICHMOND
1905 Emporium Mall. Downtown. Corner of 12th St. and Broadway. 3-story, 7,500 sq. ft. Lots of antiques and great collectibles. Soda fountain and general store. Over 25 antique shops located in this town. (815) 678-4414. *Daily, 10:30 A.M. - 5:00 P.M.*

ROCKFORD
East State Street Malls. 5411 and 5301 E. State St. These malls cover 60,000 sq. ft. Over 500 showcases filled with quality items. Antique furniture, china, pottery art glass, vintage clothing and jewelry, advertising items, country primitives. Approximately 250 dealers at both malls. Sandwich shop with ample parking. Credit cards accepted. *Daily, 10:00 A.M. - 9:00 P.M.*

ROCKWOOD
Eastwood Farm Antiques and Collectibles. Shaw Rd. Quality antiques and collectibles of all kinds. Glass, wood, metal, and paper. (815) 885-3389.

SANDWICH
Sandwich Antiques Mall. 108 N. Main St. Downtown. Quality-oriented mall, with no used or secondhand items. 30 dealers. (815) 786-7000. *Monday - Saturday, 10:00 A.M. - 5:00 P.M.; Sundays, 1:00 - 5:00 P.M.*

SAVANNA
Pulford Open House Antique Mall. Great River Rd. Hwy. 84. 27,500 sq. ft. Antiques, collectibles. 120 dealers. (815) 273-2661. *Monday - Thursday, 10:30 A.M. - 5:30 P.M.; Fridays and Saturdays, 10:30 A.M. - 8:00 P.M.*

SPARTA
Old Broadway Hotel Antique, Crafts and Flea Market. Rts. 4 and 154, corner of Broadway and St. Louis St., downtown. Mall is located in a historic hotel. Antiques, collectibles, lots of good miscellaneous "stuff." Mall also holds special events during nice weather; call for dates. (618) 443-2195.

SPRINGFIELD
Old Georgian Antique Mall. 830 S. Grand Avenue East. Quality antiques and collector items of all kinds. Glassware, china, pottery, paper and advertising items, country primitives, Victorian-era finds. (217) 753-8110. *Monday - Saturday, 10:00 A.M. - 4:00 P.M.; Sundays, noon - 3:00 P.M.*

SPRINGFIELD
Springfield Mall. 3031 Reilly Dr. I-55, Exit Stevenson Ave, north at light onto Dirksen,

> ### More Tenets of Shopper Courtesy
> 1. Don't open or reach inside display cases. Ask for assistance.
> 2. Sealed boxes should never be opened. Ask dealers to assist you if you want to get a closer look at something.
> 3. If you knock something off a table, pick it up.

then 1 mile. General line of antiques and collectibles. 50+ dealers. (217) 522-3031. *Daily, 10:00 A.M. - 6:00 P.M.*

St. Charles
Antique Markets. 3 separate malls, with over 75 dealers: (1) 11 N. Third St., (708) 377-1868; (2) 303 W. Main St., (708) 377-5818 or 377-5798; (3) 413 W. Main St., (708) 377-5599. Credit cards accepted. *Daily, 10:00 A.M. - 5:00 P.M.*

St. Charles
Consigntiques. 201 E. Cedar Ave. Antiques, collectibles, curios, furniture. (708) 584-7535.

Volvo
Volvo Antique Mall. Jan Voss, 27640 W. Rt. 120. 150 booths. Quality antiques, collectibles, lots of nice small items. Mall features over 175 classic autos on display and for sale. (815) 344-6002. *Daily, 10:00 A.M. - 5:00 P.M.; Fridays until 8:00 P.M.*

West Frankfort
West Frankfort Antique Mall. 117 W. Main St. Glassware, furniture, silver, china, linens, dolls, toys.

Wheeling
Antiques Center of Illinois. 1920 S. Wolf Rd. Wolfpoint Shopping Center. Great selection of merchandise. Antique, collectible, and specialty shops all located in one building. 50 shops. (708) 215-9418. *Daily, 10:00 A.M. - 5:00 P.M.*

Wilmington
Antiques. Water St. and Rt. 53, downtown. Glassware, furniture, clocks, china, books, advertising. (815) 476-7660.

Wyanet
Wyanet Antique Mall. 320 W. Main St. Hwys. 6 and 34. (815) 699-7256. Antiques, collectibles, crafts. *Daily, 9:00 A.M. - 5:00 P.M.*

INDIANA

ANDERSON
Anderson Antique Mall. 1407 Main St. 30,000 sq. ft, 4-story building. New mall. Glassware, collectibles, furniture, books. (800) 427-4121 or (317) 622-9517. *Monday - Saturday, 10:00 A.M. - 5:00 P.M.; Sundays, noon - 5:00 P.M.*

ANGOLA
Conklin's Olde Towne Mall. 101 W. Maumee. Antiques, collectibles, toys, glassware, gifts, furniture, country, Victorian. (219) 833-1740. *Monday - Saturday, 10:00 A.M. - 5:00 P.M.; Sundays, noon - 5:00 P.M.*

ARCADIA
Arcadia Antique Mall. 101 W. Main St. Antiques, collectibles. Mall is housed in a 2-story building that has recently been remodeled. Very attractive mall. 30+ dealers. (371) 984-7107. *Monday - Saturday, 10:00 A.M. - 6:00 P.M.; Sundays, 10:00 A.M. - 4:00 P.M.*

BLOOMINGTON
Bloomington Antique Mall. 311 W. 7th St. Laden with antiques and collectibles. 120+ booths. Credit cards accepted. (812) 332-2290. *Monday - Saturday, 10:00 A.M. - 5:00 P.M.; Fridays 10:00 A.M. - 8:00 P.M.; Sundays, noon - 5:00 P.M.*

BOSWELL
Antique Mall of Boswell. Hwy. 41. Antiques, collectibles, art, jewelry, vintage clothing, furniture. 40 dealers. (317) 869-5525. *Monday - Saturday, 10:00 A.M. - 5:00 P.M.; Sundays, noon - 5:00 P.M.*

BRAZIL
Brazil Antique Mall. 105 E. National Ave. Antiques and collectibles for every interest and budget. (812) 448-3275. *Monday - Saturday, 10:00 A.M. - 5:00 P.M.; Sundays, 1:00 - 5:00 P.M.*

BRAZIL
E-Z City Super Mall. 240 N. Depot St. Glassware, furniture, paper and advertising items, china. (812) 448-8988. *Daily, 9:00 A.M. - 5:00 P.M.*

BRAZIL
Treasure Chest Antiques Mall. 115 W. National Ave. A wide variety of antiques and collectibles, even for the most discerning collector. (812) 446-0505. *Monday - Saturday, 10:00 A.M. - 5:00 P.M.; Sundays, 1:00 - 5:00 P.M.*

BROOKSTON
Brookston Antiques. Hwy. 43. 7 miles north of I-65. 4,500 sq. ft. Antiques, collectibles,

furniture, quilts, primitives. (317) 563-3505. *Monday - Saturday, 10:00 A.M. - 5:00 P.M.; Sundays, 1:00 - 5:00 P.M.*

CARMEL
Antique Mall of Carmel. 622 Rangeline Rd. Mohawk Plaza Shopping Center. Antiques, collectibles, furniture, nice selection of wicker, jewelry, glassware. (317) 848-1280. *Monday - Saturday, 10:00 A.M. - 5:00 P.M.; Sundays, noon - 5:00 P.M.*

CENTERVILLE
Little Creek Antique Mall. Hwy. 46 West. 1/2 mile from I-65. Antiques, collectibles, quilts, primitives, dolls, linens, postcards, pottery. (812) 342-9289. *Monday - Saturday, 9:00 A.M. - 5:00 P.M.; Sundays, noon - 5:00 P.M.*

CENTERVILLE
Tom's Antique Mall. 117 E. Main St. Hwy. 40. 35 booths. Antiques, collectibles, nice selection of fine antique furniture, glassware, toys, quilts, banks, carousel horses. A complete stained-glass studio is located in the mall. (317) 855-3296. *Monday - Saturday, 10:00 A.M. - 5:00 P.M.; Sundays, 1:00 - 5:00 P.M.*

CENTERVILLE
Webb's Antique Mall. 200 W. Union St. 2 miles south of I-70, Exit 145. 70,000 sq. ft. facility. Mall features high-quality dealers selling fine furniture, collectibles, glassware, and quality items of all descriptions. No junk. Over 400 booths. This market is one of my favorite stops. (317) 855-5542. Credit cards accepted. Nice restaurant in the mall. Clean restrooms, wheelchair accessible, lots of walking. Ample parking. *Daily, 9:00 A.M. - 6:00 P.M.*

CHESTERTON
Yesterday's Treasures Antique Mall. 700 W. Broadway. 2-story building. Antiques, collectibles, art. 90+ dealers. (219) 926-2268. *Monday - Friday, 10:00 A.M. - 5:30 P.M.; Saturdays, 10:00 A.M. - 5:00 P.M.; Sundays, noon - 5:00 P.M.*

COLUMBIA CITY
The Hayloft Antique Mall. 224 W. Van Buren St. Antiques, collectibles. Mall specializes in primitives. *Monday - Saturday, 10:00 A.M. - 6:00 P.M.; Sundays, noon - 5:00 P.M.*

CORYDON
Griffin Building Antiques Mall. 113 E. Beaver St. Town square. Glassware, china, vintage clothing and jewelry, small desirables. (812) 738-3302. *Monday - Saturday, 10:00 A.M. - 5:00 P.M.; Sundays, 1:00 - 5:00 P.M.*

CORYDON
Red Barn Antique Mall. 215 Hwy. 62 West. Unique treasures of all kinds to be found at this market. Antiques and collectibles in all categories. (812) 738-2276. *Monday - Saturday, 10:00 A.M. - 5:00 P.M.; Sundays, 1:00 - 5:00 P.M.*

CRAWFORDSVILLE
Cabbages and Kings Antique Mall. 124 S. Washington St. (317) 362-2577. *Monday - Saturday, 10:00 A.M. - 5:00 P.M.; Sundays, 1:00 - 5:00 P.M.*

CROWNPOINT
Old Town Square Antique Mall. 103 W. Joliet St. Antiques, collectibles, Christmas room. (219) 662-1219. *Monday - Saturday, 10:00 A.M. - 5:00 P.M.; Sundays, noon - 5:00 P.M.*

DECATUR
Memories Past Antique Mall. 111 W. Jefferson St. Antiques, collectibles, decorator items, nice selection of furniture. (219) 728-2643. *Monday - Saturday, 9:00 A.M. - 5:00 P.M.; Sundays, noon - 4:00 P.M.*

DECATUR
Yvonne Marie's Antique Mall. 152 S. 2nd St. 3-story building. Well-stocked mall. 75+ dealers. (219) 724-2001. *Monday - Saturday, 10:00 A.M. - 5:00 P.M.; Sundays, 1:00 - 5:00 P.M.*

DELPHI
Delphi Antique Mall. 117 S. Washington St. Antiques and collectibles. (317) 546-3990. *Monday - Saturday, 11:00 A.M. - 5:00 P.M.; Sundays, 1:00 - 5:00 P.M.*

DELPHI
Town Square Mall. 110 W. Main St. Antiques, collectibles, crafts. A beauty shop and tanning-bed salon are also located in the mall. (317) 564-6317. *Monday - Saturday, 9:30 A.M. - 5:00 P.M.*

EDINBURGH
Back In Time Antique Mall. 126 E. Main Crossing. I-65, Exit 80. Antiques, collectibles. (812) 526-5409. *Monday - Saturday, 10:00 A.M. - 5:00 P.M.*

ELKHART
The Caverns of Elkhart. 111 Prairie Ct. Antiques and collectibles for every budget and taste. Glassware, country primitives, Victorian and Art Deco, Oriental. (219) 293-1484. *Monday - Saturday, 10:00 A.M. - 6:00 P.M.; Sundays, noon - 5:00 P.M.*

ELKHART
Elkhart Antique Mall. Rt. 19N. Wayne and Kay Hostetler, (219) 262-8763 or

262-3030. *Monday - Saturday, 10:00 A.M. - 5:00 P.M.; Sundays, noon - 5:00 P.M.*

ELLETTSVILLE

Ellettsville Antique Mall. Hwy. 46, downtown. Quality booths of fine antiques and collector items. (812) 876-4527. *Wednesday - Saturday, 10:00 A.M. - 6:00 P.M.; Sundays, noon - 5:00 P.M.*

EVANSVILLE

Old Evansville Antique Mall. 1419 W. Lloyd Expressway. Large, 3-story historic building. 24,000 sq. ft. Antiques, collectibles, furniture, quilts, jewelry, arts and crafts. Mall has many special promotions. 135 dealers. Air-conditioned and fully wheelchair accessible. Credit cards accepted. (812) 422-1986. *Tuesday - Saturday, 10:00 A.M. - 5:00 P.M.; Sundays, noon - 5:00 P.M.*

EVANSVILLE

Treasures Antiques and Collectibles. 800 N. Green River Rd. Eastland Mall. Large new mall, located in nice modern shopping mall. A prototype of things to come in this business. (800) 479-1363. *Monday - Saturday, 10:00 A.M. - 9:00 P.M.; Sundays, noon - 5:00 P.M.*

FRANKFORT

County Seat Antique Mall. 306 N. Jackson St. Antiques, collectibles, crafts. 20 dealers. (317) 659-5490. *Wednesday - Friday, 10:00 A.M. - 4:00 P.M.; Saturdays, 10:00 A.M. - 5:00 P.M.; Sundays, 1:00 - 4:00 P.M.*

FRANKLIN

Lighthouse Antique Mall. 62 W. Jefferson St. I-65 at the 90-mile marker. Mall features antique lighting, lots of collectible Christmas items, glassware, primitives, nice selection of furniture. (317) 738-3344. *Monday - Saturday, 10:00 A.M. - 5:00 P.M.; Sundays, noon - 5:00 P.M.*

FT. BRANCH

Windmill Antique Mall. Hwy. 41, 1/2 mile north of town. Fine antiques and sought-after collectibles. (812) 753-3053. *Monday - Saturday, 9:00 A.M. - 5:00 P.M.*

FT. WAYNE

Anna's Antique Mall. 1121 Taylor. Corner Taylor and Broadway. 18,000 sq. ft. Antiques, collectibles, jewelry, postcards, rugs, Art Deco, classic used furniture. (219) 426-4197. *Thursday - Saturday, 11:00 A.M. - 5:00 P.M.; Sundays, 10:00 A.M. - 2:00 P.M.*

Ft. Wayne
Antique Mall. 1510 Fairfield. 18,000 sq. ft., 2-story building. Antiques, collectibles, year-round Christmas shop. Specialty gift shop. This mall is the home of the Farnsworth TV Museum. 60+ dealers. Credit cards accepted. (219) 422-4030. *Monday - Saturday, 10:00 A.M. - 6:00 P.M.; Sundays, 1:00 - 5:00 P.M.*

Geneva
Jemea's Antique Mall. Hwy. 27 North. Antiques and collectibles. (219) 368-9411. *Tuesday - Saturday, 10:00 A.M. - 5:00 P.M.; Sundays, noon - 4:00 P.M.*

Goshen
Goshen Antique Mall. 107 S. Main St. Antiques, collectibles, furniture, butter churns, linens, toys, jewelry, glassware, pottery. 40 dealers. (219) 534-6141. *Monday - Saturday, 10:00 A.M. - 5:00 P.M.*

Greenfield
Sugar Creek Antique Mall. 22244 Hwy. 40. 4 miles west of town. Antiques, collectibles. Mall features a rough and "as found" furniture building. No crafts. (317) 467-4938. *Daily, 9:00 A.M. - 6:00 P.M.*

Huntington
Antiques and Not Mall. 515 N. Jefferson St. Downstairs Penny Mall Building. (219) 359-9824. *Sunday - Thursday, 11:00 A.M. - 5:00 P.M.; Fridays and Saturdays, 11:00 A.M. - 7:00 P.M.*

Huntington
Flint Creek Antique Mall. 3050 W. Park Dr. Antiques and collectibles. (219) 359-9824. *Monday - Saturday, 10:00 A.M. - 5:00 P.M.; Sundays, 1:00 - 5:00 P.M.*

Indianapolis
Diner and Antique Mall. 1105 Prospect. I-65, Exit 110. New mall, in downtown historic Fountain Square. Mall is located in an old bowling alley. (317) 686-6018. *Monday - Saturday, 10:00 A.M. - 5:00 P.M.; Sundays, noon - 5:00 P.M.*

Indianapolis
Downtown Antique Mall. 1044 Virginia Ave. Antiques, collectibles, glassware, toys, furniture, primitives. 40 dealers. Credit cards accepted. (317) 635-5336. *Monday - Saturday, 10:00 A.M. - 6:00 P.M.; Sundays, noon - 5:00 P.M.*

Indianapolis
Fountain Square Antique Mall. 1056 Virginia Ave. Large, 2-story mall, well

stocked. It also features a wonderful tea room. 70+ dealers. (317) 636-1056. *Monday - Saturday, 10:00 A.M. - 5:00 P.M.; Sundays, noon - 5:00 P.M.*

INDIANAPOLIS
Shadeland Antique Mall. 3444 N. Shadeland. I-70, Exit Shadeland St. Features antiques and collectibles. 100 dealers. (317) 542-7283. *Daily, 10:00 A.M. - 6:00 P.M.*

JASPER
Treasure Chest Antique Mall. 321 U.S. Hwy. 231 South. Southgate Shopping Center. New mall. Antiques, collectibles, primitives, quilts. Nice selection of Uhl pottery. 30 dealers. (812) 634-2986. *Monday - Friday, 10:00 A.M. - 6:00 P.M.; Saturdays, 10:00 A.M. - 4:00 P.M.; Sundays, noon - 4:00 P.M.; closed Wednesdays.*

KENTLAND
Kentland Antiques Mall. 206 N. Third St. Bill and Pat Denham, (219) 474-3221. *Monday - Saturday, 10:00 A.M. - 5:00 P.M.; Sundays, noon - 5:00 P.M.*

KNIGHTSTOWN
Heartland Antique Mall. 121 E. Main St. Credit cards accepted. (317) 345-5555. *Daily, 10:00 A.M. - 5:00 P.M.*

KNIGHTSTOWN
Knightstown Antique Mall. 136W. Carey St. Antiques, advertising items, glassware, toys, primitives, jewelry, furniture. This is a very large, well-stocked mall. (317) 345-5665. *Monday - Saturday, 10:00 A.M. - 5:00 P.M.; Sundays, 1:00 - 5:00 P.M.*

KNIGHTSTOWN
Lindon's Antique Mall. 32 E. Main St. Credit cards accepted. (317) 345-2545. *Monday - Saturday, 10:00 A.M. - 5:00 P.M.; Sundays, 1:00 - 5:00 P.M.*

KOONTZ LAKE
Keepsake Mall. Hwy. 23. Antiques, collectibles, no crafts. 25+ dealers. *Wednesday - Saturday, 10:00 A.M. - 5:00 P.M.; Sundays, noon - 5:00 P.M.*

LAFAYETTE
Antique Mall. 800 Main St. Antiques, collectibles, jewelry, furniture, art glass, primitives. Jeff Shearer, (317) 742-2469. *Monday - Saturday, 10:00 A.M. - 5:00 P.M.*

LA PORTE
Antique Junction Mall. 711 Lincolnway. Downtown. 10,000 sq. ft. (219) 324-0363. *Open daily.*

LA PORTE
Coachman Antique Mall. 500

> ### *Antiquer's Paradise*
> Madison is an antiquer's paradise. Besides the malls, there are numerous antique and specialty shops, some wonderful restaurants, bed-and-breakfast inns, art galleries, and museums. This town is a true Americana vacation in itself. For a complete package of information about Madison, contact the Convention and Visitors Bureau, 301 E. Main St., Madison, IN 47250. (800) 559-2956.

Lincolnway. 23,000 sq. ft. Antiques, collectibles, country, Victorian. A unique feature of this mall is its Carriage Shop. 100+ dealers. (219) 326-5933. *Monday - Saturday, 9:00 A.M. - 5:00 P.M.; Sundays, noon - 5:00 P.M.*

LEBANON
Cedars of Lebanon Antiques. 126 W. Washington St. Downtown. New mall. *Monday - Saturday, 10:00 A.M. - 5:00 P.M.; Sundays, noon - 5:00 P.M.*

LEBANON
Uncle Dudley's Antique Mall. 2040 Indianapolis Ave. Frank Woodruff, (317) 482-7007. *Daily, 10:00 A.M. - 6:00 P.M.*

LEO
Cellar Antique Mall. State Rt. 1, 1 block north of 4-way stop. Rear entrance and parking. Antiques, collectibles, jewelry, glassware, nice selection of furniture. (219) 627-6565. *Tuesday - Saturday, 10:00 A.M. - 5:00 P.M.; Sundays, noon - 4:00 P.M.*

LINTON
The Country Store Antique Mall. Hwy. 54, 4 miles west of town. Antiques, collectibles, glassware, gifts, and a nice selection of quality crafts. (812) 847-9023. *Monday - Saturday, 10:00 A.M. - 5:00 P.M.; Sundays, 1:00 - 5:00 P.M.*

LINTON
Linton Antique Mall. Hwy. 54, downtown. 2 buildings full of antiques, collectibles, furniture. (812) 847-8373. *Monday - Friday, 9:00 A.M. - 5:00 P.M.; Saturdays, 10:00 A.M. - 5:00 P.M.*

LOGANSPORT
Two Rivers Antique Mall. 412 E. Broadway. (219) 735-2119. *Monday - Saturday, 10:00 A.M. - 5:00 P.M.; Sundays, noon - 5:00 P.M.*

MADISON
Broadway Antique Mall. Corner 5th St. and Broadway St. Quality antiques and

collectibles. 60 dealers. (812) 265-6606. *Monday - Saturday, 10:00 A.M. - 5:00 P.M.; Sundays, noon - 5:00 P.M.*

MADISON
Lumbermill Antique Mall. 721 W. First St. 2-story facility. Quality antiques and collectibles. (812) 273-3040. *Monday - Saturday, 10:00 A.M. - 5:00 P.M.; Sundays, noon - 6:00 P.M.*

MADISON
Madison Antique Mall. 401 E. 2nd St. 3-story facility. Large selection of furniture, antiques; excellent selection of collectibles and smalls. (812) 265-6399. *Monday - Saturday, 9:00 A.M. - 6:00 P.M.; Sundays, 1:00 - 5:00 P.M.*

MADISON
Miracle Antique Mall. 301 Jefferson St. Antiques, collectibles and crafts.

MADISON
Wallace's Antique Mall. 125 E. Main St. 2-story facility. Antiques, collectibles, secondhand items, bric-a-brac. (812) 265-2473. *Daily, 11:00 A.M. - 5:00 P.M.*

MICHIGAN CITY
Antique Market. Junction I-94 and Hwy. 421. 75 dealers. (219) 879-4084. *Monday - Saturday, 10:00 A.M. - 5:00 P.M.; Sundays, noon - 5:00 P.M.*

MICHIGAN CITY
Mona's Treasure Chest and Waterford Flea Market. 4496 N. Wozniak. (219) 874-5475. *Saturdays and Sundays, 9:00 A.M. - 5:00 P.M.*

MISHAWAKA
Antiques Etc. 110 Lincolnway East. Downtown. Gallery of antique and boutique shops. 30 dealers. (219) 258-5722. *Tuesday - Saturday, 10:00 A.M. - 5:00 P.M.; Sundays, noon - 5:00 P.M.*

MITCHELL
Mitchell Antique Mall. Corner of 7th and Main Sts. Several antique shops and nice restaurants located adjacent to mall. (812) 849-4497. *Monday - Saturday, 10:00 A.M. - 5:00 P.M.; Sundays, noon - 5:00 P.M.*

MORGANTOWN
Gaslight Antique Mall. 79 W. Washington St. (812) 597-2117.

MUNCIE
Off Broadway Antique Mall. 2404 N. Broadway. Jack and Peggy Shafer, (317) 747-5000. *Open daily.*

NAPPANEE
Amishland Antique Mall. 106 W. Market St. (219) 773-4795. *Monday - Saturday, 10:00 A.M. - 5:00 P.M.*

NASHVILLE
Albert's Mall. Keith and Patti Alberts. Star Rt. 46W. 4,000 sq. ft. Antiques, collectibles, glassware, primitives, furniture, coins, clocks, china. (812) 988-2397. *Monday - Saturday, 10:00 A.M. - 5:00 P.M.; Sundays, 1:00 - 5:00 P.M.; closed Tuesdays.*

NASHVILLE
Brown County Antique Mall. State Rt. 46E. 3 miles from town. Antiques, collectibles. Mall specializes in furniture. (812) 988-1025. *Monday - Saturday, 10:00 A.M. - 5:00 P.M.; Sundays, noon - 5:00 P.M.*

NASHVILLE
Frontier Antique Mall. 82 E. Gould St. (812) 988-0800. *Daily, 10:00 A.M. - 5:00 P.M.*

NEW ALBANY
Old New Albany Antique Mall. 225 State St. 3-story building. Antiques and collectibles. (812) 948-1890. *Open daily.*

NEW ALBANY
Seller Antique Mall. 128 W. Main St. Antiques, collectibles, glassware, country, primitives, furniture. 80+ dealers. *Monday - Saturday, 10:00 A.M. - 4:00 P.M.*

NOBLESVILLE
Noblesville Antique Mall. 20 N. 9th St. Downtown courthouse square. Mall is located in a beautifully restored, three-story, 1880s building. Antiques, collectibles, furniture, books, Art Deco, nice selection of black memorabilia, glass. Larry and Jan Smith, (317) 773-5095. *Monday - Saturday, 9:00 A.M. - 5:00 P.M.; Sundays, noon - 5:00 P.M.*

PENDLETON
Pendleton Antique Mall. 123 W. State St. Antiques and collectibles. 30 dealers. (317) 778-2303. *Monday - Saturday, 10:00 A.M. - 5:00 P.M.; Sundays, 1:00 - 5:00 P.M.*

PERU
Peru Antique Mall. 21 E. Main St. Antiques and collectibles. (219) 473-8179. *Monday - Saturday, 10:00 A.M. - 5:00 P.M.; Sundays, 1:00 - 5:00 P.M.; closed Wednesdays.*

PLAINFIELD
Gilley's Antique Mall. 1209 W. Main St. Hwy. 40. Two buildings. Outdoor flea market on weekends during the summer. 300+ booths. (317) 839-8779. *Daily, 10:00 A.M. - 5:00 P.M.*

PORTLAND
Portland Antique Emporium. 105 N. Meridian St. Antiques and collectibles. Well-stocked mall, with many fine quality

items and an excellent array of collectibles. 80+ dealers. (219) 726-2712. *Monday - Saturday, 10:00 A.M. - 6:00 P.M.; Sundays, noon - 5:00 P.M.*

ROCKVILLE

Covered Bridge Mall. Downtown, East side of courthouse square. 5,000 sq. ft. mall. Antiques, collectibles, and nice selection of crafts.

ROCKVILLE

Rockville Antique Mall. 411 E. Ohio St. Hwy. 36. Antiques, collectibles, glassware, primitives, excellent selection of quality furniture. 20 dealers. (800) 585-9264 or (317) 569-6873. *Monday - Saturday, 10:00 A.M. - 5:00 P.M.; Sundays, 1:00 - 5:00 P.M.; closed Thursdays.*

ROSSVILLE

Back Through Time Antique Mall. 9 W. Main St. Antiques and collectibles in every imaginable category, from furniture to miniatures. (317) 379-3299. *Monday - Saturday, 10:00 A.M. - 5:00 P.M.*

RUSHVILLE

Rush County Mall. 700 block of W. 5th St. Antiques, collectibles. (317) 932-5227. *Monday - Saturday, 9:00 A.M. - 6:00 P.M.; Sundays, noon - 6:00 P.M.*

SCOTTSBURG

Scottsburg Antique Mall. 4 Main St. I-65, Exit 29, east 1 mile. 10,000 sq. ft., two-story facility. Well-stocked mall. Quality antiques, collectibles, and lots of smalls. (812) 752-4645. *Monday - Saturday, 9:00 A.M. - 5:00 P.M.; Sundays, noon - 5:00 P.M.*

SEYMOUR

Crossroads Antique Mall. 311 Holiday Square, behind Holiday Inn. 10,000 sq. ft. facility. Well-stocked mall, with unique and original items in all collector fields. Antiques, collectibles, country accessories. Outdoor flea market on Saturdays. Rest rooms, snack bar, wheelchair accessible. Ample parking. (812) 522-5675. *Daily, 9:00 A.M. - 5:00 P.M.*

SHIPSHEWANA

Amish Country Antique Mall. Hwy. 5. 1/2 mile north of the flea market. (219) 768-4060. *Monday - Saturday, 10:00 A.M. - 5:00 P.M.*

SOUTH BEND

Unique Antique Mall. 50981 Hwy. 33 North. Antiques, collectibles, jewelry, fine jewelry, dolls, bears, toys, glassware. Furniture: oak, walnut, cherry. 100+ dealers. (219) 271-1799. *Daily, 10:00 A.M. - 5:00 P.M.*

SWAYZEE
Swayzee Antique Mall. Rt. 13, downtown. (317) 922-7903. *Mondays, Wednesdays, and Thursdays, 10:00 A.M. - 5:00 P.M.; Fridays and Saturdays, 10:00 A.M. - 6:00 P.M.; Sundays, noon - 6:00 P.M.; closed Tuesdays.*

TERRE HAUTE
Ancient Thymes Mall. 1600 S. Third St. Hwy. 41. (812) 238-2178. *Open daily.*

TERRE HAUTE
Antiques, Crafts and Things Mall. Honey Creek Square South. (812) 232-8959. *Monday - Saturday, 10:00 A.M. - 8:00 P.M.; Sundays, noon - 5:00 P.M.*

TERRE HAUTE
Granny's Daughter Mall. 11750 S. Hwy. 41. 7 miles south of I-70. (812) 299-8277. *Monday - Saturday, 10:00 A.M. - 6:00 P.M.; Sundays, noon - 5:00 P.M.*

TERRE HAUTE
Nancy's Downtown Mall. 600 Wabash Ave. (812) 238-1129. *Monday - Saturday, 10:00 A.M. - 5:00 P.M.; Sundays, noon - 6:00 P.M.*

TERRE HAUTE
Shady Lane Antique Mall. 9247 S. Hwy. 41. Six miles south of I-70. (812) 299-1625. *Tuesday - Saturday, 10:00 A.M. - 5:00 P.M.; Sundays, 1:00 - 5:00 P.M.*

THORNTOWN
Countryside Antique Mall and Indian Trading Post. Hwy. 52. 10,000 sq. ft. Antiques, collectibles, nice selection of furniture. Large section of collector books. The trading post features an excellent selection of Indian arts, crafts, and jewelry. (317) 436-7200. *Daily, 10:00 A.M. - 5:00 P.M.*

TIPTON
Dezerland Antique World. Sweetland Ave. North. 50,000 sq. ft. facility. Quality antiques and collectibles, furniture, rough room, lots of showcases. This is a quality mall, almost a city block in size. Fifties diner. Classic cars for sale. 100+ dealers. *Tuesday - Saturday, 10:00 A.M. - 6:00 P.M.; Sundays, 10:00 A.M. - 5:00 P.M.; closed Mondays.*

TIPTON
Timeless Treasures Antique Mall. 116 S. Main St. Antiques and collectibles. (317) 675-4537. *Tuesdays, Wednesdays, Thursdays, and Sundays, noon - 5:00 P.M.; Fridays and Saturdays, 10:00 A.M. - 5:00 P.M.; closed Mondays.*

WINCHESTER
Winchester Antique Mall. 115 W. Franklin St. Town square. Antiques, collectibles, Civil War items, glassware, jewelry, furniture. Credit cards accepted. (317) 584-4100. *Monday - Saturday, 10:00 A.M. - 5:00 P.M.; Sundays, noon - 5:00 P.M.*

WOLCOTTVILLE
Wolcottville Antique Mall. 106 N. Main St. 10,000 sq. ft. Antiques, collectibles, bric-a-brac, crafts. Ted Strawser, (219) 854-3111. *Monday - Saturday, 9:00 A.M. - 5:00 P.M.*

IOWA

AMES
Memories of Main Antique Mall. 203 Main St. 11,000 sq. ft. Lots of fine antiques and collector items of all kinds. 75+ dealers. (515) 233-2519. *Open daily.*

BLOOMFIELD
Memory Lane Antique Mall. 208 E. Franklin St. Glassware, china, books, toys, banks, dolls, RR items, country primitives, kitchenware, pottery, crocks and bottles, china and silver. 60 booths. (515) 664-1714. *Monday - Saturday, 8:00 A.M. - 5:00 P.M.; Sundays, 1:00 - 5:00 P.M.*

CASEY
Pieces of Olde Antique Mall. Downtown. Glassware, china, silver, dolls, toys, linen, quilts, country items, decorator finds. (515) 746-2853. *Daily, 9:00 A.M. - 6:00 P.M.*

CENTERVILLE
Country Heart Antiques and Uniques. Downtown, north side of the town square. Antique furniture, primitives, collectibles, and crafts by local artisans. (515) 437-1687.

CLARINDA
Gabby's Treasures Antique Mall. 417 S. 8th St. Quality antiques and collectibles for every taste and budget. Air-conditioned. (712) 542-4380. *Monday - Saturday, 9:00 A.M. - 5:00 P.M.*

DES MOINES
The Brass Armadillo Antique Mall. Mall has two locations: (1) S.E. 14th St. and Indianola Rd, (515) 244-2140 or (800) 375-2140; (2) 2206 S.W. Third St., (515) 964-2003 or (800) 398-0105. Great variety of quality antiques and collectibles. Glassware, furniture, quilts, crocks, pottery, china. Over 400 dealers in both malls.

IOWA CITY
The Antique Mall. 507 S. Gilbert. I-80, Exit 244. Good

selection of quality antiques. (319) 354-1822. *Daily, 10:00 A.M. - 5:00 P.M.*

KEOKUK
Showcase Antique Mall. 800 Main St. Antiques and collectibles. Furniture, glassware, art, lots of Roseville pottery, quilts. (319) 354-1822. *Monday - Saturday, 10:00 A.M. - 5:00 P.M.; Sundays, 11:00 A.M. - 4:00 P.M.*

LOGAN
Logan Antique Mall. Hwy. 30. Vintage jewelry and clothing, glassware, art glass, pottery, decorator finds. 40 dealers. (712) 844-2781. *Open daily.*

MASON CITY
North Federal Antique Mall. 524 N. Federal St. Good variety of items. 40 dealers. (515) 423-0841. *Open daily.*

MASON CITY
Olde Central Antique Mall. 317 S. Delaware St., across from Southbridge Mall. 2 levels, 8,000 sq. ft., 40 dealers. Antiques, collectibles, gift and decorator items, jewelry, glassware, linens. Snack bar, rest rooms, wheelchair accessible. Ample parking. Dealers welcome. (515) 423-7315. *Monday - Saturday, 10:00 A.M. - 5:00 P.M; Sundays, 11:00 A.M. - 4:00 P.M.*

MISSOURI VALLEY
Antique, Arts and Crafts Mall. ½ mile west of I-29 on Hwy. 30. Vintage soda fountain. 60 antique dealers, 45 crafters. (712) 642-2125. *Monday - Saturday, 9:30 A.M. - 5:30 P.M.; Thursdays, 9:30 A.M. - 8:00 P.M.; Sundays, noon - 5:30 P.M.*

MUSCATINE
River Bend Cove Antique Mall. 418 Grandview Ave. Antiques, collectibles, lots of glassware. (319) 263-9929. *Monday - Saturday, 10:00 A.M. - 5:00 P.M.; Sundays, noon - 5:00 P.M.*

MUSCATINE
Rivers Edge Antiques. Corner of Second and Walnut Sts. Antiques, collectibles. Plenty of small desirables. Some furniture. (319) 264-2351. *Monday - Saturday, 10:00 A.M. - 6:00 P.M.; Sundays, noon - 5:00 P.M.*

ONAWA
Onawa Antique Mall. Off I-29, between Sioux City and Omaha. Antique furniture, collectibles, glassware, china, linens, coins, dolls, kitchenware. (712) 423-1487. *Monday - Saturday, 10:00 A.M. - 5:00 P.M.; Sundays, 1:00 - 5:00 P.M.*

Pacific Junction
Antique Junction Mall. 14 miles south of Council Bluffs on I-29, at Glenwood, Exit 35. 24,000 sq. ft. One of the midwest's newest and finest malls, worth visiting. 138 booths, 80+ dealers. Tearoom. Air-conditioned. Market also conducts two large flea markets, spring and fall; call for dates. (712) 622-3532. *Monday - Saturday, 10:00 A.M. - 5:00 P.M.; Sundays, noon - 5:00 P.M.*

Pella
Red Ribbon Antique Mall. 812 Washington St. Antiques and collectibles of every description. 45 dealers. (515) 628-2181. *Open daily.*

Spirit Lake
Heritage Square Antique Mall. Downtown. Antiques and collectibles only. *Open daily; closed January and February.*

Thayer
L and H Antique Mall. Hwy. 34. 14 miles west of I-35, on Hwy. 34. Antiques and collectibles. 20 dealers. (515) 338-2223. *Monday - Saturday, 10:00 A.M. - 5:00 P.M.; Sundays, noon - 5:00 P.M.*

Tripoli
Golden Age Antique Mall. 120 S. Main St. Large antique mall in a small town. Dealers welcome. (319) 882-3076. *Daily.*

Waterloo
Antique Galleries. 618 Sycamore St. Downtown. Antiques, collectibles. Glassware, kitchenware, country primitives, Victorian and Art Deco items, Oriental, china. 30 dealers. *Monday - Saturday, 10:00 A.M. - 5:30 P.M.*

Waterloo
Venice Antiques. Hwy. 92, halfway between Omaha and Waterloo. Rt. 1, Box 191 E. Antiques, glass, primitives, toys, books, jewelry, collectibles. Separate furniture building. 67 dealers. (402) 359-5782. *Monday - Saturday, 10:00 A.M. - 5:00 P.M.; Sundays, 1:00 - 5:00 P.M.*

West Amana
West Amana General Store. Antiques, collectibles, gifts, curios. Something here for every budget and interest. 12 dealers. (319) 622-3945. *Daily, 10:00 A.M. - 5:00 P.M.*

KANSAS

Augusta
Two Fools Antiques Mall. 429 State St. 67010. Mall named tongue-in-cheek for the husband-and-wife team who operate it. 60+ dealers. (316)

775-2588. *Daily, 11:00 A.M. - 9:00 P.M.; closed Thursdays.*

AUGUSTA
White Eagle Antique Mall. 2+ miles west of town on Hwy. 54. Good variety of merchandise at this mall. Antiques and collector items in all categories. 100+ dealers. Rest rooms, snack bar, wheelchair accessible. Ample parking. (316) 775-2812. *Monday - Saturday, 10:00 A.M. - 9:00 P.M.; Sundays, noon - 7:00 P.M.*

BONNER SPRINGS
Bunny Patch Craft Mall. 607 Front St. (K-32 Hwy). Next to Dolly Madison store. 60+ booths of handmade crafts. (913) 441-6043.

BONNER SPRINGS
Oak Street Antique Mall. 205 Oak St. Glassware, quilts, china, small desirables, some furniture. 25 dealers. Park and enter building from rear. (913) 441-8999.

CANEY
Blackledge Antique Mall. Junction of Hwys. 75 and 166, downtown. 25,000 sq. ft. 2 floors. Quality antiques and collectibles. This mall also has a separate craft area. (316) 879-2210 or 879-5198. *Monday - Saturday, 10:00 A.M. - 6:00 P.M.; Sundays, 1:00 - 5:00 P.M.*

CANEY
Caney Antique Mall. South edge of town, on Hwy. 75. This is a large, well-stocked mall, with good variety: dolls, toys, glassware, china, jewelry, advertising items, country primitives. 100 dealers. (316) 879-5478. *Monday - Saturday, 9:00 A.M. - 6:00 P.M.; Sundays, 1:00 - 5:00 P.M.*

CHETOPA
Mary's Flea Market. 324 Maple St. Collectibles, tools and "junque." *Open Tuesday - Saturday; closed Sundays and Mondays.*

DOUGLAS
Treasures Antiques Co. 24 miles southeast of Wichita, or 12 miles south of Augusta. Antiques, good selection of refinished furniture. (316) 746-3131. *Weekdays, 10:00 A.M. - 5:00 P.M.; Sundays, 1:00 - 5:00 P.M.; closed Tuesdays and holidays.*

ELK FALLS
Tiffany Gallery. 601 Montgomery. 1 block south of highway and 1 block east of Main St. *Open Fridays, Saturdays, Sundays, and Mondays.*

EMPORIA
Wild Rose Antique Mall. 311

Graham St. Antiques, collectibles, glass, quilts, jewelry, primitives, and lots of miscellaneous. Mall takes items on consignment. Formerly known as the Junque Yard Antique Mall. 50 dealers. (316) 343-8862 or 342-8662. *Tuesday - Saturday, 11:00 A.M. - 5:00 P.M.; Sundays, 1:00 - 5:00 P.M.; closed Mondays.*

GALENA

Old Miners Antique and Flea Market Mall. 610 S. Main St. Crafts, antiques, collectibles, baseball cards, lots of new bookcases, wide variety. (316) 733-9814. *Monday - Saturday, 9:30 A.M. - 5:00 P.M.; Sundays, noon - 5:00 P.M.*

GARNETT

Emporium on the Square. 415 Oak St. Nice antiques, crafts, collectibles. 19 booths. (913) 448-6459. *Monday - Saturday, 10:00 A.M. - 5:00 P.M.; Sundays, 1:00 - 5:00 P.M.*

HOLTON

Yesterday's Antique Mall. Downtown, East side of town square. Mall has lots of fine furniture, R.S. Prussia, Roseville, toys, quilts, and jewelry. (913) 364-3382. *Monday - Saturday, 9:00 A.M. - 5:00 P.M.*

HOWARD

Heritage House Mini Mall. 224 N. Wabash St. Antiques, coins, collectibles, crafts, and furniture. (316) 374-2309. *Monday - Friday, 9:00 A.M. - 7:00 P.M.; Saturdays, 9:00 A.M. - 5:00 P.M.; Sundays, 1:00 - 5:30 P.M.*

KANSAS CITY

Antique and Craft City. 1270 Merriam Lane. I-35, at the Lamar Exit. Coca-Cola collectibles, telephones, lamps, jewelry, good variety of stock. 70 dealers. (913) 677-0752. *Tuesday - Sunday, 9:00 A.M. - 6:00 P.M.; closed Mondays.*

LAWRENCE

Antique Mall. 830 Massachusetts. Downtown. (913) 842-1328. 16,000 sq. ft. 50+ antique and collectible dealers located on the first floor. The second floor is devoted to 50+ arts and crafts dealers in a craft mall known as The Artisans' Loft. Lots of nice quality folk art and crafts here.

LAWRENCE

Quantrill's Antique Mall. 811 New Hampshire St. Downtown. Antiques and collectibles for every taste and budget. Company also operates a flea market on the premises. Snack bar, rest rooms, wheelchair accessible. Ample parking. (913) 842-6616. *Daily, 10:00 A.M. - 5:00 P.M.*

LEAVENWORTH

11-Worth Antique Mall. Con Denney. 410 S. 5th St. If you are superstitious, it is not recommended that you stay overnight in Leavenworth. (913) 651-2424. *Tuesday - Saturday, 10:00 A.M. - 5:00 P.M.*

MANHATTAN

On The "Avenue" Antique Mall. 413 Poyntz Ave., downtown. Antiques, collectibles, furniture, vintage clothing, paper goods, jewelry, books, glassware, quilts. (913) 539-9116. *Monday - Saturday, 10:00 A.M. - 6:00 P.M.; Sundays, 1:00 - 5:00 P.M.*

MCPHERSON

Main Street Antique Mall. 119 N. Main St. 8,500 sq. ft. in a beautifully restored building. China, antiques, collectibles, jewelry, quilts, furniture, dolls, primitives, glassware. (316) 241-7272. *Monday - Saturday, 10:00 A.M. - 5:30 P.M.; Sundays, 1:00 - 5:00 P.M.*

MISSION

Lincoln Antiques. 5636 Johnson Dr. Corner Reeds Rd. and Johnson Dr. 30 dealers. (913) 384-6811. *Monday - Saturday, 10:00 A.M. - 5:30 P.M.; Sundays, noon - 5:30 P.M.*

OLATHE

Townsquare Uniques. 138-B South Clairborn. Antiques, crafts, collectibles. (913) 829-3661. *Daily, 10:00 A.M. - 6:00 P.M.; Tuesdays, 10:00 A.M. - 8:00 P.M.; closed Sundays.*

OSAGE

Section House Antiques. 609 Market St. Glassware, collectibles, furniture, lamps, clocks, china, pottery, country primitives, kitchenware. (913) 528-8198. *Tuesday - Saturday, 10:00 A.M. - 6:00 P.M.; Sundays, 1:00 - 5:00 P.M.*

OSWEGO

Circle C Trading Post. 518 Commercial St. Antiques, collectibles, crafts, leaded glass, gifts. Furniture, both new and used; lots of nice reproduction oak furniture. Snack bar, rest rooms. Ample parking. (316) 795-3081. *Tuesday - Saturday, 11:00 A.M. - 5:00 P.M.*

PAOLA

Magdalena's. Downtown, West side of town square. 10,000 sq. ft. Antiques, collectibles, and lots of old medicinal remedies. Mall also takes items on consignment. (913) 294-5048.

PAOLA

Park Square Emporium.

Downtown on west side of town square. Air-conditioned. Lots of collectibles, books, comics, records, jewelry, and toys. Mall also has a good selection of model trains, especially HO items. 50 dealers. (913) 294-9004. *Monday - Saturday, 9:00 A.M. - 5:30 P.M.; Thursdays, 9:00 A.M. - 8:00 P.M.; Sundays, noon - 5:00 P.M.*

PARSONS
Doogie's Place. 5401 Main St. Antiques and collectibles of every description, including glass, coins, paper and advertising items, linens, and quilts. (316) 421-3950. *Open daily.*

PARSONS
Old Glory Flea Market, Antiques and Craft Mall. 5021 W. Main St. Hwy. 160 West. Antiques, crafts, glassware, collectibles, primitives, decorator items, silver, linens, quilts. Longaberger basket consultant on premises. 75+ dealers. (316) 421-6326. *Monday - Saturday, 9:00 A.M. - 6:00 P.M.; Sunday, 1:00 - 6:00 P.M.*

PERRY
Perry Antique and Craft Mall. 111 Elm St. (Between Lawrence and Topeka on Hwy. 24). Antiques, jewelry, tools, and Hummels. Handmade local crafts. (913) 597-5250. *Monday - Thursday, 10:00 A.M. - 6:00 P.M.; Fridays and Saturdays, 9:00 A.M. - 5:00 P.M.; Sundays, noon - 5:00 P.M.*

PITTSBURG
Jayhawk Antique/Craft Mall and Flea Market. 4030 N. Hwy. 69. General line of antiques and collectibles. Large selection of locally made crafts and decorator items. 175+ dealers. Snack bar, rest rooms, wheelchair accessible. Ample parking. *Daily, 10:00 A.M. - 6:00 P.M.*

PRATT
Main Street Antiques and Collectibles Mall. 213 S. Main St. 7,000 sq. ft. Antiques, antique furniture, pictures, dishes, quilts, fishing, railroad and western items, books, toys, tools. Air-conditioned. (316) 672-6770. *Monday - Saturday, 10:00 A.M. -*

> **What State Has the Most Antique/Craft Malls?**
>
> According to my research, the greatest number of antique malls is located in the state of Missouri, with 115 malls, far outdistancing the state of Indiana, which has 99 malls.

5:30 P.M.; Sundays, 1:00 - 5:00 P.M.

SEVERY
Swap Shop Antique Mall. Rt. 1, Box 173. 2 miles west of 99 and Severy Junction on Hwy. 96. Antiques and collectibles. Good selection of cast iron items, furniture, dolls, toys, black memorabilia, jewelry, quilts, and marbles. Clarence Pettyjohn, (316) 736-2854. *Monday - Thursday, 9:00 A.M. - 6:00 P.M.; Sundays, 1:00 - 6:00 P.M.; closed Tuesdays and Wednesdays.*

TOPEKA
Antique Plaza of Topeka. 2935 S.W. Topeka Blvd. 29th and Topeka, Holiday Square Shopping Center. 18,000 sq. ft. This mall has an excellent selection of quality antique furniture, Flow Blue, cameo glass, stoneware, and Staffordshire. Decorator is also available on the premises. 52 booths. (913) 267-7411. *Monday - Saturday, 10:00 A.M. - 5:30 P.M.; Sundays, noon - 5:00 P.M.*

TOPEKA
Topeka Antique Mall and Flea Market. 5427 S.W. 28th Court. Furniture, stoneware, quilts, jewelry, Flow Blue, Oriental, primitives, pottery. 50 booths. Company also conducts flea market on weekends. (913) 273-2969. *Tuesday - Sunday, 10:00 A.M. - 5:00 P.M.*

TOPEKA
Washburn View Antique Mall. 22nd and Washburn Sts. I-40 Exit 5, North 2.2 miles on Burlingame. Dolls, dishes, furniture, antiques, collectibles. Special section of furniture in the rough. 50+ dealers. Credit cards accepted. (913) 234-0949. *Open daily.*

TOPEKA
Wheatland Antique Mall. 2121 S.W. 37th St. I-470 off Burlingame Rd., in the Burlingame South Shopping Center. 4500 sq. ft. Antiques and collectibles. Layaway available. Mall takes items on consignment. Excellent restaurant, "A Lite A'Fare," located next door. (913) 266-3266. *Monday - Friday, 10:00 A.M. - 5:30 P.M.; Saturdays and Sundays, 10:00 A.M. - 5:00 P.M.*

TOWANDA
Towanda Antiques Mall and Blue Moon Saloon and Restaurant. 319 N. Main St. 40 dealers in an historic setting. Lots of depression glass, jewelry, collectibles, and furniture. This mall has a unique restaurant, with an

antique soda fountain and old-fashioned entertainment on Friday and Saturday evenings (reservations recommended). (316) 536-2544. *Thursday - Saturday, 11:00 A.M. - 10:00 P.M.; Sundays, noon - 9:00 P.M.*

WASHINGTON
George and Martha's Antique Mall. 321 C St. Downtown. 4,500 sq. ft. Antiques, collectibles, glass, toys, primitives, political items, tools, furniture, pottery, china. (316) 325-2445. *Daily, 9:00 A.M. - 5:00 P.M.; Sundays, 1:00 - 5:00 P.M.*

WELLINGTON
Antique Merchants Mall. 106 S. Washington St. Antiques, collectibles, primitives. 35+ dealers. (316) 326-8484. *Tuesday - Saturday, 10:00 A.M. - 5:00 P.M.; Sundays, 1:00 - 5:00 P.M.; closed Mondays.*

WICHITA
Annie's Antique Mall. 61st St. and North Hydraulic. Park City area, 1/2 mile east of I-35. 10,000 sq. ft. Antiques, collectibles, furniture, fishing items, jewelry, lots of Coca-Cola items and toys. Air-conditioned. 80+ dealers. (316) 744-1999. *Mondays and Tuesdays, 10:00 A.M. - 6:00 P.M.; Wednesday - Saturday, 10:00 A.M. - 8:00 P.M.; Sundays, 1:00 - 6:00 P.M.*

WICHITA
Hewitt's Antique Mall. 232 N. Market St. Downtown. Advertising items, fine art, books, primitives, maps, quilts, jewelry, furniture, glassware, pottery, ephemera. (316) 263-2305. *Monday - Saturday, 9:30 A.M. - 5:00 P.M.; Sundays, 1:00 - 5:00 P.M.*

WICHITA
Park City Antique Mall. 6227 N. Broadway. I-135, take 61st St., North exit. West 1/2 mile. Mall is located in shopping center. 20,000 sq. ft. Large, clean, well-stocked antique mall. 200+ booths. (316) 744-2025. *Monday - Wednesday, 9:30 A.M. - 6:00 P.M.; Thursday - Saturday, 9:30 A.M. - 7:00 P.M.; Sundays, 9:30 A.M. - 6:00 P.M.*

WICHITA
Treasure Mall. 1255 S. Tyler. West Kellogg and Tyler. Antiques, crafts, furniture, dolls, jewelry, primitives, gifts, cookie jars. Dealers welcome. (316) 729-0560. *Wednesday - Saturday, 10:00 A.M. - 5:00 P.M.; Sundays, 1:00 - 5:00 P.M.*

WICHITA
White Eagle Antique Mall. Hwy. 54, 11 miles east of

town. Good variety of merchandise at this mall. Antiques and collector items in all categories. 100+ dealers. Rest rooms, snack bar, wheelchair accessible. Ample parking. (316) 775-2812. *Monday - Saturday, 10:00 A.M. - 9:00 P.M.; Sundays, noon - 7:00 P.M.*

WINFIELD

Antique Mall. 1400 S. Main St. Furniture, books, advertising items, toys, jewelry, coins, primitives. Nice selection of reference books for collectors. Market also has monthly outdoor flea market on Sundays. (316) 221-1065 or 221-0392. *Monday - Saturday, 10:00 A.M. - 6:30 P.M.; Sundays, 1:00 - 5:00 P.M.*

KENTUCKY

AUGUSTA

Augusta Antique Mall. Great booths full of fine antiques and collectibles in all categories. Ample parking. (608) 756-2653. *Thursday - Sunday, noon - 7:00 P.M.*

BARDSTOWN

Bardstown Antique Market. 20 N. Third St. Antiques, collectibles, crafts, Christmas items, nice selection of railroad items. (502) 348-3139. *Monday - Saturday, 10:00 A.M. - 5:00 P.M.*

BARDSTOWN

Kimberly Run Antique Center. 200 E. Nohn Rowan Blvd. Hwy. 245. Antiques, collectibles, furniture, many unusual lamps, clocks, furniture. 60 dealers. (502) 348-7555. *Monday - Saturday, 10:00 A.M. - 5:00 P.M.; Sundays, 1:00 - 5:00 P.M.*

BARDSTOWN

Town and Country Antique Mall. N. Third St. Antiques, collectibles, good selection of locally made crafts. (502) 348-7708. *Open daily.*

BEAVER DAM

Downtown Antique Mall. 103 N. Main St. Glassware, furniture, china, quilts, dolls, advertising, art. (502) 274-4774. *Open daily.*

BEREA

Chestnut Street Antique Mall. 420 Chestnut St. Antiques, collectibles, primitives, furniture, majolica, Flow Blue, R.S. Prussia, Nippon. (606) 986-2883. *Monday - Saturday, 10:00 A.M. - 5:00 P.M.; Sundays, 1:00 - 5:00 P.M.*

BEREA

Impressions Antique Mall. I-75, Exit 76. A variety of antiques and collectibles can be found at this mall to delight even the most discerning collector. (606) 988-

8177. *Monday - Saturday, 10:00 A.M. - 9:00 P.M.; Sundays, 1:00 - 5:00 P.M.*

BEREA
Todd's Antique Mall and Flea Market. Hwy. 21 West. Mainly permanent booths with antiques and collectibles. Great selection of merchandise, from Flow Blue to Griswold skillets. Rest rooms, wheelchair accessible. Ample parking. (606) 986-9961. *Daily.*

BOWLING GREEN
River Bend Antique Mall. 315 Beech Bend Rd. Antiques, collectibles, glassware, furniture, primitives. Nice selection of reference books. Credit cards accepted. (502) 781-6773. *Monday - Saturday, 10:00 A.M. - 5:00 P.M.; Sundays, noon - 5:00 P.M.*

CADIZ
Blue Moon Antique Mall. Hwy. 68 East and Bypass. Antique furniture, collectibles, dishes, primitives, china, kitchenware. (502) 522-4245. *Open daily.*

CADIZ
Cadiz Antique Mall. Business Rt. 68, downtown. A typical antique mall. Expect to find the unexpected here in quality antiques and collector items. (502) 522-7880. *Open daily.*

CADIZ
Main Street Antique Mall. Business Rt. 68, downtown. Collectibles, glassware, vintage jewelry, books, pottery. (502) 522-7665. *Open daily.*

CADIZ
Simpler Tymes Antique Mall and Frame Shop. Business Rt. 68, downtown. Treasures of all kinds: glassware, lamps, decorator items, jewelry, vintage clothing. (502) 522-0214. *Open daily.*

CADIZ
Starlight Antique Mall. Business Rt. 68, downtown. Antiques and collectibles in all categories. (502) 522-1410. *Open daily.*

DANVILLE
Antique Mall. 158 N. 3rd St. Mall is located in historic church. Antiques, collectibles. (606) 236-3026. *Tuesday - Saturday, 10:00 A.M. - 5:00 P.M.; Sundays, 1:00 - 5:00 P.M.*

ELIZABETHTOWN
Antiques and Things. 618 E. Dixie Hwy. I-65, Exit 91. Antiques, collectibles. 30 booths. Several antique shops located close to mall. (502) 769-9691. *Daily, 1:00 - 7:00 P.M.*

FRANKLIN
Heritage Antique Mall and Collectibles. 111 W. Washington St. Shop here for a variety of fine antiques and collectibles. (502) 586-3880.

FRANKLIN
Plain and Fancy Antique Mall. 272 Trotters Ln. Books, quilts, linens, lamps, coins, small desirables, some furniture. (502) 586-4833.

FRANKLIN
Strictly Country Antique Mall. 5945 Bowling Green Rd. Six individual shops located on an 1840s homestead. (502) 586-3978.

FRANKLIN
Winnies Antique Mall. 2736 Nashville Rd. Glassware, collectibles, vintage jewelry, books, advertising items, toys, dolls, military items. (502) 586-6104.

GEORGETOWN
Central Kentucky Antique Mall. 114 E. Main St. 7,000 sq. ft. Quality and variety best describe this mall, its booths full to the brim with great antiques and collectibles. 40 dealers. (502) 863-4018. *Monday - Saturday, 10:00 A.M. - 5:00 P.M.; Sundays, 1:00 - 5:00 P.M.; Wednesdays, noon - 5:00 P.M.*

GEORGETOWN
Georgetown Antique Mall. 124 W. Main St. This mall is contained in three large, separate buildings, each with a fine assortment of antiques and collectibles. Ample parking. (502) 863-1275 or 863-9033. *Monday - Saturday, 10:00 A.M. - 5:00 P.M.; Sundays, 1:00 - 5:00 P.M.*

GEORGETOWN
Wyatt's Antique Center. 149 E. Main St. Primitives, kitchenware, glassware, china, silver, pottery, quilts, books. (502) 863-0331. *Monday - Saturday, 10:00 A.M. - 5:00 P.M.*

GLASGOW
The Hidden Attic Antique Mall. 609 Columbia Ave. Antiques, collectibles, quilts, very nice selection of quality glassware. Lots of antique furniture. Mall has a special warehouse section for dealers and wholesale only. (502) 651-8829. *Monday - Saturday, 9:00 A.M. - 5:00 P.M.*

GLENDALE
Bennie's Barn Antique Mall. Behind PNC. Glassware and small desirables of all kinds, china, lamps, furniture, crocks, bottles, quilts. (502) 369-9677. *Tuesday - Saturday, noon - 9:00 P.M.; Sun-*

days and Mondays, 1:00 - 6:00 P.M.

GLENDALE
Glendale Antique Mall. 104 E. Railroad Ave. I-65, Exit 86. Antiques, collectibles, jewelry, glassware, furniture. Mall has an authentic two-story log cabin on the grounds, stocked with crafts and gift items. 45 dealers. *Open daily.*

GLENDALE
The Side Track Shops and Antique Mall. Main St. Mall features 25 individual shops located in one facility. Antiques, collectibles, wicker, Blue Ridge pottery, gifts, crafts. (502) 369-8766.

GREENSBURG
Glover's Antique Mall. 123 S. Public Square. 9,000 sq. ft. facility. Antiques, collectibles, gift items, and locally made crafts. (502) 932-5588. *Open daily.*

HARRODSBURG
The Antique Mall of Harrodsburg. 540 N. College St. Antiques and collectibles in all categories. 130+ dealers. (606) 734-5191. *Monday - Saturday, 10:00 A.M. - 5:00 P.M.; Sundays, 1:00 - 5:00 P.M.*

HAZEL
Decades Ago Antique Mall. Main St. Antiques, collectibles, primitives, country, depression glass, dolls, telephones, Victorian. 75 dealers. (502) 492-8140.

HENDERSON
Henderson Antique Mall. 325 First St. Corner of First and Green Sts. Over 50 booths and 75+ showcases. (502) 826-3007. *Monday - Saturday, 10:00 A.M. - 5:00 P.M.; Sundays, 1:00 - 5:00 P.M.*

HODGENVILLE
Lincoln Square Mall. Downtown, courthouse square. A mall for all collectors, this one. (502) 358-8513. *Monday - Saturday, 8:30 A.M. - 5:30 P.M.; Sundays, 1:00 - 5:00 P.M.*

HOPKINSVILLE
Main Street Antique Mall. 803 S. Main St. Glassware, china, coins, tokens, RR items, military memorabilia, books, dolls, jewelry. (502) 886-9869. *Monday - Saturday, 10:00 A.M. - 5:00 P.M.; Sundays, 1:00 - 5:00 P.M.*

LEITCHFIELD
Leitchfield Antique Mall. 108 W. Main St. Antiques and collectibles. Everything here from hatpins to perfumes, Fiestaware to Aladdin lamps. (502) 259-5824 or 257-2688. *Open daily.*

LEXINGTON
Antique Mall. 535 W. Short

St. Todd Square. 1 block north of Rupp Arena. Antiques, clocks, collectibles. 25 dealers. (606) 252-0296.

LEXINGTON

Country Antique Mall. 1455 Leestown Rd. Meadowthorpe Shopping Center. 14,000 sq. ft., 60 dealers. Don and Rodna Southworth. (606) 233-0075. *Monday - Saturday, 10:00 A.M. - 5:00 P.M.; Sundays, 1:00 - 5:00 P.M.*

LEXINGTON

Lexington Antique Gallery. 637 Main St. Antiques, collectibles, 18th- and 19th-century furniture, clocks, Oriental rugs, prints, silver. 40 dealers. (606) 231-8197. *Monday - Saturday, 10:00 A.M. - 5:00 P.M.*

LOUISVILLE

Louisville Antique Mall. 900 Goss Ave. 60,000 sq. ft. Large mall, with one of the finest selections of quality antiques in the entire area. Mall has a large showcase section that features the finest items. 200+ dealers. Credit cards accepted. (502) 635-2852. *Monday - Saturday, 10:00 A.M. - 6:00 P.M.; Sundays, noon - 6:00 P.M.*

LOUISVILLE

Saint Matthews Antique Market. 3900 Shelbyville Rd. Antiques, collectibles, furniture, glassware. (502) 893-7929. *Open daily.*

LOUISVILLE

Swan Street Antique Mall. 947 E. Breckinridge. 30,000 sq. ft. Features a large showcase room with quality items. Mall also has a rough room for furniture. 100 dealers. (502) 584-6255. *Monday - Saturday, 10:00 A.M. - 5:00 P.M.; Saturdays, 10:00 A.M. - 6:00 P.M.; Sundays, noon - 6:00 P.M.*

MCHENRY

Old Brick Mall. Hwy. 62. Antiques, collectibles. (502) 274-4589. *Monday - Saturday, 10:00 A.M. - 4:00 P.M.; Sundays, 1:00 - 5:00 P.M.*

NEWPORT

471 Antique Mall. 901 E. 8th St. 20,000 sq. ft. mall. Antiques, collectibles, no crafts. Ample parking, buses welcome. (606) 431-4753. *Wednesday - Saturday, 10:00 A.M. - 6:00 P.M.; Sundays, noon - 6:00 P.M.*

NICHOLASVILLE

Antiques On Main Mall. 221 N. Main St. Antiques, collectibles, glassware, primitives. (606) 887-2767. *Monday - Saturday, 10:00 A.M. - 5:00 P.M.; Sundays, 1:00 - 5:00 P.M.*

NICHOLASVILLE
Coach Light Antique Mall. 213 N. Main St. Antiques and collectibles. Large, well-stocked mall, with many quality items. (606) 887-4223. *Monday - Saturday, 10:00 A.M. - 5:00 P.M.; Sundays, 1:00 - 5:00 P.M.*

NICHOLASVILLE
The Rocking Horse Antique Mall. 120 N. Main St. Antiques, collectibles; mall specializes in "country." (606) 885-7893. *Daily, 10:00 A.M. - 5:00 P.M.*

OWENSBORO
Owensboro Antique Mall. 500 W. Third St. Antiques and collectibles. 55 dealers. (502) 684-3003. *Monday - Saturday, 10:00 A.M. - 6:00 P.M.; Sundays, noon - 5:00 P.M.*

PADUCAH
Chief Paduke Antique Mall. 300 S. Third St. Collector items for all tastes and budgets. (502) 442-6799. *Monday - Saturday, 10:00 A.M. - 5:00 P.M.; Sundays, noon - 5:00 P.M.*

PADUCAH
Sherry and Friends Antique Mall. 208 Kentucky Ave. Antiques and collector items of all kinds. Many unique finds. (502) 442-4103. *Monday - Saturday, 10:00 A.M. - 5:00 P.M.; Sundays, 1:00 - 5:00 P.M.*

RADCLIFF
Radcliff Antique Mall. 509 S. Dixie Hwy. Variety and quality are two words that best describe this mall. Booths display antiques and collectibles in all categories. (502) 351-5155. *Monday - Saturday, 10:00 A.M. - 6:00 P.M.; Sundays, 1:00 - 6:00 P.M.*

RUSSELL SPRINGS
Russell Springs Antique Mall. 224 Dan St. A typical mall, with a little of this and a little of that in fine antiques and collectibles. (502) 866-7443. *Open daily.*

RUSSELLVILLE
Russellville Antique Mall. 141 E. 5th St. Antiques, collectibles, wicker, china, glassware, furniture. (502) 726-6900. *Wednesday - Monday, 9:30 A.M. - 4:30 P.M.*

SHELBYVILLE
Main Street Antique Mall. Main St. 2-story building. Antiques and collectibles. (502) 633-0721. *Monday - Saturday, 10:00 A.M. - 5:00 P.M.; Sundays, 1:00 - 5:00 P.M.*

SHELBYVILLE
Shelbyville Antique Mall. Main St. Antiques, collectibles, glassware, furniture. (502) 633-0720. *Monday - Sat-*

> ### *Beware of Reproductions!*
> In the world of antiques and collectibles, reproductions have become a real problem—the problem being that many times, unsuspecting buyers think they are purchasing an original item and are really getting a new copy. For the most part, reproduced antiques are quite legal.
>
> The manufacturers are not guilty of patent or copyright infringement. And though their production may be quite legal, it is the sale that can cause problems if buyers are not alert.
>
> Ethical dealers will tell you that an item is a reproduction. If you are not sure, you can always ask. Only the most unscrupulous dealers will not be honest. The problem for the buyer then becomes whether to trust a dealer or not. Here, you will have to rely on gut instinct and your knowledge of the item in question. If you are really not sure, you are always safe if you refrain from making the purchase.

urday, 10:00 A.M. - 5:00 P.M.; Sundays, 1:00 - 5:00 P.M.

SOMERSET

Cumberland Antique Mall. 6111 S. Hwy. 27. Antiques and collectibles in all categories: vintage clothing and jewelry, coins, dolls, toys, lamps, banks, glassware. (606) 561-8622.

VERSAILLES

Olde Towne Antique Mall. 161 N. Main St. 2-story facility full of great antiques and collectibles. (606) 873-6326. *Monday - Saturday, 10:00 A.M. - 5:00 P.M.; Sundays, 1:00 - 5:00 P.M.*

VINE GROVE

Main Street Antique Mall. 116 W. Main St. Antiques and collectibles of all types. Glassware, china, pottery, silver, linens, primitives. (502) 877-5001. *Tuesday - Saturday, 10:00 A.M. - 5:00 P.M.; Sundays, 1:00 - 5:00 P.M.*

MICHIGAN

ADRIAN

Adrian Antique Mall. 122 N. Main St. Antiques, collectibles, oak furniture, nice selection of cookie jars. (517) 265-6266. *Monday - Saturday, 10:00 A.M. - 5:30 P.M.; Sundays, noon - 4:00 P.M.*

ADRIAN

Marsh's Antique Mall. 136 S. Winter St. Antiques, collectibles, oak and Victorian furniture. (517) 265-6266.

Monday - Saturday, 10:00 A.M. - 5:30 P.M.; Sundays, 1:00 - 5:00 P.M.; closed Wednesdays.

ALBION
Harley's Antique Mall. 4 miles east of town. I-94, Exit 127. A good variety of antiques and collectibles of all kinds. (517) 531-5300. *Daily, 10:00 A.M. - 6:00 P.M.*

ALLENDALE
Grand Valley Antique Mall. 11233 68th St., north of M45. Antiques, collectibles. (616) 892-6022. *Monday - Saturday, 9:00 A.M. - 6:00 P.M.; Sundays, noon - 5:00 P.M.*

ANN ARBOR
Antiques Mall of Ann Arbor. 2739 Plymouth Rd. Plymouth Rd. Mall. Quality-oriented mall. Very fine selection of high-grade antiques and collectibles. 40 dealers. Credit cards accepted. (313) 663-8200. *Monday - Saturday, 11:00 A.M. - 7:00 P.M.; Sundays, noon - 5:00 P.M.*

AU SABLE
A Quaint Little Antique Mall. Typical array of goods—antiques and collector items for all budgets. (517) 739-4000. *Seasonal market; open daily during the summer and fall.*

BANGOR
Bangor Antique Mall. Downtown. 4-story building with over 20,000 sq. ft. Carriage barn and 50s shop under one roof. (616) 427-8557. *Monday - Saturday, 10:00 A.M. - 5:00 P.M.; Sundays, 1:00 - 5:00 P.M.*

BAY CITY
Bay City Antiques Center. 1010 N. Water. One of the largest malls in Michigan; 41,000+ sq. ft. Large selection of fine items. New showcase section. Large assortment of stripped-pine furniture and quality country accessories. 150+ booths. Restaurant in authentic soda fountain setting. (517) 893-1116. *Daily until 5:00 P.M.*

BLISSFIELD
Blissfield Antique Mall. 101 US Hwy. 223. 2 buildings, 3 floors. Antiques, collectibles, great selection of oak furniture, glassware, toys. (517) 486-2236. *Monday - Saturday, 10:00 A.M. - 5:30 P.M.; Sundays, noon - 5:00 P.M.*

BLISSFIELD
Estes Antiques Mall. 116-118 S. Lane St. Downtown. Antiques, collectibles, cookie jars, toys, jewelry. (517) 488-4618. *Tuesday - Saturday, 10:30 A.M. - 5:00 P.M.; Sundays, noon - 5:00 P.M.*

BLISSFIELD
J and B Antique Mall. 109 W. Adrian St. U.S. Hwy. 223. Antiques and collectibles. Furniture, pottery, glass, china, tools. Large selection of Jewel Tea items. 60 dealers. Jerry and Beverly Nichols, (517) 486-3544. *Monday - Saturday, 10:00 A.M. - 5:30 P.M.; Sundays, noon - 5:00 P.M.*

BRIGHTON
Mill Pond Antique Galleries. 217 W. Main St. Antiques, collectibles, jewelry, pewter, silver, watches and clocks, Oriental rugs, glassware, art. 25+ dealers. (810) 229-8686. *Open daily.*

BRITTON
Yesteryears Antique Mall. 208 E. Chicago St. Hwy. M50. Antiques, collectibles. (517) 451-8600. *Saturdays and Mondays, 10:00 A.M. - 5:30 P.M.*

COLDWATER
Chicago Street Antique Mall. 34-36 W. Chicago St. Antiques and collectibles in all categories: glassware, china, art, furniture. 25 dealers. (517) 279-7555. *Monday - Saturday, 10:00 A.M. - 5:00 P.M.; Sundays, 11:00 A.M. - 5:00 P.M.*

DEARBORN
Village Antiques Mall. 22091 Michigan Ave. Lots of collectibles. 35 dealers. (313) 563-1230. *Open daily.*

FARMINGTON
Hickory Hill Antiques. 32315 Grand River Ave. 12,000 sq. ft. Antiques, collectibles, furniture. 75+ dealers. (313) 477-6630. *Daily, 10:00 A.M. - 6:00 P.M.*

FLAT RIVER
Flat River Antique Mall. 212 W. Main St. Downtown. 35,000 sq. ft., 4-story building. Antiques, collectibles, furniture, primitives, jewelry, wicker, toys, good selection of architectural items. Nice restaurant on premises. Rest rooms, wheelchair accessible. Credit cards accepted. (616) 897-5360. *Monday - Friday, 10:00 A.M. - 6:00 P.M.; Saturday and Sundays, 9:00 A.M. - 6:00 P.M.*

FLINT
Reminisce Antique Mall. 3514 S. Saginaw St. Booths full of great finds in antiques, collectibles, decorator items. 60 dealers. (801) 767-4152. *Daily, 9:00 A.M. - 7:00 P.M.*

FLUSHING
Antique Center. I-75, Exit 122. 2½ miles west. Antiques, collectibles. 100+ dealers. Credit cards accepted. Rosemary and Jim Allamon,

(810) 659-2663. *Daily, 10:00 A.M. - 5:00 P.M.*

GALESBURG
Grants Antique Market. 33 W. Battle Creek St. 8,000 sq. ft. Quality antiques and collectibles. 30+ dealers. *Tuesday - Saturday, 10:00 A.M. - 5:00 P.M.; Sundays, noon - 5:00 P.M.*

GRAND HAVEN
West Michigan Antique Mall. Hwy. 31. 2 miles south of town. 12,000 sq. ft. Antiques, collectibles, furniture, glassware. 75 dealers. (616) 842-0370. *Open daily.*

GRAND RAPIDS
Antiques By The Bridge. 445 Bridge St., NW. 9,000 sq. ft. Antiques, collectibles, pottery, china, Beatle and Coke memorabilia. This mall specializes in furniture. Credit cards accepted. (616) 451-3400. *Tuesday - Saturday, 10:00 A.M. - 5:00 P.M.; Sundays, noon - 5:00 P.M.*

GRAND RAPIDS
Plaza Antique Mall. 1410 28th St., S.E. 9,000 sq. ft. Antiques, collectibles, glassware, primitives, jewelry, nice selection of antique Christmas items, advertising items, furniture, toys, dolls. Well-stocked section of reference books. 65+ booths. Credit cards accepted. (616) 243-2465. *Monday - Saturday, 10:00 A.M. - 7:00 P.M.; Sundays, 1:00 - 5:00 P.M.*

GREENVILLE
Greenville Antique Center. Corner of Hwys. M-57 and M-91. 15,000 sq. ft. Historic Greenville Furniture building. Furniture, oak, primitives, Victorian, books, linens, quilts, glassware, pottery, jewelry, advertising items. Air-conditioned. Credit cards accepted. 65+ dealers. (800) 405-1155 or (616) 754-5540. *Thursdays, Fridays, and Saturdays, 11:00 A.M. - 8:00 P.M.; Sunday - Wednesday, 11:00 A.M. - 6:00 P.M.*

HOLLAND
Tulip City Antique Mall. 1145 S. Washington Ave. Antiques, collectibles, jewelry, toys, china, pottery, oak and Victorian furniture, restored radios, Indian artifacts, pump organs. 80 booths. Mall is located in one of America's most beautiful towns. Holland holds an annual tulip festival that is one of America's most popular events—a sure-fire, don't-miss happening. Credit cards accepted. (616) 396-8855. *Monday - Saturday, 10:00 A.M. - 5:30 P.M.; Sundays, noon - 5:00 P.M.*

HOLLY
Water Tower Antiques Mall. 310 Broad St. 10,000 sq. ft. Antiques and collectibles of all descriptions. Furniture, glass, pottery, china, paper and advertising items, and much more. (313) 634-3500. *Monday - Saturday, 10:00 A.M. - 5:00 P.M.; Sundays, noon - 5:00 P.M.*

HOWELL
Adams Antique Mall. 201 E. Grand River St. Antiques, collectibles, primitives, glassware, furniture. (517) 546-5360. *Monday - Saturday, 10:00 A.M. - 6:00 P.M.; Sundays, 10:00 A.M. - 5:00 P.M.*

IONIA
Ionia Antique Mall. 415 W. Main St. 6,500 sq. ft. facility. Plenty of antiques and collectibles to intrigue the most seasoned shopper. 14 dealers. (616) 527-6720. *Daily, 10:00 A.M. - 5:00 P.M.; Fridays until 8:00 P.M.*

JACKSON
Jackson Antique Mall. 201 N. Jackson St. Antiques, collectibles. (517) 784-3333. *Monday - Saturday, 10:00 A.M. - 6:00 P.M.; Sundays, noon - 5:00 P.M.*

LA SALLE
American Heritage Antique Mall. Mason Bright. 5228 S. Otter Creek Rd. I-75, Exit 9. 14,000 sq. ft. Good selection of antiques and collectibles. 50 dealers. (313) 242-3430. *Daily from 10:00 A.M.*

LAWTON
Lawton Antique Mall. 131 S. Main St. I-94, Exit 60, 3 miles south. 8,700 sq. ft. Antiques and collectibles. 50 dealers. (616) 624-6157. *Monday - Saturday, 10:00 A.M. - 5:00 P.M.; Sundays, noon - 5:00 P.M.*

LIVONIA
Town and country Antiques Mall. 31630 Plymouth Rd. I-96, Exit 175. All manner of antiques and collectibles: glassware, books, quilts, primitives, many small desirables. Approximately 50 dealers. Credit cards accepted. (313) 425-4355. *Daily, 11:00 A.M. - 6:00 P.M.*

MANCHESTER
Manchester Antique Mall. 116 E. Main St. Good selection of furniture. Also glass, collectibles, watches, primitives, and jewelry. (313) 428-9357. *Daily, 10:00 A.M. - 5:00 P.M.*

MUSKEGON
Airport Antique Mall. 1391 Peck St. All types of antiques and collectibles, for every taste and pocketbook. (616) 726-3689. *Monday - Saturday,*

11:00 A.M. - 6:00 P.M.; Sundays, noon - 6:00 P.M.

MUSKEGON
Memory Lane Antique Mall. 2073 Holton Rd. Hwy. M120. Fine antiques and collectibles in every category can be found at this mall. (616) 744-8510. *Daily, 10:00 A.M. - 6:00 P.M.*

MUSKEGON
Muskegon Antique Mall. 30 E. Clay St., downtown. Antique furniture, glassware, pottery, china, coins, dolls, toys, lamps, quilts, vintage jewelry. (616) 728-0305. *Monday - Thursday, 10:00 A.M. - 5:00 P.M.; Fridays and Saturdays, 10:00 A.M. - 7:00 P.M.; Sundays, 1:00 - 5:00 P.M.*

NEW BALTIMORE
Heritage Square Antique Mall. 3682 Green St. Hwy. M29. This mall is housed in a historical 1861 house. A variety of quality antiques and collectibles. 18 dealers. Credit cards accepted. (810) 725-2453. *Tuesday - Saturday, 10:00 A.M. - 5:00 P.M.; Sundays, 11:00 A.M. - 5:00 P.M.*

NILES
Four Flags Antique Mall. 218 N. 2nd St. Glassware, china, silver, postcards, books, RR items, country primitives, quilts, Victorian-era items. (616) 683-6681. *Monday - Friday, 10:00 A.M. - 5:00 P.M.; Saturdays, 10:00 A.M. - 6:00 P.M.; Sundays, noon - 6:00 P.M.*

NILES
Michiana Antique Mall. 2423 S. Hwy. 33. A nice mall, with booths full of quality antiques and collectibles. (616) 684-7001. *Daily, 10:00 A.M. - 6:00 P.M.*

NILES
Pickers Paradise Antique Mall. 2809 Hwy. 33 South. A good mall for dealers to shop. Prices reasonable on a wide variety of antiques and collectibles. (616) 683-6644. *Daily, 10:00 A.M. - 6:00 P.M.*

OKEMOS
Farm Village Antique Mall. 3448 Hagadorn Rd. Antiques and collectibles for every want and every budget. Credit cards accepted. (517) 337-4988. *Monday - Saturday, 11:00 A.M. - 6:00 P.M.; Sundays, noon - 6:00 P.M.*

OTSEGO
Heritage Antique Mall. 621 Hwy. M89. 2 miles west of town. Many hard-to-find antiques and collectibles. 65 dealers. (616) 694-4226. *Tuesday - Saturday, 10:00 A.M. - 5:00 P.M.; Sundays, 1:00 - 5:00 P.M.*

Owosso
Owosso Midtown Antiques Mall. 1426 N. M52. Antiques, collectibles. Primitives, quilts, kitchenware, collectibles, decorator finds. (517) 723-8604. *Open daily.*

Parma
Cracker Hill Antique Mall. 12000 Norton Rd. I-94, Exit 128. Antiques and collectibles in all categories. (517) 531-4200.

Richmond
Barb's Country Antiques Mall. 69394 Main St. Barbara and Paul McConnell. (810) 727-2826. *Daily, noon - 5:00 P.M.; closed Mondays.*

Romeo
Town Hall Antiques. 205 N. Main St. 2 buildings. A wide array of quality antiques and collectibles. Mall has a "general store" section, with 3 rooms of authentic country-store collectibles. 50 dealers. (810) 752-5422. *Daily, 10:00 A.M. - 6:00 P.M.*

Royal Oak
Antiques On Main. 115 S. Main St. Fine antiques and collectibles. 36 dealer co-op. Many fine neighboring antique shops. (313) 545-4663. *Monday - Saturday, 10:00 A.M. - 6:00 P.M.*

Saginaw
Antique Warehouse. 1910 N. Michigan Ave. 30,000 sq. ft. Antiques, collectibles, nice, well-stocked mall. 70+ dealers. Tearoom, 10 neighboring antique shops. (517) 755-4343. *Open daily.*

Saline
Saline House Antiques Mall. 116 W. Michigan. Excellent selection of antiques, collectibles, furniture, toys, primitives, glassware, art. (313) 429-5112. *Monday - Saturday, 10:00 A.M. - 5:00 P.M.; Sundays, 11:00 A.M. - 5:00 P.M.*

Saugatuck
Fannie's Antique Market With Fleas. 3604 64th St. Antiques to "junque," lots of bric-a-brac. *Tuesday - Sunday, 11:00 A.M. - 5:00 P.M.*

Schoolcraft
Schoolcraft Antique Mall. 209 N. Grand. Hwy. 131. 2-story building. Antiques, collectibles, toys, primitives. (616) 679-5282. *Monday - Saturday, 10:00 A.M. - 5:00 P.M.; Sundays, noon - 5:00 P.M.*

Spring Lake
Spring Lake Antique Mall. 801 W. Savidge. Antiques, collectibles, glassware, furniture. (616) 846-1774. *Monday - Thursday, 10:00 A.M. -*

6:00 P.M.; Fridays, 10:00 A.M. - 8:00 P.M.; Sundays, noon - 6:00 P.M.

TECUMSEH
Hitching Post Antiques Mall. 1322 E. Monroe Rd. 2 miles west of town on M50. Antiques, collectibles, hardware, good selection of reference books. Mall conducts large outdoor flea markets on Memorial Day, Fourth of July, and Labor Day. (517) 423-8277. *Daily, 10:00 A.M. - 5:30 P.M.*

TECUMSEH
L and M Antique Mall. 7811 Monroe Rd. Hwy. M50. Antiques and collectibles. (517) 423-8441. *Tuesday - Sunday; closed Mondays.*

TECUMSEH
Tecumseh Antique Mall I. 112 E. Chicago Blvd. Hwy. M50. Antiques and collectibles. 30 dealers. (517) 423-6441. *Monday - Saturday, 10:00 A.M. - 5:00 P.M.; Sundays, noon - 5:00 P.M.*

TECUMSEH
Tecumseh Antique Mall II. 111 W. Chicago Blvd. Hwy. M50. Antiques and collectibles in all collector lines. 100 dealers. (517) 429-6082. *Monday - Saturday, 10:00 A.M. - 5:00 P.M.; Sundays, noon - 5:00 P.M.*

TROY
Troy Corners Antiques. 90 E. Square Lake Rd. Antiques and collectibles. Lots of furniture - American and English country. Also primitives, chests, desks, etc. 18 dealers. (810) 879-9848. *Monday - Saturday, 10:00 A.M. - 5:00 P.M.*

WATERFORD
The Great Midwestern Antique Emporium. 5233 Dixie Hwy. U.S. Hwy. 24. 5,500 sq. ft. Quality antiques and collectibles. 50 dealers. (810) 623-7460. *Tuesday - Sunday, 10:00 A.M. - 5:00 P.M.*

WATERVLIET
Annette's Antique Mall. 340 N. Main St. Antiques and collectibles. (616) 463-3554. *Daily, 10:00 A.M. - 5:00 P.M.; closed Tuesdays.*

WATERVLIET
Historic House Antique Mall. 349 N. Main St. Antiques, collectibles, Indian artifacts, nice selection of Civil War items, furniture, graniteware, glassware. Karen and Dan Stice, (616) 463-2888. *Monday - Saturday, 10:00 A.M. - 5:30 P.M.; Sundays, noon - 5:00 P.M.*

WEST OLIVE
Lake Shore Antique Shop. 10300 W. Olive Rd. Hwy. 31. Antiques, collectibles. 60+

dealers. (616) 847-2429. *Monday - Saturday, 10:00 A.M. - 6:00 P.M.; Sundays, noon - 5:00 P.M.*

WILLIAMSTON
Antique Mall of Williamston. 1039 W. Grand River Rd. 15,000 sq. ft. Antiques and collectibles. 75 dealers. (517) 655-1350. *Monday - Saturday, 10:30 A.M. - 5:30 P.M.; Sundays, noon - 5:30 P.M.*

WILLIAMSTON
Consignments of Williamston. 115 W. Grand River Ave. Consignment shop with collectibles. This is a market where occasional treasures can be discovered. (517) 655-6064. *Tuesday - Saturday, 10:00 A.M. - 6:00 P.M.; Sundays, 1:00 - 6:00 P.M.*

WILLIAMSTON
Putnam Street Antiques Mall. 122 S. Putnam. Glassware, paper and advertising items, vintage clothing and jewelry, coins, dolls. (517) 655-4521. *Monday - Saturday, 10:30 A.M. - 5:00 P.M.; Sundays, noon - 4:00 P.M.*

YALE
Yale Antiques Mall. 110 S. Main St. New mall. 6,500 sq. ft. Quality antiques and collectibles. China, pottery, dolls, linens, quilts, glassware. (810) 387-2261. *Open daily.*

MINNESOTA

ANOKA
Antiques on Main. 212 E. Main St. 2-story building. Quality antiques and collectibles. 40 dealer mall. (612) 323-3990. *Open daily.*

BURNSVILLE
Crafters Market. 806 W. County Rd. (612) 898-4664.

CAMBRIDGE
Memories on Main. 103 S. Main St. Quality antiques and collectibles, glassware, china, silver, linens, country primitives, Victorian and Art Deco items, Oriental collectibles. (612) 689-1950. *Daily, 10:00 A.M. - 5:00 P.M.*

CANNON FALLS
Country Side Antique Mall. 51 Old Hwy. 52. 55009. Next to John Deere dealership. 12,000 sq. ft. facility. 35 dealers. Antiques and collectibles, lots of small desirables. (507) 263-0352. *Monday - Saturday, 9:30 A.M. - 5:00 P.M.; Sundays, noon - 5:00 P.M.*

EDEN PRAIRIE
Crafters Market. 12500 Plaza Dr. (612) 829-8030.

HOPKINS
Blake Antiques. 1115 Excelsior Blvd. 1 mile east, Exit 169. Good selection of antiques, bric-a-brac, collectibles. 50 dealers. (612) 930-0477. Fax (612) 933-9777. *Monday - Saturday, 11:00 A.M. - 6:00 P.M.; Sundays, noon - 5:00 P.M.*

HOPKINS
Main Street Antique Mall. 901 Main St. 20 minutes west of Minneapolis. General line of antiques and collectibles, art, prints, books. Approximately 65 exhibitors. (612) 931-9748. *Daily; closed holidays.*

HUTCHINSON
Main Street Antiques. 122 N. Main St. Booths of interesting antiques and hard to find collectibles of all kinds. 40 dealers. (612) 587-6305. *Open daily.*

ISANTI
Isanti Antique Mall. 16 W. Main St. New mall. Glassware, collectibles, lots of small desirables, china, art, furniture, Oriental items. (612) 444-5522. *Open daily.*

LITCHFIELD
Sibley Antiques. Downtown. Antiques and collectibles for everyone, from the casual to the serious collector. 25 dealers. (612) 693-7335. *Open daily.*

LOWRY
Memory Mercantile Antiques and Collectibles. Hwy. 55. 13 miles south of I-94. 20,000 sq. ft. Furniture, glassware, toys, automobiles, collectibles. (612) 283-5120. *Open daily.*

MANKATO
Earthly Remains. 731 S. Front St. Glassware and small desirables, collectibles, kitchen nostalgia, primitives, Victorian-era items, paper, advertising, vintage jewelry. 25 dealers. (507) 388-5063. *Monday - Saturday, 10:00 A.M. - 5:00 P.M.*

MINNEAPOLIS
Antiques Minnesota. 1516 E. Lake St. Furniture, glass, collectibles. Large, well-stocked mall. Furniture and clock repair shop on premises. (612) 722-6000. *Monday - Saturday, 10:00 A.M. - 5:00 P.M.; Sundays, noon - 5:00 P.M.; closed Tuesdays.*

MINNEAPOLIS
Cobblestone Antiques. 1010 W. Lake St. Corner of Dupont and Lake Sts. 22,000 sq. ft., all on one level. 90+ dealers. (612) 823-7373. *Daily, 11:00 A.M. - 6:00 P.M.*

MINNEAPOLIS
Great River Antiques. 210 3rd Ave. North. Historic ware-

house district downtown. 25,000 sq. ft. Period and estate furniture, silver and jewelry, decorative arts. Oriental rugs, prints, paintings. 40+ dealers. (612) 338-1109. *Tuesday - Saturday, 10:00 A.M. - 5:30 P.M.; Sundays, 11:00 A.M. - 5:30 P.M.*

OWATONNA
Uncle Tom's Antique Mall. Hwy. 14 W., 3/4 mile west of I-35. Antiques and collectibles. Glassware, china, quilts, Flow Blue to RR timetables. (507) 451-2254. *Monday - Friday, 10:00 A.M. - 5:00 P.M.; Saturdays, 10:00 A.M. - 4:00 P.M.; Sundays, noon - 4:00 P.M.*

ST. LOUIS PARK
International Craft Fair. 8332 Hwy. 7. (612) 930-9498.

ST. PAUL
Antiques Minnesota. 1197 University Ave. Furniture, glass, collectibles. Clock and furniture repair shop on premises. Large, well-stocked mall. *Monday - Saturday, 10:00 A.M. - 5:00 P.M.; Sundays, noon - 5:00 P.M.; closed Tuesdays.*

ST. PAUL
Payne Avenue Antique Mall. 1055 Payne Avenue. 75 dealers. (618) 772-1635. *Daily, 10:00 A.M. - 5:30 P.M.*

SHAKOPEE
The Country Collection Antiques. 213 E. First Avenue. 3,200 sq. ft. Antiques, collectibles, decoys, stoneware, folk art, great selection of country furniture and country collectibles. 15 dealers. (612) 446-1500. *Open daily.*

STILLWATER
The Mill Antiques. 410 N. Main St. 15,000 sq. ft. Mall is located in a historic sawmill. Large selection of collectibles, antiques, and lots of memorabilia. 80+ dealers. (612) 430-1816. *Daily, 10:00 A.M. - 6:00 P.M.*

STILLWATER
More Antiques. 312 N. Main St. Antiques and collectibles of all kinds, from furniture to miniatures, china to table linen. 65 dealers. (612) 439-1110. *Monday - Saturday, 10:00 A.M. - 5:00 P.M.; Sundays, 11:00 A.M. - 5:00 P.M.*

STILLWATER
Mulberry Point Antiques. 270 N. Main St. 4-level building. Furniture, china, silver, pottery, art, glassware, collectibles in all categories. 65 dealers. (612) 430-3630. *Open daily.*

MISSOURI

BEVERLY
Beverly Hills Antique Center.

Junction of Hwys. 45 and 92. Antiques and collectibles in every imaginable category. Glassware, china, silver, dolls, vintage jewelry, advertising items. (816) 546-3432. *Tuesday - Sunday, 10:00 A.M. - 5:00 P.M.*

BLUE SPRINGS
Decorator's Touch Craft Mall and Decorating Center. 1035 S. Hwy. 7. (Next to Hobby Lobby). (816) 224-9252. *Mondays, Wednesdays, Fridays, and Saturdays, 10:00 A.M. - 5:00 P.M.; Tuesdays and Thursdays, 10:00 A.M. - 8:00 P.M.; Sundays, noon - 5:00 P.M.*

BLUE SPRINGS
Once Upon A Time Collectible Mall. 411 S. Hwy. 7. Collectibles, Jewel Tea, books, Shawnee, McCoy, Wagon Wheel, Frankoma. Music rolls, records, and even a player piano. Memorabilia and fine antiques. (816) 224-2555. *Monday - Saturday, 10:00 A.M. - 7:00 P.M.; Sundays, noon - 5:00 P.M.*

BLUE SPRINGS
Victorian Rose Antique Mall. 3500 W. Hwy. 40. Glassware, linens, quilts, lamps, furniture. (816) 229-3045. *Monday - Saturday, 10:00 A.M. - 6:00 P.M.; Sundays, 1:00 - 5:00 P.M.*

> ### *More Bargaining Savvy for the Beginner*
> Make more than one offer if you still believe the item is a good deal for you. In other words, if the seller doesn't want to take your lowest offer, he might make a counteroffer. You must then decide if the item is worth the new quoted price to you. If it is—buy it. If not, you might try another number between yours and his. He might accept it and he might not, but the more practice you get, the better you will become at bargaining.

BOONEVILLE
Boone Village Antique Mall. I-70, Exit 103, 1 mile north. 50 dealers. (816) 882-7451. *Daily, 10:00 A.M. - 5:00 P.M.*

BUCKNER
Antique and Auction Center. Hwy. 24. Mall conducts monthly consignment/retail auctions. 20 dealers. (816) 373-1247 or 249-9488. *Monday - Saturday, 10:00 A.M. - 5:00 P.M.; Sundays, 1:00 - 5:00 P.M.*

BUCKNER
Granny's Attic. 323 S. Hudson, Downtown. Antiques, crafts, collectibles, miniatures,

Fenton glass. 17 dealers. (816) 249-3717. *Monday - Saturday, 10:00 A.M. - 5:30 P.M.; Sundays, noon - 5:00 P.M.*

CAPE GIRARDEAU
Antique Centre Mall. 2121 William. Behind Hardees. Furniture, lots of small desirables, glassware, silver, pottery, primitives. (314) 339-5788. *Open daily.*

CARROLLTON
Country Cellar Antique Mall. Downtown, North side of town square. Antiques, collectibles, tins, stoneware, quilts, antique jewelry, furniture. 27 dealers. (816) 542-2588. *Monday - Saturday, 10:00 A.M. - 5:00 P.M.*

CARTHAGE
Deans Antique Mall and Flea Market. 1200 Oak St. A little bit of everything antique and collectible. Glassware, furniture, books, vintage clothing and jewelry, and more. 100+ dealers. (417) 358-6104.

CARTHAGE
Goad's Unique Antique Mall. Downtown, north side of town square. Antiques, collectibles, books, primitives, furniture, glassware. (417) 358-1201. *Monday - Saturday, 10:00 A.M. - 5:00 P.M.; Sundays, 1:00 - 5:00 P.M.*

CARTHAGE
Oldies and Oddities Mall. Downtown, west side of town square. Books, decorator finds, glassware, china, art, pottery, watches, coins. Collectibles and antiques of all kinds on two floors. (417) 358-1752.

CLAYCOMO
Claycomo Antique Mall and Flea Market. Claycomo Plaza Shopping Center. 433 N.E. Hwy. 69. 10,000 sq. ft. facility. Antiques, collectibles, flea market. 125+ dealers. (816) 455-5422. *Tuesday - Sunday, 10:00 A.M. - 6:00 P.M.*

CLAYCOMO
Remember When Antiques and Collectibles. 349 Hwy. 69. Antiques, collectibles, and lots of oak furniture. (816) 455-1815. *Monday - Saturday, 10:00 A.M. - 6:00 P.M.; Sundays, 1:00 - 5:00 P.M.; closed Tuesdays and Wednesdays.*

CLINTON
Junction Antique Mall. Hwys. 7 and 13 North. Quality antique furniture, Coca-Cola memorabilia, advertising items, lots of nice glassware: Heisey, Fenton, Fostoria, Stangel, Roseville, Frankoma. Very nice craft area. Approximately 70 dealers. (816) 885-8575. *Open daily.*

COLUMBIA
Midway Antique Center and Flea Market. Exit 121, I-70 and Hwy. 40. 3 miles west of Columbia. Used merchandise, collectibles, garage sale items, crafts. Food available, rest rooms, wheelchair accessible. Ample parking. 45 dealers. (314) 445-6717. *Daily 10:00 A.M. - 5:00 P.M.*

DEARBORN
Lick Skillet Antique and Craft Mall. 210 Main St. Lots of country crafts. Good selection of toys and wind-ups, primitives, lots of country furniture. Mall also sells country food, jams, preserves, sorghum, and such. (816) 992-8776. *Monday - Saturday, 10:00 A.M. - 5:00 P.M.; Sundays, 1:00 - 5:00 P.M.*

EOLIA
Feed Store Antiques and Mall. Hwy. 61, Eolia exit (D). 1/4 mile to downtown. 6,000 sq. ft. Antiques, collectibles, furniture, primitives, glassware, gift items, quilts, and handcrafted items. (314) 485-7000. *Monday - Saturday, 9:00 A.M. - 6:00 P.M.; Sundays, 11:00 A.M. - 6:00 P.M.*

EUREKA
Ice House Mall. Downtown. Good selection of collectibles. Several neighboring shops. 14 dealers. (314) 938-6355. *Open daily.*

FARMINGTON
The Old Village Store Antique Mall. 102 S. Jackson. Antiques, collectibles, lots of quality smalls. Separate building for crafts. Large quilt store and woodworker next door. (314) 756-8060. *Monday - Saturday, 10:00 A.M. - 5:00 P.M.; Sundays, 1:00 - 5:00 P.M.*

FARMINGTON
Shopper's Paradise. Hwy. 67 North. Nice indoor mall, with new merchandise: imports, gifts, sportswear, furniture and some collectibles. (314) 756-5437. *Open daily.*

GOODMAN
Kelly Springs Antique Mall and Flea Market. Hwy. 71, south of town. Collectibles, Coca-Cola memorabilia, cast-iron items, quilts, dolls, glassware. Rest rooms. Ample parking. (417) 364-8508. *Thursday - Sunday, 10:00 A.M. - 5:00 P.M.*

GRAIN VALLEY
Main Street Mall Antiques. 518 Main St. 3 blocks south of I-70 exit. Glassware, collectibles, antique furniture, decorator finds. (816) 224-6400. *Monday - Saturday,*

10:00 A.M. - 5:00 P.M.; Sundays, noon - 5:00 P.M.

GRANDVIEW

Truman Corners Antique and Furniture Mall. 12346 S. 71 Hwy. Truman Corners, between Sam's Wholesale and Ward's Outlet Store. Hwy. 71' and Blue Ridge Exit. (Kansas City). Lots of furniture (some very high-quality pieces), police memorabilia, trunks, cookie jars, crafts, good selection of Disney items. Lots of "stuff" at this mall for treasure hunters to prowl through. (816) 761-2221. *Monday - Friday, 10:00 A.M. - 8:00 P.M.; Saturdays, 10:00 A.M. - 7:00 P.M.; Sundays, noon - 6:00 P.M.*

GREENWOOD

Greenwood Antiques and Country Tea Room. 5th and Main Sts. Country and fine antiques. Delightful country tea room on premises. (816) 537-7172. *Monday - Saturday, 10:00 A.M. - 5:00 P.M.; Sundays, noon - 5:00 P.M.*

HAMILTON

Antique Market Antique Mall. Downtown. Furniture, antiques, and collectibles of all descriptions, from hatpins to graniteware, in all price ranges. Mike Ford, (816) 583-2300.

HAMILTON

Over the Hill Mini Mall. I-35 and Hwy. 36. Box 187, Cameron, MO. (816) 632-7807. Antiques, collectibles and crafts. 60 dealers. (816) 632-7807.

HAMILTON

Penney Mall. Downtown. Antiques, collectibles, gifts.

HANNIBAL

Market Street Mall. 1408 Market St. Antiques, collectibles, quilts, furniture. 30 dealers. Historic river town, home of Mark Twain. Lots of antique shops, old homes, and museums to tour. An excellent place to spend a few days. The city also hosts several popular special events during the year. Contact the Hannibal Chamber of Commerce for more information. (314) 221-3008. *Monday - Saturday, 10:00 A.M. - 5:00 P.M.*

HARRISONVILLE

Fountain Square Antique Mall. 311 S. Independence St. Downtown, on the town square. Crafts, collectibles, primitives, good all-around selection and atmosphere. 80 dealers. (816) 884-2119. *Monday - Friday, 9:00 A.M. - 6:00 P.M.; Saturdays, 10:00 A.M. - 6:00 P.M.; Sundays, 1:00 - 5:00 P.M.*

HARRISONVILLE
Harrisonville Trade Fair. 2301 S. Commercial St. Antiques, collectibles. Lots of handmade items, especially glass and jewelry. New reproductions and used furniture. 100+ dealers. (816) 884-5413. *Monday - Saturday, 10:00 A.M. - 5:00 P.M.; Sundays, noon - 5:00 P.M.*

INDEPENDENCE
Adventure Antiques. 11432 E. Truman Rd. 10,000 sq. ft. Collectibles and furniture. (816) 833-0303. *Tuesday - Saturday, 10:00 A.M. - 5:00 P.M.; Sundays, noon - 5:00 P.M.*

INDEPENDENCE
Back Alley Antiques and Auction. 1400 W. Turner St. New shop. Antiques and collectibles only. (816) 254-5855. *Monday - Saturday, 10:00 A.M. - 5:00 P.M.; Sundays, noon - 5:00 P.M.*

INDEPENDENCE
Country Meadows Antique Mall. 17200 E. Hwy. 40. 35,000 sq. ft. Large mall, with excellent assortment of quality items. Serious collectors will like this mall. It also puts on many weekend special events that are free to the public. Quaint tea room on the premises; reservations welcome. 200+ dealers. (816) 373-0410. *Monday - Saturday, 9:00 A.M. - 9:00 P.M.; Sundays, 9:00 A.M. - 6:00 P.M.*

INDEPENDENCE
Keepsake Kupboard. 212 W. Maple St. Ceramics, rugs, florals, dolls, lamps, stained glass, woodcrafts. 80 craft booths. (816) 252-6653. *Monday - Saturday, 10:00 A.M. - 5:00 P.M.*

JOPLIN
Connie's Antiques. 3421 N. Rangeline. 64801. 5 miles north of I-44 on Hwy. 71. Large, well-stocked mall with over 500 booths of quality antiques, crafts, new items, lots of fine collector items here. This is a good place to put on your regular shopping list. Acres of attractive booths stocked by professional dealers. (417) 781-2602. *Sunday - Friday, 9:00 A.M. - 6:00 P.M.; Saturdays, 9:00 A.M. - 7:00 p.m*

JOPLIN
The Meeker Antique Mall. 1101 E. 7th St. 2 floors. Mall is located in a very large old (Meeker) factory building. Large, well-lighted, well-stocked, a very interesting place to shop. (417) 781-5533. *Monday - Thursday, 9:00 A.M. - 6:00 P.M.; Fridays and Saturdays, 9:00 A.M. - 8:00 P.M.; Sundays, 1:00 - 6:00 P.M.*

JOPLIN

North Main Street Antique/Craft Mall and Flea Market. 5 miles north of I-44 on Hwy. 43, (Main St.), behind Lumberjack Carpet. New market. 100+ booths inside with general line of antiques and collectibles. Air conditioned. Outside space available on weekends, weather permitting. Rest rooms, wheelchair accessible. Ample parking. (417) 781-9700. *Monday - Saturday, 9:00 A.M. - 5:00 P.M.; Sundays, noon - 5:00 P.M.*

JOPLIN

Southside Antique Mall. 2914 E. 32nd. 1/2 mile north of I-44 on Rangeline, at 32nd St. 18,000 sq. ft. Antiques, collectibles, Precious Moments. Large selection quality glassware: Roseville and Hull. (417) 623-1000. *Monday - Saturday, 9:00 A.M. - 6:00 P.M.; Sundays, 9:00 A.M. - 5:00 P.M.*

KANSAS CITY

Antique Mall of America. 400 E. 135th St. Antiques and collectibles of all descriptions and in all price ranges. (816) 941-2119. *Open daily.*

KANSAS CITY

Mid-America Antique Mall. 3501 Red Bridge Rd. Terrace Lake Shopping Center. 5,000 sq. ft. Quality furniture, collectibles, primitives, good selection of Hummels. (816) 763-0979. *Monday - Saturday, 10:00 A.M. - 5:30 P.M.; Sundays, noon - 5:00 P.M.*

KANSAS CITY

State Line Antique Mall. 4510 State Line. 7,000 sq. ft. Collectibles, antiques, silver, toys, Orientalia, original artwork. 40 dealers. (913) 362-2002. *Monday - Saturday, 10:00 A.M. - 5:00 P.M.; Sundays, noon - 5:00 P.M.*

KANSAS CITY

Volker Village Antique Mall. 200 Main St. Kansas City, MO. Located in Kansas City's historic downtown river market area, next to the water tower. Large mall, with over 18,000 sq. ft. of dealer-occupied space. Market has unusually large amount of firefighter memorabilia. (816) 421-0911. *Monday - Friday, 10:30 A.M. - 6:00 P.M.; Saturdays, 9:00 A.M. - 7:00 P.M.; Sundays, 10:00 A.M. - 5:00 P.M.*

KANSAS CITY

Waldo's Antiques and Flea Market. 226 W. 75th St. 25 individual antique shops offering a general line of antiques and collectibles. There is an outdoor flea market on weekends with used merchandise, garage sale items, and some new merchandise. Snack bar, rest rooms, wheelchair accessible. Ample parking. *Open daily; flea market held on Saturdays and Sundays.*

LAKE OZARK
What-Ever Antiques Flea Market. Hwy. 54 to Hwy. 42 east, 1/4 mile. Lots of furniture, dishes, records, quilts, and junk. Mall is located in a beautiful tourist area. Lake country. (314) 348-6112. *Daily, 9:00 A.M. - 5:00 P.M.*

LEADINGTON
Parkland Pavilion Antiques and Auction Gallery. Corner of Main St. and Woodlawn. Hwy. 67 to 32 West. Leadington exit. New antique mall, located in an old Pepsi-Cola plant. This is one of my favorite malls to shop. There are some real treasures here at very good prices. Very pleasant, helpful people operate this mall. Company also conducts antiques sales from its premises. (800) 827-2887 or (314) 431-6094. Fax (314) 431-7031. *Daily.*

LEES SUMMIT
American Heritage Antique Mall. 220 S. Douglas St. Primitives, folk art, furniture, jewelry, vintage clothing, lots of Fenton glassware. 40+ dealers. (816) 524-8427. *Tuesday - Saturday, 10:00 A.M. - 5:30 P.M.; Sundays, 1:00 - 5:30 P.M.*

LEES SUMMIT
Gingham Goose Antiques. 302 S.W. Main St. Antique furniture, primitives, glassware, collectibles, gnomes. (816) 524-4015. *Monday - Saturday, 10:00 A.M. - 5:30 P.M.; Sundays, 1:00 - 5:00 P.M.*

LEXINGTON
Cannon Ball Antique Mall. 900 Main St. (816) 259-6580. *Daily.*

LEXINGTON
Rivertown Antique Mall. 914 Main St. Antiques and Collectibles. (816) 259-4102. *Monday - Saturday, 10:00 A.M. - 5:00 P.M.; Sundays, 11:00 A.M. - 5:00 P.M.*

LIBERTY
Liberty Antique Mall. 1 E. Kansas St. Downtown on the town square. 2 floors. Large selection of primitives, tools, vintage clothing, collectibles. 40 dealers. *Monday - Wednesday, 10:00 A.M. - 5:00 P.M.; Thursday - Saturday, 10:00 A.M. - 8:00 P.M.; Sundays, 1:00 - 5:00 P.M.*

LOUISIANA
Old English House of Antiques Mall. 300 N. Main St. 7 blocks west of Hwy. 79. Furniture, glassware, jewelry, old dolls. Very interesting old

river town; worth a day stop here. 20 dealers. Janis Bartolin, (314) 754-5992.

MARIONVILLE
Kountry Korner Flea Market. Junction of Hwys. 60 and 265. Railroad items, antiques, primitives, furniture, glass, Indian artifacts, western items, books. Picture gallery collection. Rest rooms, wheelchair accessible. Ample RV and bus parking. Contact: Don and Ruth Rickman, (417) 463-2923. *Monday - Saturday, 10:00 A.M. - 5:00 P.M.; Sundays, 1:00 - 5:00 P.M.*

MARSHFIELD
Bobbie's Wishing Well. 222 S. Crittenden. Exit 100 off I-44. Antiques, "junque," collectibles. Lots of interesting shops in Marshfield make this a great stop. 20 dealers. Contact: Bobbie Reed, (417) 468-6380. *Monday - Saturday, 9:30 A.M. - 5:00 P.M.; Sundays, 12:30 - 5:00 P.M.*

MARSHFIELD
His Heritage Antique Mall. I-44 at Marshfield exit. Rt. 2, Box 174E. Marshfield. Primitives, furniture, antiques, radios, jewelry, collectible, lots of Coca-Cola stuff and Aladdin lamps. Custom framing and old prints. 50 booths. Soda fountain. Air-conditioned. Ben Franker, (417) 468-3303. *Monday - Saturday, 9:00 A.M. - 5:30 P.M.*

MARSHFIELD
KD's Antiques and Woodcrafts Mall. Town square, old Sears building. Lots of locally made woodcrafts. (417) 468-4469. *Monday - Saturday, 9:00 A.M. - 5:00 P.M.; Sundays, 1:00 - 5:00 P.M.*

MT. VERNON
Nana's Antique Mall. Exit 46 from I-44 and Hwy. 39. A convenient highway stop. Antiques, collectibles, crafts, flea market items. Well-stocked mall, operated in the true Ozark manner—clean, down home, and pleasant. A very enjoyable place to stop and shop. 100+ dealers. (417) 466-2646. *Open daily.*

NAPOLEON
Ma and Pa's Riverview Antique and Collectible Mall. Downtown. Lots of furniture and primitives. 25 dealers. (816) 934-2698. *Monday - Saturday, 9:30 A.M. - 5:00 P.M.; Sundays, noon - 5:00 P.M.*

NEOSHO
Neosho Gallery and Flea Market. 900 N. College St. Business Rt. 60. Antiques, furniture, collectibles, glassware, and toys. 100+ booths. Rest rooms, wheelchair

accessible. Ample parking. (417) 451-4675. *Tuesday - Sunday, 9:00 A.M. - 5:00 P.M.*

NEOSHO

Special Treasures. 902 N. College St. Glassware, furniture, consignments, toys, antiques, collectibles. 40 booths. (417) 451-3080. *Tuesday - Thursday, 10:00 A.M. - 6:00 P.M.; Friday - Sunday, 9:00 A.M. - 6:00 P.M.; closed Mondays.*

NEVADA

Crossroads Antique and Collectibles Mall. 1617 E. Ashland. (417) 667-7775. *Open daily.*

NEW HAVEN

New Haven Antique Mall. 117 Front St., downtown historic district. Antiques, collectibles, and a year-round Christmas store with many Christmas collectibles and Christmas decorator items. (314) 237-2420. *Open daily.*

NIANGUA

Niangua Antique Mall. Downtown. 10,000 sq. ft. Antiques, collectibles, and secondhand items. (417) 473-6335 or 473-6291. *Open daily.*

NIXA

Old Theater Mall. Junction of Hwys. 160 and 14. 11,500 sq. ft. Antiques, furniture, collectibles. Excellent bakery, with fresh bread and delicious pies. (417) 725-3939. *Daily, 9:00 A.M. - 6:00 P.M.*

OAK GROVE

Olde Stone Church Antiques. 200 E. 12th St. Collectibles, primitives, flea market. (816) 625-7797. *Tuesday - Saturday, 10:00 A.M. - 5:00 P.M.*

ODESSA

Country Corner Treasures Antique and Craft Mall. 102 S. 2nd St. (816) 633-4393. *Monday - Saturday, 10:00 A.M. - 5:00 P.M.; Sundays, 1:00 - 5:00 P.M.; closed Wednesdays.*

O'FALLON

I-70 Antique Mall. Exit 216, I-70. 1174 W. Terra Lane. Furniture, toys, elegant glass, jewelry, collectibles, primitives. (314) 272-0289. *Daily, 10:00 A.M. - 5:00 P.M.*

OZARK

Best Friends Antiques and Collectibles Mall. Riverview Plaza Shopping Center. Business Rt. 14. Antiques, collectibles, lots of glassware and jewelry. (417) 485-0307. *Open daily.*

OZARK

Maine Street Mall. 1994 Evangel. 2-story building, 25,000 sq. ft. Antiques, collectibles, furniture, jewelry, toys, Jewel

> ### *Rare Items in Poor Condition: "Books Don't Buy"*
>
> Although we may find some real treasures at the flea market, there is one I can't caution you too much to leave alone. That is a truly rare or unique item in poor condition.
>
> Sure, it may be listed in the book as worth a lot of money in poor-to-bad condition, but keep in mind that "books don't buy." The overwhelming majority of collectors want items in nice-to-excellent condition. In my collections, I do not want any battered, torn-up, rusty, and in general unpresentable items, and most collectors feel the same way.

Tea items, depression glassware, dolls, quilts, primitives. (800) 553-2575 or (417) 485-2575. Plenty of parking. *Daily, 9:00 A.M. - 6:00 P.M.*

OZARK

Ozark Antique Mall. 200 S. 20th St. New mall, 1 level. Primitives, toys, sporting goods, old-time ice cream shop. Wheelchair accessible. Ample parking. (417) 485-5233.

PARK HILLS

Pat's Antique Mall. 233 W. Main St. Collectibles, jewelry, smalls, dolls, china, costume jewelry, lots of Avon products. (314) 431-6950.

PARK HILLS

Southern Hills Antique Mall. 201 E. Main St. Antiques, collectibles, secondhand items, some crafts. (314) 431-3499. *Monday - Friday, 9:00 A.M. - 6:00 P.M.; Saturdays, 9:00 A.M. - 5:00 P.M.; Sundays, noon - 4:00 P.M.*

PECULIAR

Dorothy's Den Antiques. Hwy. 71 and Peculiar Exit. 15 dealers. (816) 758-6910. *Monday - Saturday, 10:00 A.M. - 5:00 P.M.; Sundays, 11:00 A.M. - 5:00 P.M.*

PECULIAR

Peculiar Antique Mall. Hwy. 71 and Peculiar Exit. Depression glass, pottery, antiques, collectibles. 40 dealers. Outdoor flea market held on second Sunday of each month during warm weather. (816) 758-9511. *Monday - Saturday, 10:00 A.M. - 5:00 P.M.; Sundays, noon - 5:00 P.M.*

PECULIAR

Vintages. 208 C Hwy. Antiques, collectibles, gifts. (816) 758-5456. *Monday - Sat-*

urday, 10:00 A.M. - 5:00 P.M.; Sundays, noon - 5:00 P.M.

PEVELY

Pevely Antique Mall. Market is located at the Pevely Flea Market, on Hwy. 61-67 at the I-55 Pevely Exit. Mall has many fine quality antiques and a good selection of quality collectibles. Flea market is held on Saturdays and Sundays, both outdoors and indoors, and is far and away Missouri's finest flea market. (314) 479-7755 or 479-3215. *Wednesday - Sunday, 9:00 A.M. - 4:00 P.M.*

PLATT CITY

I-29 Antique Mall. Junction of I-29 and HH Hwy. 6 miles north of KCI Airport. 12,000 sq. ft. Lots of advertising items, Art Deco, coin-op, country furniture, primitives, telephones, toys, quilts, and Fiestaware. 65 dealers. (816) 431-2921. *Daily, 10:00 A.M. - 6:00 P.M.*

PLATT CITY

W. D. Pickers Antique Mall. Exit 20, off I-29 at the Weston/Leavenworth Exit. Lots of Indian artifacts, advertising, furniture, primitives, granite, Coca-Cola, toys. 100+ dealers. Mall has a flea market the second weekend of each month. (816) 243-8645 or 431-3100. *Daily, 10:00 A.M. - 6:00 P.M.*

PLATTSBURG

Spease Antique Mall. 202 N. East St. Antiques, collectibles, exceptional assortment of fine Victorian furniture. (816) 539-3170. *Tuesday - Saturday, 10:00 A.M. - 5:00 P.M.; Sundays, 1:00 - 5:00 P.M.; Thursdays, 10:00 A.M. - 8:00 P.M.*

PLEASANT HILL

Simmons General Mercantile Antique Mall. 124 First St. (816) 987-5999. *Wednesday - Friday, 11:00 A.M. - 5:00 P.M.; Saturdays, 10:00 A.M. - 5:00 P.M.; Sundays, 1:00 - 5:00 P.M.*

PLEASANT HILL

Traders Market. 100 First St. Downtown. 2 floors. Toys, dolls, records, primitives, collectibles. (816) 986-5592. *Monday - Friday, 11:00 A.M. - 5:00 P.M.; Saturdays and Sundays, noon - 5:00 P.M.; closed Tuesdays.*

REPUBLIC

County Fair Mall. 420 N. Hwy. 60. New mall. Wide variety of items; lots of collectibles and new merchandise. Some locally made crafts. 200 booths. (417) 732-8821. *Daily, 10:00 A.M. - 7:00 P.M.*

ROCHEPORT

Missouri River Antique Mall. I-70, Rocheport Exit 115. Glassware, china, furniture, silver, dolls, toys. Don Brumm, (314) 698-2066.

ROCK PORT

Country Creek Mall. 323 S. Main St. Antiques, Precious Moments. Mall has an old-fashioned candy counter and a crafters' loft. (816) 744-2345. *Monday - Saturday, 9:00 A.M. - 5:00 P.M.*

SALISBURY

General Store and Antique Mall. 2nd and Broadway, downtown. Antiques, collectibles, gifts, lots of Missouri-produced food items. Religious bookstore. (816) 388-5030. *Monday - Saturday, 9:00 A.M. - 5:30 P.M.*

SEDALIA

Country Cottage Craft Mall. 105 S. Osage. Downtown. Lots of local country crafts of all types. (816) 826-2164. *Monday - Friday, 9:00 A.M. - 5:30 P.M.; Saturdays, 9:00 A.M. - 5:00 P.M.*

SEDALIA

Crafters Mall. 809 Thompson Blvd. Lots of locally made crafts. (816) 826-6606. *Monday - Saturday, 10:00 A.M. - 5:00 P.M.*

SEDALIA

Evies Country Village. 4005 S. Hwy. 65. Antiques, collectibles. 25+ dealers. (816) 827-2877.

SEDALIA

Maple Leaf Antique Mall. 106 W. Main St. Large antique mall in downtown area. Well-stocked mall, with a wide variety of good items. Also a large selection of country gifts and crafts, new merchandise, new oak and pine furniture. For the added enjoyment of shoppers, there is an excellent tearoom. The mall also has a year-round Christmas and Holiday Shoppe. (816) 826-8383. *Monday - Saturday, 10:00 A.M. - 5:00 P.M.; Sundays, 11:00 A.M. - 5:00 P.M.*

SEDALIA

Marriott Antiques. The Pink Mall. Rt. 2, Box 340. 3 miles south of junction of Hwys. 50 and 65. Furniture, glassware, nice primitives. *Monday - Saturday, 9:30 A.M. - 5:00 P.M.; Sundays, 12:30 - 5:00 P.M.*

SMITHVILLE

Down on Main Street. 113 E. Main St. Antiques, crafts, gifts. *Monday - Friday, 1:00 - 5:00 P.M.; Saturdays, 10:00 A.M. - 5:00 P.M.*

SMITHVILLE
Pack Rats Antiques. 103 E. Main St. Antiques, furniture, jewelry, and toys. (816) 532-3363. *Mondays, 9:00 A.M. - 5:00 P.M.; Tuesday - Saturday, 10:00 A.M. - 5:00 P.M.*

SPRINGFIELD
Bass Country Antique Mall. 1832 S. Campbell. Mall is located directly across the street from the Bass Pro Store, an adventure in itself. Lots of fine antiques and collectibles here. The serious shopper will like this mall. On the down side, I found some of the owners less than courteous. Anyone in need of restrooms will be out of luck here. 100+ dealers. *Monday - Saturday, 10:00 A.M. - 6:00 P.M.; Sundays, noon - 5:00 P.M.*

SPRINGFIELD
Traders Market Antiques and Gifts Mall. 1845 E. Sunshine. New indoor mall. (417) 889-1145. Fax 882-0261.

ST. CHARLES
Do Antiques Mall. 1 Charlestown Plaza. 3 miles south of I-70, on Hwy. 94. 25,000 sq. ft. Large, well-stocked mall, with wide variety, from fine antiques and collectibles to crafts and new merchandise. (314) 939-4178. *Monday - Saturday, 10:00 A.M. - 8:00 P.M.; Sundays, 11:00 A.M. - 5:00 P.M.*

ST. GENEVIEVE
Kaegel's Country Collectibles. 252 Merchant St. Collectibles, antiques, crafts. 35 dealers. Mall is located in very old, quaint, historic river town. Many fine antique and craft shops here. Worth spending a couple of days in one of the many fine bed-and-breakfast inns in the area. (314) 883-7995. *Thursday - Tuesday, 10:00 A.M. - 5:00 P.M.; closed Wednesdays.*

ST. JOSEPH
Alabama Street Mall. 715 Alabama, (Hwy. 752). Primarily collectibles. 30 dealers. *Monday - Saturday, 10:00 A.M. - 5:00 P.M.*

ST. JOSEPH
Belt Highway Antique Mall. 407 S. Belt St, 1 block south of Venture. New mall. Chandeliers and lamps, lots of WW II memorabilia, carousel horses, dolls, toys, Victorian items, crafts. Well-stocked mall. (816) 232-0568. *Monday - Saturday, 10:00 A.M. - 5:00 P.M.; Sundays, 1:00 - 5:00 P.M.*

ST. JOSEPH
Central Station Mall. 710 S. 9th St. 15,000 sq. ft. Located

in the old police/jail building. Lots of dolls and quilts, collectibles of all descriptions. Also furniture, glassware, and pottery. (816) 232-6171. *Monday - Saturday, 10:00 A.M. - 5:00 P.M.; Sundays, 1:00 - 5:00 P.M.*

ST. JOSEPH
Felix Street Mini Mall. 518 Felix St. Antiques, collectibles, crafts, primitives, glassware, and new merchandise. 50+ dealers. (816) 233-7676. *Monday - Saturday, 10:00 A.M. - 6:00 P.M.; Sundays, noon - 6:00 P.M.*

ST. JOSEPH
Horns Antique Emporium. 502 Felix St. Downtown, 1 block east of Civic Arena. Fine antiques and collectibles. 2 large furniture rooms. 65 dealers, (816) 364-3717. *Monday - Saturday, 10:00 A.M. - 5:00 P.M.; Sundays, noon - 5:00 P.M.*

ST. JOSEPH
Kaleidoscope Antique Mall. 2717 Pear St. Antiques, furniture, collectibles, art glass, pottery, jewelry. Layaways available. (816) 232-8775. *Monday - Saturday, 9:00 A.M. - 5:00 P.M.; Sundays, 1:00 - 4:00 P.M.*

ST. JOSEPH
One of a Kind Gallery and Gifts. 2239 N. Belt. Woodlawn Center. Original artwork, stained and etched glass, jewelry, pottery, lots of high-quality art and crafts. 85 artists' booths. Mall has free special events for the public every weekend. Connie Tabony, (816) 232-0441. *Monday - Friday, 10:00 A.M. - 6:00 P.M.; Saturdays, 10:00 A.M. - 5:00 P.M.*

ST. JOSEPH
Penn Street Square Antique and Craft Mall. 12th and Penn Sts. 2-story mall, located between Jesse James House and the Pony Express Stable. Across the street from the Patee House Museum. Antiques and collectibles of all kinds. Some unique and hard-to-find items amid the booth displays and bric-a-brac. (816) 232-4626. *Open daily.*

ST. JOSEPH
United Antique Mall. 6th and Felix St. Downtown. Furniture, glassware, collectibles. 100+ booths. (816) 364-2881. *Monday - Friday, 11:00 A.M. - 6:00 P.M.; Saturdays, 10:00 A.M. - 6:00 P.M., Sundays, noon - 6:00 P.M.*

ST. LOUIS
Coomers Crafts. 1668 Clarkson Rd. Very nice arts and

crafts mall. Rest rooms. Ample parking. (314) 530-1706.

ST. LOUIS
South County Antiques Mall. 13208 Tesson Ferry Rd. I-270, south 2 miles on Tesson Ferry Rd. Large, 1-level mall. Very pricy; this is one I'd pass on. 400+ booths. (314) 842-5566. *Monday - Saturday, 9:00 A.M. - 8:00 P.M.; Sundays, 10:00 A.M. - 6:00 P.M.*

SULLIVAN
Showcase Antique Mall. 201 N. Service Rd. (314) 481-1068. *Daily, 10:00 A.M. - 6:00 P.M.*

WARRENSBURG
Those Were The Days Mall. ½ mile south of town, on Hwy. BB at Hwy. 13. Collectibles and lots of secondhand items. (816) 747-8799. *Monday - Saturday, 10:00 A.M. - 5:00 P.M.; Sundays, 1:00 - 5:00 P.M.*

WARRENSBURG
Trash and Treasures Shopping Mall. 138 W. Pine St. 7,500 sq. ft. Antiques, crafts, collectibles, lots of low-dollar items and junk. (816) 747-3123. *Monday - Saturday, 9:00 A.M. - 5:00 P.M.; Saturdays, 10:00 A.M. - 4:30 P.M.*

WARSAW
Valley Flea Market and Antique Mall. Old Hwy. 65 North. Quality antiques, collectibles, furniture, primitives, glassware, jewelry, and brass. 100+ dealers. Very interesting and picturesque town, with lots of antique shops and other fun things to do. This is a nice vacation area. (816) 438-6633.

WAVERLY
Gospel Truth Antique Mall. 100 W. Kelling. Downtown. Mall is located in a historic 1800s church. Antiques, collectibles, lots of Roseville and Carnival glass. (816) 493-2354. *Monday - Saturday, 10:00 A.M. - 5:00 P.M.; Sundays, 1:00 - 5:00 P.M.*

WEST PLAINS
Downtown Antique Mall. City Square, downtown. 60 dealers. (417) 256-6487. *Monday - Saturday, 9:00 A.M. - 5:30 P.M.; Sundays, 1:00 - 5:00 P.M.*

NEBRASKA

BELLEVUE
Enamel and Lace Antiques. 908 Ft. Crook Rd. South. (Hwy. 75). Booths displaying fine antiques and collectibles of all kinds. 35 dealers. (402) 291-4781. *Monday - Friday, 10:00 A.M. - 6:00 P.M.; Saturdays, 10:00 A.M. - 5:00 P.M.; Sundays, noon - 6:00 P.M.*

EAGLE
Eagle Antiques. 517 S. 4th St. General line of antiques and collectibles, including glassware, primitives, vintage jewelry and clothing, advertising items. 30+ dealers. *Open daily.*

FAIRBURY
Fredericks Antique Mall. W. Hwy. 136. 5 buildings full of furniture, primitives, glassware, collectibles. Property has a beautiful, restored Victorian house. (402) 729-5105 or 729-5126. *Monday - Saturday, 10:00 A.M. - 5:00 P.M.; Sundays, 1:00 - 5:00 P.M.*

FREMONT
Park Avenue Antiques. 515 N. Park Ave. Downtown. Variety of antique desirables. Also a large assortment of oak and pine furniture, both finished and unfinished, and a good selection of stoneware. 25+ dealers. (402) 721-1157. *Open daily.*

KEARNEY
Granny's Antique Co-Op. 229 S. Central. Multidealer shop with a bit of everything antique and collectible to be found, from turn-of-the-century family pictures to vintage wind-up toys. *Monday - Saturday, 10:00 A.M. - 5:00 P.M.; Sundays, 1:00 - 5:00 P.M.*

KEARNEY
Plum Tree Antique Mall. 2006 E. Hwy. 30. Glassware, china, pottery, art glass, collectibles. (308) 236-5777. *Tuesday - Saturday, 10:00 A.M. - 5:00 P.M.; Sundays, noon - 5:00 P.M.*

LEXINGTON
Antique Mall. I-80, Exit 237, 1/4 mile north. Antique mall and 11 individual shops located here. (308) 324-2816. *Open daily.*

LINCOLN
Antique Corner Cooperative. 1601 S. 17th St. Collectibles and good selection of oak furniture. (402) 476-8050. *Open daily.*

LINCOLN
The Antique Market. 48th St. and Old Cheney Rd. General line of antiques and collectibles with some nice furniture. 55 dealers. Snack bar, rest rooms, wheelchair accessible. Ample parking. (402) 423-4805. *Daily.*

LINCOLN
Burlington Arcade Antique Mall. Corner 7th and "P" Sts. Antique and collector items in all categories. (402) 476-6067. *Open daily.*

LINCOLN
Lincoln O Street Mall. 1835 "O" St. Furniture, primitives,

jewelry. Credit cards accepted. 60 dealers. (402) 435-3303 or 434-3747. *Monday - Saturday, 10:00 A.M. - 6:00 P.M.; Sundays, noon - 5:00 P.M.*

LINCOLN

St. George Antique Mall. 1023 "O" St. 7,000 sq. ft. Everything for the casual collector or serious investor. Some treasures hidden here amid run-of-the mill collectibles. (402) 477-4400. *Open daily.*

McCOOK

Magic City Mall. 112 E. 2nd St. Great selection of quality collectibles. (308) 345-7473.

OMAHA

Treasure Trove Flea Mall. E. 8806 Groer St. I-80, Exit 72nd St. 16,000 sq. ft. Antiques, collectibles. (402) 397-6811. *Daily, 9:00 A.M. - 6:00 P.M.*

OMAHA

Venice Antiques. Hwy. 92, 10 miles west of town. Antiques, furniture, primitives, glass, pottery, collectibles. 60+ dealers. (402) 359-5782. *Open daily.*

NORTH DAKOTA

FARGO

North Dakota Mall. 1024 Ave N. Antique furniture, antiques, collectibles, glassware, country crafts. Mall is located in a historic 100-year-old house. (701) 237-4423. *Monday - Saturday, 10:00 A.M. - 5:30 P.M.*

JAMESTOWN

Antique Attic. 219 First Ave S. Downtown. (701) 252-6733.

MANDAN

Antique Gallery. 300 W. Main St. (701) 667-2829. *Monday - Saturday, 9:00 A.M. - 6:00 P.M.; Sundays, noon - 5:00 P.M.*

OHIO

AKRON

West Hill Antiques. 461 W. Market St. Hwy. 18. Quality line of antiques and collectibles. Mall is located in Akron's antique row, with many neighboring shops. 5 dealers. (216) 762-6633. *Daily, 10:00 A.M. - 6:00 P.M.*

ARCANUM

Olde Tyme Treasures Antiques and Collectibles Mall. Corner of West George and High Sts. Judy Holster. *Tuesday - Saturday, 10:00 A.M. - 5:00 P.M.; Sundays, noon - 5:00 P.M.*

ARCANUM

Smiths Big Antique Store. 109 W. George St. 60 dealers. (513) 692-8540. *Tuesday - Sat-*

urday, 10:00 A.M. - 5:00 P.M.; Sundays, noon - 5:00 P.M.

ARCANUM
Victorian Babes Antiques Mall. 20 W. George St. Vickie Bruss Harter, (513) 548-3349. *Tuesday - Saturday, 11:00 A.M. - 5:00 P.M.; Sundays, 1:00 - 5:00 P.M.; closed Mondays.*

ASHLAND
Antiques on Main. 143 West Main St. Downtown. (419) 289-8599.

ASHLAND
Pumphouse Antiques. 400 Orange St. 22,000 sq. ft., 3-story building. Antiques and collectibles. First floor is quality antiques from all periods. Second floor is the collectors' mart—antiques and creative art. Third floor is lost treasures and elegant "junque." 100+ dealers. Air-conditioned. Good food; Pumphouse Cafe on premises. *Open daily.*

AVON
Country Heirs. 35800 Detroit Rd. Rt. 254. Antiques, collectibles, crafts, wreaths, woodcrafts, primitives, Christmas items. 15 dealers. (216) 937-5544. *Daily, 11:00 A.M. - 5:00 P.M.*

BARNESVILLE
Barnesville Antique Mall. 202 N. Chestnut St. 3-story building. Antiques, collectibles, secondhand and used merchandise. (614) 425-2435. *Daily, 9:00 A.M. - 5:00 P.M.*

BLANCHESTER
Broadway Antique Mall. 102 S. Broadway. Antiques, collectibles. 85 booths. (513) 783-2271. *Monday - Saturday, 10:00 A.M. - 5:00 P.M.; Sundays, 12:30 - 5:00 P.M.*

BLANCHESTER
Broadway Antique Mall #2. Junction of Rts. 28, 123, and 133. 10,000 sq. ft. Antiques, collectibles, primitives, glassware, furniture, dolls, and toys. 85 booths. Mall conducts retail consignment auctions the first Thursday of each month. (513) 783-2271. *Monday - Saturday, 10:00 A.M. - 5:00 P.M.; Sundays, 12:30 - 5:00 P.M.*

CAMBRIDGE
Penny Court Antiques. 637 Wheeling Ave. Antiques and collectibles. 100+ dealers. (614) 432-4369. *Monday - Saturday, 10:00 A.M. - 6:00 P.M.; Sundays, noon - 5:00 P.M.*

CARROLL
Soper's Antique Palace Mall. Junction of Rt. 33 and Coonpath Rd., 4 miles north of Lancaster. 4 buildings full of antiques and collectibles.

Mall specializes in old furniture and jewelry. (614) 756-4411. *Wednesday - Sunday, 11:00 A.M. - 5:30 P.M.*

CASTALIA

Cloud's Antique Mall. Rt. 269. Antiques, collectibles. Very quality-oriented establishment. Mall features 35 showcases. 50 dealers. Mark and Trina Cloud, (419) 684-7566. *Daily, 10:00 A.M. - 5:00 P.M.*

CHADRON

Antiques On The Square. 101 Main St. On the town square. 20 dealers. Several antique shops neighboring. (216) 286-1912. *Monday - Saturday, 10:00 A.M. - 5:00 P.M.; Sundays, noon - 5:00 P.M.*

CHESTERLAND

Antiques of Chester. 7976 Mayfield Rd. Rt. 322. Restored 1830 farmhouse. Fine antiques, collectibles, country oak, Victorian, nautical, tools, quilts, glassware. 11 dealers. (216) 729-3395. *Tuesday - Saturday, 11:00 A.M. - 5:00 P.M.; Sundays, noon - 5:00 P.M.*

CHESTERVILLE

Chesterville Antiques. Junction of Rts. 95 and 314. 2 miles east of I-71, Exit 151. (419) 768-3979.

CINCINNATI

Antique Mall and Collectibles Market. 3742 Kellogg Ave. Hwy. 52. 30,000 sq. ft. Antiques, collectibles, fine furniture, Art Deco, vintage clothing, dolls, toys, estate jewelry. 90 dealers. Credit cards accepted. Restaurant on premises. (513) 871-5560 or 321-0919. *Wednesday - Friday, 10:00 A.M. - 5:00 P.M.; Saturdays and Sundays, 9:00 A.M. - 6:00 P.M.*

CINCINNATI

Duck Creek Antique Mall. 3715 Madison Rd. New mall. 20,000 sq. ft. Antiques, furniture, glassware, jewelry, pottery, china, toys. 130 dealers. Credit cards accepted. (513) 321-0900. *Monday - Saturday, 10:00 A.M. - 5:00 P.M.; Sundays, noon - 5:00 P.M.*

CINCINNATI

Special Things Antique Mall. 5701 Cheviot Rd. I-74, Exit 14, 1 mile north. Dealer co-op; 10-room farmhouse. Fine antiques and collectibles. (513) 741-9127. *Monday - Saturday, 10:00 A.M. - 5:00 P.M.; Sundays, noon - 5:00 P.M.*

CIRCLEVILLE

Brewer's Antique Mall. 105 W. Main St. *Monday - Saturday, 10:00 A.M. - 6:00 P.M.; Sundays, noon - 5:00 P.M.*

CLEVELAND
Craft Market Place. 13500 Pearl Rd. Arts and crafts. (216) 572-5802.

CLIFTON
Clifton Antique Mall. 301 N. Main St. Antiques and collectibles. (513) 767-2277. *Wednesday - Sunday, 11:00 A.M. - 5:00 P.M.*

CLIFTON
Weber's Antiques. Clay St. (513) 767-8581.

COLUMBUS
Greater Columbus Antique Mall. 1045 S. High St. 5-story facility; 11,000 sq. ft. Quality antiques and collectibles. 70+ dealers. Credit cards accepted. (614) 443-7858. *Daily, 11:00 A.M. - 8:00 P.M.*

COSHOCTON
Coshocton Antique Center. Clark Stuart. 309 S. 4th St. (614) 622-3223. *Monday - Saturday, 10:00 A.M. - 5:00 P.M.; Sundays, 1:00 - 5:00 P.M.*

CRIDERSVILLE
The Antique Arcade. 608 E. Main St. I-75, Exit 118. Antiques, collectibles, furniture. (419) 645-4563. *Monday - Saturday, 8:00 A.M. - 5:00 P.M.; Sundays, noon - 5:00 P.M.*

DEFIANCE
Another Man's Treasures Antique Mall. 235 Hopkins. 4,000 sq. ft. Antiques, collectibles, furniture. (419) 784-4589. *Tuesday - Friday, 10:00 A.M. - 5:00 P.M.; Sundays, noon - 4:00 P.M.*

DELPHOS
Miami-Erie Antique Mall. 132 S. Delphos St. Mall is located in 1880s train station hotel. Antiques, collectibles, lots of antique furniture displayed in the hotel's 30 rooms. (419) 695-6926. *Monday - Friday, 10:00 A.M. - 6:00 P.M.; Saturdays and Sundays, 11:00 A.M. - 4:00 P.M.*

DELTA
Delta Antiques Market. 301 Main St. Hwy. 2. (419) 335-0156. *Tuesday - Saturday, 10:30 A.M. - 5:00 P.M.; Sundays, 12:30 - 4:00 P.M.*

DENNISON
250 Antique Mall. 9043 State Rt. 250 S.E. 13,000 sq. ft. Quality line of antiques and collectibles. Mall has a year-round Christmas shop. 50+ dealers. (800) 247-3704 or (614) 922-3811. *Daily, 10:00 A.M. - 5:00 P.M.*

DEXTER CITY
Dexter City Antique Mall. Hwy. 821. I-77, Exit 16, 2 miles north. 2-story building. Large selection of furniture at this mall; general line of antiques and collectibles.

> ### *Beware of Reproductions!*
> Price is a good measure of whether an item is an original or a reproduction. Again, you will have to be somewhat knowledgeable about the general category.
>
> If you find a piece of pink depression glass marked $40, and, in the same booth, one almost identical for $12, odds are the $12 item is either a broken original or a reproduction. If it isn't broken, you probably know the answer.
>
> Reproductions have flooded the marketplace and have turned up in many categories. So, in the field of collectibles, the educated shopper is the wise shopper.

Lots of quality glassware. 45 dealers. (614) 783-5921. *Monday - Saturday, 10:00 A.M. - 6:00 P.M.; Sundays, noon - 6:00 P.M.*

DOVER
Dover Antique Mall. 416 W. 8th St. Rear of building. Antiques and collectibles. *Monday - Saturday, 10:00 A.M. - 5:00 P.M.*

ETNA
H and R Antique Mall. 1063 Pike St. I-70, Exit 118. 1/2 mile north to Pike. Antiques and collectibles. (614) 927-4053. *Wednesday - Saturday, 10:00 A.M. - 5:00 P.M.; Sundays, 1:00 - 5:00 P.M.*

FINDLAY
Clover Farms Antiques Emporium. 130 E. Sandusky St. Mall is located in historic old building. Antiques, collectibles, nice selection of oak, walnut, cherry furniture. Lots of architectural antiques. (419) 424-8833. *Tuesday - Saturday, 11:00 A.M. - 5:00 P.M.; Sundays, 1:00 - 5:00 P.M.*

FINDLAY
Jeffrey's Antique Gallery. Bryan Jrick. 11326 Township Rd. 99. I-75, Exit 161. Large, well-stocked mall; many high-quality and investment-grade pieces here. 300+ dealers. Credit cards accepted. (419) 429-7500. *Daily, 10:00 A.M. - 6:00 P.M.*

FOSTORIA
Fostoria Town Center Antique Mall. 116 N. Main St. (419) 435-1989. *Tuesday - Saturday, 10:00 A.M. - 6:00 P.M.; Sundays, noon - 5:00 P.M.*

GREENTOWN
Union Station Antiques. 9815 Cleveland Ave. N.W. Located at Coach House Square. 4,000 sq. ft. 2-story building. 15 dealers. Credit cards

accepted. (216) 966-0658. *Monday - Saturday, 10:00 A.M. - 5:00 P.M.; Sundays, noon - 5:00 P.M.*

GREENVILLE
Biddlestone Antique Mall. 126 W. 4th St. Antiques, collectibles. (513) 548-3180. *Monday - Saturday, 10:00 A.M. - 5:00 P.M.; Sundays, 1:00 - 5:00 P.M.*

HARPSTER
Old General Store Antique Mall. 7223 State Rt. 294. Antiques, collectibles. (614) 496-2532. *Monday - Friday, 11:00 A.M. - 6:00 P.M.; Sundays, 1:00 - 5:00 P.M.*

HILLSBORO
Old Parts Factory Mall. 135 N. West St. Nice selection of quality antiques and collectibles. (513) 393-8934. *Monday - Saturday, 10:00 A.M. - 6:00 P.M.; Sundays, 1:00 - 5:00 P.M.*

HOMERVILLE
Homerville Antique Mall. Junction of Hwys. 224 and 301. Antiques, collectibles, country, kitchen items, primitives, furniture, depression glass, decorator items. (216) 625-2500. *Thursdays, 11:00 A.M. - 5:00 P.M.; Fridays and Saturdays, 11:00 A.M. - 7:00 P.M.; Sundays, 11:00 A.M. - 5:00 P.M.*

JOHNSTOWN
Village Antique Mall. 42 S. Main St. 6,000 sq. ft. Antiques, collectibles, pottery, books, depression glass, primitives, cookie jars. (614) 967-0048. *Monday - Saturday, 9:00 A.M. - 6:00 P.M.*

KIDRON
Village Antique Mall. 4750 Kidron Rd. Antiques and collectibles, 20 dealers. (216) 857-1040. *Monday - Saturday, 10:00 A.M. - 5:00 P.M.*

KUNKLE
Kunkle Schoolhouse Antique Mall. 119 Elm St. New mall. Don Ackley, (419) 737-2571.

LANCASTER
Lancaster Antique Emporium. 201 W. Main St. (614) 653-1973. *Open daily.*

LEBANON
Broadway Antique Mall. 17 S. Broadway. 10,000 sq. ft. Antiques and collectibles. 80 dealers. (513) 932-1410. *Monday - Saturday, 10:00 A.M. - 5:00 P.M.; Sundays, noon - 5:00 P.M.*

LEBANON
Lebanon Antique Exchange. 15 E. Main St. (513) 933-9935. *Monday - Saturday, 10:00 A.M. - 5:00 P.M.; Sundays, noon - 5:00 P.M.*

LITHOPOLIS
Lithopolis Antique Mart. 9 E.

Columbus St. 5,000 sq. ft, 4 levels. Antiques, collectibles, furniture. 50 dealers. (614) 837-9683. *Tuesdays, 10:00 A.M. - 8:00 P.M.; Wednesday - Saturday, 10:00 A.M. - 5:00 P.M.; Sundays, 1:00 - 5:00 P.M.*

LOGAN

Logan Antique Mall. 145 W. Main St. 3-story building. 60 dealers. (614) 385-2061. *Monday - Saturday, 10:00 A.M. - 5:30 P.M.; Sundays, noon - 5:00 P.M.*

MANSFIELD

Mid-Ohio Antique Mall. 155 Cline Ave. Corner of Cline and Lexington Aves. Rt. 42S. 2-story building. (419) 756-5852. *Daily, 10:00 A.M. - 5:00 P.M.*

MEDINA

Brothers Antique Mall. 6132 Wooster Pike. Rt. 3. 5 miles north on I-76, Exit 2. Antiques, great selection of cookie jars, Watt pottery, 40s and 50s collectibles. Mall does furniture stripping, repair, and refinishing. (216) 723-7580. *Monday - Saturday, 10:00 A.M. - 5:00 P.M.; Sundays, noon - 5:00 P.M.*

MENTOR

Mentor Village Antiques. 8619 Mentor Ave. Rt. 20. Furniture, linens, glass, primitives, pottery, paper, porcelains. (216) 255-1438. *Monday - Saturday, 11:00 A.M. - 5:00 P.M.*

MILLERSBURG

Antique Emporium. 113 W. Jackson. Antiques, collectibles, country furniture, china, Victorian, glassware, primitives. Country crafts and decorator items. (216) 674-0510. *Monday - Saturday, 10:00 A.M. - 5:00 P.M.; Sundays, 10:00 A.M. - 4:00 P.M.*

MONTPELIER

Village Trading Post. 123 Empire St. Credit cards accepted. (419) 485-4996. *Monday - Saturday, 10:00 A.M. - 5:00 P.M.; Sundays, 1:00 - 5:00 P.M.*

NEW BALTIMORE

Mack's Barn Old-Tiques and Ant. State Rt. 44, between Rts. 619 and 224. Antiques and collectibles. Cheryl Himebaugh, (216) 935-2746. *Monday - Saturday, 11:00 A.M. - 5:00 P.M.; Sundays, noon - 5:00 P.M.; closed Tuesdays.*

NEW PHILADELPHIA

Riverfront Antique Mall. 1203 Front St. I-77, Exit 81. 80,000 sq. ft., all on one floor. One of the largest and best-stocked malls in the country. Many showcases and room settings, very attractively displayed. Dealer quality throughout the mall is very high. This mall is almost a vacation in itself. 250+ dealers. (800) 926-9806 or (216) 339-4448. *Monday - Saturday, 10:00 A.M. - 8:00 P.M.; Sundays, 10:00 A.M. - 6:00 P.M.*

New Vienna
Village Antique Mall. 191 Main St. 4,000 sq. ft. Antiques and collectibles. (513) 987-2932. *Monday - Saturday, 10:00 A.M. - 5:00 P.M.; Sundays, 1:00 - 5:00 P.M.*

North Ridgeville
Hatchery Antique Mall. 7474 Avon Belden Rd. 5,000 sq. ft. Mall features a 16-showcase room filled with very desirable smalls. 30 dealers. (216) 327-9808. *Daily, 10:00 A.M. - 6:00 P.M.*

Olmsted Falls
Trackside Antique Mall. 9545 Columbia Rd. Rt. 252. Antiques, collectibles, early toys, glass, advertising items, china. (216) 235-1166. *Daily, 11:00 A.M. - 4:30 P.M.*

Perrysburg
Perrysburg Antiques Market. 118 Louisiana Ave. Antiques, collectibles, furniture, jewelry, watches. Always a nice selection of fireplace mantels. 15 dealers. Marty Kruser, (419) 872-0231. *Tuesday - Saturday, 10:30 A.M. - 5:30 P.M.; Sundays, 11:00 A.M. - 4:00 P.M.*

Pioneer
Pioneer Antique Mall. 103 Baubice St. Credit cards accepted. (419) 737-2341. *Monday - Saturday, 10:00 A.M. - 6:00 P.M.; Sundays, 1:00 - 5:00 P.M.*

Pioneer
Tri-State Antique Mall. State Rt. 15. Ohio Turnpike, Exit 2, 1 mile north. Credit cards accepted. (419) 485-5610. *Tuesday - Saturday, 10:00 A.M. - 5:30 P.M.; Sundays, 1:00 - 5:00 P.M.*

Powell
Depot Street Antique Mall. 41 and 47 Depot St. 2 buildings, 6,000 sq. ft. Antiques and collectibles. Credit cards accepted. Merrill and Bunny Wells, (614) 885-6034. *Tuesday - Saturday, 10:00 A.M. - 5:00 P.M.; Sundays, noon - 5:00 P.M.*

Ripley
Olde Piano Factory Antique Mall. 307 N. 2nd St. Antiques, collectibles, furniture. (513) 392-9243. *Monday - Saturday, 10:00 A.M. - 4:00 P.M.; Sundays, noon - 5:00 P.M.*

Ross
Early Days Antiques. 71 W. Olentangy St. Antiques, collectibles, gifts. (614) 848-4747.

Tuesday - Saturday, 11:00 A.M. - 5:00 P.M.; Sundays, 1:00 - 5:00 P.M.

ROSS
Liberty Antique Mall. 22 N. Liberty St. Antiques, collectibles, furniture, toys, paper, jewelry, glassware. 30 dealers. (614) 885-5588. *Tuesday - Saturday, noon - 5:00 P.M.; Sundays, 1:00 - 5:00 P.M.*

ROSS
Venice Antique Mall. Junction of State Rts. 128 and 126. 12,000 sq. ft., 3 floors. Antiques and collectibles. 70+ dealers. (513) 738-8180. *Daily, 11:00 A.M. - 7:00 P.M.*

SMITHVILLE
Smithville Antique Mall. 637 E. Main St. Hwy. 585. Antiques and collectibles. (216) 669-3332. *Monday - Saturday, 10:00 A.M. - 5:00 P.M.; Sundays, noon - 5:00 P.M.*

SOUTH BLOOMFIELD
South Bloomfield Antique Mall. Rt. 23 North. General line of antiques and collectibles. 25 dealers. (614) 983-4300. *Monday - Saturday, 10:00 A.M. - 5:00 P.M.; Sundays, noon - 5:00 P.M.*

SPENCERVILLE
Ohio Antique Market. 113 S. Broadway. Antiques and collectibles. 40 dealers. (419) 647-6237. *Monday - Saturday, 10:00 A.M. - 6:00 P.M.; Sundays, noon - 5:00 P.M.; closed Wednesdays.*

SPENCERVILLE
Spencerville Antique Mall. 127 N. Broadway. Antiques and collectibles. (419) 647-4050. *Monday - Saturday, 11:00 A.M. - 5:00 P.M.; Sundays, 1:00 - 5:00 P.M.; closed Thursdays.*

SPRINGFIELD
AAA I-70 Antique Mall. 4700 S. Charleston Pike. New mall. Deli in mall. Credit cards accepted. (513) 324-8448. *Daily, 10:00 A.M. - 6:00 P.M.*

STRASBURG
Strasburg 77 Antiques and Collectibles. 780 S. Wooster. I-77, Exit 87. 1/4 mile west. Antique mall, 3 antique shops, and 2 weekend indoor flea markets are all located at this stop. Leave the kids at Hardee's, across the street, and spend the day here. (216) 878-7726. *Tuesday - Sunday, 11:00 A.M. - 5:00 P.M.*

SUGARCREEK
Dutch Valley Antique Mall. Old Rt. 39. 4,000 sq. ft. Antiques and collectibles. Great restaurant next door. (216) 852-4026. *Monday - Saturday, 9:00 A.M. - 8:00 P.M.*

SUNBURY
Sun-Berry Antique Mall. 20 S. Vernon St. Country, collectibles, jewelry. 20 dealers. (614) 965-2279. *Monday - Saturday, 10:00 A.M. - 5:00 P.M.; Sundays, 1:00 - 5:00 P.M.*

SUNBURY
Weidners Village Square Antique Mall. 31 E. Granville St. Quality antiques, coins, furniture, artifacts. Mall has a large selection of display cases and accessories. 40 dealers. (614) 965-4377. *Monday - Saturday, 10:00 A.M. - 6:00 P.M.; Sundays, 1:00 - 5:00 P.M.*

TOLEDO
Cobblestone Antique Mall. 2635 W. Central Ave. Antiques, collectibles. 40+ dealers. (419) 475-4761. *Monday - Saturday, 10:00 A.M. - 5:00 P.M.; Sundays, noon - 5:00 P.M.*

TOLEDO
Downtown Antiques and Collectibles Mall. 333 N. Superior St. Antiques, collectibles, books, coins, glassware, estate jewelry, pottery, dolls. Jim Wagner, (419) 255-5252. *Monday - Saturday, 10:00 A.M. - 6:00 P.M.; Sundays, 10:00 A.M. - 4:00 P.M.*

TOLEDO
Old West End Collector's Corner. 2502 Collingwood Blvd. 12,000 sq. ft. consignment center. Antiques, collectibles. Credit cards accepted. *Monday - Friday, noon - 6:00 P.M.; Saturdays, 10:00 A.M. - 6:00 P.M.*

VAN WERT
Years Ago Antique Mall. 108 W. Main St. Antiques, collectibles. (419) 238-3362. *Monday - Friday, 9:00 A.M. - 5:00 P.M.*

WADSWORTH
Wadsworth Antique Mall. 332 College St. Good selection of quality antiques and collectibles. (216) 336-8620. *Wednesday - Friday, 10:00 A.M. - 5:00 P.M.; Saturdays, 10:00 A.M. - 3:00 P.M.; Sundays, 1:00 - 5:00 P.M.*

WAPAKONETA
Auglaize Antique Mall. 116 W. Auglaize St. 17,000 sq. ft, 2 levels. Credit cards accepted. (419) 738-8004. *Monday - Saturday, 10:00 A.M. - 5:00 P.M.; Sundays, noon - 5:00 P.M.*

WATERVILLE
Mill Race Antiques Mall. 217 Mechanic St. Antiques, collectibles. (419) 878-6822.

WAYNESVILLE
Bittersweet Antiques Mall. 57

S. Main St. Antiques, collectibles. 20 dealers.

WAYNESVILLE
Waynesville Antique Mall. 69 S. Main St. Antiques and collectibles. 20+ dealers. (513) 897-6937. (513) 897-6937. *Daily, 11:00 A.M. - 5:00 P.M.*

WESTERVILLE
Heart's Content Antique Mall. 7 N. State St. Country furniture, restored trunks, classic fountain pens, bottles, linens, kitchen collectibles. (614) 891-6050. *Monday - Saturday, 10:00 A.M. - 5:00 P.M.*

WESTERVILLE
Westerville Antique Mall. 34 E. College Ave. Antique clocks, Victorian linens, quilts, furniture, primitives, glass, china, collectibles. (614) 891-6966. *Monday - Saturday, 10:00 A.M. - 5:00 P.M.*

ZANESVILLE
Old Towne Antique Mall. 529 Main St. Rt. 40. 20,000 sq. ft. Quality line of antiques and collectibles. Good selection of antique furniture and quality pottery. Mall atmosphere is set in 1890s western town, with a general store and an auction house. 80 dealers. Many neighboring antique shops. (614) 452-1527. *Open daily.*

SOUTH DAKOTA

DEADWOOD
Gold Belt Mercantile Antiques and Fancy Goods. 93 Sherman St. 20 antique dealers. (605) 578-2202.

FLANDREAU
Bend in the River Antique Mall. 119 E. 2nd Ave. Antiques, collectibles, refinishing, repair, chair weaving and caning. (605) 997-5177.

RAPID CITY
Antique Mall. 2101 W. 41st St. (605) 335-7134.

ST. JOE
St. Joe Antiques Mall and Gift Shop. 615-A St. Joseph St. 40 antique dealers and a gift shop. (605) 341-1073. *Monday - Saturday, 9:30 A.M.- 5:30 P.M.*

WISCONSIN

APPLETON
Fox River Antique Mall. 1074 S. Van Dyke Road. 20,000 sq. ft. New mall. Large selection of antiques and collectibles. 130+ dealers. (414) 731-9699. *Daily, 10:00 A.M. - 6:00 P.M.*

BEAVER DAM
General Store Antique Mall. Highway 33 and Business 151. Great buys in quality antiques and popular collect-

ibles. Advertising items, country primitives, Victorian, Art Deco, Oriental items, glassware, books. 60 dealers. (414) 887-1116. *Open 10:00 A.M. - 5:00 P.M.*

BELOIT
Elegant Chicken Antique Mall. 412 Prospect. Country accessories and gifts. Also plenty of fine antiques and collector items for every taste and budget. (608) 364-4791. *Monday - Saturday, 10:00 A.M. - 4:00 P.M.*

BELOIT
Riverfront Antiques Mall. 306 State St. Antiques, furniture, lamps. glassware, jewelry, primitives. (608) 362-7368. *Monday - Saturday, 10:00 A.M. - 5:00 P.M.; Sundays, noon - 4:00 P.M.*

CLINTON
Nana's House of Antiques. 244 Allen St. 1 mile south of Hwy. 43. Approximately 50 dealers. (608) 676-5535. *Monday - Saturday, 10:00 A.M. - 4:00 P.M.; Sundays, 11:00 A.M. - 4:00 P.M.*

COLUMBUS
Columbus Antique Mall and Museum. 65,000 sq. ft. mall. Well stocked with excellent-quality items. 150 dealers and 300 booths. Museum is devoted to Christopher Columbus and things relating to his voyages and life. Includes many Columbian Exposition items. Admission charge $1. (414) 623-1992. *Daily, 8:30 A.M. - 4:00 P.M.*

EAU CLAIRE
Antique Emporium. 306 Main St, downtown. Lots of American and Victorian furniture. Glassware and plenty of small collectibles. 20 dealers. (715) 832-2494. *Monday - Saturday, 10:00 A.M. - 5:30 P.M.*

FOUNTAIN CITY
Antique Market. 27 N. Shore Drive. Collectibles, secondhand and bric-a-brac. 6 dealers. (608) 687-7600. *Open daily.*

KEWASKUM
General Store Antique Mall. Junction of Hwys. 45 and 28. A bit of everything for both new and serious collectors. 75 dealers. (414) 626-2885. *Daily, 10:00 A.M. - 5:00 P.M.*

LA CROSSE
Antique Center. 110 S. Third. Downtown. 3 floors. Antique furniture, china, silver, coins, vintage jewelry, lamps, linen, quilts, primitives. 75 booths. *Monday - Saturday, 9:00 A.M. - 5:30 P.M.; Sundays, 11:00 A.M. - 4:00 P.M.*

Madison
Mapletree Antique Mall. 1293 N. Sherman St. 20,000 sq. ft. General line of antiques and collectibles. Separate craft section. (608) 241-2599. *Open daily.*

Milton
Campus Antique Mall. 609 Campus St. Antiques and collectibles of all descriptions. (608) 888-3324. *Monday - Saturday, 10:00 A.M. - 5:00 P.M.; Sundays, noon - 5:00 P.M.*

Milwaukee
Milwaukee Antiques Center. 341 N. Milwaukee St. 3 floors full of great antiques and collectibles. Give yourself plenty of time to poke around in this mall. 75 dealers. (414) 276-0605.

Montello
Granite City Antique Mall and Flea Market. 145 Clay St. Good selection of antiques and collectibles. Outdoor flea market on weekends. (608) 297-7925. *Daily.*

Oshkosh
Original's Mall of Antiques. 1475 S. Washburn. Hwy. 41. West Frontage Road at 9th St. Quality antiques and collectibles. Approximately 80 booths. (414) 235-0495. *Daily, 10:00 A.M. - 6:00 P.M.*

Phelps
Rainy Day Antique Mall. Downtown. Even though it operates on a relatively short schedule, this mall has many nice antiques and collector items. (715) 547-3114. *May - October; daily.*

Portage
Antiques Mall. 114 W. Cook St. Glassware, kitchen collectibles, boudoir items, china, glassware, collector finds of all kinds. (608) 742-1640. *Open daily.*

Reedsburg
Big Store Plaza Antique Malls. 195 Main St. Hwys. 23 and 33. Downtown. 3 antique malls with a nice restaurant. Quality antiques, collectibles. Lots of smalls and unusual items. A colorful, quirky, and interesting stop. 80 dealers total. (608) 524-4141.

Richland Center
Valley Antique Mall. 178 S. Central Ave. Antiques and collector items for everyone, from the newest to the most seasoned collector. 20 dealers. (608) 647-3793. *Open daily.*

Sturtevant
School Days Mall. 9500 Durand Ave. Hwy. 11. 2 miles east of I-94. 12,000 sq. ft. 7

specialty shops under one roof. 50 dealers. (414) 886-1069. *Tuesday - Saturday, 10:00 A.M. - 8:00 P.M.; Sundays, noon - 5:00 P.M.*

TOMAH
Antique Mall of Tomah. P.O. Box 721. I-94 and Hwy. 21E, Exit #143. Quality antique furniture, primitives, collectibles, jewelry, coins. 40 dealers. Mall welcomes dealers. (608) 372-7853. *April - January; daily, 9:00 A.M. - 5:00 P.M.*

UNION GROVE
Storm Hall Antique Mall. Hwy. 45, 5 miles west of I-94. Quality antiques and collectibles. (414) 878-1644.

WALWORTH
Freddy Bears Antique Mall. 2819 Beck Drive. 8,000 sq. ft. 45 dealers. 414) 534-BEAR. *Daily, 9:30 A.M. - 5:00 P.M.*

WALWORTH
On The Square Antique Mall. Junction Routes 14 and 67. Quality antiques and collectibles. 85+ dealers. (414) 275-9858. *Daily, 10:00 A.M. - 5:00 P.M.*

WAUKESHA
A Dickens of a Place Antique Center. 521 Wisconsin Ave. Quality furniture, jewelry, collectibles, primitives, glassware, vintage clothing, and general line of antiques. 35 dealers. (414) 542-0702. *Monday - Saturday, 10:00 A.M. - 5:00 P.M.; Sundays, noon - 5:00 P.M.*

WEST BEND
Half Mile Antique Fair Mall. 7003 Hwy. 144 North. Nice antiques and quality collectibles. Country primitives, Victorian-era items, glassware, dolls, books, china, vintage jewelry, paper and advertising memorabilia, linens, quilts, boudoir items. (414) 338-6282. *Daily.*

AUCTIONS

(Includes Public Auctions and Dealer Auctions)

Public Auctions

The following companies conduct retail auctions, also known as 'sales.' One note of caution: Some auction houses are now charging buyers a ten percent premium. This means that a ten percent surcharge will be added to the total amount of your purchases. I refuse to attend any auction that charges a premium, and I recommend that others follow my example. Remember, always call before traveling long distances.

ILLINOIS

ALTON
Hilltop Auction Co. Fosterburg Rd., Alton, IL. (618) 462-6458. Company conducts weekly retail consignment auctions with good representation of antiques and collectibles.

AURORA PARK
Conwill Auction. Pete Conwill, Van Der Karr Rd. and Bridge St., Aurora Park, IL. (815) 937-9171. Company conducts wholesale dealer auctions and several monthly retail public consignment auctions from its premises. Call for dates.

BELLEVILLE
Garrett Galleries. 222 West B St., Belleville, IL 62220. (800) 707-3434, (618) 277-0192. Company conducts many fine-antique sales and specializes in English containers of furniture. Charges a 10% buyers' premium.

BELOIT
Antique and Collector Consignment Auction. 2237 Alton Rd, Beloit, IL. Sales conducted on Thursdays and Fridays at noon.

BLOOMINGTON
Fine Arts Brokers, Auctioneers and Appraisers. The Gallery, 300 E. Grove St., Bloomington, IL 61701. (309) 828-5533, Fax (309) 829-2266. Company conducts high-quality auctions—investment items, collections, art, rare books and prints, collections from its gallery.

CHICAGO
Auction USA, Inc. 1423 W. Fullerton Ave., Chicago, IL 60614. (312) 871-7200. Company conducts monthly

> ### *A Word to the Wise: Arrive Early!*
>
> Auctions can be tricky places to buy if you aren't on your toes. When an item goes on the block, when your hand goes up and the auctioneer's gavel comes down, you'd better know what you just bought and be prepared to pay for it.
>
> It is never the auctioneer's fault if what you just bought isn't what you thought it was. That means chips, dings, dents, and all.
>
> Smart auction-goers plan to arrive at least forty-five minutes to an hour prior to the start of the sale. The reasons? 1. You want to stake out a good seat, where you will have a clear view of the auctioneer and the selling ring. 2. You need time to examine the merchandise.
>
> When you find something you think you will want to bid on, look it over carefully. In this way you won't be surprised—or, worst of all, disappointed—when it comes time to pay for your new acquisition.

wholesale dealers' auction of general merchandise.

CHICAGO
Chase Gilmore Art Galleries. 724 W. Washington St., Chicago, IL 60606. (312) 648-1690.

CHICAGO
Elliott's Country Faire, Techspace Inc., 222 S. Morgan St. 1-D, Chicago, IL 60607. Monthly estate auctions from January - April on the last Tuesday of the month.

CHICAGO
Hanzel Galleries. 1120 S. Michigan Ave., Chicago, IL 60605. (312) 922-6234.

CHICAGO
Leslie Hindman Auctions. 215 W. Ohio St., Chicago, IL 60610. (312) 670-0010, Fax (312) 670-4248.

DIXON
Auction City Sales. Lee Hollingsworth, 2305 W. 4th St., Dixon, IL. (815) 288-5814. Company conducts antique and collectible sales from its premises.

ELGIN
Dunnings Auction Service, Inc. 755 Church Rd., Elgin, IL 60123. (708) 741-3483, Fax (708) 741-3589. Company conducts fine-antique auctions on its premises.

Mazon
Hintze Auction Service. Mazon, IL. (815) 448-2368 or 448-5551. Company conducts many fine-antique and specialty auctions in Northern Illinois.

Newton
Art Schackman Auction Specialist. Newton, IL. (618) 783-2084. Conducts estate sales in the area.

Northbrook
Ipc Levy Auctioneers. 1535 Lake Cook Rd., #306, Northbrook, IL 60062. (708) 205-1280, Fax (708) 205-1286. Company conducts large industrial auctions and liquidations throughout the U.S. Mack Realty and Auction Co. Wally Kilker. (815) 938-2185. Company conducts retail auctions and antique auctions.

Orion
Anderson Auction. Bruce Anderson, Orion, IL. (309) 522-5897. Company conducts many fine, specialized sales, including oil paintings, etchings, photos, and prints. Sales are usually conducted at the Anderson Auction Building.

Palatine
Andre Ammelounx. Box 136, Palatine, IL 60078. (708) 991-5927, Fax (708) 991-5947. Company conducts many specialized sales, such as beer stein auctions.

Pecatonica
Henry Hachmeister, Auctioneer. Pecatonica, Illinois. (815) 239-1436. Conducts antique and estate auctions in the area.

Putnam
Signature Marketplace and Auction. Rt. 29. Putnam, IL. (815) 437-2025. Company conducts antique and collectible sales and general consignment auctions.

Roscoe
Dealer Auction. Roscoe Auction Center, 11631 Main St. Roscoe, IL. (815) 623-8232. Retail public consignment auctions from its premises throughout the month.

Roscoe
Roscoe Auction House. Hwy. 251 and Elevator Rd., Roscoe, IL. (815) 623-8232 or 654-7762. Company conducts retail consignment auctions on Friday nights at 7:00 P.M.

Shipman
Harman Auction Center. Shipman, IL. (618) 836-7355. Company conducts many large antique and collectible auctions on its premises; also operates weekly retail consignment auctions.

Sparta

Willard Buckhorn. 10720 Blair Rd., Sparta, IL 62286. (618) 443-3905. Company conducts antique and general auctions throughout southern Illinois, along with general consignment sales from its lovely farm in southern Illinois. Lots of real treasures at these sales.

Vergennes

Doerr Auction Service. P.O. Box 37, Vergennes, IL 62994. (618) 684-6315 or 687-3744. Company conducts retail consignment sales on Tuesday and Friday evenings, and a once-a-month auction of fine antiques and collectibles on its premises. Excellent, well-conducted auction, with lots of quality items. Note that this is a nonsmoking facility.

Waterloo

Asselmeier and May Auctioneers. 6903 Asselmeier Dr., Waterloo, IL 62298. (618) 473-2273. Conducts antique, collectible, and estate auctions in the Illinois/Missouri area.

West Frankford

Monday Dealers Auction. Hwy. 37 South, West Frankford, IL. Company conducts weekly consignment auction on Friday nights. Sale starts at 6:00 P.M.

INDIANA

Anderson

Jackson's Auction Gallery, Inc. Dennis Jackson, 5330 Pendleton Ave., Anderson, IN. (317) 642-7563. Company conducts antique and estate auctions at its auction house.

Brookston

Ron's Auction Center. Ronald Schmierer, Brookston, IN. (317) 563-6656. Company conducts many general, household, and farm auctions from its auction barn.

Brookville

Dave White. Brookville Sale Barn, P. O. Box 53, Brookville, IN 47012. (317) 647-3574. Company conducts livestock auctions.

Cicero

Chaudions Auction Co. 50 W. Buckeye, Box 438, Cicero, IN 46034. (317) 984-4125. Company conducts antique auctions, furniture, and collectible auctions from its sale barn.

Connersville

Koons Auction and Realty Co. 1324 E. Fifth St., Connersville, IN 47331. (317) 825-3594. Company conducts many quality estate auctions, antique and collectible auctions, and general auctions in the area.

Danville
Dave Petree Auction Co. Danville, IN (317) 317-745-5166. Company conducts many antique, collectible, and estate auctions.

Evansville
Curan Miller Auction and Realty Inc. Hugh Miller, 13020 N. State Hwy. 67, Evansville, IN 47711. (800) 280-8970. Company conducts large liquidations and many fine-quality antique auctions throughout the midwest.

Greenwood
Christy's of Greenwood. Greenwood, IN 46142. (317) 887-3499. Company conducts many estate, antique, and general auctions in the area.

Huntington
Ness Brothers Real Estate and Auction Co. 18 W. Washington St., Huntington, IN 46750. (219) 356-3911 or 672-2668. Company conducts many general, farm, farm-item, household, antique, and collectible sales in the area.

Indianapolis
Earl's Auction Co. Earl Cornwell, Sr., (317) 291-5843, Indianapolis, IN. Company conducts many fine-quality antique and estate auctions throughout the Indianapolis area.

Jeffersonville
Main Street Auction House. 334 W. Maple St., Jeffersonville, IN 47130. (812) 283-7294. Corner of East Third and Main St. Company conducts a weekly wholesale dealer auction on Fridays at 7:00 P.M., and a large public auction on the first Sunday of each month at 2:00 P.M.

Madison
Minor Auction Service. Sara Minor, 813 Holcroft Dr., Madison, IN 47250. (812) 273-6169. Company conducts general consignment auctions in the area.

Noblesville
Bailey Auction Service. Don Bailey, Noblesville, IN. (317) 773-4456. Company conducts many quality antique sales in the area.

North Webster
Sparks Auction Service. Kay Sparks, P.O. Box 108, North Webster, IN 46555. (219) 834-7528 or 834-2336. Company conducts general sales, fine-antiques, and specialty sales, including many fine pottery and ceramic auctions.

Shipshewana
Shipshewana Antique and Collectible Auction. Shipshewana Flea Market. Shipshewana, IN. (219) 789-4129.

Market conducts large consignment sales weekly during the flea market. Livestock, miscellaneous, antiques, collectibles, farm items. During the summer months, as many as five auctioneers are selling at the same time. Plan on spending a full day here.

SOLSBERRY

Kenny Bland Auctions. Rt. 2, Box 232, Solsberry, IN 47459. (812) 876-4486. Company conducts estate, farm, household, business, and general sales from its country pavilion sale facility.

IOWA

CEDAR FALLS

Jackson's Auctioneers and Appraisers. 2227 Lincoln St., Cedar Falls, IA 50613. (319) 277-2256, Fax (319) 277-1252. Company conducts antique auctions and many specialized auctions, such as steins.

CORALVILLE

Classic American Auctions. Mike Hammes, Coralville, IA (319) 351-5766. Company conducts fine-antique auctions in the Iowa area.

DES MOINES

Greenfield's Professional Auction Service. 4330 Hubbell Ave., Des Moines, IA 50317. (515) 265-2429. Company conducts many antique, collectible, estate, and general sales in the general area.

IOWA CITY

Sharpless Auctions. Mark Sharpless, I-80, Hoover Hwy., Exit 249, Iowa City. Company conducts various types of sales from its auction barn, one of the largest in the midwest.

MARSHALLTOWN

Gene Harris Antique Auction Center. 203 S. 18th Ave, Box 476, Marshalltown, IA 50158. (515) 752-0600, Fax (515) 753-0226. Conducts fine antique and collectible auctions and specialty auctions, including toys, at its auction house.

TRAER

Boldt Auction Co. Marvin Boldt, Traer, IA. (319) 478-2809. Company conducts general retail sales, antique and collectible, and specialty auctions.

KANSAS

CALDWELL

Cochran Real Estate and Auction Co. Deborah Cochran, Rt. 2, Box 23, Caldwell, KS 67022. (316) 845-2155. Company conducts estate sales and antique auctions in the general area.

> **When Attending Auctions, Be Sure to:**
> When attending auctions, be sure to take identification with you. A lot of auctions will not allow you to register and receive a bidding number if you do not have a valid photo ID, such as your driver's license.
>
> A lot of auctions do not take checks or credit cards. Some take checks from known customers, and a few accept credit cards. However, do not count on it if you have not been to that auction before.
>
> To be on the safe side, take plenty of green Yankee currency. It is such a widely spoken language.

DOUGLAS
Woody Auction Company. Box 618, Douglas, KS. (316) 746-2694, Fax (316) 746-2145. Specializes in carnival and cut-glass auctions. Holds many estate auctions and other fine-antique and collectible auctions.

GARDNER
Strickner's Auction Co. 16775 N. Gardner Rd., Gardner, KS. One mile north of town. (913) 856-7074. Company conducts large, two-ring weekly retail auction on Mondays, starting at 6:00 P.M. Company has been in business since 1970. No checks (probably a good reason for its longevity.)

HAYS
Legere Auction and Realty Co. Don Legere, Box 456, Hays, KS 67601. (800) 447-2545 or (913) 625-2545. Company conducts many large real-estate auctions throughout the southwest.

KANSAS CITY
Mainion's International Auction House. P.O. Box 12214, Kansas City, KS 69112. (913) 299-6692. Company conducts large mail auctions of quality collectibles.

KINGMAN
Koch Auction Services. 325 N. Main St., Kingman, KS 67068. (316) 532-3878 or 532-2259. Company conducts antique, estate, and general sales in the area.

MULLINVILLE
Brown Auction and Real Estate. Mullinville, KS 67109. (316) 723-2111 or 548-2681. Company conducts antique sales in the general area.

OVERLAND PARK
LFK Art and Antiques Auction Co. Box 7364, Overland

Park, KS 66207. (800) 243-5211 or (913) 262-7860. Conducts antique, art, and quilt auctions in the midwest.

PRAIRIE VILLAGE
Tom Stroud Auctioneer. P.O. Box 8671, Prairie Village, KS 66208. (913) 381-0114. Company conducts many fine-antique and specialty auctions in the Kansas City area.

WICHITA
Rick Kaufman Auctioneer. Wichita KS. (316) 943-0715 or (316) 686-2699. Company conducts antique and jewelry sales in the Wichita area.

KENTUCKY

BOWLING GREEN
Auction Concepts. Thomas Hunt, 661-A, 31-W Bypass, Bowling Green, KY 42101. (502) 782-2200 or (800) 543-2083, Fax (502) 843-843-8780.

CALHOUN
Price Buster Dealer Auction. Hwy. 81., Main St., Calhoun, KY. (502) 736-5043. Company conducts wholesale dealer auction on Mondays. Sale starts at 6:30 P.M.

CYNTHIANA
Kentucky Realty and Auction Co. 115 N. Main St., Cynthiana, KY (606) 834-3820 or 234-6714. Company conducts real estate, general, antique, and collectible auctions throughout the area.

LIVERMORE
Coke Auction. Hwy. 431 N. Livermore, KY. (502) 733-4444. Company conducts weekly wholesale dealer auction on Mondays and a public consignment auction on Friday evenings from its premises.

LOUISVILLE
Auction Unlimited. Mid-City Mall, 1250 Batchtown, Louisville, KY. (502) 459-2110. Company conducts weekly wholesale dealer auctions on Wednesdays and public auctions throughout the week from its premises.

LOUISVILLE
Fairdale Auction Co. Carl Roution. 10713 W. Manslick Rd., Louisville, KY 40188. (502) 366-2790. Company conducts many large quality antique and collectible auctions throughout the area.

LOUISVILLE
White's Kentucky Auction Service. Jim White, Jr., 506 Huron St., Louisville, KY. (502) 375-3450. Company conducts many large—some two-day—antique auctions in the general area.

MICHIGAN

COLDWATER
David A. Norton Auctioneer. 50 W. Pearl, Coldwater, MI. (517) 279-9063. Company conducts major auctions throughout the U. S.

DETROIT
Du Mouchelles Auctioneering. 409 E. Jefferson Ave., Detroit, MI 48226. (313) 963-6255, Fax (313) 963-8199.

DETROIT
Gallery of Antiques. 7105 Michigan, Detroit, MI. (313) 554-1012.

DETROIT
Edward J. Kaye Auctioneers. 5641 Conner, Detroit, MI. (313) 571-4400, Fax (313) 571-4400. Commercial and industrial auction company.

EAU CLAIRE
Glassman's Auctioneers. Eau Claire, MI. (616) 461-6271. Conducts antique auctions in the area.

ESSEXVILLE
Dan Van Sumeren and Associates. 519 W. Center Rd., Essexville, MI 48732. (517) 894-2859. Company conducts real-estate, commercial, machinery, agricultural, and industrial sales throughout the area.

FREELAND
Wegner Auctioneers. 7450 Lawndale, Freeland, MI. (517) 793-8689.

HEMLOCK
Besner Auction Team. 13785 Swan Creek Rd., Hemlock, MI. (517) 642-8158.

HILLSDALE
Andy Adams Auctioneer. Andy Adams Sale Barn, Broad St., Hillsdale, MI. (517) 437-7230. Retail auction, including livestock, conducted each Saturday, 9:00 A.M.

JACKSON
Spikes Flea Market. 2190 Brooklyn Rd., Jackson, MI. (517) 423-6312. Company conducts weekly public auction from its premises.

NILES
AAA Straight Up Auction Service. Roger Lucas, 2725 Geyer Rd., Niles, MI 49120. (616) 695-7701. Company conducts quality sales of antiques, collectibles, collections, furniture.

PORTLAND
McAllister Auctions. Mike McAllister, 958 Maynard Rd., Portland, MI 48875. (517) 647-7482. Company conducts estate sales, general auctions, and quality antique auctions.

> **Auction Tip #1**
> Arrive early to get a good seat in front of the auctioneer—one with a good view of the auction block and the items to be sold.

RAVENNA
Ravenna Flea Market. Folcum Rd. 2 miles north of the Ravenna Livestock Sales Grounds. I-96, Coopersville exit, north 13 miles. Jim Lund, 1685 19-Mile Rd., Cedar Springs, MI 49319. (616) 696-1247 or 853-2952. Market conducts retail consignment auction on Mondays.

SAGINAW
Butler Auction Service. Rod Butler, 630 S. Frost Dr., Saginaw, MI. (517) 799-4181. Company conducts estate, household, farm, business, antique, and liquidation sales throughout the area.

SAGINAW
Furlo Auction Service. 490 E. Brooks, Saginaw, MI. (800) 673-8756.

SAGINAW
United States Property Auctions. 2835 Bay Rd., Saginaw, MI. (517) 799-4500.

SOUTHFIELD
Norman Levy Associates, Inc. 21415 Civic Center Dr., Southfield, MI 48076. (313) 353-8640, Fax (313) 353-1442. Company conducts many large liquidations and industrial auctions throughout the U.S.

TRUFANT
Trufant Auction and Flea Market. 303 North St. Maurice Peterson, Rt. 1, Box 201, Trufant, MI 49347. (616) 984-2168. Weekly.

VERNONVILLE
Stanton's Auctioneers and Realtors. Box 146, 144 S. Main St., Vernonville, MI 49096. (517) 725-0181, Fax (517) 726-0060. Company conducts antique, estate, and general sales.

MINNESOTA

BLOOMINGTON
Quickie Auction Service. Bloomington, MN. (612) 428-4217.

COON RAPIDS
Harvey Auction Service, Inc. 2907 N.W. Coon Rapids Blvd., Coon Rapids, MN. (612) 421-1687.

LAKELAND
Valley Auction Co. 370 S. St. Croix Trail, Lakeland, MN. (612) 436-6020.

LAKEVILLE
Ritchie Brothers Auctioneers

International. 22100 Pillsbury Ave., Lakeville, MI. (612) 469-1700.

MINNEAPOLIS
Classic Sporting Collectibles. One Appletree Square, Minneapolis, MN 55425. (800) 477-4867 or (612) 854-5229, Fax (612) 853-1486. Company conducts mail auctions of gun-related collectibles.

MINNEAPOLIS
Kloster Industrial Auctioneers. Minneapolis, MN. (612) 931-9013. Company conducts major machine, equipment, and commercial auctions throughout the U.S.

PRINCETON
Wayne Pike Auction Co. P.O. Box 387, Princeton, MN. (800) 657-4678.

ROSEMONT
Alliance Auctions and Realty Services. 14000 Robert Trail, Rosemont, MN. (612) 423-5400. Company conducts many retail auctions in the local area and from its 10-acre facility.

ROSEVILLE
Rose Galleries. 1123 W. County Rd. B, at Lexington. Roseville, MN (612) 484-1415. Quality antique and estate auctions every Wednesday on the premises. Also does fine estate, jewelry, art, antique, doll, and toy auctions.

ST. PAUL
Rode Galleries. 2717 Lincoln Dr., St. Paul, MN. (612) 484-1415. Company specializes in gallery auctions of antiques, fine home furnishings, jewelry, and art objects. Sales every Wednesday.

ST. PAUL
Royal Star. 7565 E. Concord, St. Paul, MN. (612) 455-1931. Company conducts many retail consignment sales in the area and at its facility. Conducts a wholesale dealer auction on Mondays at 1:00 P.M.

ST. PAUL
Tracy Luther Auctions and Antiques. St. Paul, MN. (612) 770-6175.

ST. PAUL
Wally Lawmeyer Auction Co. 3324 E. 75th Ct., St. Paul, MN. (612) 455-9547. Company conducts antique, estate, business, and real-estate auctions in the general area.

WINNEBAGO
Auction America. Robert Morris. Box 3668, Winnebago, MN 56098. (507) 893-4216. Conducts antique and collectible auctions.

MISSOURI

CARL JUNCTION
Richard Larson. Rt. 1, Box 87, Carl Junction, MO. (417) 649-7222. Company conducts many public auctions in the general area.

CARTHAGE
Ytell Auction Service. 1244 Glenwood Place, Carthage, MO 64836. (417) 358-7024 or (800) 537-6617. Company conducts many large public and estate sales throughout the Missouri Ozarks region.

EXCELSIOR
Gary Ryther Auctioneering, Inc. Excelsior Springs, MO. (800) 858-2586. Company conducts many fine gun, civil war, and antique firearm auctions.

GRANVIEW
Longview Auction. Longview Rd. Exit and Hwy. 71. Longview, MO. (816) 761-0004. Company conducts antique auctions on its premises.

HARRISBURG
Voorheis Auction and Realty. R. E. Voorheis, Harrisburg, MO. (314) 874-5987. Company conducts antique auctions in central Missouri.

HOLDEN
Calton's Auction House. Hwy. 50, 12 miles west of Warrensburg. Holden, MO. (816) 732-6686. Company conducts retail/consignment auctions on Friday nights. Sale starts at 6:30 P.M. Company is also available for estate, farm, coin, antique, and liquidation sales throughout the area.

JAMESPORT
Midstate Auction Service. Jamesport, MO. (816) 684-8343.

JOPLIN
Diamond Auto Auctions. Hwy. 71 Alt., 1 mile south of I-44. Joplin, MO. (417) 781-SELL. Company conducts public and dealer auto auctions on Mondays at 7:00 P.M., and dealers-only auction on Tuesdays at 7:00 P.M. Credit cards accepted.

JOPLIN
Bill Horton. Joplin, MO. (417) 451-5103. Company conducts many estate and farm auctions throughout the area.

JOPLIN
The Pavilion Galleries. Ron Johnston, Rt. 2, Box 216, Joplin, MO 64804. Company conducts many fine-antique auctions from its premises.

KANSAS CITY
Dealers Auction. Heart of America Trade Center.

Kansas City, MO. (816) 861-6900. Company conducts monthly wholesale sale. Held in conjunction with Collectors Whatever Trade Show.

LEADINGTON
Parkland Pavilion Antiques and Auction Gallery. Corner of Main St. and Woodlawn. Hwy. 67 to 32 West. Leadington exit. (800) 827-2887 or (314) 431-6094. Fax (314) 431-7031. Company conducts antique sales from its premises.

LIBERTY
Pence Auction Co. Rick Pence, 417 Camelot, Liberty, MO 64068. (816) 781-4218. Company conducts large estate and antique sales throughout the midwest.

MARIONVILLE
Square Deal Auctions. Town square, Marionville. (417) 463-2018. Company conducts retail/consignment sales on Friday nights at 6:30 P.M.

NEOSHO
Bob Lasswell and Associates. Bob Lasswell. P.O. Box 58, Neosho, MO 64850. (417) 451-7357. Company conducts retail public sales, real-estate sales, and general auctions throughout the area.

OZARK
Blansits Sale Pavilion. 15 miles south of Springfield, on US Hwy. 65. Ozark, MO. Tom Hartley. (417) 485-6093, Fax (417) 485-7822. Livestock sale barn.

PHILLIPSBURG
Hog Eye Auction Service. Zachary McCaslin, P.O. Box 648, Phillipsburg, MO 65722. (417) 589-4125 or 589-4320. Company conducts many antique, estate, and general sales in the area.

REPUBLIC
Don Sissel Auction Service. Rt. 1, Box 25, Republic, MO 65738. (417) 732-8687. Company conducts estate sales, antique sales, and general retail auctions throughout the Ozark area.

RUTLEDGE
Dog, Gun, Hillbilly Consignment Auction and Flea Market. Contact: Irvin Johnson, (816) 883-5816 or 883-5322. Monthly.

ST. LOUIS
Belle Starr Auction Co. 13379 Manchester Rd., St. Louis, MO. (316) 966-0244 or 965-3966. Company conducts weekly retail consignment sales on its premises, with

some antiques and collectibles.

St. Louis
Robert Merry Auction Co. 5501 Milburn Rd., St. Louis, MO 63129. (314) 487-3992, Fax (314) 487-4080. Conducts fine-antique and collectibles auctions in the Missouri and Illinois areas.

Sarcoxie
Sarcoxie Livestock Auction. Sale barn in Sarcoxie, MO. (417) 548-6750. Livestock sale every Thursday at 7:30 P.M. Concession on premises.

Sikeston
Sikeston Auction Co. 112 Dale St., Rt. 5. Sikeston, MO. (314) 471-3952. Company conducts consignment auction on the third Monday of each month. Usually a lot of small antiques, some furniture, and some collectibles in each sale.

Springfield
Industrial Liquidators. Les Mace. 2432 N. Eastgate, #7, Springfield, MO 65803. (417) 866-6887 or 881-4826. Company conducts industrial sales and liquidations throughout the U.S.

Springfield
R. Ness Auction Gallery. Richard Ness or Diane Ness, 3500 E. Kearney. Springfield, MO 65803. (417) 866-0407. Company conducts fine-antique auctions in the Ozarks.

Strafford
Joe Mueller. Rt. 2, Box 66A, Strafford, MO 65757. (417) 962-8794. Company conducts general auctions throughout the area.

NEBRASKA

Brady
Tommy Palmer Auctioneer. Brady, NE 69123. (308) 584-3411. Conducts antique and estate auctions in the area.

Gering
The Auction House. 1605 11th St., Gering, NE. (308) 436-3271. Company conducts wholesale dealer auctions each Thursday.

Ravenna
Loup Valley Auction. Box 15, Ravenna, NE 68869. (308) 467-2335. Conducts antique auctions in Nebraska and surrounding area.

Scottsbluff

Asmus Brothers Auctioneers. Scottsbluff, NE. (308) 635-3133. Company conducts antique auctions in the general area.

York

Bailey and Associates Realty and Auction. York, NE. (402) 362-7653. Conducts antique auctions in Nebraska and surrounding area.

NORTH DAKOTA

Bismarck

Dacotah Auction and Liquidation. 310 Dover Dr., Bismarck, ND. (701) 224-9755 or 223-1343. Company conducts farm, household, estate, antique, real-estate, livestock, and general-consignment auctions in the general area.

Bismarck

Lamertz Auction Service. Bismarck, ND. (701) 258-7287.

Bismarck

Ramblin' Auctioneers. 1218 Pocatello Dr., Bismarck, ND. (701) 222-0140.

Cavalier

Dennis Biliske Auctioneers. P.O. Box W, Hwy. 5 East, Cavalier, ND. (800) 726-1655.

Harvey

Lien Auction and Realty Service. 915 Lincoln Ave., Harvey, ND. (701) 324-4401.

Mandan

Northland Auction and Clerking Service. 2100 Third St. S.E., Mandan, ND. (701) 663-1561.

Auction Tip #2
Inspect the merchandise carefully before the sale, to note any imperfections in the items you want to bid on.

OHIO

Aurora

Aurora Farms Auction. Rt. 42. (216) 562-2000. Company conducts several monthly public auctions from its premises. Call for dates.

Cambridge

DeHays Auctions. Box 1482, Cambridge, OH 43725. (614) 432-4755. Company conducts many antique, household, farm, and estate sales throughout the area.

Cambridge

Jim Rogers Auctioneer. Box 973, Cambridge, OH 43725. (614) 432-4454. Company conducts glass, pottery, collectibles, estate, furniture, and book sales in the area.

CANTON
KIKO Auction and Real Estate Service. Russ Kiko, 2805 Fulton Dr. N.W., Canton, OH 44718. (218) 455-9357 or 453-9187.

CINCINNATI
Ace Antiques. 6108 Vine St., Cincinnati, OH. (513) 242-4494. Company conducts antique and collectible sales throughout the area.

CINCINNATI
Cincinnati Art Gallery. 635 Main St., Cincinnati, OH 45202. (513) 381-2128. Company specializes in fine paintings, watercolors, and American art pottery sales. Company conducts America's largest Rookwood Pottery auctions.

CINCINNATI
Cincinnati Wholesale Auction. Marty Martineck, Gongworth Hall, Cincinnati, OH. (513) 542-4950. Company conducts large wholesale auction on Mondays. Sale is primarily antiques and collectibles.

CINCINNATI
Main Auction Galleries Inc. 137 W. Fourth St., Cincinnati, OH. (513) 621-1280. Company has been in business since 1871.

CINCINNATI
Don Treadway Gallery. 2128 Madison Rd., Cincinnati, OH 45208. (513) 321-6742, Fax (513) 871-7722.

CLEVELAND
Rosen and Co. The Arcade. Cleveland, OH. (216) 621-1860. Company conducts auctions of real estate, machinery, and equipment throughout the U.S.

CLEVELAND
Wolf's Auctioneers. 1239 W. 6th St., Cleveland, OH 44113. (216) 575-9653, Fax (216) 621-8011. Company conducts estate liquidations, antique, and household auctions.

COLUMBIANA
Gardeners Auction Service. Columbiana, OH 44408. (216) 726-0658. Company conducts retail/consignment auction at Theron's Country Flea Market on Saturday nights at 7:00 P.M.

COLUMBUS
Trader Ned's Auction. (614) 876-8883. Company conducts several monthly public auctions from its premises. Call for dates.

DELAWARE
Garth's Auctions. 2690 Stratford Rd., Delaware OH 43015. (614) 362-4771.

East Rochester
NCA Wholesale Auction. 6940 Rochester Rd., East Rochester, OH 44625. (216) 525-7255. Company conducts wholesale dealer auction on Wednesdays. Sale starts at 9:00 A.M.

Eaton
Eaton Wholesale Auction Co. 210 Nation Ave., Eaton, OH. (513) 456-4768. Company conducts weekly wholesale dealer auction on Wednesdays. Sale starts at noon.

Findlay
Farthing Real Estate and Auctioneers. 804 Tiffin Ave., Findlay, OH. (419) 423-0765, Fax (419) 423-4316. Company conducts many antique, collectible, household, estate, farm, and general consignment sales throughout the area.

Germantown
Lindy's Auction Barn. Rt. 725, Germantown, OH.

Goshen
Ross Conley Auctioneers. P.O. Box 144, Goshen, OH. 45122. (513) 625-9707. Company conducts specialized sales of collections, such as Hummel and other fine collections.

Greenville
Midwest Auctioneers and Marketers. Mike Baker, 7603 Celina Rd., Greenville, OH. (513) 548-2640. Company conducts estate, antique, collection, and general sales in the area.

Grover Hill
Porters Auction. 102 N. Main St., Grover Hill, OH. (419) 587-3511. Company conducts weekly wholesale dealer auction on Thursdays. Sale starts at noon.

Hamilton
Robert Vaughn Auctions. 1100 Millville, Hamilton, OH. (513) 844-1411. Company conducts general auctions throughout the tri-state area.

Health
M and S Auction Inc. Mark Moore, 7432 Hamilton Ave., Health, OH. (513) 931-1728. Company conducts fine-antique, estate, art, and household sales.

Lafayette
Anderson Flea Market. 20 Elisdorf St., (317) 474-6114. Retail auctions conducted on the first and third Saturdays of each month.

Lockland
A-Auction by Jer. Jerry Rogers, 501 Westview Ave., Lockland, OH. (513) 769-4150. Company conducts antique, estate, household, art, and

> ### Auction Tip #3
> Bring a pencil and paper to keep a list of what you buy and what you pay for it. The back of your bidding number card also works great for this. A small pocket calculator can be helpful.

business liquidations throughout the area.

MARION
Higgins Auction House. 280282 Copeland Ave., Marion, OH 43302. (614) 387-5111. Company conducts weekly wholesale dealer auction on Wednesdays. Sale starts at 4:00 P.M.

MILFORD
Early Auction Co. 123 Main St., Milford, OH 45150. (513) 831-4833. Company conducts many antique and collectible auctions throughout the general area.

MINFORD
Allens Auctions. Norman Allen, Box 67, Minford, OH 45653. (614) 820-2728 or 820-2725. Company conducts many antique, estate, farm, and general household auctions throughout the area.

MULBERRY
First American Auction Co. 1011 Hwy. 28, Mulberry, OH. (513) 821-5900. Company conducts general retail consignment auction each Friday night at its premises, beginning at 6:30 P.M.

NEW WATERFORD
Rogers Community Auction and Open Air Market. 4640 Raley Rd., Rt. 154 West. (216) 227-3233. One of the midwest's better auction houses. Company conducts large public auction on Fridays at 6:00 P.M.

NORTH BLOOMFIELD
North Bloomfield Auction and Flea Market. Approximately 1 mile west of Bloom Center on Hwy. 87. Charles Roscoe, 8183 Rt. 193, Farmdale, OH 44417. (216) 876-4993. Monthly.

PERRYSBURG
Tim and Glenn Speck. Perrysburg, OH. (419) 874-4272. Conducts antique auctions in Ohio and surrounding area.

PLAIN CITY
Plain City Auction Service. 145 E. Main St., Plain City, OH 43064. (614) 873-5622 or 873-5217. Company conducts antique and collectible sales throughout the area.

ROSS
Strickers Grove Auctionmania. Betty DuPree, Rt. 128, Between Ross and Miami-

town. (513) 738-3268. Company conducts general consignment sales from its sale barn every Tuesday. Sale starts at 6:00 P.M. Good place to find treasures in among the junk.

RUSHVILLE
Mike Clum. Box 2, Rushville, OH 43150. (614) 536-9220. Conducts antique auctions in Ohio.

SYCAMORE
Ned Gregg Realty Co. Ned F. Gregg, 6761 Crawford-Wyandot County Line Rd., Sycamore, OH 44882. (419) 927-5492. Company conducts antique, estate, and farm sales throughout the general area.

TOLEDO
BJ's Wholesale Auction. 701 N. Wheeling, Toledo, OH. Company conducts weekly wholesale dealer auction on Mondays. Sale starts at 4:30 P.M.

TOLEDO
Langolis Auction House. 640 N. Lallendorf Rd., Toledo, OH. (419) 698-3412.

VAN WERT
North Western Ohio Land and Auction Co. Les Strickler, 147 E. Main St., Van Wert, OH 45891. (419) 495-2578. Company conducts many large estate, farm, land, and antique auctions in the general area.

VICKERY
Baker Bonnigson Auctioneers. William Baker, 4488 State Rt. 412, Vickery, OH 43464. (419) 547-9218. Company conducts estate, antique, farm, and general sales throughout the area.

WASHINGTON
E. J. Weade Associates. Rone Weade, 313 E. Court St., Washington, OH 43160. (614) 335-2210. Company conducts antique, estate, collectible, and general household sales in the area.

WESTLAKE
Richard D. Davis Auctioneer. (216) 779-5210. Company conducts estate, household, antique, farm, and industry auctions throughout the area.

WORTHINGTON
David Bowers. Worthington, OH. (614) 766-SALE. Conducts sports and baseball item auctions in central Ohio.

SOUTH DAKOTA

BALTIC
Sluiter's Country Auction. Rt. 1, Box 100, Baltic, SD. (605) 529-5229.

CUSTER
Bradeen Auctions and Real Estate. 8 Mt. Rushmore Rd., Custer, SD. (605) 673-2629.

HURON
Holty Auction Service. W. L. Barnes, Rt. 4, Huron, SD 57350. (605) 352-6380 or 352-2781. Company conducts antique, farm, gun, estate, and general sales in the local area.

MARION
Wieman Land and Auction Co. 35 N. Broadway, Marion, SD. (605) 648-3111.

OLIVET
Ken Wintersteen. Olivet, SD (605) 387-2418. Company conducts many large, high-quality sales in the high plains states.

PIEDMONT
Haley's Tri-State Auction. Jack Moravec, P.O. Box 254, Piedmont, SD 57769. (605) 787-4283.

RAPID CITY
A-1 Auction House. 2413 S. Hwy. 79, Rapid City, SD. (605) 341-5656. Company conducts weekly consignment auctions from its premises.

RAPID CITY
Martin Jurisch and Associates. P.O. Box 1867, Rapid City, SD 57709. (605), Company conducts real-estate, farm and ranch, antique, household, and estate sales throughout the area.

RAPID CITY
Larson Auctioneering. Rt. 8, Box 3750, Rapid City, SD. (605) 343-3602.

RAPID CITY
McPherson Auction Co. Dale McPherson, P.O. Box 8204, Rapid City, SD 57708. (800) 685-1369 or (605) 348-1369. Company conducts farm and ranch auctions, livestock sales, estate, and real-estate auctions throughout the high plains area.

RAPID CITY
Penfield Auction Service. 1829 Hillsview Dr., Rapid City, SD. (605) 342-7286.

RAPID CITY
Trade Winds Auction Co. 1208 E. North St., Rapid City, SD. (605) 342-7286.

RAPID CITY
Wingler's Furniture and Auction Co. 611 N. Main, Rapid City, SD. (605) 332-5682.

STURGIS
Casteel Auction Service. 866 Lazelle St., Sturgis, SD. (605) 347-5110.

WALL
Anderson Auction Service 18460 Anderson Hill Rd., Wall, SD. (605) 279-2235

WISCONSIN

BURLINGTON
Town Crier Auctions. Tom Burbey, N7595 Bell School Rd., Burlington, WI 52105. (414) 642-9517. Company conducts antique auctions in the area. Many of its sales are quite large and run for more than one day.

EVANSVILLE
George Auction Co. Paul George, Box 135, Evansville, WI 53536. (608) 455-7912. Company conducts farm auctions, antique, household, commercial, and estate sales in the general area.

FOND DU LAC
Dealers' Auction. American Legion Hall, 400 Fond du Lac Ave., Fond du Lac, WI. (414) 922-7225. Company conducts wholesale dealer auction on the second and fourth Wednesdays of each month.

GRASS LAKE
Wholesale Dealers Auction. Grass Lake, WI. (608) 254-8691. Company conducts weekly wholesale dealers' auction on Tuesdays.

HUDSON
Mike Kranz. 463 Stageline Rd., Hudson, WI 54016. (715) 386-7333. Company specializes in mail auctions of black memorabilia.

KEWASKU
Dealers' Auction. Amerahan Hall, Hwy. 45, Kewasku, WI. Company conducts wholesale dealer auction on the second and fourth Mondays of each month. Sale starts at 6:30 P.M.

LADYSMITH
Ladysmith Flea Market. Hwy. 8, Ladysmith, WI. (715) 532-3661. Market conducts retail auctions the first and third weeks of each month.

MILWAUKEE
Milwaukee Auction Galleries. 4747 W. Bradley Rd., Milwaukee, WI 53223. (414) 355-5054.

MILWAUKEE
Schrager Auction Galleries. 2915 N. Sherman Blvd., Milwaukee, WI 53210. (414) 873-3738, Fax (414) 873-5229. Company conducts many high-quality antique and specialty sales on its premises.

OSHKOSH
Dealers' Auction. 3116 Algoma Blvd., Oshkosh, WI. (414) 231-3030 or 426-5555. Company conducts weekly wholesale dealer auction on Tuesdays. Sale restricted to new merchandise. Sale starts at 1:00 P.M.

> ### *Auction Tip #4*
> Know what the auctioneer's requirements are for removing items after the sale—especially at estate sales, where removal is generally expected at the conclusion of the auction on the day of the sale. If you want to purchase something large and have no way to move it, talk to the auctioneer before the sale begins. See if he provides any type of delivery service.
>
> Buyer, beware if you leave an item at the sale to pick up at a later date. As soon as the auctioneer's hammer hits that block, ownership of an item transfers hands, and all further responsibility becomes that of the purchaser. Most auctioneers will try to accommodate you if they can. This job is made easier if the auction is being held in the auctioneer's own building. But the ultimate responsibility is yours and yours alone.

VERONA

Tim Unterholzner Auctions. P.O. Box 930216, Verona. (608) 523-1064. Company conducts antique, collectible, and specialized auctions in the general area. Has been in business since 1971.

WILD ROSE

Wild Rose Auction Co. P.O. Box 224, Wild Rose, WI 54984. (414) 622-4000. Company conducts antique auctions and is also a wholesale house for antiques, by the single piece or container.

WISCONSIN DELLS

Dealers' Auction. Lee Murray, Wisconsin Dells, WI. (608) 254-8691. Company conducts weekly wholesale dealer auction.

WISCONSIN DELLS

Lee Murray Auction Service. Wisconsin Dells, WI. (608) 254-8691. Company conducts weekly retail auctions.

MISCELLANEOUS

America West Archives, Warren Anderson, Box 100, Cedar City, UT 84721. (801) 586-9497. Publishes quarterly illustrated catalog of auction information relating to both early and historical documents and other paper-related items.

Auction Hotline. 1-900-287-5156. $1 per minute. Info: (219) 347-8980.

Auctioneer Classes, Perkins Auction Co. (417) 468-7860.

Continental Auction School,

P.O. Box 346, Mankato, MN. (507) 625-5595.

Knotts Auctioneering School, P.O. Box 786, Gallipolis, OH 45613.

Mendenhall School of Auctioneering, P.O. Box 7344, High Point, NC 27264. (919) 887-3602.

Missouri Auction School, 1600 Genessee, Kansas City, MO 64102. (816) 421-7117. The nation's largest and most respected school of auctioneering. School has an excellent line of auction supplies of all types.

Southeastern School of Auctioneering, P.O. Box 9124, Greenville, SC 29604. (803) 947-2000.

Walton Auction School, 3860 Paradise Rd., Medina, OH 44256. (800) 369-2818.

Western College of Auctioneering. P.O. Box 50310. Located in Metra Inn. Billings, MT. (406) 252-7066.

World Wide College of Auctioneering, Gordon Taylor, P.O. Box 949, Mason City, IA, 50402. (515) 423-5242.

Dealer Auctions

Dealer auctions are wholesale and high-volume by nature. Most items are sold by the case, lot, gross, or some other large measure. Often the price of the individual item will be given, plus the number of such items offered for sale by the auctioneer. To calculate what you can expect to pay, simply multiply the price of the individual item by the total number of those items for sale. Be sure you know what and how many items you are bidding on at these sales! And remember, if you do not have a state resale tax number, you probably will have to pay state sales tax. Always call first before traveling to these dealer auctions.

ILLINOIS

AURORA PARK
Conwill Auction. Corner of Van Der Karr Road and Bridge Street. Contact: Pete Conwill, (815) 937-9171. *Tuesdays, 6:30 P.M.*

CHICAGO
Auction USA, Inc. 1423 W. Fullerton Ave., Chicago, IL 60614. (312) 871-7200. *Monthly.*

ROSCOE
Dealer Auction. Roscoe Auction Center, 11631 Main Street. (815) 623-8232. *Mondays.*

WEST FRANKFORD
Monday Dealers Auction. Highway 37 South. *Mondays, 6:00 P.M.*

ZION
Waukegan-Zion Dealers Auction. Sheridan Road. Contact: Vern Mathson, (312) 249-4242. Company conducts weekly wholesale dealer auction. *Mondays, 1:00 P.M.*

INDIANA

BOSWELL
Dealer Auction. Boswell Trade Center. Contact: Paul Tolen, (317) 869-5702 or 869-5516. Fax (317) 869-5411. *Wednesdays, 10:00 A.M.*

HOWARDS GROVE
Dealers Auction. Kraemers Korner Balls Hall. Highway 42. *Weekly.*

INDIANAPOLIS
Dealer Auction. Tradewinds Auction House, 1422 W. Washington St. (317) 632-0742. *Mondays.*

INDIANAPOLIS
Indy Merchandise Clearing House Auction. Corner of I-70 East and Shadyland Ave. (317) 353-2350. *Tuesdays, 10:00 A.M.*

JEFFERSONVILLE
Main Street Auction House. 334 W. Maple St., Jeffersonville, IN 47130. (812) 283-7294. Corner of East Third and Main St. Company conducts a weekly wholesale dealer auction on Fridays at 7:00 P.M., and a large public auction on the first Sunday of each month at 2:00 P.M.

KENTUCKY

CALHOUN
Pricebuster Dealer Auction. Main St. (Hwy. 81). (502) 736-5043. *Mondays, 6:30 P.M.*

LIVERMORE
Coke Auction. Highway 431 N. (502) 733-4444. *Mondays.*

LOUISVILLE
Auction Unlimited. Mid-City Mall, 1250 Batchtown. (502) 459-2110. *Wednesdays.*

MICHIGAN

GRASSLAKE
Dealers Auction. 242 Burtch Road. (517) 722-8810. *Weekly.*

> **Auction Tip #5**
> Bring a box or boxes, and some newspaper to wrap your breakable purchases in.

MISSOURI

CROCKER
Hawkeye Dealers Auction. 8 miles west of Crocker on Highway 'U'. (314) 736-5236. *First and third Tuesdays of each month.*

KANSAS CITY
Dealers Auction. Heart of America Trade Center, (816) 861-6900. Held in conjunction with Collectors Whatever Trade Show. *Second Sunday of each month.*

NEBRASKA

GERING
The Auction House. 1605 11th St. (308) 436-3271. *Thursdays.*

OHIO

AURORA
Aurora Farms Auction. Rt. 42. (216) 562-2000. *Wednesdays.*

CINCINNATI
Cincinnati Wholesale Auction. Gongworth Hall. Contact: Marty Martineck, (513)

> **Auction Tip #6**
> At outdoor auctions, expect a lot of standing. For comfort, you might want to take a lawn chair along with you.

542-4950. Primarily antiques & collectibles. *Mondays.*

COLUMBUS
Trader Ned's Auction. (614) 876-8883. *Saturdays.*

EAST ROCHESTER
NCA Wholesale Auction. 6940 Rochester Road, East Rochester, OH 44625. (216) 525-7255. *Wednesdays, 9:00 A.M.*

EATON
Dealer Auction. Contact: Eaton Wholesale Auction, 210 Nation Ave. (513) 456-4768. *Wednesdays, 12:00 p.m.*

GROVER HILL
Porters Auction. 102 N. Main Street. Contact: Porters Auction, Rt. 1, Box 223, Grover Hill, OH 45849. (419) 587-3511. *Thursdays, 12:00 P.M.*

MARION
Higgins Auction House. 280282 Copeland Ave., Marion, OH 43302. (614) 387-5111. *Wednesdays, 4:00 P.M.*

TOLEDO
BJ's Wholesale Auction. 701 N. Wheeling. (419) 697-1506. *Mondays, 4:30 P.M.*

WISCONSIN

FOND DU LAC
Dealers Auction. American Legion Hall, 400 Fond du Lac Ave. (414) 922-7225. *Second and fourth Wednesdays.*

GRASS LAKE
Wholesale Dealers Auction. (608) 254-8691. *Tuesdays.*

KEWASKUM
Dealers Auction. Amerahan Hall, Highway 45. *Second and fourth Mondays, 6:30 P.M.*

OSHKOSH
Dealer Auction. 3116 Algoma Blvd. (414) 231-3030 or 426-5555. Sale restricted to new merchandise. *Tuesdays, 1:00 P.M.*

WISCONSIN DELLS
Dealers Auction. Contact: Lee Murray, (608) 254-8691. *Weekly.*

REFERENCES

ASSOCIATIONS, ORGANIZATIONS, CLUBS

Aluminum Collector's Society. Daniel Woodard, P.O. Box 1347, Weatherford, TX 76086. (817) 594-4680.

American Barbed Wire Collector's Society. John Mantz, 1023 Baldwin Rd., Bakersfield, CA (805) 397-9572.

American Game Collector's Association. Joe Angiolillo, 4628 Barlow Dr., Bartlesville, OK 74006.

Antique and Art Glass Salt Shaker Collector's Society. 2832 Rapidan Trail, Maitland, FL 32751.

Antique Bottle Club. P.O. Box 571, Lake Geneva, WI 53417.

Antique Mall Owners Association. Antoinette Kopp, P.O. Box 219, Western Springs, IL 60558. (708) 246-4990.

Antique Radio Club of America. 81 Steeplechase Rd., Devon, PA 19333.

Antique Stove Association. Clifford Boram, 417 N. Main St., Monticello, IN 47960.

Appraisers Information Exchange. International Society of Appraisers, P.O. Box 726, Hoffman Estates, IL 60195. (708) 882-0706.

Big Little Book Collector's Club. Larry Lowery, P.O. Box 1242, Danville, CA 94526. (415) 837-2086.

Candy Container Collector's of America. P.O. Box 1088, Washington, PA 15301.

Cat Collector's Club. 33161 Wendy Dr., Sterling Heights, MI 48310.

Coca-Cola Collector's Club. P.O. Box 49166. Atlanta, GA 30359.

The Cola Clan. Alice Fisher, 2084 Continental Dr. N.E., Atlanta, GA 30345.

Cookie Cutters Collector's Club. Ruth Capper, 1167 Teal Rd. S.W., Delroy, OH (216) 735-2839.

Early American Industries Association. J. Watson, P.O. Box 2128, Empire State Plaza Station, Albany, NY 12220. Information on early tools and trades.

Ephemera Society of America. P.O. Box 37, Schoharie, NY 12157. (518) 295-7978.

Ertl Collector's Club. Mike Meyer, Hwys. 136 and 20, Dyersville, IA 52040. (319) 875-2000.

Fenton Glass Collectors of America. P.O. Box 384, Williamstown, WV 26187. (304) 375-6196

Fostoria Glass Society of America. P.O. Box 826, Moundsville, WV 26041.

Haviland Collectors International. Jean Kendall, Iowa Memorial Union, University of Iowa, Iowa City, IA 52242. (319) 335-3513.

Heisey Collector's of America. National Heisey Glass Museum, 169 W. Church St.. Newark, OH 43055. (614) 345-2932.

International Carnival Glass Association. Lee Markley, Rt. 1, Box 14, Mentone, IN 46539. (219) 353-7678.

International Rose O'Neill Club. Karen Steward, P.O. Box 668, Branson, MO 65616.

Midwest Antique Fruit Jar and Bottle Club. P.O. Box 38, Flat Rock, IN 47234.

Morgantown Collector's of America. Jerry Gallagher, 420 First Avenue N.W., Plainview, MN 55964.

Mouse Club East. P.O. Box 3195, Wakefield, MA 01880. Club for Disney collectors.

Mystic Lights of the Aladdin Knights. J. W. Courter, Rt. 1, Simpson, IL 62985. (618) 949-3884. Association and newsletter for collectors of Aladdin lamps.

National Association of Avon Collectors. Connie Clark, 6100 Walnut, Kansas City, MO 64113.

National Association of Breweriana Advertising. John Murray, 475 Old Surrey Rd., Hinsdale, IL 60521.

National Association of Milk Bottle Collectors. Thomas Gallagher, #4 Ox Bow Rd., Westport, CT 06880. (203) 277-5244.

National Association of Paper and Advertising Collectors. P.O. Box 500, Mt. Joy, PA 17552. (717) 653-4300.

National Association of Watch and Clock Collectors. Thomas Bartels, 514 Poplar St., Columbia, PA 17512. (717) 684-8621.

National Bit, Spur, and Saddle Collector's Association. P.O. Box 3098, Colorado Springs, CO 80934.

National Cambridge Collectors. P.O. Box 416, Cambridge, OH 43725.

National Depression Glass Association. Anita Wood, P.O. Box 69843, Odessa, TX 79769. (915) 337-1297.

National Early American Glass Club. P.O. Box 8489, Silver Spring, MD 20907.

National Fantasy Fan Club. P.O. Box 19212, Irvine, CA 92713. Club for Disney collectors.

National Graniteware Society. P.O. Box 10013, Cedar Rapids, IA 52410.

National Imperial Glass Collector's Society. P.O. Box 534, Bellarie, OH 43906.

National Milk Glass Collector's Society. Helen Storey, 46 Almond Dr., Cocoa Townes, Hershey, PA 17033.

National Reamer Association. Larry Branstad, Rt. 3, Box 67, Frederic, WI 54837.

National Scouting Collector's Society. 806 E. Scott St., Tuscola, IL 61953.

New England Society of Open Salt Collectors. Mimi Waible, P.O. Box 177, Sudbury, MA.

Novelty Salt and Pepper Club. Irene Thornburg, 581 Joy Rd., Battle Creek, MI 49017.

The Occupied Japan Club. Florence Archambault, 29 Freeborr St., Newport, RI 02840.

Paperweight Collector's Association. P.O. Box 1059, Easthampton, MA 01027. (413) 527-2598.

Peanuts Collector Club. Andrea Podley, P.O. Box 94, North Hollywood, CA 91603.

Perfume and Scent Bottle Collectors. Jeane Parris, 2022 E. Charleston Blvd., Las Vegas, NV 89104. (702) 385-6059.

Pie Birds Unlimited. Lillian Cole. 14 Harmony School Rd., Flemington, NJ 08822.

Planters Peanuts Collector's Club. 804 Hickory Grade Rd., Bridgeville, PA 15017. (412) 221-7599.

Postcard History Society. John McClintock, P.O. Box 1765, Manassas, VA 22110. (703) 368-2757.

Roy Rogers-Dale Evans Collector's Association. Nancy Horsley, P.O. Box 1166, Portsmouth, OH 45662.

Shawnee Pottery Collectors Club. P.O. Box 713, New Smyrna Beach, FL 32170.

The Shot Glass Club of America. Mark Pickvet, P.O. Box 90404, Flint, MI 48509.

The Smurf Collector's Club. 24 Cabot Rd. W., Massapequa, NY 11758.

Society of Inkwell Collectors. Vince McGraw, 5136 Thomas Ave. S., Minneapolis, MN 55410. (612) 922-2792.

Statue of Liberty Collector's Club. Iris November, P.O. Box 535, Chautauqua, NY 14722.

Steiff Collector's Club. Beth Savino, 7856 Hill Avenue, Holland, OH 43528. (419) 865-3899.

Thimble Collectors International. 6411 Montego Rd., Louisville, KY 40228.

Tin Container Collector's Association. Clark Secrest, P.O. Box 4555, Denver, CO 80204.

Westmoreland Glass Society. Jim Fisher, 513 Fifth Avenue, Coralville, IA 52241. (319) 354-5011.

Worlds Fair Collector's Society. Michael Pender, P.O. Box 20806, Sarasota, FL 34238.

Zane Grey's West Society. Carolyn Timmerman, 708 Warwick Avenue, Ft. Wayne, IN 46825. (219) 484-2904.

Newspapers, Newsletters

Action Toys Newsletter. P.O. Box 31551, Billings, MT 59107. (406) 248-4121.

American Carnival Glass News. Dennis Runk, P.O. Box 235, Littlestown, PA 17340. (717) 359-7205.

American Ceramic Journal. P.O. Box 1495, Grand Central Station, New York, NY 10163.

American Lock Collector's Newsletter. Charles Chandler, 36076 Grennada, Livonia, MI 48154. (313) 522-0920.

American Pottery Journal. P.O. Box 14255, Parkville, MO 64152. (816) 587-9179.

American Quilter Magazine. P.O. Box 3290, Paducah, KY 42002.

American Willow Report. Lisa Kay Henze, P.O. Box 900, Oakridge, OR 97463.

Antique and Collectible News. P.O. Box 529, Anna, IL 62906. Monthly.

Antique and Collector's Reproduction News. Mark Cherenka, P.O. Box 71174, Des Moines, IA 50325. (800) 227-5531.

Antique Gazette. 6949 Charlotte Pike, #106, Nashville, TN 37209. Monthly.

Antique Monthly. Stephen Croft, 2100 Powers Ferry Rd., Atlanta, GA 30339. (404) 955-5656.

Antique Press of Florida. 12403 N. Florida Avenue, Tampa, FL 33612.

Antique Souvenir Collector's News. Gary Levelle, P.O. Box 562, Great Barrington, MA 01230.

Antique Trader. P.O. Box 1050, Dubuque, IA 52004. Considered by many to be the nation's leading newspaper on antiques, collecting, auctions, and events. Weekly.

Antique Week. Tom Hoepf, P.O. Box 90, Knightstown, IN 46148. (800) 876-5133. Excellent newspaper for antiques, collecting, auctions, and events. Company publishes two separate editions, Eastern and Central. Weekly.

Antiques and Collecting. 1006 S. Michigan Avenue, Chicago, IL 60605. Monthly.

Art Deco Reflections. Barry Van Hook, 2149 W. Jibsail Loop, Mesa, AZ 85202. (602) 838-6971.

Arts and Crafts Quarterly. P.O. Box 3592, Trenton, NJ 08629. (800) 541-5787.

Auction Block Newspaper. P.O. Box 337, Iola, WI 54945. (715) 445-5000.

Avon Times. Dwight Young. P.O. Box 273, Effort, PA 18330.

Barbie Bazaar Newsletter. 5617 Sixth Avenue, Kenosha, WI 53140. (414) 658-1004.

The Baum Bugle. Fred Meyer. 220 N. 11th St., Escanaba, MI 49829. Newsletter for Wizard of Oz collectors.

Beam Around the World. Shirley Sumbles, 5013 Chase Avenue, Downers Grove, IL 60515. (708) 963-8980. Newsletter for Jim Beam collectors.

Beer Can Collector's News. Don Hicks, 747 Merus Court, Fenton, MO 63026. (314) 343-6486.

Bulletin. 14 Chestnut Rd., Westford, MA 01886. (617) 692-8392. Magazine for doll collectors.

California Pottery Newsletter. Verlangieri Gallery, 816 Main St., W. Cambria, CA 93428. (800) 292-2153.

The Carousel News and Trader. 87 Park Avenue W. #206, Mansfield, OH 44902. Newsletter for carousel collectors. Monthly.

Collecting Tips Newsletter. Meredith Williams, P.O. Box 633, Joplin, MO 64802. (417) 781-3855. Magazine for fast-food collectibles.

The Cookie Jar Collector's News. Louise Daking, 595 Cross River Rd., Katonah, NY 10563. (914) 232-0383.

The Courier. 2503 Delaware Avenue, Buffalo, NY 14216. (716) 873-2594. Newsletter for Civil War collectors. Bimonthly.

The Cutting Edge. Adrienne Escoe, P.O. Box 342, Los Alamitos, CA 90720. Newsletter for glass knife collectors. Quarterly.

Depression Glass Daze. Teri Steel, P.O. Box 57, Otisville, MI 48463. Newsletter for glass, china, and pottery.

Dept. 56 Collectors. Roger Bain, 1625 Myott Avenue, Rockford, IL 61103.

Farm Antique News. Gary Van Hoozer, 812 N. Third St., Tarkio, MO 64491. (816) 736-4528.

The Fenton Flyer. P.O. Box 4008, Marietta, OH 45750. Newsletter for collectors of Fenton glassware.

Fiesta Collector's Quarterly. China Specialties Inc., 19238 Dorchester Circle, Strongville, OH 44136.

Flea Marketeer. P.O. Box 686, Southfield, MI 48037. (313) 351-9910.

Golf Club Collector's Newsletter. Dick Moore, 640 E. Liberty St., Girard, OH 44420.

Gone with the Wind Collector's Newsletter. 8105 Woodview Rd., Ellicott City, MD 21043. (301) 465-4632.

Hall China Collector's Newsletter. P.O. Box 36-488, Cleveland, OH 44136.

The Heisey News. 169 W. Church St., Newark, OH 43055. (612) 345-2932.

Hobby News. P.O. Box 258, Ozone Park, NY 11416.

Hopalong Cassidy Newsletter. P.O. Box 1361, Boyes Hot Springs, CA 95416.

Inside Antiques. Robert Reed. P.O. Box 204, Knightstown, IN 46148. Newspaper dealing with antiques and collectibles. Monthly.

Kitchen Antiques and Collectibles Newsletter. Dana DeMore, 4645 Laurel Ridge Dr., Harrisburg, PA 17110. (717) 545-7320.

Madame Alexander Newsletter. Earl Meisinger, 11 S. 767 Book Rd., Naperville, IL 60564.

Maine Antique Digest. Sam Pennington, P.O. Box 645, Waldoboro, ME 04572. (207) 832-7534.

Majolica Newsletter. Michael Strawser, 1275 First Ave., #103, New York, NY 10021.

Marble Mania. Stanley Block, P.O. Box 222, Trumbull, CT 06611. (203) 261-3223.

Master Collector. Fun Publications, 12513 Birchfalls Dr., Raleigh, NC 27614. (800) 772-6673. Excellent newspaper for doll, bear, and toy collectors. Weekly.

McDonald's Collector Newsletter. Tenna Greenberg, 5400 Waterbury Rd., Des Moines, IA 50312. (515) 279-0741.

The Melting Pot. P.O. Box 256, Findlay, OH 45840. Newsletter for Findlay glass collectors. Quarterly.

Mid-Atlantic Antiques Magazine. Lydia Tucker, P.O. Box 908, Henderson, NC 27536. (919) 492-4001. East Coast magazine covering antiques, shops, collecting, auctions and events. Monthly.

Model and Toy Collector Magazine. 137 Casterton Ave, Akron, OH 44303. (216) 836-0668.

Movie Advertising Collector Magazine. George Reed, P.O. Box 28587, Philadelphia, PA 19149.

News and Views. Anita Wood, P.O. Box 69843, Odessa, TX 79769. (915) 337-1297. Newsletter for collectors of depression glass.

Olympic Collector's Newsletter. Bill Nelson, P.O. Box 41630, Tucson, AZ 85717.

Our McCoy Matters. Kathy Lynch, McCoy Publications, P.O. Box 14255, Parkville, MO 64152. (816) 587-9179.

Pepsi-Cola Collector's Newsletter. Bob Stoddard, P.O. Box 1275, Covina, CA 91722. (714) 593-8750.

Pottery Lovers Newsletter. Pat Sallaz, 4969 Hudson Dr., Stow, OH 44224.

Precious Collectibles. Rosie Wells, Rt. 1, Canton, IL 61520. Magazine for Precious Moments collectors.

Quint News. P.O. Box 2527, Woburn, MA 01888. (617) 933-2219. Newsletter for Dionne Quint collectors.

Red Wing Collector's Newsletter. David Newkirk, Rt. 3, Box 146, Monticello, MN 55362.

Roseville's of the Past Newsletter. Jack Bomm, P.O. Box 681117, Orlando, FL 32868.

Royal Doulton International Collector's Club Newsletter. Royal Doulton, P.O. Box 1815, Somerset, NJ 08873. (908) 356-7929.

The Shirley Temple Collector's News. Rita Dubas, 8811 Colonial Rd., Brooklyn, NY 11209.

Singing Wires. George Howard, 19 N. Cherry Dr., Oswego, IL 60543. (708) 554-8154.

Tobacco Jar Newsletter. Charlotte Tarses, 3011 Falstaff Rd., #307, Baltimore, MD 21209.

Toy Gun Collectors of America Newsletter. Jim Buskirk, 312 Starling Way, Anaheim, CA 92807. (714) 998-9615.

Toys and Prices Magazine. 700 E. State St., Iola, WI 54990. (715) 445-2214. Monthly.

Trainmaster Newsletter. P.O. Box 1499, Gainesville, FL 32602. (904) 377-7439.

Vintage Clothing Newsletter. Terry McCormick, P.O. Box 1422, Corvallis, OR 97339. (503) 752-7456.

Vintage Fashion and Costume Jewelry Newsletter. Davida Baron, P.O. Box 265, Glen Oaks, NY 11004. (718) 969-2320.

Wat's News. Susan Morris, P.O. Box 708, Mason City, IA 50401.

Recommended Resources

I highly recommend the following reference books. A good reference book is a necessity for serious collecting. It not only establishes a ballpark value for items, it will also keep you from overpaying and help you make sure you are buying authentic items and not reproductions. Whatever your specialty, and no matter the level of your expertise, you should buy the book. Take it from me, it's worth the money.

The following list is only a sampling of the many fine books available at most book stores. The prices listed are suggested retail.

American Militaria Sourcebook. (Available by mail order only.) Terry Hannon, P.O. Box 245, Lyon Station, PA 19536. (800) 446-0909.

American Premium Guide to Pocket Knives. 3rd ed. Jim Sargent. 508p. 1992. pap. $22.95. Bks. Americana.

Antique Tools: Our American Heritage. Kathryn McNerney. (Illus.) 153p. 1991. pap. $9.95. Collector Bks.

Avon Bottle Collectibles Encyclopedia. 13th ed. Bud Hastin. 1994. $19.95. Nostalgia Pblg.

Book of Country. Vol. 1 and 2. Don and Carol Raycraft. (Illus.). 160p. 1988. $19.95. Collector Bks.

Bottle Pricing Guide. 3rd ed. Hugh Cleveland. 1994. $7.95. Nostalgia Pblg.

Cambridge Glass, 1949-1953. Bill Smith. 1986. pap. $14.95. Collector Bks.

Collectible Glassware of the 40's, 50's, 60's. Vol. 2. Gene Florence. 1994. $19.95. Collector Bks.

Collecting Toys: An Identification and Value Guide, No.6. Richard O'Brien. (Illus.). 608p. 1992. pap. $22.95. Bks. Americana.

Collector's Encyclopedia of American Art Glass. John Shuman. 1994. $29.95. Nostalgia Pblg.

Collector's Encyclopedia of American Furniture. Robert Swedberg. 1991. $24.95. Collector Bks.

Collector's Encyclopedia of Cookie Jars. Fred Roerig. 1991. $24.95. Collector Bks.

Collector's Encyclopedia of Depression Glass. Gene Florence. 1994. $19.95. Collector Bks.

Collector's Encyclopedia of Disneyana. Michael Stern. 272p. 1991. $24.95. Collector Bks.

Collector's Encyclopedia of Fiesta. 7th ed. Bob Huxford. 1991. $19.95. Collector Bks.

Collector's Encyclopedia of Heisey Glass, 1925-1938. Neila Bredehoft. (Illus.). 462p. 1991. $24.95. Collector Bks.

Collector's Encyclopedia of Occupied Japan Collectibles. Gene Florence. (Illus.). 108p. 1990. $14.95. Collector Bks.

Collector's Encyclopedia of RS Prussia: Second Series. Mary F. Gaston. (Illus.). 232p. 1986. $24.95. Collector Bks.

Collector's Encyclopedia of Roseville Pottery. Sharon and Bob Huxford. (Illus.). 192p. 1991. $19.95. Collector Bks.

Collector's Encyclopedia of Roseville Pottery: Second Series. Sharon and Bob Huxford. (Illus.). 208p. 1991. $19.95. Collector Bks.

Collector's Guide to Hull Pottery-the Dinnerware Lines: Identification and Values. Barbara L. Gick-Burke. 144p. 1993. pap. $16.95. Collector Bks.

Collector's Guide to Shawnee Pottery. Duane Vanderbilt. 144p. 1992. $19.95. Collector Bks.

Fostoria. Vol. 1. Ann Kerr. 232p. 1993. $24.95. Nostalgia Pblg.

Furniture of the Depression Era. Robert and Harriet Swedberg. 144p. 1990. $19.95. Collector Bks.

Illustrated Value Guide to Cookie Jars, Bk. II. Ermagene Westfall. 240p. 1993. pap. $19.95. Collector Bks.

Imperial Glass Identification and Value Guide. Vol. 1. Archer. 212p. 1994. $14.95. Schroeder Pblg.

Keen Kutter Collectibles. Jerry and Elaine Heuring. 1990. pap. $14.95. Collector Bks.

Kitchen Glassware of the Depression Years. 4th ed. Gene Florence. 224p. 1990. $19.95. Collector Bks.

Kovel's Antiques and Collectibles Price List. Ralph and Terry Kovel. 1995. pap. $13.00. Crown Pblg. Group.

North American Indian Artifacts. 5th ed. Lar Hothem. 416p. 1993. pap. $22.95. Bks. Americana.

100 Years of Collectible Jewelry. Lillian Baker. (Illus.) 169p. 1989. pap. $9.95. Collector Bks.

Salt and Pepper Shakers. Helene Guarnaccia. (Illus.). 176p. 1990. pap. $9.95. Collector Bks.

Salt and Pepper Shakers II. Helene Guarnaccia. 1990. pap. $14.95. Collector Bks.

Salt and Pepper Shakers III. Helene Guarnaccia. 1991. pap. $14.95. Collector Bks.

Salt and Pepper Shakers IV: Identification and Values. Helene Guarnaccia. 224p. 1993. pap. $18.95. Collector Bks.

Schroeder's Antiques Price Guide. 11th ed. 608p. 1992. pap. $12.95. Collector Bks.

Standard Carnival Glass Price Guide. 9th ed. Bill Edwards. $9.95. Nostalgia Pblg.

Standard Knife Collector's Guide. 2nd ed. Ron Stewart. 608p. 1992. pap. $12.95. Collector Bks.

Vintage Fashion Source Book. Kristina Harris. 1994. hc. $40.00. Nostalgia Pblg.

INDEX

ILLINOIS

A and M Indoor Flea Market, 25
A. M. Bargain Bazaar Flea Market, 27
Albany Antique Mart, 185
Anderson Auction, 265
Andre Ammelounx, 265
Antique Alley Mall, 188
Antique and Collector Consignment Auction 263
Antique and Treasure Trove, 187
Antique Flea Market (Le Grange), 27
Antique Gallery Mall, 185
Antique Mall, The (Chenoa), 186
Antique Markets (St. Charles), 193
Antique Mini Mall and Flea Market, 188
Antique Show and Flea Market (Amboy), 18
Antique Show and Flea Market (Peotone), 31
Antique Warehouse, 188
Antique World Annex, 186
Antique World, 189
Antiques Center of Illinois, 193
Antiques Mart, 187
Antiques, 193
Arches Antique Marketplace, The, 188
Archview Flea Market, 33
Armitage Antique Gallery, 186
Art Achackman Auction Specialist, 265
Ashland Avenue Swap-O-Rama, 27
Asselmeier and May Auctioneers, 266
Auction City Sales, 264
Auction USA, Inc., 263, 286
Avon Antique Mall, 185
Beardstown Antique Mall, 185
Belleville Flea Market, 17, 18
Big John's Flea Market, 27
Biggest Indoor Flea Market, The, 30
Brighton Park Swap-O-Rama, 19
Brinton Avenue Antique Mall, 187
Broadway Antique Mall, 191
Bull Dog Antiques, 189
Buyers Market, The, 17, 19
Cal-Jean Shops, 190
Casa Blanca Flea Market, 21
Chase Gilmore Art Galleries, 264
Cicero Swap-O-Rama, 21
Clinton Antique Mall, 187
Commercial House Antiques, 189
Consigntiques, 193
Conwill Auction, 263, 286
Country Boy Flea Market, 31
Country Seed House Antique Mall, 190
County Line Swap-O-Rama, 28
Court Street Flea Market, 25
Dealer Auction, 265, 286
Derald's Indoor Flea Market, 25
Dix Flea Market, 22
Doerr Auction Service, 266
Don's Flea Market, 19
Double Drive-In Flea Market, 20

Du Page Antique and Flea Market, 35
Dundee Drive-In Flea Market, 22
Dunnings Auction Service, 264
East State Street Malls, 192
Eastwood Farm Antiques and Collectibles, 192
Elliott's Country Faire, 264
Emporium Antiques, 185
Ferry Street Mall, 190
Fine Arts Brokers, Auctioneers and Appraisers, 263
Flea Market (Bismarck), 18
Flea Market (Downers Grove), 22
Flea Market (Elmhurst), 23
Flea Market (Fairfield), 23
Flea Market (Godfrey), 24
Flea Market (Grayslake), 24
Flea Market (Hartford), 25
Flea Market (Harvey), 25
Flea Market (Havana), 25
Flea Market (Herrin), 25
Flea Market (Kankakee), 26
Flea Market (Marion), 27
Flea Market (Melrose Park), 27
Flea Market (Northbrook), 29
Flea Market (Pinckneyville), 31
Flea Market (Royalton), 32
Flea Market (Springfield Drive-In), 33
Flea Market (Springfield, MacArthur St.), 33
Flea Market (Springfield, W. Lawrence), 33
Flea Market (Vergennes), 35
Flea Market (Wapella), 35
Flea Market (Warren), 35
Flea Market (Waterloo), 35
Flea Market (Yorkville), 36

Flea Market and Arts and Crafts Show (Grafton), 24
Flea Market and Bazaar (Ottawa), 30
Flea Market and Crafts Show (Nauvoo), 29
Flea Market City, 25
Flea Market, Antiques and Crafts (Warren), 35
Fourth Sunday Flea Market (Mendota), 28
Fourth Sunday Flea Market (Mt Prospect), 28
Frank's Gigantic Flea Market, 33
Garrett Galleries, 263
Genesseo Antique Mall, 188
Geneva Antiques Market, 188
"Giant Flea Market" (Champaign), 19
"Giant Flea Market" (Decatur), 22
"Giant Flea Market" (Duquoin), 22
"Giant Flea Market" (Kankakee), 26
"Giant Flea Market" (Normal), 29
"Giant Flea Market" (Peoria), 30
"Giant Flea Market" (Springfield), 34
Grayslake Indoor Mart, 24
Grayslake Swap-O-Rama, 24
Great American Flea Market, 20
Greater Rockford indoor/Outdoor Antique and Flea Market, 31
Hanzel Galleries, 264
Harman Auction Center, 265
Heartland Antique Mall, 188

Hello Open Air Flea Market
and Farmers Market, 17
Henry Hachmeister,
Auctioneer, 265
Highland Flea Market, 25
Hilltop Auction Co., 263
Hintze Auction Service, 265
I-80 Collectibles and Flea
Market, 34
Illinois Antique Center, 191
Indian Oaks Antique Mall, 186
International Amphitheater
Swap-O-Rama, 20
Ipc Levy Auctioneers, 265
J and S antiques Mall, 188
Jack's Flea Market, 31
Jacksonville Antique Mall, 189
Jerry's Variety Flea Market, 24
Judy's Flea Market, 34
Kane County Flea Market,
17, 32
Kankakee Antique Mall, 189
Landmark Antiques, 187
Leslie Hindman Auctions, 264
Lisa's Antique Mall, 187
Little Flower Flea Market, 22
Marketplace Flea Market, 20
Maryville Antique Mall, 190
Mattoon Antique Mart, 190
Maxwell Street Flea Market, 20
Melrose Park Swap-O-Rama, 28
Memory Lane Antique
Mall, 186
Monday Dealers Auction,
266, 286
North Vermillion Flea
Market, 21
Northlake Swap-O-Rama, 29
Old Broadway Hotel Antique,
Crafts and Flea
Market, 192

Old Georgian Antique
Mall, 192
Olde Hotel Flea Market and
Auction, 33
On the Park Antiques, 189
1905 Emporium Mall, 192
Oswego, 191
Peddler's Days, 18
Peddlers Place Flea Market,
The, 27
Petersburg Peddlers, 191
Plainfield Antique Mart, 191
Pleasant Hill Antique Mall and
Tea Room, 187
Pulford Open House Antique
Mall, 192
Regency Flea Market, 20
River Valley Antique Mall, 189
Rockford Flea Market, 31
Roscoe Auction House, 265
Route 66 Antique Mall
(Atlanta), 185
Route 66 Antique Mall
(Lincoln), 189
Ruby Sled Antique and Art
Mart, 34
Sandwich Antiques Mall, 192
Sandwich Antiques Market,
17, 32
Second Story Antique
Mall, 190
Second Sunday Flea Market
(Princeton), 31
Sherwood Antique Mall, 191
Signature Marketplace and
Auction, 265
Silo Antiques, 191
South Jacksonville Antique
Mall, 189
Southern Illinois Trade
Fair, 28
Southfork Antique Mall, 190

Springfield Mall, 192
Swap-O-Rama (Bensenville), 18
Swap-O-Rama (Griffith), 24
TG's Antique Mall, 191
Trading Fair, 29
Trash to Treasures Flea Market, 27
Tri-State Swap-O-Rama, 17
Twin Flea Market, 36
Urbana Antiques and Flea Market, 34
VFW Flea Market, 22
Village Green Antique and Gift Mall, 190
Vintage Antiques, 186
Volvo Antique Mall, 193
Volvo Sales Flea Market, 35
Waukegan Drive-In Theater Flea Market, 21
Waukegan Swap `N Shop Flea Market, 35
Waukegan-Zion Dealers Auction, 286
Weekend Flea Market, 21
West Frankfort Antique Mall, 193
Wildwood Flea Market, 19
Willard Buckhorn, 266
World Bazaar Giant Indoor/Outdoor Flea Market, 24
Wrigleyville Antique Mall, 187
Wyanet Antique Mall, 193
Yesteryear Antique Mall, 191

INDIANA

Albany Flea Market Mall, 37
Albert's Mall, 202
Amish Country Antique Mall, 203
Amishland Antique Mall, 201
Ancient Thymes Mall, 204
Anderson Antique Mall, 194
Anna's Antique Mall, 197
Antique Flea Market (Indianapolis), 46
Antique Junction Mall, 199
Antique Mall (Ft. Wayne), 198
Antique Mall (Lafayette), 199
Antique Mall of Boswell, 194
Antique Mall of Carmel, 195
Antique Market (Michigan City), 201
Antique Show and Flea Market (Portland), 56
Antiques and Collectibles Flea Market (Attica), 38
Antiques and Collectibles Flea Market (Petersburg), 56
Antiques and Not Mall, 198
Antiques Center and Flea Market (Jeffersonville), 48
Antiques Etc., 201
Antiques, Crafts and Thins Mall, 204
Arcadia Antique Mall, 194
Aurora Flea Market, 38
Back in Time Antique Mall, 196
Back Through Time Antique Mall, 203
Bailey Auction Service, 267
Bargersville Flea Market, 38
Barn and Field Flea Market, 40
Beechwood Pavilion Flea Market, 40
Big Bear Flea Market, 41
Big Red Flea Market, 46
Big Top Flea Market, 46
Bloomington Antique Mall, 194
Bloomington Antique Show and Flea Market, 39
Borden Flea Market, 39

Borkholder Dutch Village Market, 54
Brazil Antique Mall, 194
Broadway Antique Mall, 200
Brookston Antiques, 194
Brown County Antique Mall, 202
Burtons Farmers and Collectors Flea Market, 51
Cabbages and Kings Antique Mall, 196
Carlisle Flea Market, 40
Caverns of Elkhart, The, 196
Cedars of Lebanon Antiques, 200
Cellar Antique Mall, 200
Central Avenue Flea Market, 49
Charlestown Flea Market, 41
Chaudions Auction Co., 266
Christy's of Greenwood, 267
Coachman Antique Mall, 199
Collector's Fair, The, 51
Conklin's Olde Towne Mall, 194
Country Corner Flea Market, 41
Country Store Antique Mall, The, 200
Country Village Flea Market and Craft Show, 45
Countryside Antique Mall and Indian Trading Post, 204
County Seat Antique Mall, 197
Covered Bridge Mall, 203
Cracker Ridge Flea Market, 52
Crossroads Antique Mall, 58, 203
Curan Miller Auction and Realty Inc., 267
Dave Petree Auction Co., 267
Dave White, 266

Dealer Auction (Boswell), 286
Dealer Auction (Indianapolis), 286
Dealers Auction (Howards Grove), 286
Delphi Antique Mall, 196
Dezerland Antique World, 204
Diamond Flea Market, 42
Diner and Antique Mall, 198
Downtown Antique Mall, 198
Dunes Swap-O-Rama, 50
E-Z City Super Mall, 194
Earl's Auction Co., 267
East Drive-In Flea Market, 49
Eastern Indiana Flea Market, 56
Ed's Gift Shop and Flea Market, 52
Elkhart Antique Mall, 196
Ellettsville Antique Mall, 197
Evansville Flea Market, 42
Farmers Flea Market (Salem), 58
Festival Flea Market, 48
Flea Market (Attica), 38
Flea Market (Austin), 38
Flea Market (Avon), 38
Flea Market (Birdseye), 38
Flea Market (Carlisle), 40
Flea Market (Columbia City), 41
Flea Market (Connersville), 42
Flea Market (Decatur), 42
Flea Market (Flora), 42
Flea Market (Franklin), 43
Flea Market (Highland), 45
Flea Market (Indianapolis, E. 10th St.), 46
Flea Market (Indianapolis, LaFayette Rd.), 47
Flea Market (Indianapolis, S. Tibb Ave.), 46

INDEX **305**

Flea Market (Indianapolis, W. Washington), 47
Flea Market (Jacksonburg), 48
Flea Market (Kingsland), 49
Flea Market (Kokomo), 49
Flea Market (Lafayette), 49
Flea Market (Morgantown), 53
Flea Market (Muncie), 53
Flea Market (New Albany), 54
Flea Market (New Castle), 55
Flea Market (North Linton), 55
Flea Market (North Webster), 56
Flea Market (Powell), 50
Flea Market (Roanoke), 57
Flea Market (Rochester), 57
Flea Market (Zanesville), 60
Flea Marketeers, The, 41
Flint Creek Antique Mall, 198
41 Swap-O-Rama, 45
Fountain Square Antique Mall, 198
Fountaintown Emporium, 43
Franklin Antique Show and Flea Market, 43
Friendship Flea Market, 43
Frontier Antique Mall, 202
Ft. Wayne Antique and Collectors Market, 44
Ft. Wayne Flea Market, 44
Gallery Flea Market, The, 42
Gaslight Antique Mall, 201
Gilley's Antique Mall, 202
Goshen Antique Mall, 198
Granny's Daughter Mall, 204
Green County Hill Flea Market, 59
Green Meadows Flea Market, 55
Greenwalts Flea Market, 53
Griffin Building Antiques Mall, 195

Halfway Flea Market, 52
Hayloft Antique Mall, The, 195
Heartland Antique Mall, 199
Highway 20 Flea Market, 56
Holdiay's Barn Market, 46
Hoosier Swap-O-Rama, 52
Indiana Avenue Flea Market, 42
Indiana Flea Market, 37, 47
Indoor Flea Market (New Haven), 55
Indy Merchandise Clearing House Auction, 287
Inside Flea Market (Rushville), 57
International Park Consumer Center, 44
Jackson County Flea Market, 40
Jackson's Auction Gallery, 266
Jemea's Antique Mall, 198
Kamms Island Antique and Flea Market, 52
Keepsake Mall, 199
Kenny Bland Auctions, 268
Kentland Antiques Mall, 199
Kilgore Flea Market, 53
Knightstown Antique Mall, 199
Koons Auction and Realty Co., 266
Lafayette Road Flea Market, 47
Liberty Bell Flea Market, 47
Lighthouse Antique Mall, 197
Lilac Park Country Fair Craft and Flea Market, 52
Lindon's Antique Mall, 199
Linton Antique Mall, 200
Little Creek Antique Mall, 195
Livery Stable Antique Mart, 51
Lumbermill Antique Mall, 201
Madison Antique Mall, 201

Main Street Auction House, 267, 287
Main Street Flea Market, 53
Marion Flea Market, 51
Market City Flea Market, 45
Memories Past Antique Mall, 196
Merchants Market, The, 49
Minor Auction Service, 267
Miracle Antique Mall, 201
Mitchell Antique Mall, 201
Mona's Treasure Chest and Waterford Flea Market, 201
Monthly Flea Market (Hoagland), 46
Moonglo Treasure Chest Flea Market, 58
Moonlite Flea Market and Crafts Show, 43
Nancy's Downtown Mall, 204
Ness Brothers Real Estate and Auction Co., 267
New Haven Flea Market, 44
New Whiteland Flea Market, 55
Noblesville Antique Mall, 202
Norway Flea Market, 53
Off Broadway Antique Mall, 201
Old Canyon Works Flea Market, 50
Old Evansville Antique Mall, 197
Old New Albany Antique Mall, 202
Old Time Flea Market, 54
Old Town Square Antique Mall, 196
Olympia Expo Center Flea Market, 37
Open Air Flea Market, 51
Parkers Flea Market, 51
Parlor City Flea Market, 39
Peddlers Acre, 50
Peddlers Flea Market, 45
Pendleton Antique Mall, 202
Peru Antique Mall, 202
Pine Ridge Flea Market, 55
Portland Antique Emporium, 202
Pumpkin Vine Junction, 58
Red Barn Antique Mall, 196
Rennselaer Antique and Flea Market, 56
Reservation Campground Flea Market, 56
Rivertown Flea Market, 51
Rockville Antique Mall, 203
Ron's Auction Center, 266
Rush County Mall, 203
Scottsburg Antique Mall, 203
Seller Antique Mall, 202
Shadeland Antique Mall, 199
Shady Lane Antique Mall, 204
Shiloh Country Flea Market, 44
Shipshewana Antique and Collectible Auction, 267
Shipshewana Auction and Flea Market, 37, 58
Sky-Hi Flea Market, 54
Sparks Auction Service, 267
Speedway Mall Flea Market, 44
Spring Street Flea Market, 55
Starlite Drive-In Theater Flea Market, 39
Sugar Creek Antique Mall, 198
Swayzee Antique Mall, 204
Terre Haute Flea Market, 59
Thieves Market, 59
Timeless Treasures Antique Mall, 204
Tom's Antique Mall, 195
Town Square Mall, 196

Trading Fair, 41
Trafalgar Antique Market, 59
Treasure Chest Antique Mall (Jasper), 199
Treasure Chest Antiques Mall (Brazil), 194
Treasures Antiques and Collectibles, 197
Tri-State Antique Market, 50
Twin Drive-In Theater Flea Market, 48
Twin Lakes Flea Market, 53
Two Rivers Antique Mall, 200
Uncle Dudley's Antique Mall, 200
Uncle John's Flea Market, 40
Unique Antique Mall, 203
Village Flea Market, 45
Wallace's Antique Mall, 201
Wayne County Flea Market, 56
Webb's Antique Mall, 41, 195
West Washington Flea Market, 48
White Farmers Market, 37, 39
White River Flea Market, 54
Wildwood Park Farm and Flea Market, 50
Wilson Corners Flea Market, 59
Winchester Antique Mall, 205
Windmill Antique Mall, 197
Wolcottville Antique Mall, 205
Y and W Drive-In Flea Market, 52
Y and W Drive-In Theater Flea Market, 39
Ye Olde Central House Flea Market, 54
Yesterday's Treasures Antique Mall, 195
Yesteryears Antique and Collectible Mall and Flea Market, 57
Yvonne Marie's Antique Mall, 196

IOWA

Antique Galleries, 207
Antique Junction Mall, 64, 207
Antique Mall, The, 205
Antique, Arts and Crafts Mall, 206
Boldt Auction Co., 268
Brass Armadillo, The, 205
Bryants Flea Market, 61, 62
Central Iowa Flea Market, 63
Classic American Auctions, 268
Collector's Fair, 63
Collectors Paradise Flea Market, 61, 64
Country Heart Antiques and Uniques, 205
Crystal Lake Flea Market, 62
Flea Market (Des Moines, S.E. 30th St.), 62
Flea Market (Des Moines, State Fairgrounds), 61, 62
Flea Market (Dubuque), 62
Flea Market (La Porte City), 63
Flea Market (Manley), 63
Flea Market (Sioux City), 64
Gene Harris Antique Auction Center, 268
"Giant Flea Market" (Council Bluffs), 61
"Giant Flea Market" (Davenport), 62
Golden Age Antique Mall, 207
Greenfield's Professional Auction Service, 268

Heritage Square Antique Mall, 207
Jackson's Auctioneers and Appraisers, 268
King's Flea Market, 63
Kozy Corner Flea Market, 64
L and H Antique Mall, 207
Ledges Road Flea Market, 61
Logan Antique Mall, 206
Memories of Main Antique Mall, 205
Memory Lane Antique Mall, 205
Midway Shop and Swap, 64
North Federal Antique Mall, 206
Olde Central Antique Mall, 63, 206
Onawa Antique Mall, 206
Original Hillbilly Flea Market and Auction, 61
Pieces of Olde Antique Mall, 205
Red Ribbon Antique Mall, 207
River Bend Cove Antique Mall, 206
Rivers Edge Antiques, 206
Sharpless Auctions, 268
Showcase Antique Mall, 206
Tomes Flea Market, 61
Venice Antiques, 207
Vincent Antique Galleries, 64
West Amana General Store, 207
World Wide College of Auctioneering, 285

KANSAS

Airport Flea Market, 67
Annie's Antique Mall, 213
Antique and Craft City, 209
Antique Mall (Lawrence), 209
Antique Mall (Winfield), 214
Antique Merchants Mall, 213
Antique Plaza of Topeka, 212
Arkansas City Flea Market, 65
Armourdale Collectibles and Flea Market, 67
Blackledge Antique Mall, 208
Boulevard Drive-In Swap Shop, 67
Brown Auction and Real Estate, 269
Bunny Patch Craft Mall, 208
Caney Antique Mall, 208
Chautouqua Flea Market, 65
Circle C Trading Post, 68, 210
Cochran Real Estate and Auction Co., 268
Concordia Flea Market, 66
Country Cupboard Antiques Flea Market, 66
Country Flea Market and Antique Mall, 66
Doogie's Place, 211
11-Worth Antique Mall, 210
Emporium on the Square, 209
Flea Market (Junction City), 67
Flea Market (Kansas City), 67
Flea Market (Topeka), 65, 69
Garnett Flea Market, 66
George and Martha's Antique Mall, 213
Heavitt's Antique Mall, 213
Helen's Market, 66
Heritage House Mini Mall, 209
Highland Crest Flea Market, 69
Hutchinson Flea Market, 65, 66
Jayhawk Antique/Craft Mall and Flea Market, 68, 211
Koch Auction Services, 269

INDEX **309**

Legere Auction and Realty Co., 269
LFK Art and Antiques Auction Co., 269
Lincoln Antiques, 210
Magdalena's, 210
Main Street Antique Mall, 210
Main Street Antiques and Collectibles Mall, 211
Mainion's International Auction House, 269
Market, The, 70
Mary's Flea Market, 208
Needful Things Flea Market, 69
New Ponderosa Flea Market, 70
Oak Street Antique Mall, 208
Old Glory Flea Market, Antiques and Crafts Mall, 68, 211
Old Miners Antique and Flea Market Mall, 209
On The "Avenue" Antique Mall, 210
Opolis Flea Market, 68
Oswego Flea Market, 68
Ottawa Flea Market, 68
Park City Antique Mall, 213
Park Square Emporium, 210
Perry Antique and Craft Mall, 211
Peters Flea Market, 66
Quantrill's Antique Mall, 67, 209
Rick Kaufman Auctioneer, 270
Section house Antiques, 210
Strickner's Auction Co., 269
Swap Shop Antique Mall, 212
Tiffany Gallery, 208
Tom Stroud Auctioneer, 270
Topeka Antique Mall and Flea Market, 69, 212
Towanda Antiques Mall and Blue Moon Saloon and Restaurant, 212
Townsquare Uniques, 210
Treasure Mall, 213
Treasure Plaza Flea Market, 70
Treasures Antiques Co., 208
Two Fools Antiques Mall, 207
Village Flea Market, 70
Warehouse, The, 69
Washburn View Antique Mall, 212
Wheatland Antique Mall, 212
White Eagle Antique Mall, 208, 213
Wichita Flea Market, 65, 70
Wild Rose Antique Mall, 208
Woody Auction Company, 269
Yesterday's Antique Mall, 209

KENTUCKY
A B and D Flea Market, 71
American Legion Flea Market, 74
Antique Flea Market (Glasgow), 76
Antique Flea Market (Kuttawa), 78
Antique Mall (Danville), 215
Antique Mall (Lexington), 217
Antique Mall of Harrodsburg, The, 217
Antiques and Things, 215
Antiques on Main Mall, 218
Auction Concepts, 270
Auction Unlimited, 270, 287
Augusta Antique Mall, 214
Bardstown Antique Market, 214
Bargain Bazaar, 79

Bennie's Barn Antique Mall, 216
Beverly Flea Market, 84
Blue Moon Antique Mall, 215
Boonville Flea Market, 73
Bowling Lanes Flea Market, 74
Bratcher's Flea Market, 78
Bullett County Flea Market, 83
Burlington Antique Flea Market, 71, 73
By Buy Enterprise Flea Market, 74
Cadiz Antique Mall, 215
Camp Nelson Flea Market, 73
Carroll County Flea Market, 73
Central Kentucky Antique Mall, 216
Chestnut Street Antique Mall, 214
Chief Paduke Antique Mall, 219
Clarksville Flea Market, 73
Clay Street Flea Market, 79
Coach Light Antique Mall, 219
Coke Auction, 270, 287
Country Antique Mall, 218
Country Fair and Flea Market, 79
Country World Flea Market, 71, 76
Cumberland Antique Mall, 220
Dean Tobacco Warehouse Flea Market, 79
Decades Ago Antique Mall, 217
Derby Park Traders Circle Flea Market, 79
Downtown Antique Mall, 214
Drive-In Theater Flea Market, 78
Ellis Park Flea Market, 77
Fairdale Auction Co., 270
Flea for All Flea Market, 75
Flea Market (Beaver Dam), 72
Flea Market (Central City), 73
Flea Market (Crestwood), 74
Flea Market (Florence), 75
Flea Market (Henderson, Hwy. 41), 77
Flea Market (Henderson, S. Green St.), 77
Flea Market (Louisville), 80
Flea Market (Owensboro), 82
Flea Market (Paintsville), 82
Flea Market (Wayne), 84
Flea Market Mall, 75
Flea World Flea Market, 79
471 Antique Mall, 218
Georgetown Antique Mall, 216
Glendale Antique Mall, 217
Glover's Antique Mall, 217
Hardin County Flea Market, 82
Helping Hand Flea Market, 84
Henderson Antique Mall, 217
Heritage Antique Mall and Collectibles, 216
Hidden Attic Antique Mall, The, 216
High Grove Antiques and Flea Market, 80
Hillbilly Flea Market (Ashland), 71
Hillbilly Flea Market (Russell), 83
Hillbilly Peddlers Flea Market, 72
Hog Heaven Flea Market, 82
Horse Park Flea Market, 76
Impressions Antique Mall, 214
Kay's Flea Market, 72
Kay's Fleaground, 81
Kentucky Flea Market, 71, 80
Kentucky Realty and Auction Co., 271

Kimberly Run Antique Center, 214
Lakewide Flea Market, 84
Leitchfield Antique Mall, 217
Lexington Antique and Flea Market, 78
Lexington Antique Gallery, 218
Lily Trading Post and Flea Market, 73
Lincoln Square Mall, 217
Louisville Antique Mall, 218
Main Street Antique Mall (Cadiz), 215
Main Street Antique Mall (Shelbyville), 219
Main Street Antique Mall (Vine Grove), 220
Main Street Antiques Mall (Hopkinsville), 217
Mayfield-Graves County Park Flea Market, 81
Mid-State Flea Market, 78
Mt. Sterling Flea Market, 81
Murray Drive-In Theater Flea Market, 81
New London Flea Market, 81
North Kentucky Flea Market, 78
Old Brick Mall, 218
Old Southern Flea Market, 74
Olde Towne Antique Mall, 220
Owensboro Antique Mall, 219
Plain and Fancy Antique Mall, 216
Price Buster Dealer Auction, 270
Pricebuster Dealer Auction, 287
Radcliff Antique Mall, 219
Richwood Flea Market, 71, 82
Ridners Flea Market, 73
Risk Flea Market, 83
River Bend Antique Mall, 215
Robbie's Antique and Flea Market, 72
Robby's Flea Market, 72
Rochester Flea Market, 83
Rocking Horse Antique Mall, The, 219
Russell Springs Antique Mall, 219
Russell Springs Flea Market, 83
Russellville Antique Mall, 219
Saint Matthews Antique Market, 218
Sammy's Flea Market and Auction, 74
Shelby County Flea Market, 84
Shelbyville Antique Mall, 219
Shelbyville Flea Market, 83
Sherry and Friends Antique Mall, 219
Show and Sell Flea Market, 78
Side Track Shops and Antique Mall, The, 217
Simpler Tymes Antique Mall and Frame Shop, 215
South Central Kentucky Flea Market, 75
Southern Kentucky Flea Market, 77
Starlight Antique Mall, 215
Starlite Drive-In Theater Flea Market, 75
Strictly Country Antique Mall, 216
Swan Street Antique Mall, 218
Todd's Antique Mall and Flea Market, 72, 215
Town and Country Antique Mall, 214
Town and Country Flea Market, 76

Twin Street Flea Market, 77
Union City Flea Market, 84
Welk's Flea Market, 76
White's Flea Market, 72
White's Kentucky Auction
    Service, 270
Winchester Flea Market
    (Oliver Rd.), 84
Winchester Flea Market (W.
    Lexington Ave.), 85
Windmill Flea Market, 82
Winnies Antique Mall, 216
Wyatt's antique Center, 216

MICHIGAN

A Quaint Little Antique
    Mall, 221
AAA Straight Up Auction
    Service, 271
Adams Antique Mall, 224
Adrian Antique Mall, 220
Airport Antique Mall, 224
American Heritage Antique
    Mall, 224
Andy Adams Auctioneer, 271
Andy Adams Sale Barn Flea
    and Farmers Market, 91
Ann Arbor Antiques
    Market, 86
Annette's Antique Mall, 227
Antique Center (Flushing), 222
Antique Flea Market
    (Mason), 94
Antique Mall of
    Williamston, 228
Antique Warehouse, 226
Antiques By The Bridge, 223
Antiques Mall of Ann
    Arbor, 221
Antiques On Main, 226
Armada Outdoor Flea
    Market, 87

B and B Flea Market, 89
Bangor Antique Mall, 221
Barb's Country Antiques
    Mall, 226
Bay City Antiques Center, 221
Becks Farm Market, 100
Beltline Drive-In Flea Market,
    90, 102
Besner Auction Team, 271
Big D Flea Market, 89
Blissfield Antique Mall, 221
Bunky's Flea Market, 102
Burley Park Swap Meet, 92
Butler Auction Service, 272
C.V. Auction and Flea
    Market, 91
Caravan Antiques Market,
    86, 87
Chicago Street Antique
    Mall, 222
Close Out - Blow Out Flea
    Market, 89
Consignments of
    Williamston, 228
Copemish Flea Market, 88
Country Fair Antique Flea
    Market (Warren), 101
Country Fair Flea Market
    (Utica), 101
Country Store Antique Flea
    Market, 92
Cracker Hill Antique Mall, 226
Dallas Corner Flea Market, 94
Dan Van Sumeren and
    Associates, 271
David A. Norton
    Auctioneer, 271
Dealers Auction
    (Grasslake), 287
Dixieland Flea Market, 97
Dowagiac Flea Market, 90

Du Mouchelles Auctioneering, 271
Eastland Outdoor Market, 93
Edward J. Kaye Auctioneers, 271
8 Mile Trade Center, 89
Elba Flea Market, 90
Estes Antiques Mall, 221
Fannie's Antique Market With Fleas, 226
Farm Village Antique Mall, 225
Farmers and Flea Market, 98
Farmers Market (Coloma), 88
Farmers Market Flea Market (Muskegon Heights), 96
Featherbone Flea Market, 101
Flat River Antique Mall, 222
Flea and Farmers Market (Royal Oak), 99
Flea Market (Ann Arbor), 87
Flea Market (Birch Run), 87
Flea Market (Hillsdale), 91
Flea Market (Holly), 91
Flea Market (Houghton Lake), 92
Flea Market (Lansing), 93
Flea Market (Six Lakes), 100
Flea Market (Sterling Heights), 100
Four Flags Antique Mall, 225
Four Flats Flea Market, 96
Furlo Auction Service, 272
Gallery of Antiques, 271
"Giant Flea Market" (Burton), 87
Giant Flea Market (Ypsilanti), 102
Giant Public Market, 99
Giant Trade Center Flea Market, 86, 90
Gibraltar Trade Center, 95, 100

Glassman's Auctioneers, 271
Gold Token Flea Market, 95
Grand Valley Antique Mall, 221
Grants Antique Market, 223
Grasslake Mini-Mall flea Market, 91
Great American Market Place, The, 96
Great Midwestern Antique Emporium, The, 227
Green Line Road Flea Market, 99
Greenville Antique Center, 223
Harley's Antique Mall, 221
Heritage Antique Mall, 225
Heritage Square Antique Mall, 225
Hickory Hill Antiques, 222
Historic House Antique Mall, 227
Hitching Post Antiques Mall, 227
Howell Flea and Farmers Market, 92
Ionia Antique and Collectibles Market, 86, 92
Ionia Antique Mall, 224
J and B Antique Mall, 222
J and V Flea Market, 100
Jackie's I-69 Super Flea Market, 88
Jackson Antique Mall, 224
Jo's Ceramic Art and Flea Market, 93
L and M Antique Mall, 227
La Rue's Flea Market, 97
Lake City Flea Market, 93
Lake Shore Antique Shop, 227
Lambertville Antique Market, 93
Lansing Classic Flea Market, 93

Lansing Flea Market, 94
Lawton Antique Mall, 224
Lexington Harbor Bazaar, 94
Lions Club Flea Market, 94
Manchester Antique Mall, 224
Marsh's Antique Mall, 220
McAllister Auctions, 271
Memory Lane Antique Mall, 225
Merri Trail Market (Wayne), 101
Merri-Trail Flea Market (Westland), 102
Michiana Antique Mall, 225
Midway Flea Market, 89
Mill Pond Antique Galleries, 222
Mt. Morris Mini Market, 95
Muskegon Antique Mall, 225
Norman Levy Associates, 272
North Star Flea Market, 100
Northern Exchange Flea Market, 87
Northland Flea Market, 89
Old Timers Flea Market, 95
1761 Flea Market, 88
Owosso Midtown Antiques Mall, 226
Penn-Huron Flea Market, 89, 96
Pickers Paradise Antique Mall, 225
Plaza Antique Mall, 223
Portland Flea Market, 98
Purple Flea, The, 90
Putnam Street Antiques Mall, 228
Ravenna Flea Market, 98, 272
Reits Flea Market, 86, 97
Reminisce Antique Mall, 222
Richfield Center Flea Market, 89

Saginaw flea Market, 99
Saline House Antiques Mall, 226
Saugatuck Flea Market, 99
Schoolcraft Antique Mall, 226
Select Auditorium Flea Market, 96
Shelby Pavilion Flea Market, 100
Spikes Flea Market, 93, 271
Sports Flea Market, 87
Spring Lake Antique Mall, 226
Stanton's Auctioneers and Realtors, 272
Tecumseh Antique Mall I, 227
Tecumseh Antique Mall II, 227
Thurstons Flea Market, 91
Tillies Treasures Flea Market, 94
Town and Country Antiques Mall, 224
Town Hall Antiques, 226
Tri-City Trade Center, 99
Troy Corners Antiques, 227
Trufant Auction and Flea Market, 101, 272
Tulip City Antique Mall, 223
U.S. 10 and M-66 Flea Market, 100
United States Property Auctions, 272
Village Antiques Mall, 222
Water Tower Antiques Mall, 224
Wayne Farmers and Flea Market, 101
Weekend Flea Market, 88
Wegner Auctioneers, 271
West Michigan Antique Mall, 223
Wurzel Flea Market, Inc., 98
Yale Antiques Mall, 228

INDEX **315**

Yesteryears Antique Mall, 222

MINNESOTA

Alliance Auctions and Realty Services, 273
Antiques Minnesota (Minneapolis), 229
Antiques Minnesota (St. Paul), 230
Antiques on Main, 228
Auction America, 273
Auctions Unlimited Flea Market, 104
Blaine Flea Market, 103
Blake Antiques, 229
Buds Flea Market, 106
Carol's Flea Market, 107
Classic Sporting Collectibles, 273
Cobblestone Antiques, 229
Continental Auction School, 284
Country Collection Antiques, The, 230
Country Side Antique Mall, 228
Crafters Market (Burnsville), 228
Crafters Market (Eden Prairie), 228
Earthly Remains, 229
Flea Market (Fairbault), 104
Flea Market (Hackensack), 104
Flea Market (Jenkins), 105
Flea Market (Minneapolis, Lyndale St.), 106
Flea Market (Minneapolis, Midway Shopping Center), 106
Flea Market (Nisswa), 106
Flea Market (Pine City), 107
Flea Market (Redwing), 107
Flea Market (St. Cloud), 107
Flea Market (St. Paul), 107
Flea Market (Twin Cities), 107
Flea Market (Winona), 108
Great River Antiques, 229
Harvey Auction Service, Inc., 272
Hinckley Flea Market, 104
International Craft Fair, 230
Isanti Antique Mall, 229
Kloster Industrial Auctioneers, 273
Main Street Antique Mall, 105, 229
Main Street Antiques, 229
Mann-France Drive-In theater Flea Market, 104
Meeker County Swap Area, 105
Memories on Main, 228
Memory Mercantile Antiques and Collectibles, 229
Mill Antiques, The, 230
More Antiques, 230
Mulberry Point Antiques, 230
Olmstead County Gold Rush Antique Show and Flea Market, 103, 107
Orchard Fun Market, 103, 106
Payne Avenue Antique Mall, 230
Quickie Auction Service, 272
Rainbow Bait Flea Market, 103
Ritchie Brothers Auctioneers International, 272
Rode Galleries, 273
Rose Galleries, 273
Royal Star, 273
Searcy Flea Market, 104
Shady Hollow Flea Market, 104
Sibley Antiques, 229
Smitty's Flea Market, 103, 105

Tracy Luther Auctions and Antiques, 273
Traders Market, 103, 106
Uncle Tom's Antique Mall, 230
Valley Auction Co., 272
Wabasha Indoor/Outdoor Flea Market, 108
Wally Lawmeyer Auction Co., 273
Wayne Pike Auction Co., 273
Wild Cat Swap Meet, 106
Wright County Swap Meet, 103

MISSOURI

Adventure Antiques, 235
AJ's Trade Fair, 127
Alabama Street Mall, 243
American Heritage Antique Mall, 237
Antique and Auction Center, 231
Antique Centre Mall, 232
Antique Flea Market (Cape Girardeau), 112
Antique Mall of America, 236
Antique Market Antique Mall, 234
Antique Mart, 126
Antiques and Uniques Flea Market, 114
B and B Swap and Shop Flea Market, 127
Back Alley Antiques and Auction, 235
Barnhart Flea Market, 110
Bass Country Antique Mall, 243
Bear Ridge Antique and Collectible Flea Market, 113
Belle Starr Auction Co., 275
Belt Highway Antique Mall, 243
Belton Antique Mall and Flea Market, 111
Best Friends Antiques and Collectibles Mall, 239
Beverly Hills Antique Center, 230
Bill Horton, 274
Blansits Sale Pavilion, 275
Bob Lasswell and Associates, 275
Bobbie's Wishing Well, 119, 238
Bonanza Flea Market, 115
Boone Village Antique Mall, 231
Caldwells Flea Market, 111
Calton's Auction House, 274
Camel Back Antiques and Flea Market, 121
Cannon Ball Antique Mall, 237
Carthage Route 66 Antique Mall and Flea Market, 112
Central Station Mall, 243
Chea's Place, 120
Cherry Tree Flea Market, 123
Claycomo Antique Mall and Flea Market, 232
Coffelt Country Crossroads, 111
Connie's Antiques, 235
Coomers Crafts, 244
Country Cellar Antique Mall, 232
Country Corner Flea Market and Antiques, The, 118
Country Corner Flea Market, 123
Country Corner Treasures Antique and Craft Mall, 239
Country Cottage Craft Mall, 242
Country Creek Mall, 242

Country Junction Flea Market and Baird's Antiques, 121
Country Meadows Antique Mall, 235
County Fair Mall, 241
Crafters Mall, 242
Crossroads Antique and Collectibles Mall, 239
De Ole Garage Antique Mall, 112
Dealers Auction (Kansas City), 274, 287
Deans Antique Mall and Flea Market, 232
Deants Antique Mall and Flea Market, 112
Decorator's Touch Craft Mall and Decorating Center, 231
Diamond Auto Auctions, 274
Do Antiques Mall, 243
Dog, Gun, Hillbilly Consignment Auction and Flea Market, 122, 275
Don Sissel Auction Service, 275
Dorothy's Den Antiques, 240
Down on Main Street, 242
Downtown Antique Mall, 245
E and E Flea Market, 112
Eldon Flea Market, 114
Evies Country Village, 242
Fairgrounds Flea Market, 114
Feed Store Antiques and Mall, 232
Felix Street Mini Mall, 244
Flea Bag Market, 111
Flea Market (Carthage), 112
Flea Market (Cole Camp), 113
Flea Market (Knob Noster), 118
Flea Market (Macon), 119
Flea Market (Poplar Bluff), 122
Flea Market (St. Louis), 126
Flea Market and Antique Show (St. Louis), 126
Flea Market and Swap Meet, 123
Fountain Square Antique Mall, 234
Freddy Bees Flea Market, 127
Frisom Flea Market, 126
G and W Antiques and Collectible Flea Market, 123
Gary Ryther Auctioneering Inc., 274
General Store and Antique Mall, 242
Gingham Goose Antiques, 237
Goad's Unique Antique Mall, 232
Gospel Truth Antique Mall, 245
Granby Flea Market, 114
Granny's Attic Flea Market, 110
Granny's Attic, 231
Great Discoveries Flea Market and Antique Furniture, 124
Greenwood Antiques and Country Tea Room, 234
Hammers Junktique Flea Market and Swap Meet, 110
Harrisonville Trade Fair, 235
Hawkeye Dealers Auction, 287
Heart Swap Meet, 116
Hickory Hills Flea Market, 116
Hidden Treasures Antiques and Flea Market, 119
Hidden Treasures Flea Market, 111
Highway 37 Flea Market, 122
Highway 39 Merchants Flea Market, 110
Hillbilly Al's Flea Market, 118
Hillbilly Park Flea Market, 115

His Heritage Antique Mall, 238
Hog Eye Auction Service, 275
Holstein Antiques and Flea Market, 111
Horns Antique Emporium, 244
Houn Dawg Flea Market, 110
I-29 Antique Mall, 241
I-44 Swap Meet, 124
I-70 Antique Mall, 239
Ice House Mall, 233
Indoor Flea Market (Bonne Terre), 111
Indoor Flea Market (Doolittle), 114
Industrial Liquidators, 276
Inge's Oak Grove Flea Market, 121
Iron Kettle Antiques and Flea Market, 115
J and L Flea Market, 118
Jeff Williams Original Kansas City Flea Market, 109, 107
Joe Mueller, 276
Joplin Flea Market, 115
Jose's Flea Market, 121
Junction Antique Mall, 232
Kaegel's Country Collectibles, 243
Kaleidoscope Antique Mall, 244
Kansas City Flea Market, The, 117
KD's Antiques and Woodcrafts Mall, 238
Keepsake Kupboard, 235
Kelly Springs Antique Mall and Flea Market, 114
Kelly Springs Antique Mall and Flea Market, 233
Kennet Flea Market, 118
Knob Noster Flea Market, 118
Kountry Korner Flea Market (Marionville), 119, 238
Kountry Korner Flea Market (Springfield), 124
Liberty Antique Mall, 237
Lick Skillet Antique and Craft Mall, 232
Little Red School House flea Market, The, 122
Living Rock Sell R' Swap, 122
Lloyd's Flea Market ((Houston), 115
Lloyds Flea Market (Cabool), 112
Longview Auction, 274
Ma and Pa's Riverview Antique and Collectible Mall, 238
Main Street Mall Antiques, 233
Maine Street Mall, 239
Mainstreet Market, 122
Maple Leaf Antique Mall, 242
Market Street Mall, 234
Marriott Antiques, 242
Mason-Dixon Line Flea Market, 127
Meeker Antique Mall, The, 235
Mid-America Antique Mall, 236
Midstate Auction Service, 274
Midway Antique Center and Flea Market, 113, 233
Missouri Auction School, 285
Missouri River Antique Mall, 242
Monthly Flea Market (West Plains), 128
Morton's Flea Market, 113
Mt. Vernon Flea Market, 120
Nana's Antique Mall, 109, 238
Nate's 63rd Street Swap Meet, 117

Neosho Gallery and Flea Market, 120, 238
New Haven Antique Mall, 239
Niangua Antique Mall, 239
North 65 Swap and Show, 113
North Main Street Antique/Craft Mall and Flea Market, 115, 236
Northtown Flea Mart, 125
Old English House of Antiques Mall, 237
Old Mill Flea Market, 114
Old Theater Mall, 239
Old Timers Flea Market, 114
Old Village Store Antique Mall, The, 233
Olde Stone Church Antiques, 239
Olde Towne Flea Market, 125
Oldies and Oddities Mall, 232
Once Upon A Time Collectible Mall, 231
One of a Kind Gallery and Gifts, 244
111 Mile Junction Flea Market, 112
Over the Hill Mini Mall, 234
Ozark Antique Mall, 240
Ozark Flea Market, 121
Pack Rats Antiques, 243
Park Central Flea Market, 125
Parkland Pavilion Antiques and Auction Gallery, 109, 237, 275
Pat's Antique Mall, 240
Pavilion Galleries, The, 274
Peculiar Antique Mall, 240
Pence Auction Co., 275
Penn Street Square Antique and Craft Mall, 244
Penney Mall, 234
Perkins Auction Co., 285

Pevely Antique Mall, 241
Pevely Flea Market, 109, 122, 127
R. Ness Auction Gallery, 276
Red Barn Flea Market and Antiques, 121
Remember When Antiques and Collectibles, 232
Remember When Flea Market, 118
Richard Larson, 274
Rivertown Antique Mall, 237
Robert Merry Auction Co., 276
Rusty Nail Flea Market, 115
S.T.D. East Flea Market, 126
S.T.D. West Flea Market, 126
Sac River Trade and Antique Mall, 125
Sarcoxie Livestock Auction, 276
Sedalia Flea Market, 122
71 Craft and Flea, 120
71 Flea Market, 112
Shopper's Paradise, 233
Showcase Antique Mall, 245
Sikeston Auction Co, 276
Sikeston Trade Fair, 123
Simmons General Mercantile Antique Mall, 241
South County Antiques Mall, 245
South Peer Antique Mall and Flea Market, 125
Southern Hills Antique Mall, 240
Southside Antique Mall, 236
Southtown Flea Market, 125
Spease Antique Mall, 241
Special Treasures, 239
Springfield Flea Market, 125
Square Deal Auctions, 275
Stacey Flea Market, 112

Starlite Flea Market, 121
State Line Antique Mall, 236
Stateline Trade Center and Flea Market, 109
Stop N Scratch Flea Market and Antiques, 113
Things Unlimited, 117
Those Were The Days Mall, 245
Trade Fair Market, 121
Traders Market Antiques and Gifts Mall, 243
Traders Market, 241
Tradewinds Flea Market, 123
Trash and Treasures Shopping Mall, 245
Treasure Finders Antiques and Flea Market, 126
Treasure Seekers Antique Mall and Flea Market, 118
Truman Corners Antique and Furniture Mall, 234
United Antique Mall, 244
Valley Flea Market and Antique Mall, 245
Verns Flea Market, 120
Victorian Rose Antique Mall, 231
Viking Flea Market, 126
Vintages, 240
Volker Village Antique Mall, 236
Voorheis Auction and Realty, 274
W. D. Pickers Antique Mall, 241
Waldo's Antiques and Flea Market, 117, 236
Washington Flea Market, 128
Weavers Auction and Flea Market, 119
Wentzville Flea Market, 128
West County Flea Market, 122
Westport Flea Market, 117
What-Ever Antiques Flea Market, 237
Wisner's Flea Market and Antiques, 121
Ytell Auction Service, 274

NEBRASKA

Antique Corner Cooperative, 246
Antique Mall (Lexington), 246
Antique Market, The, 130, 246
Antique Place, The (North Platte), 131
Asmus Brothers Auctioneers, 277
Auction House, The, 276, 288
Bailey and Associates Realty and Auction, 277
Burlington Arcade Antique Mall, 246
CLBC Flea Market, 131
Columbus Flea Market, 129
County Collectibles Market, 130
Eagle Antiques, 246
Enamel and Lace Antiques, 245
Flea Market (Omaha), 131
Flea Market (South Sioux City), 129, 132
Flea Market (Valentine), 132
Foxy Grandma's Flea Market, 130
Fredericks Antique Mall, 246
Granny's Antique Co-Op, 246
Great Exchange Indoor Flea Market, 129
Indoor Flea Market, 129, 130
Invale Flea Market, 130
Lincoln O Street Mall, 246
Loup Valley Auction, 276

Magic City Mall, 247
Maurices Flea Market, 131
New City Flea Market, 131
Park Avenue Antiques, 246
Plum Tree Antique Mall, 246
Siouxland Flea Market, 132
St. George Antique Mall, 247
Sunrise Sunset Flea Market, 129, 131
Swap and Flea Market, 132
Tommy Palmer, Auctioneer, 276
Treasure Trove Flea Mall, 247
Venice Antiques, 247

NORTH DAKOTA
Antique Attic, 246
Antique Gallery, 246
Dacotah Auction and Liquidation, 277
Dakota Midwest Flea Market and Antique Show, 133
Dennis Biliske Auctioneers, 277
Farmers and Flea Market (Fargo), 133
Flea Market and Craft Show (Grand Forks), 133
Greater Grand Forks Area Flea Market, 134
Lamertz Auction Service, 277
Lien Auction and Realty Service, 277
Magic City Flea Market, 133, 134
Midwest Flea Market and Antique Show, 134
North Dakota Mall, 246
Northland Auction and Clerking Service, 277
Ramblin' Auctioneers, 277

OHIO
A-Auction by Jer, 279
AAA I-70 Antique Mall, 255
Ace Antiques, 278
Allens Auctions, 280
Alliance Flea Market, 136
Anderson Flea Market, 153, 279
Another Man's Treasures Antique Mall, 250
Antique and Collectible Flea Market (Piqua), 160
Antique and Collectible Market (Medina), 156
Antique and Flea Market (Perrysburg), 160
Antique Arcade, The, 250
Antique Emporium, 253
Antique Mall and Collectibles Market (Cincinnati), 249
Antique Show and Flea Market (Marion), 155
Antique Show and Flea Markets (Urbana), 166
Antiques and Collectibles Show (Columbus), 145
Antiques of Chester, 249
Antiques on Main (Ashland), 248
Antiques On The Square, 249
Auglaize Antique Mall, 256
Aurora Farms Auction, 277, 287
Aurora Farms Flea Market, 135, 137
Austintown Flea Market, 168
Baker Bonnigson Auctioneers, 281
Barnesville Antique Mall, 248
Bassett Flea Market, 164
Bazaar, The (Cleveland), 144
Bellefontaine Flea Market, 138
Bethel Flea Market, 138
Biddlestone Antique Mall, 252

Big B's Flea Market, 164
Big Red's Flea Market, 168
Bittersweet Antiques Mall, 256
BJ's Wholesale Auction, 281, 288
Bloomfield Auction and Flea Market, 138
Bowling Green Flea Market, 138
Brandt Pike Flea Market, 152
Brewer's Antique Mall, 249
Broadway Antique Mall (Lebanon), 252
Broadway Antique Mall, 248
Broadway Antique Mall #2, 248
Broadway Flea Market, 144
Brothers Antique Mall, 253
Buyers Flea Market, 152
C and G Flea Market, 155
Caesar Creek Flea Market, 140
Canton Flea Market, 141
Chesterville Antiques, 249
Cincinnati Art Gallery, 278
Cincinnati Wholesale Auction, 278, 287
Clark Avenue Flea Market, 144
Clifton Antique Mall, 250
Cloud's Antique Mall, 249
Clover Farms Antiques Emporium, 251
Cloverland Drive-In Theater Flea Market, 144
Cobblestone Antique Mall, 256
Columbus Flea Market, 146
Company B NCO Club Flea Market, 152
Congress Inn Antiques and Flea Market, 156
Coshocton Antique Center, 250
Country Bazaar, 148
Country Heirs, 248

Country Lane Flea Market, 158
Craft Market Place, 250
David Bowers, 281
Dayton Traffic Circle Flea Market, 147
Dealer Auction (Eaton), 288
DeHays Auctions, 277
Delta Antiques Market, 250
Depot Street Antique Mall, 254
Dexter City Antique Mall, 250
Dixie Flea Market, 156
Dixie Stop Flea Market, 148
Don Treadway Gallery, 278
Dover Antique Mall, 251
Dover Flea Market, 149
Downtown Antiques and Collectibles Mall, 256
Duck Creek Antique Mall, 249
Dumontville Flea Market, 154
Dutch Valley Antique Mall, 255
E. J. Weade Associates, 281
Early Auction Co., 280
Early Days Antiques, 254
East Lake Drive-In Theater Flea Market, 145
East Oberlin Flea Market, 159
Eaton Wholesale Auction Co., 279
Etna Flea Mart, 150
Fairborn Flea Market, 150
Fairgrounds Flea Market (Montpelier), 157
Fairgrounds Flea Market (Painesville), 159
Farmers and Flea Market (Toledo), 164
Farmers Auction and Flea Market, 135
Farthing Real Estate and Auctioneers, 279

INDEX **323**

Findley Flea Market and Antique Show, 150
Finneytown Flea Market, 141
Fireland Public Market, 158
Firelands Flea Market, 156
First American Auction Co., 280
Flea Market (Amende), 136
Flea Market (Brooklyn), 139
Flea Market (Bryan, Holiday Inn), 139
Flea Market (Bryan, Hwy. 6), 140
Flea Market (Cambridge), 140
Flea Market (Canton), 141
Flea Market (Dayton), 148
Flea Market (Eaton), 149
Flea Market (Germantown), 151
Flea Market (Grand Rapids), 151
Flea Market (Malvern), 155
Flea Market (Marietta), 155
Flea Market (St. Clairsville), 163
Flea Market (Toledo), 165
Flea Market (Troy), 165
Flea Market (Waldo), 166
Flea Market (Westchester), 167
Flea Market and Antique Show (Canton), 141
Flea Market and Auction (Montpelier), 157
Flea Market and Swap Shop (Ravenna), 161
Flea Market Bazaar (Valley View), 166
Flea Mart, The (St. Marys), 163
Fort Firelands Flea Market, 153
Fostoria Town Center Antique Mall, 251
40 East Drive-In Theater Flea Market, 161
Four Seasons Flea and Farmers Market, 168
Fremont Flea Market, 151
French 500 Flea Market, 151
French Creek Flea Market, 137
Gala Flea Market, 135
Gallipolis Flea Market, 151
Gardeners Auction Service, 279
Gardners Warehouse Flea Market, 140
Garth's Auctions, 278
Garver Flea Market, 163
"Giant" Outdoor Flea Market, 165
Grand Oaks Flea Market, 154
Greater Columbus Antique Mall, 250
Groesbeck Flea Market, 141
H and R Antique Mall, 251
Halls Flea Market, 150
Harrison Flea Market, 152
Hartville Flea Market, 135, 152
Hatchery Antique Mall, 254
Heart's Content Antique Mall, 257
Higgins Auction House, 280, 288
Highway 62 Drive-In Theater Flea Market, 139
Hills and Dales Flea Market, 153
Homerville Antique Mall, 252
Howland Drive-In Flea Market, 158
Hubbard Liberty Flea Market, 152

Indoor Flea Market (Astabula), 137
Indoor Flea Market (Navarre), 157
Jamies Flea Market, 136, 162
Jeffrey's Antique Gallery, 251
Jim Rogers Auctioneer, 277
Kellogg Flea Market, 142
KIKO Auction and Real Estate Service, 278
Kingman Drive-In Theater Flea Market, 149
Knotts Auctioneering School, 285
Kunkie Schoolhouse Antique Mall, 252
Lakeview Hall Flea Market, 160
Lancaster Antique Emporium, 252
Langolis Auction House, 281
Lebanon Antique Exchange, 252
Lee Road International Market, 145
Lens Odds and Ends, 159
Liberty Antique Mall, 255
Lil Rebel Flea Market, 167
Lima Antique Show and Flea Market, 154
Lindy's Auction Barn, 279
Lisa Maries Flea Market and Antique Mall, 136
Lithopolis Antique Mart, 252
Livingston Court Indoor Flea Market, 146
Logan Antique Mall, 253
London Flea Market, 148
London Village Flea Market, 142
Loveland Flea Market, 154
M and S Auction Inc., 279

Mack's Barn Old-Tiques and Antiques, 253
Main Auction Galleries Inc., 278
Mansfield Flea Market, 155
Memphis Drive-In Theater Flea Market, 145
Mentor Village Antiques, 253
Miami-Erie Antique Mall, 250
Mid-Ohio Antique Mall, 253
Middlefield Farmers and Flea Market, 156
Midtown Flea Market, 142
Midwest Auctioneers and Marketers, 279
Mike Clum, 281
Mill Race Antiques Mall, 256
Montrose Drive-In Flea Market, 136
NCA Wholesale Auction, 279, 288
Ned Gregg Realty Co., 281
Newark Flea Market, 157
Nikana Flea Market, 162
North Bloomfield Auction and Flea Market, 158, 280
North Western Ohio Land and Auction Co., 281
Northfield Flea Market, 158
Northland Plaza Shopping Center Flea Market, 154
Oakwood Antiques and Collectibles Market, 147
Ohio Antique Market, 255
Old General Store Antique Mall, 252
Old Parts Factory Mall, 252
Old Towne Antique Mall, 257
Old West End Collector's Corner, 256
Olde Piano Factory Antique Mall, 254

INDEX **325**

Olde Tyme Treasures Antiques and Collectibles Mall, 247
Outdoor Flea Market (Toledo), 165
Paris Flea Market (Cincinnati), 142
Paris Flea Market (Dayton), 148
Park 'N Swap Flea Market, 150
Peddlers Flea Market, 142
Penny Court Antiques, 248
Perrysburg Antiques Market, 254
Pickaway County Flea Market, 144
Pikeston Flea Market, 160
Pioneer Antique Mall, 254
Pisgah Flea Market, 160
Plain City Auction Service, 280
Poland Flea Market, 161
Portage Flea Market, 161
Porters Auction, 279, 288
Preble County Flea Market, 149
Proctorville Flea Market, 161
Pumphouse Antiques, 248
Pymatuning Lake Drive-In Flea Market, 135, 137
Radsons Flea Market, 167
Rainbow's Giant Amos Indoor Flea Market, 146
Ravenna Flea Market, 161
Red Barn Flea Market, 159
Red Barn Flea Market, The, 146
Rich Mart Flea Mart, 160
Richard D. Davis, Auctioneer, 281
Rinks Flea Market, 142
Riverfront Antique Mall, 253
Robert Vaughn Auctions, 279
Rogers Community Auction and Open Air Market, 157, 281
Rosen and Co., 278
Ross Conley Auctioneers, 279
Ross County Flea Market, 141
Route 30 Flea Market, 159
Sabina Antique Village and Flea Market, 162
Schome Flea Market, 151
Shady Rest Flea Market, 138
Skyway Drive-In Flea Market, 167
Smiths Big Antique Store, 247
Smithville Antique Mall, 255
Soper's Antique Palace Mall, 248
South Bloomfield Antique Mall, 255
South Drive-In Theater Flea Market, The, 146
South Point Flea Market, 166
Special Things Antique Mall, 249
Spencerville Antique Mall, 255
Springfield Antique Show and Flea Market, 135, 162
Stagecoach Antique Mall Market, 159
Stickers Grove Flea Market, 143
Strasburg 77 Antiques and Collectibles, 255
Straw Factory Flea Market, 155
Strickers Grove Auctionmania, 280
Strickers Grove Flea Market, 162
Sun-Berry Antique Mall, 256
Sunny Acres Flea Market, 149
Swap and Shop Flea Market, 147
Swap Shop and Flea Market, 146

Tannery Hill Farmers Flea Market, 137
Theron's Country Flea Market, 145
Tiffin Flea Market, 164
Tiffin Mall Flea Market, 164
Tim and Glen Speck, 280
Toledo Trade Market, 165
Trackside Antique Mall, 254
Trader Ned's Auction, 278, 288
Trader Ned's Flea Market, 147
Traders World, 143, 156
Tri-State Antique Mall, 254
Tri-State Jockey Lot Flea Market, 165
Turtle Creek Flea Market, 143
250 Antique Mall, 250
Union Station Antiques, 251
Venice Antique Mall, 255
Victorian Babes Antiques Mall, 248
Village Antique Mall (Johnstown), 252
Village Antique Mall (Kidron), 252
Village Antique Mall (New Vienna), 254
Village Flea Market, 144
Village Trading Post, 253
Walton Auction School, 285
Warren Flea Market, 167
Washington Court House Flea Market, 135, 167
Waynesville Antique Mall, 257
Weadsworth Antique Mall, 256
Web Flea Market, 150
Weber's Antiques, 250
Weidners Village Square Antique Mall, 256
West Hill Antiques, 247
Westerville Antique Mall, 257
Westland Indoor Flea Market, 147
Wheel and Deal Indoor Flea Market, 148
Wolf's Auctioneers, 278
Wood County Indoor and Outdoor Antiques and Flea Market, 138
Wooster Bargain Barn, 161
Years Ago Antique Mall, 256

SOUTH DAKOTA
A-1 Auction House, 282
Anderson Auction Service, 282
Antique Mall (Rapid City), 257
Antiques and Flea Market (Sioux Falls), 170
Bend in the River Antique Mall, 257
Blackhills Flea Market, 169
Bradeen Auctions and Real Estate, 282
Casteel Auction Service, 282
Flea Market (Sioux Falls, Cliff Ave.), 170
Flea Market (Sioux Falls, Expo Bldg.), 169, 170
Flea Market (Yankton), 170
Gold Belt Mercantile, 257
Haley's Tri-State Auction, 282
Holty Auction Service, 282
Ken Wintersteen, 282
Larson Auctioneering, 282
Lewis and Clark Traders, 170
Martin Jurisch and Associates, 282
McPherson Auction Co., 282
Penfield Auction Service, 282
Rapid City Flea Market, 169
Sluiter's Country Auction, 281
St. Joe Antiques Mall and Gift Shop, 257

Trade Winds Auction Co., 282
Wieman Land and Auction Co., 282
Wingler's Furniture and Auction Co., 282
Yankton Flea Market, 171

WISCONSIN
A Dickens of a Place Antique Center, 260
Adams Flea Market, 172
Adams Flea Market, 173
Antique and Flea Market (Elkhorn), 174
Antique Center (La Crosse), 258
Antique Emporium, 258
Antique Mall of Tomah, 260
Antique Market (Fountain City), 258
Antiques Mall (Portage), 259
Bargain Bin Flea Market, 177
Bargain Showcase Indoor/Outdoor Market, 176
Barn Flea Market, 175
Big Store Plaza Antique Malls, 259
Campus Antique Mall, 259
Candy's Flea Market, 178
Columbus Antique Mall and Museum, 258
Dealers' Auction (Fond Du Lac), 283, 288
Dealers' Auction (Kewaskum), 283, 288
Dealers' Auction (Oshkosh), 283, 288
Dealers' Auction (Wisconsin Dells), 284, 288
Elegant Chicken Antique Mall, 258

Flea Market (Abbotsford, 172
Flea Market (Fond Du Lac, Fairgrounds), 174
Flea Market (Fond Du Lac, Wescott Plaza Mall), 174
Flea Market (Gillett), 174
Flea Market (Milwaukee), 177
Flea Market (St. Germaine), 180
Forum Flea Market and Collectors Show, The, 176
Fox River Antique Mall, 257
Freddy Bears Antique Mall, 260
G and L Auction Company Flea Market, 178
General Store Antique Mall (Beaver Dam), 257
General Store Antique Mall (Kewaskum), 258
George Auction Co., 283
Golden Indoor/Outdoor Flea Market, The, 173
Granite City Antique Mall and Flea Market, 178, 259
Half Mile Antique Fair Mall, 260
Hayward Flea Market, 175
Jamesville Flea Market, 175
Jefferson Bargain Fair, 175
Kenosha Flea Market, 176
Ladysmith Flea Market, 283
Lee Murray Auction Service, 284
Mapletree Antique Mall, 259
Marathon Park Indoor Flea Market, 180
Mauston Antique Mall and Flea Market, 177
Maze Flea Market, 1778
Mega Market, 177

Mid-City Outdoor Theater Flea Market, 176
Mike Kranz, 283
Millard's Flea Market, 179
Milwaukee Antiques Center, 259
Milwaukee Auction Galleries, 283
Minocqua Flea Market, 178
Nana's House of Antiques, 258
North Town Trade Center, 179
Northeastern Wisconsin's Biggest Craft Sale and Flea Market, 172, 174
On The Square Antique Mall, 260
Original's Mall of Antiques, 259
Oxford Flea Market, 179
Pea Picking Flea Market, 179
Pin River Amusement Park Flea Market, 178
Princeton Flea Market, 179
Rainy Day Antique Mall, 259
Riverfront Antiques Mall, 258
Rummage-O-Rama, 172, 177
School Days Mall, 259
Schrager Auction Galleries, 283
7 Mile Fair, 172, 173
Shawano Flea Market, 172, 179
St. Joseph's Flea Market, 175
St. Martin Flea Market, 174
Starlite Swap-O-Rama, 177
Storm Hall Antique Mall, 260
Sunday Flea Market, 173
Tim Unterholzner Auctions, 284
Town Crier Auctions, 283
Valley Antique Mall, 259
Van Wey's Community Auction and Flea Market, 176
Wautoma Flea Market, 180
Westfield Flea Market, 181
Westover Drive-In Theater Flea Market, 181
White Horse Flea Market, 173
Wholesale Dealers Auction (Grass Lake), 283, 288
Wild Rose Auction Co., 284
Wisconsin Flea Market, 173
Woodstock Antique and Flea Market, 181

MISCELLANEOUS
America West Archives, 284
Auction Hotline, 284
Auctioneer Classes, Perkins Auction Co., 284
Mendenhall School of Auctioneering, 285
Southeastern School of Auctioneering, 285
Western College of Auctioneering, 285

ATTENTION FLEA MARKET OWNERS AND MANAGERS: CUSTOMERS AND VENDORS ARE LOOKING FOR YOU!

If you would like your listing to appear in the next edition of this book, simply fill out the survey form below and return to:

Goodridge's Guide to Flea Markets
**c/o Adams Publishing
260 Center Street
Holbrook, MA 02343**

City: _____ State: _____

Name of Market: _____

Street Address: _____

_____

_____

Directions: _____

_____

_____

_____

Contact Person: _____

Telephone # (_____)_____

Address: _____

_____

_____

City/State/Zip: _____

Vendor Name: _____

Basic Merchandise Make-Up: New _____ Used _____

Antique/Collectible _____

Average Daily Attendance: _____

Average Weekly Attendance: _____

Number of Vendors: _____

Restaurant/Food: _____

Parking Available: Yes _____ Cost _____ Free _____ No _____

　　　　　　　　Ample _____ Restricted _____

Admission Charge: Yes _____ Cost _____ No _____

Space Cost: _____ Tables Available: _____

Reservations: Recommended _____ Required _____

　　　　　　　Not Necessary _____

Inside Space Available: Yes _____ Cost _____ No _____

Overnight Camping: Yes _____ Cost _____ Free _____ No _____

Showers on Site: Yes _____ No _____

Electricity Available: Yes _____ No _____

Merchandise Restrictions or Comments: _____

_____

_____

_____

_____

_____

Restrictions and License: _____

_____

_____

_____

Days and Hours Held: _____

YOU BE THE JUDGE IN THE ANNUAL "TOP 10 ALL-AMERICAN MARKETPLACE AWARD"

Cast your vote today and help us honor the "Top 10" markets that have shown outstanding service to the industry during the past twelve months.

OFFICIAL BALLOT

___ Yes, here's my vote for the "Top 10 All-American Marketplace Award"

Name of Market: _____

Address: _____

_____

_____

Phone: (_____) _____

Comments: _____

_____

_____

_____

_____

_____

Please mail your entries to:

Goodridge's Guide to Flea Markets
c/o Adams Publishing
260 Center Street
Holbrook, MA 02343

ABOUT THE AUTHOR

For over twenty-five years, Jim Goodridge has worked as a professional flea market dealer, selling his wares from coast to coast. Experience and opportunity led him into owning and operating a large antique mall in St. Louis which came to an untimely end when it was destroyed in the Great Flood of '93. As Jim so aptly puts it, "During the flood, we really took a bath." Jim Goodridge is the founder of the Independent Dealer's Association of America, publisher of the *Fair Times* newspaper, and author of *The Dealer's Desk Reference*. He lives with his wife Georgia in Arnold, Missouri.

Other regional editions of
Goodridge's Guide to Flea Markets

Northeast/Mid-Atlantic Edition
Includes: Connecticut, Delaware, District of Columbia, Maine, Maryland, Massachusetts, New Hampshire, New Jersey, New York, Pennsylvania, Rhode Island, and Vermont

Southeast Edition
Includes: Alabama, Arkansas, Florida, Georgia, Louisiana, Mississippi, North Carolina, South Carolina, Tennessee, Virginia, and West Virginia

West/Southwest Edition
Includes: Alaska, Arizona, California, Colorado, Hawaii, Idaho, Montana, Nevada, New Mexico, Oklahoma, Oregon, Texas, Utah, Washington, and Wyoming

---

If you cannot find these titles at your bookstore, you may order them directly from the publisher. The price of each book is $9.95. BY PHONE: Call 1-800-872-5627 (in Massachusetts 617-767-8100). We accept Visa, Mastercard, and American Express. $4.50 will be added to your total order for shipping and handling. BY MAIL: Write out the full title of the books you'd like to order and send payment, including $4.50 for shipping and handling to: Adams Publishing, 260 Center Street, Holbrook, MA 02343.

PLEASE CHECK AT YOUR LOCAL BOOKSTORE FIRST.